A State of Nations

A STATE OF NATIONS

*Empire and Nation-Making in the
Age of Lenin and Stalin*

EDITED BY
RONALD GRIGOR SUNY
TERRY MARTIN

UNIVERSITY PRESS

2001

OXFORD
UNIVERSITY PRESS

Oxford   New York
Athens   Auckland   Bangkok   Bogotá   Buenos Aires   Cape Town
Chennai   Dar es Salaam   Delhi   Florence   Hong Kong   Istanbul   Karachi
Kolkata   Kuala Lumpur   Madrid   Melbourne   Mexico City   Mumbai   Nairobi
Paris   São Paulo   Shanghai   Singapore   Taipei   Tokyo   Toronto   Warsaw

and associated companies in
Berlin   Ibadan

Library of Congress Cataloging-in-Publication Data
A state of nations : empire and nation-making in the age of Lenin and Stalin
edited by Ronald Grigor Suny and Terry Martin.
        p.   cm.
Includes bibliographical references and index.
ISBN-13 978-0-19-514422-2; 978-0-19-514423-9 (pbk.)
ISBN 0-19-514422-8; ISBN 0-19-514423-6 (pbk)
1. Soviet Union—Politics and government.   2. Soviet Union—Ethnic relations.
3. Ethnicity—Soviet Union.   4. Nationalism—Soviet Union.   I. Suny, Ronald Grigor.
II. Martin, Terry.
DK266.S8   2002
947—dc21   2001021712

9 8 7 6 5 4 3

Printed in the United States of America
on acid-free paper

To David and Sheila,

intellectual explorers in the Chicago tradition

Preface

A CASUAL CONVERSATION BETWEEN THE EDITORS, waiting for an elevator in Cologne in June 1995, led to plans to bring together the growing number of scholars working on nation formation and state policies in the first decades of Soviet power. Terry Martin, then a graduate student at the University of Chicago, and Ron Suny, newly appointed professor of political science, organized a conference in the modest setting of Wilder House on the Chicago campus in October 1997. The Gorbachev reforms and the subsequent breakup of the Soviet Union had created an unprecedented opportunity for scholars to do archival research into questions on which information had previously not been accessible. Not only were the resources of the central party and the state archives exploited, but historians also combed regional and republic archives to come up with new stories of how the Soviet state managed the cultural, social, and political development of more than one hundred different ethnic populations. The conference and this volume are the fruits of that research, the first efforts to rewrite the multinational history of the first state to found its federation on the basis of territorialized nationality. How an anti-imperial enterprise aimed at the emancipation of nations metamorphosed into an empire of national states is the central theme of this book.

Funding for the conference came from the Council on Advanced Studies on Peace and International Cooperation (CASPIC), whose chairman at the time was David D. Laitin. Besides the participants in this volume, other scholars participated in the three days of intense discussion: Mark Beissinger, John Bushnell, Prasenjit Duara, Sheila Fitzpatrick, Michael Geyer, Francine Hirsch, Hiroaki Kuromiya, Michael Khodarkovsky, David Laitin, Volodymyr Pristaiko, Yuri Shapoval, and Amir Weiner. The editors are deeply grateful to the funders, to the paper givers, and to the commentators whose contributions made possible this collective effort. The unique setting of the University of Chicago, with its special commitment to the life of the mind, the graduate students who also attended and spoke at the conference, and the particular intimacy of Wilder House all added to the intellectual experience. A special thanks goes to our editor at Oxford University Press, Susan Ferber, who diligently shaped our essays into a graceful, compelling narrative. Ron begs forgiveness of his family—Anoush, Sevan, and Armena—for having even less time available for them than usual. Terry thanks Sally yet again for her patience and support, and Eli for making the comparative study of dinosaurs predominate over that of nations in the Martin household.

Ann Arbor, Michigan   R. S.
Belmont, Massachusetts   T. M.
February 2001   ·

Contents

Contributors

PETER A. BLITSTEIN is a graduate of the University of California, Berkeley, working on Soviet nationalities policy in the late Stalinist years.

DAVID BRANDENBERGER is a graduate of Harvard University, working on Russian nationalism and the writing of history in the Stalinist 1930s.

PETER HOLQUIST, a graduate of Columbia University, is assistant professor of history at Cornell University. His work centers on the revolution and the civil war in the Cossack country of southern Russia, and he is the author of numerous published articles on modernity and early Soviet society.

ADEEB KHALID, a graduate of the University of Wisconsin, is assistant professor of history at Carleton College and the author of *The Politics of Muslim Cultural Reform: Jadidism in Central Asia* (1998).

TERRY MARTIN, a graduate of the University of Chicago, is associate professor of history at Harvard University. He is the author of *The Affirmative Action Empire: Nations and Nationalism in the Soviet Union, 1923–1939* (2001).

DOUGLAS NORTHROP, a graduate of Stanford University, is assistant professor of history at the University of Georgia. His work is on gender and social change in Uzbekistan in the 1930s.

MATT PAYNE, a graduate of the University of Chicago, is assistant professor of history at Emory University. His work is on labor and ethnic relations during the building of the Turkestan-Siberian (Turksib) railroad in the 1920s and 1930s.

JOSHUA SANBORN, a graduate of the University of Chicago, is assistant professor of history at Lafayette College. His work is on military mobilization, nationalism, and ideas of masculinity in tsarist Russia and the Soviet Union.

DANIEL E. SCHAFER, a graduate of the University of Michigan, is assistant professor of history at Belmont University. His work focuses on the revolution and the civil war in the Tatar and the Bashkir republics.

RONALD GRIGOR SUNY, a graduate of Columbia University, is professor of political science at the University of Chicago and was formerly the Alex Manoogian Professor of Modern Armenian History at the University of Michigan. He is the author and editor of numerous books, among them *The Revenge of the Past: Nationalism, Revolution, and the Collapse of the Soviet Union* (1993) and *The Soviet Experiment: Russia, the USSR, and the Successor States* (Oxford University Press, 1998).

A State of Nations

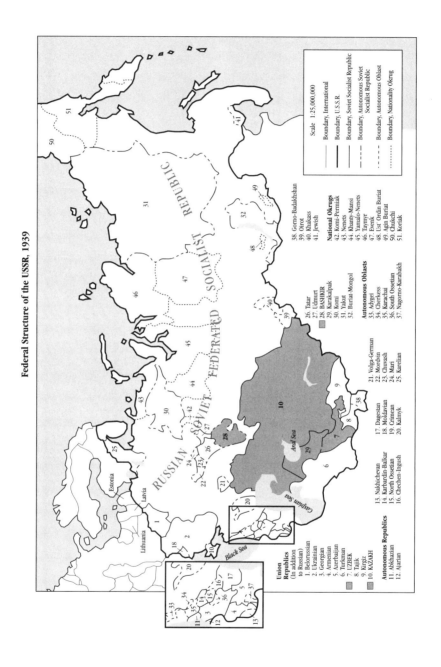

Federal Structure of the USSR, 1939

RONALD GRIGOR SUNY

TERRY MARTIN

Introduction

T HE KEY WORDS THAT HAVE INTRIGUED HISTORIANS of the Soviet Union
have changed over time. State and society, intelligentsia and gentry, proletariat and bourgeoisie have each in turn been examined in a series of debates.
But as scholars began to doubt the relative stability of social categories and to
question what categories should be employed, their attention has turned toward
issues of identity, narrative, and meaning. In the process, key words that had
served well in the past became problematic. Interest in class has declined among
Soviet historians, and nation, a topic that earlier received extraordinarily little
attention, has become a new focus for research. After decades of Russocentric
exclusion, historians in significant numbers have ventured into the non-Russian
peripheries or examined metropolitan policies toward nationalities.[1] In this collection, empire and nation join state as key words through which to explore
relations of power and representations of authority among the peoples of the
USSR. This volume is a first take, an introduction, to what its editors and authors
hope will be a new history of the Soviet Union as a multiethnic state.

Serious scholarly study of the Soviet Union began with the onset of the Cold
War as part of an effort to understand Communist Eastern Europe. Students
rushed into "area studies," coupling Soviet studies with studies of the countries
of East Central Europe in reflection of the new political division of the continent.
But, ironically, those who tilled the vineyards of the "other Europe" often restricted their work to a single country, and "Russianists" tended to cultivate only
their own plots, content to leave fallow the outlying lands of non-Russians.[2] Just
as it was then considered acceptable for scholars to treat all humankind as if it
were male, so the study of imperial Russia and the Soviet Union was often treated
unapologetically as if these ethnically and religiously diverse states were homo-
geneously Russian. Nor was the category of Russianness considered worthy of
analysis.[3] At the core of the study of Russia and the USSR was an unexamined
history of Russian and non-Russian national identities. Prior to the mid-1970s,

3

mainstream "Sovietologists" focused on high politics, economic growth, and foreign policy, while studies of nationalities were peripheral, both geographically and intellectually. With few exceptions, non-Russians were either left out of the mainstream narrative or treated as objects of political manipulation and central direction, sometimes as victims of Russification, other times as pathetic, archaic resisters to the modernizing program of the central authorities. Nationalities were homogenized; distinctions between them and within them were underplayed; and political repression and economic development, with little attention to ethnocultural mediation, appeared adequate to explain the fate of non-Russian peoples within the Soviet system. Since studying many nationalities was prohibitively costly and linguistically unfeasible, one nationality was often chosen to stand in for the rest.[4]

When Western scholars did turn their attention to the non-Russians in the early 1950s, their conclusions stood in stark contrast to the Soviet claim to have solved the "national question." Whether expressed in the extremely charged language of the Munich Institute for the Study of the USSR or the more modulated words of the influential Walter Kolarz or Richard Pipes, the Soviet state was presented as a fundamentally imperial arrangement, a colonial connection between Russia and its borderlands.[5] The conception of the Soviet Union as an empire made comparative sense, but the nature of this peculiar empire required a more detailed investigation and theorization. In particular, most scholars then treated the nation as an unproblematic category and national consciousness and nationalism as natural reflections and expressions of a national essence that needed little historical explanation. The essays in this book—while they do not all conform to a single idea of empire or even agree that the USSR should be labeled an empire—all engage with the problem of imperial rule, while taking into account the historically contingent and evolving character of nationalism and national identity.

By far the most influential early treatment of the nationalities question by a historian was Richard Pipes's *The Formation of the Soviet Union*, which, with its enormous source base and magisterial sweep of most of the borderlands, established the standard account of the origins of the "nationality problem" for most Russian historians. Though it seemed to eschew interpretation, *The Formation* had a clear and compelling thesis: that the revolution pitted communism against nationalism and that the Bolshevik victory was a military conquest by Russians over the authentic national and separatist aspirations of non-Russians. In retrospect, from the post-1991 perspective, Pipes's thesis seems to be vindicated—the artificial, illegitimate, forced annexation of non-Russian borderlands by a brutally centralizing regime was reversed at a moment of central government weakness, and the "natural" aspirations of the imprisoned peoples were finally realized in independent statehood. The desires and conflicts evident between 1917 and 1921 were taken up again by the border peoples as if the seventy-year interruption of Soviet power had not occurred. Legitimacy and morality were on one side, and cynical manipulation of ideals in the interest of naked power was on the other.

In such a scheme, it was hard to imagine that Bolshevism was not everywhere the enemy of non-Russian actors, that at times Bolshevism was seen by some non-Russians as a preferable alternative to a national independence promoted by a small nationalist elite in the name of a peasant majority, and that complex alliances were made by reformers, "national Bolsheviks," and even plain nationalists in the storm of civil war and in its aftermath. Largely left out of this vision of Soviet nationality policies was any discussion of state programs directed at preservation and development of national cultures within the USSR. Indeed, in the decade following Pipes's pioneering work, few discussions of Soviet nationality policy dealt with the indigenization (*korenizatsiia*) policies of the Soviet state in the 1920s.[6] Nevertheless, Pipes's focus on non-Russian separatism was a reminder that the Bolsheviks inherited a serious nationalities problem that lay at the foundation of their multinational state and provided a source of instability.

Pipes's approach stood in direct contrast to that of his colleagues at Harvard in the social sciences, who subscribed to the then hegemonic modernization theory, which asserted that industrialization and modern science, whether in capitalist or in communist form, fundamentally transformed traditional societies in similar ways. One such way was the tendency of substate "ethnic" or "tribal" identities to give way to a common civic national identity. The classic of this genre was Inkeles and Bauer's *The Soviet Citizen*, which, on the basis of the data collected by the massive Harvard interview project, concluded "that ethnic identity is of comparatively minor importance relative to social class membership as a predictor of the individual's life chances, his attitude toward the regime, and many of his general socio-political values."[7] This did not mean that nationality was irrelevant in all matters. Nationality was felt to be a salient feature of their lives more by Ukrainians than by Russians. Ukrainians, for instance, were about twice as likely as Russians to recommend dropping an atom bomb on Moscow! The project did conclude, however, that the USSR was a relatively stable society and that the nationality issue was not one that threatened that stability.[8]

The modernization approach gained ground in the 1960s as many scholars felt it described Khrushchev's USSR better than the rival totalitarian model. Indeed, in the 1960s, the USSR was often seen as an alternative model for national development. Reflecting this 1960s interest in problems of "development," two British scholars, Alec Nove and J. A. Newth, compared Soviet economic and social achievements against those of its neighbors to the south and asserted that association with Russia had been a net benefit for the southern Soviet republics. Far from there being any economic exploitation, they claimed that the evidence showed that industrialization, especially in Central Asia, had been financed with money raised in Russia proper. Reluctant to call the relationship between center and periphery "colonial" in the sense of being economically exploitative, Nove and Newth nevertheless pointed out that all real decision-making power rested with Moscow: "Therefore, if we do not call the present relationship colonialism, we ought to invent a new name to describe something which represents subordination and yet is genuinely different from the imperialism of the past."[9]

Whether largely negative in its assessments of Soviet nationality policies or more positive, Sovietological research was often shaped by the intense public moralizing about the Soviet experience. A more neutral, detached stance by a researcher was itself suspect in the eyes of much of the profession. Nevertheless, by the 1970s, scholarly work on the early Soviet nationality policy and on specific nationalities had prepared the ground for a "paradigm shift" from a story of cynical manipulation and repression and the erasure of nationality through Russification and modernization to a dialectical narrative of preservation and transformation, both nation-making and nation-destroying.[10] Some political scientists and sociologists undertook deeply textured historical research into the 1920s, most notably Zvi Gitelman in his analysis of the Communist party's Jewish Sections and Gregory Massell in his exploration of Soviet policies toward women in Central Asia. Gitelman and Massell both told a story of Communist attempts to modernize a traditionalist ethnic community, and both found that the attempt "to combine modernization and ethnic maintenance" was a failure, largely because of the poor fit between the developmental plans of the party and the reservoir of traditions and interests of the ethnic population.[11] Secular Jewish Communists were unable to destroy the Jewish religion, while native and Russian Communists in Central Asia were even more surprisingly unable to eradicate the veil and other "feudal" practices and eventually had to settle for a curious accommodation with traditional society.

By the mid-1970s, it was clear to unprejudiced observers that the nationalities issue was not disappearing in the Soviet Union but instead seemed to have become a permanent fact of Soviet politics. A key contribution was Teresa Rakowska-Harmstone's widely read 1974 article on the nation-making aspects of Soviet policy, which combined historical depth and social scientific sophistication.[12] Using a "dialectical" approach to explain the "increasingly assertive ethnic nationalism among the non-Russian minorities," she illustrated how "powerful integrative forces . . . released through the process of industrialization and the accompanying expansion of mass education and intensive socialization" were countered by "the retention of a federal administrative framework" that "safeguarded the territorial loci and formal ethnocultural institutions of most minorities, thereby preserving the bases for potential manifestations of national attitudes." Distinguishing between "orthodox" and "unorthodox" nationalism, the first permitted within the system, the second advocating secession, independence, and/or the rejection of the system's ideological mold, she demonstrated how indigenous ethnic elites in republics sought "sources of legitimacy in their own unique national heritage" and established ties with their own nationality through the skillful manipulation of permissible "nationalism." The consolidation of ethnic power and consciousness in many (though by no means all) of the non-Russian republics was inhibited by "the continued political, economic, and cultural hegemony enjoyed by the Great Russian majority and the national chauvinism manifested by this group vis-à-vis the minority nationalities." Whatever the policy goals of the regime, in actuality national cohesion and nationalist expression were growing and were "on a collision course with party policies."[13] The following decade witnessed such a deluge of works by political scientists on the nationalities question that, by 1984, Gail Lapidus had to begin her fine article on the nationalities question with an apology for again covering this well-trod ground.[14]

Nevertheless, the shift in the theoretical literature on nationalism and nations that commenced in the 1950s and 1960s with the work of Elie Kedourie, Ernest Gellner, and Karl Deutsch and had by the mid-1990s become the prevalent view among specialists initially had a limited resonance among Sovietologists and next to none among Soviet historians. From a tendency to view nations as ancient and natural divisions of the human race, with a deep continuity extending into modern times and underlying the emergence of political nationalism, analysts of nationalism developed a model of nations as quintessentially modern social and cultural constructions. The newer approach to nationness argued that, far from being a natural component of human relations, something like kinship or family, nationality and the nation are created (or invented) in a complex social and political process in which intellectuals and activists play a formative role, as well as broader socioeconomic forces. Whether the product of pernicious ideas (Kedourie) or a functional requirement of industrialism (Gellner) or the result of increased "social communication" (Deutsch), nations were here conceived as products of human interventions that only in the nineteenth and twentieth centuries achieved powerful resonances among masses of people.[15] Rather than the nation giving rise to nationalism, these writers suggest, it is nationalism that gave rise to the nation.

In its largely atheoretical treatment of nationality, much, though not the best, Sovietological thought had accepted uncritically a commonsense view of nationality as a relatively observable, objective phenomenon based on a community of language, culture, shared myths of origin or kinship, and perhaps territory.[16] The eruption of nationalisms in the Gorbachev era at just the time that the new theories of nationalism were gaining sway initiated a second paradigm shift. The mass media and some scholars interpreted these events in the old manner, as a reawakening of repressed desires and interests, a kettle boiling over after the lid had been removed (or blown off because of irresistible pressure).[17] However, much more interesting, there was a move to wed the new social scientific approach to nationality with informed historical inquiry. The political scientists Philip Roeder and Rogers Brubaker each produced institutionalist analyses that emphasized the role of Bolshevik-created national institutions and elites in preserving national consciousness and in providing institutions that allowed for rapid nationalist mobilization.[18] The historians Ronald Suny and Yuri Slezkine, drawing on the research from their previous monographs, provided overarching accounts of the ways in which the Bolsheviks had encouraged national consciousness and a sense of inherent primordial ethnicity.[19] However, historians generally work more slowly, and this volume represents work from the first generation of archivally based research on nationalities and empire during the first half of the Soviet period.[20]

The Bolsheviks inherited not only their "nationalities problem" from the old regime but also took over a state and a bureaucracy with its own traditions for dealing with, or ignoring, that problem. Therefore, our volume begins with Ronald Suny's wide-ranging analysis of prerevolutionary Russia's imperial and national strategies of rule. Suny outlines an ideal type of empire as a composite state that employs ethnic distinction and inequitable hierarchy. He then uses that model to distinguish nation-building processes in overseas empires, in which a metropolitan *nation-state* dominates geographically distinct colonial societies, from the much less studied land empires, such as the Russian, Habsburg, and Ottoman empires, in which the imperial and colonial peoples tended to mix and imperial and national identities consequently were more blurred. Moreover, given Russia's historic backwardness, the tsars had made much less progress in linguistic and cultural homogenization than had Western monarchies such as England, France, and Spain prior to the rise of nationalism in the nineteenth century. As a result, when the tsars did occasionally engage in a paroxysm of Russification, the result was typically stiff nationalist resistance from the more advanced nationalist movements—Polish, Finnish, Ukrainian, Latvian, Georgian, Armenian—of the empire's western and southern peripheries. Suny concludes that tsarist Russia failed to develop a strong, coherent, widely accepted national identity autonomous from religious, dynastic, or state identifications, which in turn contributed to its collapse in 1917 under the extreme pressures of World War I.

When the Bolsheviks came to power in October 1917, then, they took possession of a disintegrating multiethnic state with quite strong nationalist movements on its western and southern peripheries, weak or nonexistent ones in the east, and a relatively undeveloped national consciousness among the central and numerically dominant Russians. However, as Terry Martin's essay shows, Lenin and Stalin interpreted the existing situation quite differently. They were very impressed by the collapse of the Austro-Hungarian Empire and so agreed, particularly after three years of bitter civil war, that the nationalist threat was indeed a serious one. But they also saw Russian nationalism as exceptionally strong and as an even more serious threat to state unity, since it would provoke defensive nationalism among the non-Russians. Therefore, they self-consciously attempted to create an anti-imperial state, or, in Martin's phrase, an "affirmative action empire." They supported the creation and development of non-Russian territories, elites, languages, and cultural institutions, while systematically downplaying and even scapegoating Russian national institutions and culture. They believed this strategy would defuse nationalism and allow them to build a centralized, highly interventionist, multiethnic socialist state. The Bolsheviks kept the principle of ethnic distinction that Ronald Suny finds in all empires but reversed the traditional ethnic hierarchy that placed the "state-bearing" nation's prestige far above those of the "colonial" peoples. In this way, they hoped to preserve the territorial integrity of the former Russian empire into the postimperial age of nationalism.

Many analysts have been puzzled by the Soviet leadership's failure to try to build a national identity at the all-Union Soviet level.[21] Nationality was instead confined to the substate level. Unlike in Britain, Yugoslavia, India, or America, "Soviet" was never considered an ethnic or a national identity. In some sense, this continued the tsarist pattern of nation-building outlined by Suny. Joshua Sanborn's essay, however, takes issue with this interpretive line. He warns his readers not to conflate nation with ethnic nation and proposes that in both the tsarist and the Soviet states leaders sought a civic national, rather than an imperial or ethnonational, base for the political community. Modernizing military men in particular, faced by the daunting tasks of conscription and mobilization for war, attempted to build a nonethnic national cohesion. Both tsarist and Soviet officers employed the metaphor of family to build affinitive bonds among soldiers and linked family to the military by providing rations for families of servicemen. Sanborn traces a shift from patriarchal to fraternal imagery, beginning in tsarist times and extending across the revolution, that emphasized solidarity, equality, and loyalty—all themes resonant in the rhetoric of nationhood. Sanborn's analysis suggests that the creation of a Soviet political community was analogous to other nation-making projects, even if it renounced the crucial term of "nation" itself.[22]

The essays of Daniel Schafer, Adeeb Khalid, Matt Payne, and Douglas Northrop provide nuanced case studies that shed new light on the nature and the often unintended social consequences of the Soviet government's policy of supporting the formation of national territories, elites, languages, and cultures. Schafer's study of the formation and dissolution of the Tatar-Bashkir republic demonstrates just how complex and ambiguous the process of territorializing ethnicity was at ground zero. His essay forces reconsideration of earlier scholarly judgments about a Soviet policy of divide and conquer.[23] Instead of careful, long-term planning aimed at dividing one Muslim people from another, Soviet policy in the years of civil war appears here more like improvisation, though improvisation guided by an overarching commitment to national territories. And its *divide et impera* was directed not against a Turkic nation-in-formation but against the anti-Bolshevik movement as a whole. Schafer does not agree that Bashkir identity was instrumentally created by the Soviet elite and instead argues that it was based on the Bashkirs' nomadic past, their corporate rights to the land, and their particular relations with the Russians. As in Central Asia (see Khalid's essay), the political contest in Bashkortostan was multipolar, with local Bashkirs, local Russian Communists, central Soviet authorities, White forces, and Russian settlers all providing the context in which deception, misunderstanding, and defection all became possible. Schafer's essay also demonstrates how the formation of national territories in mixed ethnic regions was a recipe for ethnic mobilization and a dramatic increase in national consciousness. Prior to 1917, Bashkir identity may have been weak and latent, but once Bolshevik policy had endorsed the formation of national territories, the Bashkir leader, Ahmed Zeki Validov, could rally a significant popular following behind the one principal conviction of Bashkir identity: that they were not Tatars. The process Schafer describes in Bashkortostan was repeated thousands of times across the entire Soviet Union in the 1920s as tens of thousands of national territories, many as small as a few villages, were established. The result was a not undesired growth in national consciousness but also a very unwelcome growth in ethnic conflict and national mobilization.[24]

Adeeb Khalid shifts our geographic focus from the Turkic Muslims of the middle Volga to the fundamentally different Turkic Muslim culture of Central Asia, as well as our topical focus from national territories to national elites. Taking advantage of Turkic language sources to interrogate the Russian sources on which earlier scholars had relied, Khalid moves from the usual bipolar narrative of Russians against Muslims to a multipolar tale of Jadids (Muslim reformers) in conflict with the conservative Muslim *ulema* (religious leaders), Central Asian Russian settlers attacking Muslims, local Russian-dominated soviets in conflict with Moscow, and a strategic alliance by 1919 between Soviet Russia and the radicalized anti-imperialist Jadids. This marriage of convenience suited the Bolsheviks, who acquired invaluable educated Central Asians to staff their newly created national territories, and the Jadids, who used the Bolsheviks to gain political power for their reforming ideas after having lost the battle for popular opinion with their conservative Muslim opponents. As with Schafer's account of territorialization, Khalid's story also repeated itself, in different forms, across the entire Soviet Union in the 1920s. In virtually every national republic, the Bolsheviks could find the educated, qualified national "cadres" required by their indigenization programs only among the pre-existing non-Bolshevik national (and often nationalist) elites, while local nationalists found a surprising ally for their nation-building projects in Moscow's new radical rulers. This was, however, an unequal marriage. As the Bolsheviks succeeded in educating and training a new loyal, non-Russian elite, they gradually removed—in very many cases, arrested—most of their early national allies in a series of purges in 1928–1930, 1932–1934, and 1937–1938. The commitment to national elites, which would endure through the Stalin years and beyond, was not a license for nationalist autonomy or even for "national communism."

Douglas Northrop's essay on gender and ethnicity in Uzbekistan addresses the complicated issue of national culture and the Soviet project of "cultural revolution." Sheila Fitzpatrick borrowed this Bolshevik phrase to refer to the period from 1928 to 1931, when Stalin launched his "socialist offensive" that involved rapid industrialization, the abolition of private enterprise and private trade, the collectivization of agriculture, and a thoroughgoing Bolshevization of the public, academic, and professional spheres.[25] Cultural revolution refers both to a method—class warfare and an encouragement of vigilante actions by militant Bolshevik supporters—and a mood: a widespread utopian belief in the ability to immediately transform a backward society into an advanced, socialist state. Nowhere was the project of "cultural revolution" more relevant than in what the Bolsheviks called, in the language of the times, their "culturally backward eastern" national regions. Suny's essay notes that the project of helping "develop" "backward" colonial cultures is a typical late-imperial move to justify empire in the age of nationalism, so it is unsurprising that the Soviet affirmative action empire took such developmentalism to an extreme. Northrop illustrates a deep contradiction in Soviet policy in Uzbekistan. On the one hand, Uzbek nationality was defined in terms of gender relations and customs of female seclusion that were marked as backward, dirty, and oppressive. Yet to modernize and civilize the Soviet East, the Communists would have to eradicate precisely those social practices that were fundamental to national identity. This allowed those who resisted the Soviet modernization program to wrap themselves in the flag of the "nation." Northrop's account of the striking failure to penetrate and change Uzbek gender relations points to the limitations faced by even the most violent and "totalitarian" state action in transforming patterns of traditional everyday life.

Matt Payne provides a counterintuitive but instructive story of the early stages of the formation of a Bolshevik national elite in Kazakhstan. In the 1920s, as part of their class-based ideology, the Bolsheviks preferred to recruit workers to fill the many bureaucratic jobs they had both inherited and were busily creating. However, in Kazakhstan and in many other non-Russian regions, there simply was no native proletariat, so, paradoxically, the first stage of elite formation was proletarianization. Payne tells how the state authorities preferentially recruited Kazakhs into the workforce to build the Turkestan-Siberian railroad. But the transformation of nomads into waged workers met resistance from traditionalist Kazakhs, Turksib railroad managers, and European workers. The program of affirmative action for Kazakhs created resentment among non-Kazakh workers. Discrimination, ethnic stereotyping, and plain old competition for limited jobs and benefits led to fist fights, vicious beatings, and riots. This part of Payne's story was widespread throughout the Soviet Union's eastern national regions, though nowhere was ethnic conflict quite so volatile as in Kazakhstan. Facing a hostile and bewildering environment, new Kazakh proletarians found allies in veteran, internationalist Russian workers, who helped them adapt to their new environment in the only way they could: by teaching them to be linguistically and culturally "Russian." Thus, a completely good-faith effort by the Soviet state to create a Kazakh proletariat ended up promoting a strongly Russificatory outcome. Although unintended, this was, from the Soviet perspective, not undesired, as the USSR acquired both good "Kazakhs" and "Bolsheviks," many of whom would go on to staff important positions in the Kazakh government.

The end of the cultural revolution in 1932 was followed by a striking conservative turn in social and cultural policy that included, among other changes, the end of progressive education, the criminalization of abortion, and a shift from avant-garde to realist art.[26] This period also witnessed a fundamental transformation of the Soviet strategy for ruling its multiethnic state. In part, this reflected the broader conservative trend. But, in part, it was also a result of the tensions and unintended consequences—as outlined in the essays of Schafer, Khalid, Payne, and Northrop—that the original Soviet policy had produced. The territorialization of ethnicity aimed to defuse nationalism but instead often intensified it and exacerbated ethnic conflict. Affirmative action programs had similar results. Soviet developmentalism in Central Asia produced resistance and recalcitrance, rather than gratitude. The now well-known phenomenon of strategic ethnicity, where individuals manipulate their ethnic identity to take advantage of national preferences, also struck the Bolsheviks as unseemly and ungrateful opportunism, rather than rational behavior.[27] All of these problems are endemic to multiethnic states in the modern era; the nationalities issue is one to be managed, not solved. However, the Bolsheviks saw things differently. Perhaps most disturbing to Stalin was his growing conviction that the alliance with national elites was leading to a nationalization of Bolshevism, rather than a Bolshevization of nationals. This suspicion climaxed during the great famine of 1932–1933, when the central government interpreted the resistance of local Ukrainian officials to central grain requisitions as a consequence of Ukrainian national communism and passed an important Politburo resolution on December 14, 1932, edited by Stalin himself, condemning errors in the implementation of Ukrainization. This resolution triggered a major revision of the Soviet nationalities policy.[28]

Scholars have often interpreted this change in course as marking the end of indigenization and a turn toward Russification. This is a considerable exaggeration. As Peter Blitstein's detailed case study of a 1938 law that mandated Russian language education for non-Russians clearly demonstrates, the intent of the law was neither linguistic nor cultural Russification but rather a strengthening of Russian's role as the lingua franca of the multinational Soviet state. The law did not eliminate native language education; it mandated only that Russian be taught as a compulsory subject in grade schools. More striking than the passage of such a law is the fact that, as late as 1938, Russian was not being taught *at all* in a sizable number of non-Russian schools. Moreover, as Blitstein again shows, the poverty of resources put into the Russian language program led to abysmally low levels of competence in Russian after the law's passage. Moreover, there was another, more important compulsory language policy in Soviet education that lasted until Stalin's death (and quite clearly reflected his wishes): the requirement that titular nationals (e.g., Uzbeks in Uzbekistan, Tatars in Tatarstan) attend native-language schools. Though this policy was often breached in practice, it was only in the post-Stalin period, with the school reform of 1958, that non-Russians were given the *choice* to educate their children in Russian, rather than in their native languages. Whereas during Stalin's rule, educational policy probably acted as a brake on linguistic Russification, in the Khrushchev and the Brezhnev periods hundreds of thousands of non-Russian parents sent their children to Russian-language schools in order to ease the path to social advancement.

David Brandenberger's essay discusses one of the most dramatic developments that took place after the December 1932 Politburo decree and that intensified enormously during World War II: the rehabilitation of traditional Russian culture and the aggressive celebration of the Russians as the Soviet Union's leading nationality, "the first among equals," as they were now called. Brandenberger explains this development as a policy of state-building and legitimation, the creation of a Great Power (*derzhava*), rather than explicit nationalism. In Stalin's view, the original strategy of downplaying Russian culture and discouraging Russian national consciousness had failed in its task of producing state unity. A new principle of unity was needed. Brandenberger looks at the uses of history in mobilizing the public for war, the invocation of "our great ancestors" (all of whom were Russian), and the celebration of the formerly anathemized Russian imperialism (the "lesser evil" theory). A number of Russocentric historians pushed for a Russophilic, statist interpretation of the tsarist and Soviet past. When the prominent historian Anna Pankratova and her team produced a history of Kazakhstan that was critical of Russian colonialism, it was condemned as anti-Russian. She was forced to reconsider her views, as the war years marked a further retreat from a historiography informed by Marxism to a more Russian nationalist position. Again, this strategy did not mean Russification. At the same time that Russian heroes and Russian history were being celebrated across the entire Soviet union, non-Russian heroes and history were being praised in the non-Russian republics, but with the difference underscored in the Pankratova example: the non-Russian heroes and historical episodes could never be anti-Russian but rather must support the new canonical multiethnic image of the Soviet Union as a "Friendship of the Peoples," but a friendship in which the Russians occupied the central, unifying role.[29]

This transformation of the status of the Russians, and along with it the entire principle of unity for the Soviet state, represented one aspect of the new turn in Soviet policies in the 1930s. The second aspect was the emergence of the category of "enemy nations" and a growing practice of terror directed against individuals and entire nations on the basis of their ethnic identity alone. Peter Holquist's essay ambitiously seeks to identify the root causes of such destructive policies, whether they targeted class, racial, ethnic, or other social categories. He shows how, in nineteenth-century Europe, state officials and other professionals began to conceive of the citizenry as composed of aggregate populations to be measured and counted, in order to allow the state to intervene scientifically to shape and sculpt the population, a process Holquist calls "population politics." Such social engineering could take a "positive" form, as in the class-and nationality-based affirmative action policies of the early Soviet Union, or, as in Holquist's essay, they could be "negative" interventions designed to eliminate, eradicate, or exterminate unwanted population categories: Circassians (Cherkess tribes) from the Western Caucasus in the early 1860s; indigenous peoples from parts of Central Asia during World War I; Cossacks from the Don and Terek in 1919–1920; "bandits" from Chechnia in 1925; and whole nationalities deemed traitors during World War II. Holquist concludes that violence that has seemed to most observers quintessentially Bolshevik should be viewed through a wider lens and seen as a product of new forms of conceiving society and new techniques of state intervention.

In the early Soviet period, nations were not a target of such negative population politics. Cossacks were repressed as a counterrevolutionary *soslovie* (estate), not as an ethnic group. In fact, in the 1920s, the Soviet government practiced a "positive" relocation of scattered ethnic groups—Jews, above all, but many others as well—in order to concentrate them geographically and so be able to form national territories. Yet, in the 1930s, certain nationalities became targets for negative population politics: ethnic cleansing, arrest, and mass execution.[30] The key factor was the Soviet policy of using its positive nation-building policies to attempt to project Soviet influence into neighboring countries, especially along the country's western border, where Finns/Karelians, Belorussians, Ukrainians, and Romanians/Moldavians lived on both sides of the Soviet border. In the 1920s, it was hoped that the Soviet nationalities policy would help revolutionize ethnic minorities in neighboring Finland, Poland, and Romania. And, to a considerable extent, it did. However, the belief in the political salience of cross-border ethnic ties implied that the influence could flow in the opposite direction, as well. With the triumph of extreme nationalism across almost all of eastern and central Europe in the 1930s, and with a growing xenophobia in the Soviet Union itself, the Soviet leadership became convinced that the subversive influence was now flowing from west to east. As a result, from 1935 to 1938, at least nine "diaspora" nationalities—Finns, Estonians, Latvians, Lithuanians, Poles, Germans, Kurds, Chinese, and Koreans—were forcibly resettled away from the Soviet Union's border regions. During the Great Terror of 1937–1938, the regime specifically targeted these same diaspora nationalities (and others, such as Greeks and Bulgarians) for mass arrest and execution on the basis of their ethnic identity alone. Almost half of the approximately 680,000 executions in those two years were part of these "national operations." Indeed, in the last months of the Great Terror, diaspora nationalities were the almost exclusive target of the Great Terror.[31] This was an extraordinary and unexpected development.

As with Russocentric propaganda, Soviet nationalities-based terror also expanded dramatically during World War II.[32] The German invasion, in June 1941, led to the immediate deportation of the Soviet Union's entire German population. In 1943 and 1944, after the expulsion of the German armies, six entire Soviet nations—every man, woman, and child—were deported to Siberia or Central Asia on the charge of having collaborated with the enemy: the Crimean Tatars, Meskhetian Turks, Kabardinians, Ingush, Chechens, and Kalmyks. While the first three were Turkic-speaking and so could be and were, with a great stretch, interpreted as a Turkish diaspora population, the last three were clearly indigenous Soviet nations. Their deportation marked a new escalation in the practice of Soviet national terror. The Sovietization of the newly acquired territories of Estonia, Latvia, Lithuania, western Belarus, western Ukraine, and Moldova also led to a wave of mass deportations from 1944 to 1952. Strictly speaking, these were not national deportations. Rather, they replicated the mass arrests and deportations carried out across the entire Soviet Union in 1918–1921 and 1928–1933. However, since the postwar deportations did not target Russians and since the Soviet state had now identified itself to a considerable degree with its core Russian nationality, these deportations were *perceived* by their victims as *national* repression by an *imperial* Russian power.

Nor was this perception entirely groundless. In November 1948, an important law divided the Soviet Union's permanent exile population (the *spetspereselentsy*) into two categories: the temporarily exiled and the "eternally" exiled. The first category included mostly nonnational deportees, in particular "kulaks" deported in the 1930s and "Vlasovites" (those who fought with the German army) deported in the 1940s—and the majority of these were indeed freed before Stalin's death. The second included all the deported nations, as well as all Estonians, Latvians, Lithuanians, western Belorussians, western Ukrainians, and Moldavians, despite the fact that these individuals had been deported as kulaks, Vlasovites, or "bandits." In this way, their exile was nationalized, and, by the time of Stalin's death, almost the entire Soviet exile population was being confined due to national identity alone. Finally, the postwar period witnessed a shocking return to state-sponsored anti-Semitic repression, even though during the early Soviet period anti-Semitism had been considered utterly reactionary, counterrevolutionary, vulgar, and taboo. A quiet campaign of arrests and executions targeted the Yiddish-language intelligentsia, while a noisy "anticosmopolitan" campaign sought to intimidate and stigmatize assimilated Jewish intellectuals and their putative non-Jewish cosmopolitan allies.

The turn in the mid-1930s toward Russian nationalist propaganda and a practice of selective nation-destroying had a crucial long-term role in undermining the viability of the multiethnic Soviet state. As Mark Beissinger has convincingly argued, in the age of nationalism, to be labeled an empire by one's citizens and one's neighbors is frequently fatal, for it is assumed that empires are antiquated, artificial constructs that will eventually fragment into their natural nation-state components.[33] India is not now labeled an empire, but if we start to hear it described widely as one, we can assume its disintegration has suddenly become much more likely. The brilliant theorist of nationalism and ardent Scottish nationalist Tom Nairn understands this connection quite well and so has spent more than two decades trying to convince his countrymen and the world—not without some success—that Great Britain is an artificial imperial construct and is therefore doomed.[34] Lenin and Stalin also understood this dynamic very well. As Terry Martin shows in his essay, the affirmative action empire was a self-conscious strategy to avoid, at all costs, the subjective perception of empire. In the 1930s, Stalin decided the costs were too high. But his reforms had high costs as well. In the modern world, there are perhaps two things most associated with the malevolence of empire: national repression and forced assimilation. Stalin's nationally targeted repression, in fact, affected only a small percentage of non-Russians, but it nevertheless conveyed an image to all non-Russians of imperial behavior. Stalin's Russificatory measures were likewise comparatively mild, and state-supported nation-building efforts continued through to his death, but the ostentatious and often insulting Russocentric propaganda he endorsed created a false impression of a Russificatory regime and cost the state much, though far from all, of the good will acquired by its indigenization and affirmative action policies.

If we wish to characterize the Soviet strategy for running a multiethnic state as of March 1953, it would only be a slight exaggeration to say that the USSR was simultaneously pursuing a policy of nation-building and inculcating a subjective perception of empire. Khrushchev did end Stalin's nation-destroying policies, though he only partially undid their consequences, as the Crimean Tatars, Germans, and Meskhetian Turks were not allowed to return home and a lower-level nonviolent anti-Semitism became institutionalized. Khrushchev ended the overtly chauvinist Russian nationalist rhetoric but left the Russians as "elder brother" and actually increased the state's Russificatory pressure. The Brezhnev leadership largely continued this line, while growing more and more disenchanted with the nationalities policy it had inherited. But it was too late to change, or, if it wasn't, the regime now lacked the energy to do so. If, in the 1920s, indigenization was imposed from the center on reluctant Russified Communist parties, in the 1960s and 1970s there was an increasing trend toward indigenization from below, as the processes of nation-building, as well as those of industrialization, urbanization, and mass education, produced thoroughly Communized national elites that successfully contested for control of their republics. By the 1980s, survey data reveal that both Russians and titular nationals believed that in most of the union republics—Belorussia, Ukraine, and Moldavia being the exceptions—titular nationals were favored in employment and educational opportunities. The offspring of Russians and titular nationals most often chose to register as non-Russians.[35] As the Communist ideology atrophied and the authority of the central state was systematically undermined by Gorbachev's reforms, a rash of publications about Stalin's crimes against the non-Russians led to a surge in the subjective perception of empire. Even many Russians became momentarily convinced that they too were a persecuted nationality and supported Yeltsin's campaign to replace the Soviet empire with a non-imperial Russian nation-state.

There are many ironies to Soviet history. Certainly a principal one must be that a radical socialist elite that proclaimed an internationalist agenda that was to transcend the bourgeois nationalist stage of history in fact ended up by institutionalizing nations within its own political body. Another irony is that, although the promotion of nationhood was part of a sophisticated strategy for avoiding the modern world's fatal attribution of imperialism, the Soviet state ultimately fell victim to the subjective perception of empire. The dual effects of Soviet nationality policies—its nation-making and its nation-breaking aspects—were evident in the spring of the last year of Soviet power, as six republics—Armenia, Estonia, Georgia, Latvia, Lithuania, and Moldova—expressed their desire to leave the Soviet Union, and the other nine—Azerbaijan, Belarus, Kazakhstan, Kyrgyzstan, Russia, Tajikistan, Turkmenistan, Ukraine, and Uzbekistan—voted overwhelmingly to remain within a reformed federation. When, in the coup of August 1991, the Soviet center "committed suicide,"[36] the last links holding together the Bolsheviks' superstate dissolved. A final, fortunate irony was that Lenin's and Stalin's policy of drawing boundaries along national lines made the division of the Soviet Union relatively easy and peaceful. Where that principle had been violated—in

Nagorno-Karabakh and right-bank Moldova—there was bloodshed. Where eth-nonationalism of the dominant nationality turned into mini-imperialism against minorities—in Abkhazia and South Ossetia—people resorted to violence. Yet much of the work of decolonization had already occurred within the Soviet Union. Ahead, in the void of the future, lay the hard work of creating sovereign nation-states.

Notes

1. The following is an undoubtedly incomplete list of works that have taken advantage of the opening of the Soviet archives. Terry Martin, *The Affirmative Action Empire: Nations and Nationalism in the Soviet Union, 1923–1939* (Ithaca, N.Y.: Cornell University Press, 2001); Amir Weiner, *Making Sense of War: The Second World War and the Fate of the Bolshevik Revolution* (Princeton: Princeton University Press, 2001); Alaina Lemon, *Between Two Fires: Gypsy Performance and Romani Memory from Pushkin to Postsocialism* (Durham, N.C.: Duke University Press, 2000); Jeremy Smith, *The Bolsheviks and the National Question, 1917–23* (New York: St. Martin's, 1999); Michael Smith, *Language and Power in the Creation of the USSR, 1917–1953* (New York: Mouton de Gruyter, 1998); Adeeb Khalid, *The Politics of Muslim Cultural Reform: Jadidism in Central Asia* (Berkeley: University of California Press, 1998). Dissertations include David Brandenberger, "National Bolshevism: Stalinist Mass Culture and the Formation of Modern Russian National Identity, 1931–1956" (Ph.D. diss., Harvard University, 2000); Serguei Ekelchik, "History, Culture, and Nationhood under High Stalinism: Soviet Ukraine, 1939–1954" (Ph.D. diss., University of Alberta, 2000); Adrienne Edgar, "The Creation of Soviet Turkmenistan, 1924–1938" (Ph.D. diss., University of California at Berkeley, 1999); Peter Blitstein, "Stalin's Nations: Soviet Nationality Policy between Planning and Primordialism, 1936–1953" (Ph.D. diss., University of California at Berkeley, 1999); Douglas Northrop, "Uzbek Women and the Veil: Gender and Power in Stalinist Central Asia" (Ph.D. diss., Stanford University, 1999); Michaela Pohl, "The Virgin Lands between Memory and Forgetting: People and Transformation in the Soviet Union, 1954–1960" (Ph.D. diss., Indiana University, 1999); Joshua Sanborn, "Drafting the Nation: Military Conscription and the Formation of a Modern Polity in Tsarist and Soviet Russia, 1905–1925" (Ph.D. diss., University of Chicago, 1998); Francine Hirsch, "Empire of Nations: Colonial Technologies and the Making of the Soviet Union, 1917–1939" (Ph.D. diss., Princeton University, 1998); Paula Anne Michaels, "Shamans and Surgeons: The Politics of Health Care in Soviet Kazakhstan, 1928–1941" (Ph.D. diss., University of North Carolina at Chapel Hill, 1997); Peter Holquist, "A Russian Vendee: The Practice of Revolutionary Politics in the Don Countryside, 1917–1921" (Ph.D. diss., Columbia University, 1995); and Matthew Payne, "Turksib: The Building of the Turkestan-Siberian Railroad and the Politics of Production during the Cultural Revolution" (Ph.D. diss., University of Chicago, 1995).

2. The historiographic review includes some material from Ronald Grigor Suny, "Rethinking Soviet Studies: Bringing the Non-Russians Back In," in Daniel Orlovsky, ed., *Beyond Soviet Studies* (Washington, D.C.: Woodrow Wilson Center Press, 1995), pp. 105–134.

3. A notable exception to this generalization were the essays of Roman Szporluk,

now collected in Roman Szporluk, *Russia, Ukraine, and the Breakup of the Soviet Union* (Stanford Calif.: Hoover Institute, 2000).

4. The Ukrainians played this role in the case of the Harvard Project on the Soviet Social System. See Alex Inkeles and Raymond A. Bauer, *The Soviet Citizen: Daily Life in a Totalitarian Society* (Cambridge, Mass.: Harvard University Press, 1961).

5. Walter Kolarz, *Russia and Her Colonies* (New York: Praeger, 1952); Richard Pipes, *The Formation of the Soviet Union: Communism and Nationalism, 1917–1923* (Cambridge, Mass: Harvard University Press, 1954). For variations on the theme of empire, see also Olaf Caroe, *Soviet Empire: The Turks of Central Asia and Stalinism* (New York: St Martin's, 1953); Robert Conquest, *The Soviet Deportation of Nationalities* (London: Macmillan, 1960), reprinted and expanded as *The Nation Killers: The Soviet Deportation of Nationalities* (London: Macmillan, 1970); Hugh Seton-Watson, *The New Imperialism* (East Totowa, N.J.: Rowman and Littlefield, 1971); and, outside scholarship, U.S. Congress, Senate Committee on the Judiciary, *The Soviet Empire* (Washington, D.C., 1958; rev. ed., 1965).

6. A notable exception being the work of Mary Matossian, *The Impact of Soviet Policies in Armenia* (Leiden: Brill, 1962).

7. Alex Inkeles and Raymond A. Bauer, *The Soviet Citizen: Daily Life in a Totalitarian Society* (Cambridge, Mass.: Harvard University Press, 1961), p. 351.

8. Raymond A. Bauer, Alex Inkeles, and Clyde Kluckhohn, *How the Soviet System Works: Cultural, Psychological and Social Themes* (New York: Vintage, 1961), pp. 239–240, 243, 236, 243.

9. Alec Nove and J. A. Newth, *The Soviet Middle East: A Model for Development?* (London: Allen & Unwin, 1967), pp. 45, 97, 114, 122. For an interesting contrast, these conclusions might be compared to those of Vsevolod Holubnychy, who argued that "wholly inexplicable gaps" in economic development existed among Soviet republics, with the RSFSR faring better than the rest, and that this confirmed the image of a colonial relationship between Russia and the non-Russian republics ("Some Economic Aspects of Relations among the Soviet Republics," in Erich Goldhagen, ed., *Ethnic Minorities in the Soviet Union* [New York: Praeger, 1968], pp. 50–120). However distinctive Soviet imperialism may have been, its emphasis on development would have been familiar to imperialists of other empires, and the form of that development was decided almost exclusively in the metropole, with the needs of the empire paramount and those of the peoples of the periphery secondary.

10. The essential primacy of nation over other social categories, particularly class, was challenged by Ronald Suny's study of the revolution in multiethnic Baku (*The Baku Commune, 1917–1918: Class and Nationality in the Russian Revolution* [Princeton N.J.: Princeton University Press, 1972]). Suny's approach here, and in his subsequent works, emphasized the changing nature of nationality, rather than its continuity and stability through time. However, in his early work he saw nationality as having an objective, material content that was productive of nationalism.

11. Zvi Y. Gitelman, *Jewish Nationality and Soviet Politics: The Jewish Sections of the CPSU, 1917–1930* (Princeton, N.J.: Princeton University Press, 1972); Gregory J. Massell, *The Surrogate Proletariat: Moslem Women and Revolutionary Strategies in Soviet Central Asia, 1919–1929* (Princeton N.J.: Princeton University Press, 1974).

12. Teresa Rakowska-Harmstone, "The Dialectics of Nationalism in the USSR," *Problems of Communism* 23, no. 3 (May–June 1974): 1–22.

13. Ibid., pp. 1–2, 10, 21.

14. Gail W. Lapidus, "Ethnonationalism and Political Stability: The Soviet Case," *World Politics* 36, no. 4 (July 1984): 355–380. For examples of some of the better works, see Barbara A. Anderson and Brian D. Silver, "Estimating Russification of Ethnic Identity among Non-Russians in the USSR," *Demography*, 20, no. 4 (November 1983): 461–489; "Equality, Efficiency, and Politics in Soviet Bilingual Education Policy, 1934–1980," *American Political Science Review* 78 (1984): 1019–1039; Rasma Karklins, *Ethnic Relations in the USSR: The Perspective from Below* (Boston: Allen & Unwin, 1986); Gerhard Simon, *Nationalismus und Nationalitatenpolitik in der Sowjetunion* (Baden-Baden: Nomos Verlagsgesellschaft, 1986); Victor Zaslavsky, *The Neo-Stalinist State: Class, Ethnicity and Consensus in Soviet Society* (Armonk, N.Y.: Sharpe, 1982); Mark Beissinger and Lubko Hajda, eds., *The Nationality Factor in Soviet Society and Politics: Current Trends and Future Prospects* (Boulder, Colo.: Westview, 1989).

15. Among the key works in this shift in thinking about nations and nationalism were Elie Kedourie, *Nationalism* (London: Hutchinson, 1960); Karl Deutsch, *Nationalism and Social Communication: An Inquiry into the Foundations of Nationality* (Cambridge, Mass.: MIT Press, 1966; 1st ed., 1953); Benedict Anderson, *Imagined Communities: Reflections on the Origin and Spread of Nationalism* (London: Verso, 1983; rev. ed., 1991); Ernst Gellner, *Nations and Nationalism* (Ithaca, N.Y.: Cornell University Press, 1983).

16. Besides neglecting the macrohistorical theorizing of nations and nationalism, Sovietologists generally did not invoke the work of the theorists of ethnic identity and conflict such as Fredrik Barth, ed., *Ethnic Groups and Boundaries* (Boston: Little, Brown, 1969), and Donald L. Horowitz, *Ethnic Groups in Conflict* (Berkeley: University of California Press, 1985).

17. Perhaps most typical would be Hélène Carrère d'Encausse, *The End of the Soviet Empire: The Triumph of the Nations* (New York: Basic Books, 1993). So as not to slander journalists, one should note the sophisticated and highly valuable works by the British journalist Anatol Lieven, *The Baltic Revolution* (New Haven, Conn.: Yale University Press, 1993) and *Chechnya: Tombstone of Russian Power* (New Haven, Conn.: Yale University Press, 1998).

18. Philip Roeder, "Soviet Federalism and Ethnic Mobilization," *World Politics* 43 (1991): 196–232; Rogers Brubaker, "Nationhood and the National Question in the Soviet Union and Its Successor States: An Institutionalist Account," in his *Nationalism Reframed: Nationhood and the National Question in the New Europe* (Cambridge: Cambridge University Press, 1996), pp. 23–54.

19. Ronald Grigor Suny, *The Revenge of the Past: Nationalism, Revolution, and the Collapse of the Soviet Union* (Stanford, Calif.: Stanford University Press, 1993); Yuri Slezkine, "The USSR as a Communal Apartment, or How a Socialist State Promoted Ethnic Particularism," *Slavic Review* 53, no. 2 (Summer 1994): 414–452, and his *Arctic Mirrors: Russia and the Small Peoples of the North* (Ithaca, N.Y.: Cornell University Press, 1994).

20. For a general, archivally based study of the 1920s and 1930s, see Terry Martin, *The Affirmative Action Empire*.

21. This position is argued by Brubaker, Martin, Roeder, Slezkine, and Suny. See the works in the previous three notes.

22. For further discussion of these issues, see Joshua Sanborn, "The Mobilization of 1914 and the Question of the Russian Nation: A Reexamination," *Slavic Review*, 59, no. 2 (Summer 2000): 267–289; Scott J. Seregny, "Zemstvos, Peasants, and Citizenship: The Russian Adult Education Movement and World War I," *Slavic Review* 59, no. 2 (Summer 2000): 290–315; S. A. Smith, "Citizenship and the Russian Nation during

World War I: A Comment," *Slavic Review* 59, no. 2 (Summer 2000): 316–329; and the replies by Sanborn and Seregny, *Slavic Review* 59, no.2 (Summer 2000): 330–342.

23. A good example would be Alexandre A. Bennigsen and S. Enders Wimbush, *Muslim National Communism in the Soviet Union* (Chicago: University of Chicago Press, 1979).

24. For the all-Union story, see Terry Martin, "Borders and Ethnic Conflict: The Soviet Experiment in Ethno-Territorial Proliferation," *Jahrbücher für Geschichte Osteuropas* 47 (September 1999): 538–555.

25. Sheila Fitzpatrick, ed., *Cultural Revolution in Russia, 1928–1931* (Bloomington: Indiana University Press, 1981).

26. The classic account is Nicholas Timasheff, *The Great Retreat: The Growth and Decline of Communism in Russia* (New York: Dutton, 1946).

27. On strategic ethnicity, see Abner Cohen, *Custom and Politics in Urban Africa: A Study of Hausa Migrants in Yoruba Towns* (Berkeley: University of California Press, 1969).

28. This paragraph summarizes analysis found in Martin, *The Affirmative Action Empire*, chapter 7.

29. On the trend toward creating a deep historic past—a primordial ethnicity—for all Soviet nationalities in this period, see Slezkine, "The USSR as a Communal Apartment"; Terry Martin, "Modernization or Neo-Traditionalism? Ascribed Nationality and Soviet Primordialism," in Sheila Fitzpatrick, ed., *Stalinism: New Directions* (London: Routledge, 2000), pp. 348–367; and the brilliant but little known work of the late Mark Saroyan, *Minorities, Mullahs, and Modernity: Reshaping Community in the Former Soviet Union* (Berkeley, Calif.: IAS, 1997), pp. 125–166.

30. This paragraph summarizes Terry Martin, "The Origins of Soviet Ethnic Cleansing," *Journal of Modern History* 70 (1998): 813–861.

31. On the other hand, there is no convincing evidence to suggest that any other Soviet nationalities, including Jews, were specifically targeted in 1937–1938 as a result of their nationality. For a discussion of the evidence, see Martin, *The Affirmative Action Empire*, chapter 8.

32. On Soviet national deportations, see N. F. Bugai, *L. Beriia—I. Stalinu: "Soglasno vashemu ukazaniiu . . ."* (Moscow: AIRO-XX, 1995). The following two paragraphs are based on Terry Martin, "Stalinist Forced Relocation Practices: Patterns, Causes, Consequences," in Myron Weiner and Sharon Stonton Russell, eds., *Demography and National Security* (New York: Berghahn, 2001).

33. Mark Beissinger, "The Persisting Ambiguity of Empire," *Post-Soviet Affairs* 11, no. 2 (April–June 1995).

34. Tom Nairn, *The Break-up of Britain: Crisis and Neo-nationalism* (London: NLB, 1977), and *After Britain: New Labour and the Return of Scotland* (London: Granta, 2000).

35. This evidence is collected and summarized in Robert Kaiser, *The Geography of Nationalism in Russia and the USSR* (Princeton N.J.: Princeton University Press, 1994), pp. 250–324.

36. The phrase belongs to Levon Ter Petrosian, then the chairman of the Supreme Soviet of the Armenian Soviet Socialist Republic.

PART I

Empire and Nations

The Empire Strikes Out

*Imperial Russia, "National" Identity, and
Theories of Empire*

AT THE TIME WHEN RUSSIAN POLITICIANS re-employed the term *derzhava* (Great Power) to provide a vision of a future Russia, Western writers resurrected the metaphor of "empire" to describe the former Soviet Union, and even post-Soviet Russia.[1] Earlier uses of "empire" either referred to the external relationship between the USSR and its East European dependencies or, if used for the internal relations between Moscow and the non-Russian peoples, usually had a highly partisan valence and signaled to the reader a conservative, anti-Soviet interpretation of nationality policy.[2] Consistent with Ronald Reagan's references to the USSR as the "Evil Empire," "empire" applied to states that were considered internally repressive and externally expansionist. But, in the late 1980s, with the rise of nationalist and separatist movements within the Soviet Union, the term was used more widely as a seemingly transparent empirical description of a particular form of multinational state.[3] As political scientist Mark R. Beissinger noted, "What once was routinely referred to as a state suddenly came to be universally condemned as an empire."[4] Though free of any theorization at first, the concept of a "Soviet empire" implied a state that had lost its legitimacy and was destined to collapse. Rather than expansion, implosion was heightened. Beissinger pointed to the circular nature of this label: "The general consensus now appears to be that the Soviet Union was an empire and therefore it broke up. However, it is also routinely referred to as an empire precisely because it did break up."[5] This sense of the lack of legitimacy and disposition to disintegration continues to be part of the imperial metaphor, but those examining the policies of Yeltsin's Russia toward the so-called Near Abroad in recent years have once again employed "empire" in its original expansionist meaning.

Whatever its power of explanation or prediction, the concept of empire has been the organizing metaphor for a series of conferences and projected volumes and for ongoing debate in the journals.[6] At the same moment that scholars confidently predict the end of the age of empires, they have found a new growth industry in the comparative study of the extinct species. This chapter investigates empire as a problem in the internal construction of states, as in contiguous state empires, a set of states that has been far less discussed in comparative and theoretical literature than overseas colonial empires. Looking at problems of state maintenance, decay, and collapse through the interplay of nations and empires, I argue that understanding empire requires historical contextualization, since an empire's viability is related to the operative discourses of legitimation and the international environment in which empires are located. In this chapter I first elaborate theories of imperial survival, decay, and collapse that I hope will give us some purchase on understanding the dynamics and the collapse of the Russian and Soviet empires. Then, I employ ideal types of empire and nation to help understand the structure, evolution, and failure of the tsarist empire to construct a viable "national" identity. I begin with some definitions.

Among the various kinds of political communities and units that have existed historically, empires have been among the most ubiquitous, in many ways the precursors of the modern bureaucratic state. Historian Anthony Pagden has traced the various meanings attached to empire in European discourses. In its original meaning in classical times, *imperium* described the executive authority of Roman magistrates and eventually came to refer to "nonsubordinate power." Such a usage can be found in the first line of Machiavelli's *The Prince*: "All the states and dominions which have had and have empire over men . . ."[7] By the sixteenth century, empire took on the meaning of *status,* state, the political relationships that held groups of people together in an extended system, but from Roman times on it already possessed one of the modern senses of empire as an immense state, an "extended territorial dominion."[8] Finally, "to claim to be an *imperator* [from Augustus's time] was to claim a degree, and eventually a kind of power, denied to mere kings."[9] Absolute or autocratic rule was then identified with empire, along with the idea that an empire referred to "a diversity of territories under a single authority."[10] Pagden emphasizes the durability of these discursive traditions. "All these three senses of the term *imperium*—as limited and independent or 'perfect' rule, as a territory embracing more than one political community, and as the absolute sovereignty of a single individual—survived into the late eighteenth century and sometimes well beyond. All three derived from the discursive practices of the Roman empire, and to a lesser extent the Athenian and Macedonian empires."[11] Moreover, empire was connected with "the notion of a single exclusive world domain," both in Roman times and later, and the great European overseas empires, especially that of Spain, never quite abandoned "this legacy of universalism, developed over centuries and reinforced by a powerfully articulate learned elite."[12]

Though sensitive to the variety of historical meanings attached to empire, social scientists have attempted a more limited understanding of empire as a political relationship. Michael W. Doyle's definition—"Empire . . . is a relationship, formal or informal, in which one state controls the effective political sovereignty of another political society"—is extremely useful, even though he is concerned almost exclusively with noncontiguous empires.[13] Elaborating further he argues that empire is "a system of interaction between two political entities, one of which, the dominant metropole, exerts political control over the internal and external policy—the effective sovereignty—of the other, the subordinate periphery."[14] John A. Armstrong, as well, speaks of empire as "a compound polity that has incorporated lesser ones."[15] For my purposes, looking at contiguous empire-states that do not necessarily have states within them, political society must be defined more loosely than as state.[16]

Borrowing from Armstrong and Doyle, I define empire as a particular form of domination or control between two units set apart in a hierarchical, inequitable relationship, more precisely a composite state in which a metropole dominates a periphery to the disadvantage of the periphery. Rather than limit empires and imperialism (the building and maintaining of empires) to relations between polities, I extend the definition of imperialism to the deliberate act or policy that furthers a state's extension or maintenance for the purpose of aggrandizement of that kind of direct or indirect political or economic control over any other inhabited territory that involves the inequitable treatment of those inhabitants in comparison with its own citizens or subjects. Like Doyle, I emphasize that an imperial state differs from the broader category of multinational states, confederations, or federations in that it "is not organized on the basis of political equality among societies or individuals. The domain of empire is a people subject to unequal rule."[17] Not all multinational, multicultural, or multireligious states are necessarily empires, but where distinctions remain and treatment is unequal, as in areas that remain ethnically distinct, then the relationship continues to be imperial. Inequitable treatment might involve forms of cultural or linguistic discrimination or disadvantageous redistributive practices from the periphery to the metropole (but not necessarily, as, for example, in the Soviet empire). This ideal type of empire, then, is fundamentally different from the ideal type of the nation-state. While empire is inequitable rule over something different, nation-state rule is, at least in theory if not always in practice, the same for all members of the nation. Citizens of the nation, equal under the law, have a different relationship with their state than do the subjects of empire.

Besides inequality and subordination, the relationship of the metropole to the periphery is marked by difference—by ethnicity, geographic separation, and administrative distinction.[18] If peripheries are fully integrated into the metropole, as various medieval Russian principalities were into Muscovy, and treated as well or badly as the metropolitan provinces, then the relationship is not imperial. Very important, the metropole need not be defined ethnically or geographically. It is the ruling institution. In several empires, rather than a geographic or ethnic distinction from the periphery, the ruling institution had a status or class character, a specially endowed nobility or political class, like the Osmanli in the Ottoman Empire, or the imperial family and upper layers of the landed gentry and bureaucracy in the Russian Empire, or, analogously, the Communist *nomenklatura* in the Soviet Union. In my understanding, neither tsarist Russia nor the Soviet Union was an ethnically "Russian empire," with the metropole completely identified with a ruling Russian nationality. Rather, the ruling institution—nobility in one case, the Communist party elite in the other—was multinational, though they were primarily Russian *and* ruled imperially over Russian and non-Russian subjects alike. In empire, unlike nations, the distance and difference of the rulers was part of the ideological justification for the superordination of the ruling institution. The right to rule in empire resides with the ruling institution, not in the consent of the governed.

All states have centers, capital cities, and central elites, which in some ways are superior to the other parts of the state, but in empires the metropole is uniquely sovereign, able to override routinely the desires and decisions of peripheral units.[19] The flow of goods, information, and power runs from periphery to metropole and back to periphery but seldom from periphery to periphery. The degree of dependence of periphery on metropole is far greater and more encompassing than in other kinds of states. Roads and railroads run to the capital; elaborate architectural and monumental displays mark the imperial center off from other centers; and the central imperial elite distinguishes itself in a variety of ways from both peripheral elites, often their servants and agents, and the ruled population.[20] The metropole benefits from the periphery in an inequitable way; there is "exploitation," or at least there is the perception of such exploitation. That, indeed, is the essence of what being colonized means.

While subordination, inequitable treatment, and exploitation might be measured in a variety of ways, they are always inflected subjectively and normatively. As Beissinger has suggested: "Any attempt to define empire in 'objective' terms—as a system of stratification, as a policy based on force, as a system of exploitation—fails in the end to capture what is undoubtedly the most important dimension of any imperial situation: perception. . . . Empires and states are set apart not primarily by exploitation, nor even by the use of force, but essentially by whether politics and policies are accepted as 'ours' or are rejected as 'theirs.' "[21]

To this should be added that the perception of empire is about the attitude not only of peripheries but of metropoles as well. Empire exists even if peripheral populations are convinced that the result of their association with the empire is beneficial rather than exploitative, as long as the two conditions of distinction and subordination obtain. Indeed, much of the "postcolonialism" literature has dealt precisely with the ways in which hegemonic cultures of difference and development have sanctioned imperial relations and mediated resistance.

To sum up, empire is a composite state structure in which the metropole is distinct in some way from the periphery and the relationship between the two is conceived or perceived by metropolitan or peripheral actors as one of justifiable or unjustifiable inequity, subordination, and/or exploitation. "Empire" is not merely a form of polity but also a value-laden appellation that as late as the nineteenth century (and even in some usages well into our own) was thought of as the sublime form of political existence (think of New York as the "empire state") but that at the beginning of the twenty-first century casts doubts about the legitimacy of a polity and even predicts its eventual, indeed inevitable, demise.[22] Thus, the Soviet Union, which a quarter of a century ago would have been described by most social scientists as a state and only occasionally, and usually by quite conservative analysts, as an empire, is almost universally described after its demise as an empire, since it now appears to have been an illegitimate, composite polity unable to contain the rising nations within it.

Recognizing that forms of the state as well as concepts of the state have changed over time, I adopt a fairly basic definition of "state" as a set of common political institutions capable of monopolizing legitimate violence and distributing some goods and services within a demarcated territory. As Rogers Brubaker has noted, the generation of modern statehood meant a movement from what was essentially "a network of persons" in the medieval sense to "territorialization of rule," as the world was transformed into a set of bounded and mutually exclusive citizenries.[23] The modern "state" (basically post-fifteenth century) is characterized by relatively fixed territorial boundaries, a single sovereignty over its territory, and a permanent bureaucratic and military apparatus. As states homogenized their territories in the late medieval and early modern periods, eliminating competing sovereignties and standardizing administration, a number of states that at first looked a lot like the empires described earlier consolidated a relatively coherent internal community, on either linguistic, ethnocultural, or religious lines, that made an idea of "nation" conceivable with the coming of the late-eighteenth-century revolutions and the subsequent "age of nationalism."[24] At the same time, less homogeneous states, those that emerged into the modern period as contiguous empires, tightened their internal interconnections in order to be competitive in the new international environment but without achieving the degree of internal homogeneity of proto-nation-states like Portugal or France.

In his study of "internal colonialism," Michael Hechter argues that it is only after the fact that one can determine whether (nation)-state–building or empire-building has occurred. If the core has been successful in integrating the population of its expanding territory into accepting the legitimacy of the central authority, then (nation)-state–building has occurred, but if the population rejects or resists that authority, than the center has succeeded only in creating an empire.[25] Many, if not most, of the oldest nation-states of our own time began their historic evolution as heterogeneous dynastic conglomerates with the characteristics of imperial relationships between metropole and periphery, and only after the hard work of nationalizing homogenization by state authorities were hierarchical empires transformed into relatively egalitarian nation-states based on a horizontal notion of equal citizenship. Yet, in the age of nationalism, that very process of nationalization stimulated the ethnonational consciousness of some populations able to distinguish themselves (or having been distinguished by others) who then resisted assimilation into the ruling nationality, became defined as a "minority," and ended up in a colonial relationship with the metropolitan nation. In these cases, "nation-making" laid bare the underlying imperialism of the state.

Following the lead of recent theorists of the nation, I define a nation as a group of people that imagines itself to be a political community that is distinct from the rest of humankind, believes that it shares characteristics, perhaps origins, values, historical experiences, language, territory, or any of many other elements, and on the basis of its defined culture deserves self-determination, which usually entails control of its own territory (the "homeland") and a state of its own.[26] Neither natural nor primordial but the result of hard constitutive intellectual and political work of elites and masses, nations exist in particular understandings of history, stories in which the nation is seen as the subject moving continuously through time, coming to self-awareness over many centuries.[27] Though there may be examples of political communities in the distant past that approach our notions of modern nations, in the modern era political communities exist within a discourse that came together in the late eighteenth and early nineteenth centuries around the notion of bounded territorial sovereignties in which the "people" constituted as a nation provide the legitimacy to the political order. From roughly the late eighteenth century to the present, the state merged with the "nation," and almost all modern states claimed to be nation-states, in either an ethnic or a civic sense, with governments deriving power from and exercising it in the interest of the nation. Modern states legitimized themselves in reference to the nation and the claims to popular sovereignty implicit in the discourse of the nation.[28]

Though the discourse of the nation began as an expression of state patriotism, through the nineteenth century it increasingly became ethnicized, until the "national community" was understood to be a cultural community of shared language, religion, and/or other characteristics with a durable, antique past, shared kinship, common origins, and narratives of progress through time. Lost to time was the ways in which notions of shared pasts and common origins were constructed and reimagined, how primary languages themselves were selected from dialects and elevated to dominance through print and schooling, and how history itself was employed to justify claims to the world's real estate. Nationalists strove to make the nation and the state congruent, an almost utopian goal, and it is not a great stretch to argue that much of modern history has been about making nations and states fit together in a world where the two almost never match.

By the twentieth century, such imagined communities were the most legitimate basis for the constitution of states, displacing dynastic, religious, and class discourses—and coincidentally challenging alternative formulas for legitimation, like those underpinning empires. Once-viable imperial states became increasingly vulnerable to nationalist movements that in turn gained strength from the new understanding that states ought to represent, if not coincide with, nations. The simultaneous rise of notions of democratic representation of subaltern interests accentuated the fundamental tension between inequitable imperial relationships and horizontal conceptions of national citizenship. Though liberal states with representative institutions, styling themselves as democracies, could be (and were) effective imperial powers in the overseas empires of Great Britain, France, Belgium, and the Netherlands, the great contiguous empires resisted democratization that would have undermined the right to rule of the dominant imperial elite and the very hierarchical and inequitable relationship between metropole and periphery in the empire. While empires were among the most ubiquitous and long-lived polities in premodern history, they were progressively subverted in modern times by the powerful combination of nationalism and democracy.[29]

Some macrohistorical accounts of state and nation development argue that there has been a universal process of territorial consolidation, homogenization of population and institutions, and concentration of power and sovereignty that laid the groundwork for the modern nation-state. While such accounts certainly capture a principal pattern of state formation in the early modern period, that powerful metanarrative neglects the persistence and durability under certain conditions of less "modern" political forms such as empires. The question arises, why did the last empires of Europe not evolve into nation-states in the nineteenth and twentieth centuries? How did the practices and preferences of imperial elites prevent nation-making, even when becoming a nation might have made their state more competitive in the international arena? In several contiguous empires, state authorities in fact attempted to homogenize the differences within the state in order to achieve the kinds of efficiencies that accompanied the more homogeneous nation-states, yet what had once been possible in medieval and early modern times when quite heterogeneous populations assimilated into relatively homogeneous proto-nations, perhaps around common religious or dynastic loyalties, became in the "age of nationalism" nearly impossible. Even though networks of communication became more dense in modern times, in the contiguous empires of nineteenth-century Europe the most binding social and discursive consolidations took place below the level of the imperial state. The same would occur a century later in the USSR. The available discourse of the nation, with all its attendant attractions of progress, representation, and statehood, became available for all linguistic and cultural groups to claim. The appeals of popular sovereignty and democracy implied in the nation-form challenged the inequity, hierarchy, and discrimination inherent in empire, undermining its very raison d'être. Modern empires were caught between maintaining the privileges and distinctions that kept the traditional elites in power and considering reforms along liberal lines that would have undermined the old ruling classes. While the great "bourgeois" overseas empires of the nineteenth century were able to liberalize, even democratize in the metropoles, at the same time maintaining harsh repressive regimes in the colonies, pursuing different policies in core and periphery was far more difficult in contiguous empires than in noncontiguous ones. A democratic metropole and colonized peripheries managed to coexist in overseas empires, as the examples of Britain, France, and Belgium show, but maintaining autocracy along with constitutionalism or liberal democracy in part of the realm proved far more destabilizing in contiguous empires. In Russia, the privileges enjoyed by the Grand Duchy of Finland, or even the constitution granted to Bulgaria, an independent state outside the empire, constantly reminded the tsar's educated subjects of his refusal to allow them similar institutions. Here is a major tension of contiguous empires. Some kind of separation, apartheid, is essential to maintain a democratic and nondemocratic political order in a single state. But this is a highly unstable compromise, as the governments of South Africa and Israel discovered in the twentieth century.

In contiguous empires, where the distinction between the nation and the empire is more easily muddled than in overseas empires, ruling elites may attempt to construct hybrid notions of an empire-nation, as in tsarist Russia or in the Ottoman Empire in the nineteenth century.[30] Responding to the challenges presented by the efficiencies of the new national states, imperial elites promoted a transition from "ancien regime" empires to "modern" empires, from a more polycentric and differentiated polity in which regions maintained quite different legal, economic, and even political structures to a more centralized, bureaucratized state in which laws, economic practices, and even customs and dialects were homogenized by state elites. The more modern empires adopted a number of strategies to restabilize their rule. In Russia, the monarchy became more "national" in its self-image and public representation, drawing it closer to the people it ruled. In Austro-Hungary the central state devolved power to several of the nonruling peoples, moving the empire toward becoming a more egalitarian multinational state. In the Ottoman Empire, modernizing bureaucrats abandoned certain traditional hierarchical practices that privileged Muslims over non-Muslims, and in the reforming era known as *Tanzimat* they attempted to create a civic nation of all peoples of the empire, an Ottomanist idea of a new imperial community. In the last two decades of the nineteenth century, the tsarist government attempted yet another strategy, a policy of administrative and cultural Russification that privileged a single nationality. The Young Turks after 1908 experimented with everything from an Ottomanist liberalism to pan-Islamic, pan-Turkic, and increasingly nationalist reconfigurations of their empire.[31] But modernizing imperialists were caught between these new projects of homogenization and rationalization on one hand and policies and structures that maintained distance and difference from their subjects as well as differentiations and disadvantages among the peoples of the empire on the other. Modernizing empires searched for new legitimation formulas that softened rhetorics of conquest and divine sanction and instead emphasized the civilizing mission of the imperial metropole, its essential competence in a new project of development.

Given the unevenness of the economic transformations of the nineteenth and twentieth centuries, all within a highly competitive international environment, most states, even quite conservative imperial states like the Ottoman and Romanov empires, undertook state programs of economic and social "modernization." Developmentalism was soon deeply embedded both in national and in imperial state policies. Needing to justify the rule of foreigners over peoples who were constituting themselves as nations, the idea of developing inferior or unciv-ilized peoples became a dominant source of imperial legitimation and continued well into the twentieth century.[32]

There is a subversive dialectic in developmentalism, however. Its successes create the conditions for imperial failure. If the developmentalist program suc-ceeds among the colonized people, realizing material well-being and intellectual sophistication, urbanism and industrialism, social mobility and knowledge of the world, the justification for foreign imperial rule over a "backward" people evap-orates. Indeed, rather than suppressing nationmaking and nationalism, imperi-alism far more often provides conditions and stimulation for the construction of new nations. Populations are ethnographically described, statistically enumerated, ascribed characteristics and functions, and reconceive themselves in ways that qualify them as "nations." Not accidentally, the map of the world at the end of the twentieth century was marked by dozens of states with boundaries drawn by imperialism. And if clearly defined and articulated nations do not exist within these states by the moment of independence, then state elites busily set about creating national political communities to fill out the fledgling state.

Developmentalism, of course, was the project not only of "bourgeois" nation-states and empires but also of self-styled socialist ones. The problem grew when empires, which justified their rule as agents of modernity and modernization, as instruments of development and progress, achieved their stated task too well, supplied their subordinated populations with languages of aspiration and resis-tance, and indeed created subjects who no longer required empire in the way the colonizers claimed. This dialectical reversal of the justification for empire, em-bedded in the theory and practice of modernization, was, in my view, also at the very core of the progressive decay of the Soviet empire. In a real sense the Communist party effectively made itself irrelevant. Who needed a "vanguard" when you now had an urban, educated, mobile, self-motivated society? Who needed imperial control from Moscow when national elites and their constituents were able to articulate their own interests in terms sanctioned by Marxism-Leninism in the idea of national self-determination?

Earlier in the twentieth century, when the problem of imperialism gripped scholars and theorists as well as politicians, their attention focused on the causes and dynamics of empire-making—expansion and conquest, incorporation and annexation.[33] More recently, theorists have elaborated the conditions under which empires successfully maintain themselves. Following a suggestion by the classical historian M. I. Finley, Doyle looks at a series of premodern empires—Athens, Rome, Spain, England, and the Ottoman—and argues that among the factors that make empire possible, sustainable, and, more dynamically, expansionist are a differential of power, greater in the metropole, less in the peripheries; political unity of the imperial or hegemonic metropole, which involves not only a strong, united central government but a broader sense of legitimacy and community among the imperial elite; and some form of transnational connection—forces or actors, religion, ideology, economy, a form of society based in the metropole and capable of extending itself to subject societies. Athens had such a transnational society and became imperial, while Sparta did not have one and could exercise only hegemony over other states.[34]

The greater "power" of the unified metropole over the peripheries ought to be understood not merely as greater coercive power but as greater discursive power, as well. Recently, scholars have moved beyond material and structural analyses to investigate how empires maintained themselves, not only by the obvious means of physical force but also through a kind of manufactured consent. "Colonial" and "postcolonial" scholars have explored the ways in which coercive power was supplemented and sanctioned by discursive power. "Colonialism," one recent collection asserts, "(like its counterpart, racism), then, is an operation of discourse, and as an operation of discourse it interpellates colonial subjects by incorporating them in a system of representation. They are always already written by that system of representation."[35] Whether it was the story of *The Water Babies*, the adventure stories of Robert Dixon or Rudyard Kipling, or the tales of Babar the Elephant, the fantasies elaborated contained naturalized images of superior and inferior races and nations. One of the most telling sets of arguments from colonial studies has been the way in which colonialism and its attendant racism not only inscribed the position of the colonized but also fundamentally shaped the self-representation of the colonizer. The problem for imperialism was creating and maintaining difference and distance between ruler and ruled. In a discussion that began with Edward Said's seminal work, *Orientalism*, and continued with his more recent *Culture and Imperialism*, scholars have investigated the ways in which Europe understood itself in terms of what it was not, the colonized world.[36] In their collection of essays, *Tensions of Empire*, Ann Laura Stoler and Frederick Cooper reverse the usual way of looking at influences: "Europe was made by its imperial projects, as much as colonial encounters were shaped by conflicts within Europe itself."[37] Yet, at the base of European self-understandings lay the underlying problem of constructing and reproducing the categories of the colonized and the colonizer, keeping them distinct, one inferior to the other. The great nineteenth-century European overseas empires were "bourgeois" empires in which "ruling elites trying to claim power on the basis of generalized citizenship and inclusive social rights were forced to confront a basic question: whether those principles were applicable—and to whom—in old overseas empires and in newly conquered territory that were now becoming the dependencies of nation-states."[38] European ideas of citizenship were about membership in the nation, but that membership implied culture and learning. Attitudes toward both domestic lower classes and subject peoples in the colonies were bound up in serious questions of the boundaries of the nation—who should be included, and on what basis, and who should be excluded. European notions of egalitarianism clashed with imposed hierarchies; notions of democratic participation with authoritarian exclusion from decision making; ideas of universal reason with "native" understanding. To reinforce European authority, power, and privilege, difference between ruler and ruled had to be maintained, protected, and policed. Race was the most powerful inscription of difference, related to the language of class within Europe, which already "drew on a range of images and metaphors that were racialized to the core."[39] Ruling classes had to reaffirm their difference from the ruled, which became ever more difficult as the extension of democracy opened the way for the popular classes to enter politics. In the nineteenth century, discourses of civility and respectability distinguished those with the cultural competence to govern from those who merely needed to be represented.[40]

No polity exists forever, and many historians and social scientists have been most interested in why empires decline and collapse. Several have concluded that crisis and collapse of empires is written into their very nature.[41] Alexander J. Motyl concludes that "imperial decay appears to be inevitable. . . . Empires, in a word, are inherently contradictory political relationships; they self-destruct, and they do so in a very particular, by no means accidental and distinctly political, manner." Collapse stems "from the policies that the imperial elites adopt in order to halt state decline." Whether it was war, in the case of the Habsburgs, the Romanovs, and the Ottomans, that crushed the central state, or the revolution from above, as in the case of Gorbachev's Soviet Union, the implosion of the center allowed the subordinate peripheries to "search for independent solutions to their problems."[42] Yet, unless one sees an inevitable tendency in empires to enter losing wars, something that can happen to any state, or one believes that events like the selection of Gorbachev as party leader or the adoption of his particular form of reform was unavoidable rather than contingent, then there is no inevitability in the collapse of empires because of policy choices. Rather, the likelihood of collapse stems, as I have tried to suggest, from two factors: the delegitimizing power of nationalism and democracy that severely undermines imperial justifications and the subversive effect of other legitimizing formulas, like developmentalism, that produce precisely the conditions under which imperial hierarchies and discriminations are no longer required.

Decolonization is far more difficult for a contiguous empire than for an overseas empire, for it changes the very shape of the state itself. Downsizing the state means abandoning certain ideas of the very enterprise that had maintained that state and searching for new sources of legitimation. Contiguous empires, like the Habsburg, Ottoman, tsarist Russian, and Soviet, did not have hard borders within the empire, and therefore migration created a mixed population, a highly integrated economy, and shared historical experiences and cultural features—all of which make extrication of the core or any of the peripheries from the empire extremely difficult without complete state collapse. Understandably, in three of the four cases at hand—the Habsburg, Ottoman, and tsarist—defeat in war preceded the end of the empire. And, while secession of peripheries weakened these empires, in two of the four cases, the Ottoman and the Soviet, it was the secession of the core from the empire—Kemal's nationalist Turkey in Anatolia and Yeltsin's Russia—that dealt the final blow to the old imperial state.[43]

To conclude this theoretical discussion, I argue that the collapse of empires in our own times can only be understood in the context of the institutional and discursive shifts that have taken place with the rise of the nation-state. Historically, many of the most successful states began as empires, with dynastic cores extending outward by marriage or conquest to incorporate peripheries that over time were gradually assimilated into a single, relatively homogeneous polity. By the late nineteenth century, empires were those polities that were either uninterested or that had failed in the project of creating a nation-state. The fragility of twentieth-century empires was related to the particular development of nationalism, the way it shifted from civil to ethnic in the nineteenth century, and the making of nations, which in time fused with the state, so that in the past two centuries the general project of most modern states has been a nationalizing one, that is, the making of a nation within the state and the achievement of the fusion of nation and state, the creation of a nation-state. As the discourse of the nation became the dominant universe of political legitimation, its claims of popular sovereignty with its inherently democratic thrust and its call for a cultural rootedness alien to the transnational cosmopolitanism, such as those practiced earlier by European aristocracies, acted like a time bomb placed at the feet of empire.

As it spread from France, nationalism carried with it the claim that a cultural community possessed political rights over a specific territory that justified independence from alien rulers. Whether or not a monarch or a nobility was of the same nationality as the people, it could be defined as part of the nation or alien to it. As nationalism shifted from state patriotism to identification with ethnic communities, themselves the product of long historical and cultural evolutions, the seeming longevity, indeed antiquity, of ethnicity provided an argument for the naturalness, the primordiality, of the nation, against which the artificial claims of dynasties or religious institutions paled. Over time, any state that wished to survive had to become a nationalizing state, to link itself with a nation in order to acquire legitimacy in the new universal discourse of the nation. In the age of nationalism, certainly by the First World War, the term empire had in many cases (though hardly all; think of where the sun never set) gained the opprobrium of which Beissinger speaks. The Wilsonian and Leninist promotion of national self-determination powerfully subverted the legitimacy of empires, even as each of the states that Wilson and Lenin headed managed empires of one kind or another through another half century.

This leads us, finally, to consider the ways in which the international context contributes to the stability and fragility of empires, not only in the sense that a highly competitive international environment presents empires with difficult challenges economically and militarily but also at the level of dominant understandings of what constitutes legitimacy for states. In the past century, when the nation gave legitimacy to states, international law and international organizations, such as the United Nations, established new norms that sanctioned national self-determination, nonintervention into the affairs of other states, and the sovereign equality of states. After both world wars, new states and former colonies quickly were accepted as fully independent actors in the international arena. This acceptance set the stage for 1991, when the former Soviet republics—but no political units below them—were quickly recognized as independent states with all the rights and privileges appertaining. In the post-1945 period particularly, the wave of decolonizations constructed empires as antiquated forms of government, justifiable only as transitory arrangements that might aid in the development of full nation-states. This justification of empires was read back into the retrospective histories of empires. As Miles Kahler puts it, "The empire-dominated system of the early twentieth century swiftly tipped toward a nation-state dominated system after World War II; in dramatic contrast to the 1920s and 1930s empires were quickly defined as beleaguered and outdated institutional forms."[44] Kahler notes that the two dominant powers of the post–World War II period, the USA and the USSR, were both "rhetorically anti-colonial, despite their own imperial legacies," and American economic dominance, with its liberal, free trade approach, "reduced the advantages of empires as large-scale economic units."[45] Thus, both on the level of discourse and on the level of international politics and economics, the late twentieth century appeared to be a most inhospitable time both for formal external empires and contiguous empire-states.

Until quite recently, historians of imperial Russia concentrated much of their attention on Russian state-building, either eliding altogether the question of nation or collapsing it into a concept of state. Neither much empirical nor theoretical work was done on the nature of tsarism as empire, or of Russia as a nation. This may in part have been the consequence of the early identification of Russia more as a dynastic realm than as an ethnonational or religious community. As Paul Bushkovitch points out, the earliest Russian histories are tales of the deeds of the ruling princes, and the foundation legends are about the dynasty. Russia was understood, from the end of the fifteenth century until the reign of Aleksei Mikhailovich in the mid-seventeenth century, to be the territories controlled by the Riurikid and later the Romanov dynasties.[46] In his study of the rites, rituals, and myths generated by and about the Russian monarchy, Richard S. Wortman argues that the imagery of the monarchy from the fifteenth to the late nineteenth century was of foreignness, separation of the ruler and the elite from the common people.[47] The origin of the rulers was said to be foreign (the Varangians were from beyond the Baltic Sea), and they were likened to foreign rulers of the West. "In expressing the political and cultural preeminence of the ruler, foreign traits carried a positive valuation, native traits a neutral or negative one."[48] Even the models of rulership were foreign—Byzantium and the Mongol khans—and foreignness conveyed superiority. Later, in the eighteenth and nineteenth centuries, the myth of the ruler as conqueror was used to express the monarchy's bringing to Russia the benefits of civilization and progress, and the ruler was portrayed as a selfless hero who had saved Russia from despotism and ruin.

What kind of early identity, or identities, formed among "Russians"? From the earliest records the peoples of what became Russia were culturally and linguistically diverse.[49] The Primary Chronicle notes that Slavs, Balts, Turkic, and Finnic peoples lived in the region and that the Slavs were divided into distinct groups. As the Chronicle tells the tale, the various Eastern Slavic peoples drew together only after the Varangians, called Rus', came to "Russia." Those few scholars who have asked this question generally agree that from the adoption and spread of Orthodox Christianity in 988 (traditional date) through the next few centuries, Russians constituted a community that fused the notions of Orthodoxy and Russianness and saw themselves as distinct from both the Catholics of Poland and Lithuania and the non-Christian nomadic peoples of the Volga region and Siberia.[50] Affiliation with a dynastic lord was important, but this should not be confused with loyalty to a state. Indeed, the word "realm" might be preferred to "state," for in these early times the people as community was not conceived of separately from political authority. As Valerie Kivelson notes,

> The grand princes of Kiev appear to have had little or no conception of a state as a bounded territorial unit governed by a single sovereign entity, aspiring to administer, tax and control its people. Rather, the territory of the Kievan polity remained amorphous and fluid. The concept and title of "grand prince" of a unitary Kievan realm entered Kievan vocabulary and political consciousness slowly, as an import from Byzantium. The polity itself (if there was one) was constituted imprecisely around a loosely defined people ('the Rus') and was ruled piecemeal by interconnected competing and conflicting branches of the princely line. Grand princely deathbed testaments demonstrate that the goal of princely politics remained personal, familial, rather than encompassing any broader aspirations toward unified sovereignty or territorial rule.[51]

Identity was formed both internally by the consolidation of religion, the Church, and eventually by a single Muscovite state (from roughly the fifteenth century) and at the frontiers in the struggles with peoples seen to be different. From its beginning, then, Russian identity was bound up with the supranational world of belief, the political world loosely defined by the ruling dynasty, and was contrasted to "others" at the periphery.[52] Religion served in those pre- and early modern times much as ethnicity does today, as the available vocabulary of identity. It was within the realm of religion and the polity that contestations over what constituted membership and what behavior was proper or improper took place.[53] As the historian Richard Hellie puts it, "The Muscovites defined themselves as *pravoslavnye* (Orthodox) more frequently than as *russkie,* which of course many of them were not."[54] Even as the realm became increasingly heterogeneous ethnically and religiously, the "test" for belonging in Muscovy was profession of Orthodoxy. Yet, for all its isolation and oft-touted xenophobia, Russia was surprisingly ecumenical in its attitudes toward foreigners. "The conversion to orthodoxy by any foreigner automatically made him a Muscovite, fully accepted by the central authorities and seemingly the native populace as well."[55]

If not from the very beginning, then in the next few centuries Russian identity became closely tied with religion, a shifting, expanding territory, and the state. When Ivan III the Great took on the titles *tsar* and *samoderzhets* (autocrat) in the mid-fifteenth century, he was making a claim to be the sovereign ruler of Russia. Moscow, which had often been favored among Russian principalities, even promoted, by the Mongols in the previous century, now "replaced the Golden Horde as the sovereign power within the Rus' lands" and adopted the "mantle of Chingisid imperial legitimacy."[56] "Imperial sovereignty," writes Wortman, "was the only true sovereignty" in Russian understanding.[57] At the same time, appropriating and modifying the double-headed eagle of Byzantium and the Holy Roman Empire, Ivan claimed parity with the monarchs of the West. Tracing their ancestry back to Riurik, the Muscovite princes took on foreign roots, separating themselves from the Russian people. Their allies, the Orthodox clergy, collaborated in the construction of an imperial myth, which was elaborately visualized in the coronation rites: "Ceremony turned the fiction of imperial succession into sacred truth."[58] Michael Cherniavsky saw this ideological amalgam of khan and basileus as a playful, somewhat inconsistent synthesizing of various traditions. "Hence, the Russian grand prince as khan, as Roman emperor, as *the* Orthodox sovereign, and as descendant of the dynasty of Ivan I (a loyal subject of the khan) were concepts that existed simultaneously, not contradicting but reinforcing each other."[59]

With Ivan IV's conquests of Kazan and Astrakhan in the the mid-sixteenth century, the Muscovite state incorporated ethnically compact non-Russian territories, indeed an alien polity, and transformed a relatively homogenized Russia into a multinational empire. The tsars adopted the designation *Rossiia* for their realm instead of *Rus'*, which referred to the core Russian areas. But, unlike the Byzantine Emperor or the Mongol khan, the Russian tsar was ruler not of the whole universe but only the absolute and sovereign ruler of all of Russia (*tsar' vseia Rusi*).[60] Yet, as conqueror of Kazan and Astrakhan, the Muscovite tsar acquired some of the prestige of the Mongol khans, and as he pushed further south and east he sought the allegiance and subordination of the lesser rulers of Siberia and the North Caucasus. As Michael Khodarkovsky has shown, when the Shamkhal of Daghestan or the Kabardinian princes made an agreement with the tsar, they believed they had concluded a treaty between equals, but the Russians uniformly mistranslated the agreement as one of an inferior's supplication to the Russian sovereign.[61]

Russian imperial power went into the frontier world as a sovereign superior to whatever lesser lords and peoples it encountered. Conquest and annexation of the frontier lands was the extension of the tsar's sovereignty, exercised through his household or the court and conceived as another stage in the "gathering of the Russian lands." The non-Russian elites were generally coopted into the Russian nobility, as were the Kazan and Astrakhan notables, but part of the obligations of the peasantry were now diverted to Moscow. Once a region was brought into the empire, the tsarist state was prepared to use brutal force to prevent its loss. Rebellion was suppressed mercilessly. But, when the problem of security was settled, Moscow allowed local elites, though no longer sovereign, to rule and traditional customs and laws to continue in force. As these frontier regions became integrated in some ways into the empire as borderlands, many of them remained distinct administratively, though always subordinate to the center.[62]

Russian expansion was overdetermined, driven by economic, ideological, and security interests. The lure of furs in Siberia and of mineral wealth in the Urals, the threats from nomadic incursions along the Volga or the southern steppe, the peasants' hunger for agricultural land, and the pull of freedom in the frontier regions stimulated appetites for expansion. Missionary zeal, however, was not a primary motivation, though after conquest missionaries followed. When in the east and south Russians engaged in trade that brought them into contact with the myriad peoples of Siberia, the Kalmyks of the southern steppe, and the Caucasians of the mountains, differences of religion, custom, foods, and smells were duly noted. Though some, like the Cossack traders on the eastern frontier, were largely indifferent to what was foreign, others, particularly clerics, sought to spread Orthodoxy among the heathen.[63] Once converted, foreigners were easily assimilated into the Russian community. "Slaves, wives, or state servitors, the new Christians seem to have been accepted as Christians and Russians. . . . Thus, the tribute-paying foreigners who wished to remain foreigners were welcome to stay in the woods and pay tribute, whereas those who were convinced or compelled to become Russian could do so if they played by the rules."[64]

At the same time that peoples with different religions and ways of life remained distinct from and subordinate to the imperial power, the tsar's ruling institution also distinguished itself from the people (*narod*) of the empire. With the internal collapse of Russia in the Time of Troubles of the early seventeenth century, some people reconceived of Russia not simply as the possession of the Muscovite tsar but as a state ruled by the tsar and including the people. But the newly chosen Romanov dynasty did not adopt this new conception after 1613, and, rather than emphasizing election by a popular assembly, the new rulers depicted the election as divinely inspired. Again, the dynasty distanced itself from the people, claiming descent from Riurik and St. Vladimir, prince of Kievan Rus'.[65]

With the annexation of Ukraine (1654) and Vilnius (1656), the imperial claims were bolstered, and the monarch was proclaimed "tsar of all Great, Little, and White Russia."[66] The state seal of Aleksei Mikhailovich, adopted in 1667, depicted an eagle with raised wings, topped with three crowns, symbolizing Kazan, Astrakhan, and Siberia, and bordered by three sets of columns, representing Great, Little, and White Russia. The tsar, now also called *sviatoi* (holy), further distanced himself from his subjects "by appearing as the supreme worshiper of the realm, whose piety exceeded theirs."[67] Finally, toward the end of the century, Tsar Fedor referred to the "Great Russian Tsardom" (*Velikorossiiskoe tsarstvie*), "a term denoting an imperial, absolutist state, subordinating Russian as well as non-Russian territories."[68] In this late seventeenth-century vision of empire, Great Russia, the tsar, and the state were all merged in a single conception of sovereignty and absolutism. State, empire, and autocratic tsar were combined in an elaborate system of reinforcing legitimations. In Russia, according to Wortman, "The word *empire* carried several interrelated though distinct meanings. First, it meant imperial dominion or supreme power unencumbered by other authority. Second, it implied imperial expansion, extensive conquests, encompassing non-Russian lands. Third, it referred to the Christian Empire, the heritage of the Byzantine emperor as the defender of Orthodoxy. These meanings were conflated and served to reinforce one another."[69]

But the tsar was not only the holy ruler, a Christian monarch, the most pious head of the Church, but also a powerful secular ruler of a burgeoning bureaucratic state, a conqueror, and the commander of nobles and armies. With Peter the Great, the Christian emperor and the Christian empire gave way to a much more secular "Western myth of conquest and power."[70] "Peter's advents gave notice that the Russian tsar owed his power to his exploits on the battlefield, not to divinely ordained traditions of succession. . . . The image of conqueror disposed of the old fictions of descent."[71] Peter carried the image of foreignness to new extremes, imposing on Russia his preference for beardlessness, foreign dress, Baroque architecture, and Dutch, German, and English technology. He built a new capital as a "window on the West." He created a new polite society for Russia, bringing women out of seclusion into public life, culminating in the coronation of his second wife, the commoner Katerina, as empress of Russia. He took on the title *imperator* in 1721 and made Russia an *imperiia*. "Peter's ideology was very much of the age of rationalism, his contribution to the 'general welfare' of Russia legitimating his rule."[72] The emperor was "father of the fatherland" (*Otets otechestva*), and "now the relationship between sovereign and subjects was to be based not on hereditary right and personal obligation, but on the obligation to serve the state."[73]

Some historians have read national consciousness back into the Russian seventeenth century, or at least to the time of Peter. Michael Cherniavsky, for example, argues that a dual consciousness emerged with the Church schism of the late seventeenth century and the reforms of Peter I: that of the Europeanizing gentry, which identified itself with "Russia" and considered what it was doing as "by definition, Russian," and the consciousness of the Old Believers, and peasants in general, who "began to insist on beards, traditional clothes, and old rituals—creating, in reaction, their own Russian identity."[74] In this view, "national consciousness emerged as a popular reaction to the self-identity of the absolutist state, with the threat that those things which challenged it—the absolutist consciousness of tsar, empire, and Orthodoxy—could be excluded from Russian self-identity."[75] But, in a useful corrective, James Cracraft points out that much of the reaction to the Nikonian and Petrine reforms, rather than constituting xenophobia or national consciousness, was in large part "an anguished opposition to a pattern of behavior which did great violence to a world view that was still essentially religious."[76] Ideas about what constituted Russia and Russians competed between and within social groups in a confused, shifting, unsystematized play of identities in which religious and ethnocultural distinctions overlapped and reinforced one another. Russian continued to be closely identified with being Orthodox Christian but also with living in the tsar's realm. As the state moved away from the more traditional ethnoreligious sense of community toward a nonethnic, cosmopolitan, European sense of political civilization, people were pulled between these two understandings of the "Russian" community.

By the eighteenth century, Russia was an empire in the multiple senses of a great state whose ruler exercised full, absolute sovereign power over its diverse territory and subjects. Its theorists consciously identified this polity with the language and imagery of past empires. Peter the Great established an image of emperor as hero and god, someone who stood above other men and worked for the general welfare of his subjects.[77] He bequeathed his successors, four of whom were women, a stable and secure governing class of aristocrats. Despite several attempted and successful coups, tsar and nobility assisted each other in a symbiotic arrangement in which the interests of the imperial court and the nobility were configured as the general welfare of the country.[78] The eighteenth-century monarchs combined aspects of the conqueror and renovator, while at the same time preserving both serfdom and the serf-holding nobility.[79] In this cosmopolitan world, ethnicity and religion were secondary to the privileges and disadvantages of birth.

Though a number of specialists, most notably Hans Rogger, have written about national consciousness in eighteenth-century Russia, identification with Russia, at least among nobles and the educated population, was largely contained in a sense of state patriotism, that is, identification with the state and its ruler, rather than with the nation, a broader political community conceived separately from the state. As Cynthia Hyla Whittaker demonstrates, the forty-five amateur historians of eighteenth-century Russia were principally concerned with replacing religious with new secular justifications for autocracy, on the basis of dynastic continuity, dynamism of the ruler, his or her concern for the welfare of the people, or superiority of autocracy over alternative forms of government.[80] And, though some historians, such as Vasilii Tatishchev (1686–1750), argued that an originary contract had been forged between people and tsar, even they believed that once that agreement had been made it could "be destroyed by no one."[81] Historians were commissioned by the rulers to counteract the "lies" and "falsehoods" spread by foreigners. Russians of every social level probably had a sense of identity that either positively or negatively contrasted things Russian with those German or Polish or French. Russian writers shared in the general European practice of remarking on national distinctions, or what would be called "national character," something in which Enlightenment figures from Voltaire and Montesquieu to Johann Gottfried Von Herder and Johann Blumenbach engaged. This sensitivity to difference was evidenced by the resistance and resentment of "Russian" nobles to "foreigners" who advanced too high in state service. When this principle was breached during the reign of Anna, Russian nobles protested the visibility of the German barons surrounding the empress. Here patriotism was a way not only of protecting privilege and discouraging competition for power but also, more positively of nurturing solidarities within one group against another. In conscious reaction against the Germano-philia of Anna or Peter III, the coronations of Elizabeth and Catherine II were conceived as acts of restoration, bringing back the glories of Peter the Great. In the view of these monarchs, Peter now represented the authentic Russia, and Elizabeth made the most of being the daughter of Peter and Catherine I. The German princess who became Catherine II may have been a usurper with no legitimate right to rule, yet her seizure of power was sanctioned as an act of de-liverance from a tyrant with foreign airs. Besides being portrayed as Minerva, the embodiment of enlightenment, she was seen as one who loved Russia and respected its Orthodox religion. Although enveloped in a cosmopolitan culture that preferred speaking French to Russian, the noble elite was not above sen-timental attachments to elements of Russian ethnic culture: "Imperial patriotism with a Great Russian coloration was a theme of late-eighteenth-century history and literature."[82] At Catherine's court, nobles of various ethnic backgrounds wore the same dress, and the empress introduced a "Russian dress" with native features for the women.

Russia followed a particular logic of empire building. After acquiring territory, usually by conquest, often by expanding settlement, the agents of the tsar coopted local elites into the service of the empire.[83] But, in many peripheries, such as the Volga, Siberia, Transcaucasia, and Central Asia, integration stopped with the elites (and only partially involved them) and did not include the basic peasant or nomadic populations, which retained their tribal, ethnic, and religious identities. Some elites, like the Tatar and Ukrainian nobles, dissolved into the Russian *dvo-riantsvo* (nobility), but others, like the German barons of the Baltic or the Swedish aristocrats of Finland, retained privileges and separate identities. "Nationalizing," homogenizing policies, integrating disparate peoples into a common "Russian" community (particularly among the nobles), coexisted with policies of discrimi-nation and distinction. After subduing their khanate, Russia gave the Bashkirs rights as a military host in the Volga region. Some peoples, like the Georgians, were allowed to keep their customary laws; German barons and Greek and Ar-menian merchants enjoyed economic and legal benefits, while Jews were restricted from migrating out of the Pale of Settlement. The religious and social life of Muslims was regulated by the state.

Religion remained the principal marker of difference between Russians and non-Russians, and religious identity was believed to reveal essential qualities that helped to predict behavior. Orthodox Christians were expected to be more loyal than the duplicitous Muslims. "Enlightened" state officials frequently argued that conversion to Orthodox Christianity would strengthen the empire as well as bring civilization to the benighted populations of the borderlands.[84] Though efforts at such religious "Russification" were haphazard, they reinforced the perceptual connection between Russianness and Orthodoxy. Beginning with Peter's efforts to modernize Russia, the state and the Church intensified the previously sporadic attempts to bring the benefits of Orthodoxy and Western learning to the be-nighted non-Russians of the east and south.[85]

As Europe went through the fallout from 1789, Russia represented "the most imperial of nations, comprising more peoples than any other." The academician Heinrich Storch boasted of the ethnographic variety of Russia in 1797, commenting that "no other state on earth contains such a variety of inhabitants."[86] In its own imagery, Russia was the Roman Empire reborn. As the discourse of the nation took shape in and after the French Revolution and the Napoleonic wars, as concepts of "the people" and popular sovereignty spread through Europe, the traditional monarchical concepts of the foreign tsar held at bay any concession to the new national populism. Russian resistance to Napoleon, as well as the expansion of the empire into the Caucasus and Finland, only accentuated the imperial image of irresistible power, displayed physically on both battlefield and parade ground by the martinet tsars of the early nineteenth century.[87] At the moment of the French invasion of Russia in 1812, Alexander I issued a rescript that concluded, "I will not lay down arms while the last enemy soldier remains in my empire."[88] No mention was made of the Russian people, and the empire was presented as a possession of the emperor. Even as the French moved toward Moscow, Alexander had to be convinced by his advisers to go to Moscow and to take on the role of national leader. His manifestos, written by the conservative poet Admiral A. S. Shishkov, "appealed to the people's patriotic and religious feelings."[89] The tsar was depicted by writers of the time as the "Angel of God," "Our Father," loved by his subject people for whom he feels great love, and, after the French had retreated from Russia, both the "powerful valor of the people entrusted to Us by God" and Divine Providence were seen as responsible for ridding Russia of its enemies.[90] Russian authorities resisted portraying the great victory as a popular triumph and instead projected it as a divinely ordained triumph of autocracy supported by a devoted people. As Wortman puts it, "The people's involvement in the imperial scenario threatened the tsar's image as a superordinate force, whose title came from outside or from above, from divine mandate, or the emanations of reason. In social terms it was impossible to present the people as a historical agent in a scenario that glorified the monarch's authority as the idealization of the ruling elite."[91]

Russia emerged from the Napoleonic wars even more imperial than it had been in the eighteenth century. Now the possessor of the Grand Duchy of Finland, the emperor served there as a constitutional monarch and was to observe the public law of the Grand Duchy, and in the Kingdom of Poland (1815–1832) he served as *Tsar' Polskii*, the constitutional king of Poland. According to the Fundamental Laws codified in 1832, "the Emperor of Russia is an autocratic (*samoderzhavnyi*) and unlimited (*neogranichennyi*) monarch," but his realm was governed by laws, a *Rechtsstaat*, and was distinct from the despotisms of the East.[92] The tsar stood apart and above his people; his people remained diverse not only ethnically but in terms of the institutions through which they were ruled. Victorious Russia, the conservative bulwark against the principles of the French Revolution, was in many ways the antithesis of nationalism. Alexander I expressed this personally in his scheme for a Holy Alliance in which various states would consider themselves members "of a single Christian nation" ruled over by the "Autocrat of the Christian People," Jesus Christ.[93]

Four reasons for the failure to create a Russian nation might be suggested. One was deeply rooted in the vast geography, limited resources, and lack of population and communication density of tsarist Russia.[94] There was no thickening web of economic, legal, and cultural links on the scale of those, say, in early modern France.[95] Russia was so large, its road system so poor, and its urban settlements so few and far between that it was extraordinarily difficult for the state to exercise its will on its subjects very frequently. Peasants largely ran their own affairs, dealt with local lords or, more likely, their stewards instead of state authorities, and felt the state's weight only when the military recruiter appeared or they failed to pay taxes or dues. Indirect rule over non-Russians was often the norm, and little effort was made until very late in the nineteenth century to interfere with the culture of the non-Russians.

This leads to the second reason for the failure to form a nation in the empire— the misfortune of timing. By the early nineteenth century, with the emergence of the discourse of the nation, subaltern elites could conceptualize of their peoples as "nations," with all the attendant claims to cultural recognition, political rights, territory, and even statehood. With the legitimation of nationalism, the process of assimilating other peoples into the dominant nationality became progressively more difficult.

The third reason was that imperial state structures and practices, from the autocratic concentration of power to the estate hierarchy and built-in ideas of social and ethnic superiority and inferiority, worked as forces of resistance against horizontal, egalitarian nation making. As much of the recent literature on nation formation and nationalism suggests, the making of nations is the social and cultural construction of a new kind of space. Not only are nations usually spatially and conceptually larger than older politics, most notably the fractured and particularized spaces of the ancien regime in Western Europe, but they are consciously and deliberately emptied of particularization, traditional or customary divisions, certain older forms of hierarchy, and vested privilege and turned into what William H. Sewell, Jr., calls "homogeneous empty space."[96] What the French Revolution did to ancien régime France, ridding it of provincial and local privileges, abolishing internal duties and tariffs, standardizing weights and measures over a broader space, was only in part accomplished under tsarism.

The "modernizing" practices of eighteenth- and nineteenth-century Russian emperors and bureaucrats that homogenized disparate economic and legal practices were certainly significant, but they must be placed against programs and policies that moved in another direction, creating new or reinforcing old differences, distinctions, privileges, and disadvantages based on social class, region, ethnicity, or religion. Among Russians, the literary elite developed a sense of national distinction in the eighteenth century, but through the first half of the next century there was very little sense of nation in the developing Western conception of a political community in which the people were the source of legitimacy and even sovereignty. Russia was a state and an empire whose population was divided horizontally among dozens of ethnicities and religions and vertically between ruling and privileged estates and the great mass of the peasant population. These divisions were formalized in the law and fixed most people and peoples in positions of discrimination and disadvantage. Such hierarchies and separations inhibited the development of the kinds of horizontal bonds of fraternity and solidarity that already marked the rhetoric of the nation in the West. To the very last days of the empire, the Romanov regime remained imperial in this sense, a complex, differentiated, hierarchical, traditional ancient regime, with structures and laws that restricted efforts at equalization and homogenization. The horizontal, fraternal ties that ideally mark citizenship in the nation-form could not be established in a system so embedded in hierarchy and distinction, disdain and distance from the great mass of the population.

And, finally, the fourth reason was the failure of Russian elites to articulate a clear idea of the Russian nation, to elaborate an identity distinct from a religious (orthodox), imperial, state, or narrowly ethnic identity. Russia was never equated with ethnic Russia; almost from the beginning it was something larger, a multinational "Russian" state with vaguely conceived commonalities—religion, perhaps, or loyalty to the tsar—but the debate among intellectuals and state actors failed to develop a convincing, attractive notion of Russianness separate from the ethnic on the one hand and the imperial state on the other. Notions of nation dissolved into religion and the state and did not take on a powerful presence as a community separate from the state or the orthodox community.

The sources for discerning popular identities are elusive indeed, but looking at what ordinary Russians read confirms many of the points made about Russian identities. As Jeffrey Brooks points out, "We know little about the popular conception of what it meant to be Russian in premodern Russia, but," he goes on, "the early lubok tales suggest that the Orthodox Church, and, to a lesser extent, the tsar were the foremost emblems of Russianness throughout the nineteenth century. These two symbols of nationality recur in the early stories and their treatment by the authors implies that to be Russian was to be loyal to the tsar and faithful to the Orthodox Church."[97] Brooks's reading of popular literature confirms that "the concept of a nation of peoples with shared loyalties was not well developed."[98] Yet there were several hints of "national" identity indicated in the lubok tales.[99] Conversion to Orthodoxy and allegiance to the tsar signaled inclusion within the Russian community and permitted intermarriage. At the same time, there was a sense of the empire as a vast geographical space with diverse landscapes and peoples in which Russians were contrasted with the other peoples within the empire. Difference from and fear of the "other," particularly the Islamic other, was emphasized in portrayals of Turks and Tatars and in popular captivity tales.[100]

With the emergence of an autonomous intelligentsia in the second third of the nineteenth century, an intense discussion developed on the nature of Russia and on its relation with the West and with Asia, as well as with its internal "others," the nonethnic Russians within the empire. As with other peoples and states of Europe in the postrevolutionary period, intellectuals, particularly historians, were in a sense thinking nations into existence or at least elaborating and propagating the contours, characteristics, symbols, and signs that would make the nation familiar to a broader public. From Nikolai Karamzin's *Istoriia gosudarstva rossiiskogo* (1816–1826) through the great synthetic works of Sergei Solov'ev and Vasilii Kliuchevskii, historians treated Russia as something like a nation-state, in many ways reflected in the West European models but uniquely multiethnic in its composition. Karamzin's contribution was particularly significant, for his work was extremely popular among educated readers, and it provided a colorful, patriotic narrative of Russia's past up to the Time of Troubles. As he also emphasized in his secret memorandum to Alexander I, *Memoir on Ancient and Modern Russia* (1811), Karamzin believed that autocracy and a poweful state were responsible for Russia's greatness.[101] Though an adequate discussion of Russian historiography's contribution to the national imaginary cannot be elaborated at length in this essay, one should note that it coincided with the development of an ideology of imperialism, in journals like *Vestnik Evropy* and *Russkii vestnik*, the emergence of a Russian schools of ethnography and geography, and the flowering of poetry, novels and short stories, music, and the visual arts.[102] Convinced of their cultural, not to mention material, superiority over the southern and eastern peoples of their empire, Russian intellectuals and statesmen evolved a modernist program of developing, civilizing, categorizing, and rationalizing through regulations, laws, statistical surveys, and censuses the non-Russian peoples of the borderlands. Whatever sense of inferiority Russians might have felt toward Europeans, particularly the Germans and the English, they more than made up for in their condescension toward their own colonized peoples. And Russians frequently mentioned that they were much better imperialists than the British or the French.[103] Occasionally, however, the immensity of the civilizing mission impressed even the most enthusiastic advocates of expansion. Mikhail Orlov, for example, wearily (and prophetically) remarked, "It is just as hard to subjugate the Chechens and other peoples of this region as to level the Caucasian range. This is something to achieve not with bayonets but with time and enlightenment, in such short supply in our country."[104]

The early nineteenth century was a moment of imperial expansion to the south, into Caucasia. As Russian soldiers moved over the mountains into the Georgian principalities, the Muslim khanates, and Armenia, Russian writers created their own "literary Caucasus" that contributed to the Russian discourses of empire and national identity that shaped perceptions and self-understandings of the Russian nineteenth-century elite. Pushkin's evocative poem, "The Prisoner of the Caucasus," was at one and the same time travelogue, ethnography, geography, and even war correspondence. In Pushkin's imaginative geography, the communion with nature "averted the eye from military conquest" and largely disregarded the native peoples of the Caucasus, who represented a vague menace to the Russian's lyrical relationship with the wilderness. His epilogue to the poem celebrated the military conquest of the Caucasus and introduced a dissonant note into his celebration of the purity, generosity, and liberty of the mountaineers. To paraphrase Viazemskii's telling rebuke, here poetry became an ally of butchers.[105]

The Russian colonial encounter with the Caucasus coincided with an intense phase of the intelligentsia's discussion of Russia's place between Europe and Asia. In the first decades of the nineteenth century, scholars laid the foundations of Russian orientalism, and, through their perception of the Asian "other," Russians conceptualized ideas of themselves. Russian "civilization," usually taken to be inferior to that of the West, was at least superior to the "savagery" of the Caucasian mountaineers or Central Asian nomads. A compensatory pride marked the complex and contradictory attitudes toward and images of the Caucasian Orient. Emotional intensity and primitive poetry mixed with macho violence. For some, the "civilizing mission" of Russia in the south and east was paramount; for others, including military volunteers, adventure and a "license to kill" were what they sought. In the young Mikhail Lermontov's "Izmail-Bey" and in Elizaveta Gan's oriental tales, the mountaineers also become sexual aggressors, "real men" both terrifying and seductive, a threat to the wounded masculine pride of the more restrained Russian. For Belinskii, "a woman is created by nature for love," but the Caucasians go too far, making them exclusively objects of passion. Russian writers treated Georgia as a dangerous woman, capable of murder, who had to be dominated for her own good.[106] While Muslim tribesmen were featured as heroes, Christian Georgian men played no role in Russian literature except as the impotent or absent opposites of virile Russian empire-builders. History seemed to reinforce the vulnerability felt by Russian men. When the historic leader of the mountain people's war against Russia, Shamil, married an Armenian captive, she converted to Islam and stayed with him in a loving relationship for life. The eroticism that companioned imperialism was contained in the Russian fear of the physical prowess of the Caucasians that extended from the battlefield to the bedroom.

In more popular hack literature of the 1830s, the ambiguities of Russia's colonial encounters were lost, and an unabashedly celebratory account of imperialism contended with earlier visions until the young Lev Tolstoi challenged the dominant literary tradition of romanticizing and sentimentalizing the Russian-Caucasian encounter. Yet his stories written between the 1850s and the 1870s—"The Raid," "The Wood-felling," "The Cossacks," and his own "Prisoner of the Caucasus"—along with the developing Caucasian scholarship of regional specialists that criticized the "romance of noble primitivity" did not have the impact of the still-popular Romantic writers.[107] The public feted the defeated Shamil, who made a triumphal tour of Russia and was treated nostalgically as a noble warrior.

While expanding in territory and upholding the traditional principles of autocracy and orthodoxy, the Russian monarchy, at least up to the time of Nicholas I, imagined Russia as a modern Western state. But the "West" had changed since

Peter's time. No longer embracing the ideal of absolutism, Europe increasingly embodied the principles of nationality and popular sovereignty, industrialism and free labor, constitutionalism and representative government. The task for the ideologists of empire in midcentury was to reconceive Russia as "modern" and to rethink its relationship to its own imagined "West." Setting out the terms of what would become an interminable debate, the conservative Moscow university professor S. Shevyrev wrote in 1841, "The West and Russia, Russia and the West—here is the result that follows from the entire past; here is the last word of history; here are the two facts for the future."[108] As attractive at times as European ideas and practices were for reforming monarchs and intellectuals, in the last years of Catherine II's reign and again in the period after 1815, the emperors and their advisers saw foreign influences as alien, dangerous, and subversive. The threat presented by innovative ideas to absolutism became palpable with the Decembrist rebellion, and state officials themselves attempted to construct their own Russian idea of nation, one that differed from the dominant discourse of the nation in the West.

Nicholas's ideological formulation, known as "Official Nationality," was summed up in the official slogan "Orthodoxy, Autocracy, Nationality [*narodnost'*]." Elaborated by the conservative minister of education Sergei Uvarov, Official Nationality emphasized the close ties between the tsar and the people, a bond said to go back to Muscovy. Russians, it was claimed, had chosen their foreign rulers, the Varangians, and worshipped their successors. Russia was distinct in the love of the people for the Westernized autocracy and in their devotion to the church. The link that joined autocracy, Orthodoxy, and the people was present at Russia's creation, claimed the journalist Fedor Bulgarin: "Faith and autocracy created the Russian state and the one common fatherland for the Russian Slavs. . . . This immense colossus, Russia, almost a separate continent, which contains within itself all the climates and all the tribes of mankind, can be held in balance only by faith and autocracy. That is why in Russia there could never and cannot exist any other nationality, except the nationality founded on Orthodoxy and on autocracy.[109]

At the heart of Official Nationality lay the image of Russia as "a single family in which the ruler is the father and the subjects the children. The father retains complete authority over the children while he allows them to have full freedom. Between the father and the children there can be no suspicion, no treason; their fate, their happiness and their peace they share in common."[110] "Nationality," the most obscure and the most contested of the official trinity, was intimately linked with ideas of obedience, submission, and loyalty. As an authentically Christian people, Russians were said to be marked by renunciation and sacrifice, calm and contemplation, a deep affection for their sovereign, and dedicated resistance to revolution. At his coronation, which was delayed because of the Decembrist mutiny of progressive nobles, Nicholas bowed three times to the people, inventing a new tradition that continued until the dynasty's fall. At the same time, he nationalized the monarchy more intensively. At the ball that followed the coronation, nobles danced in national costumes surrounded by Muscovite decor. Russian was to be used at court; Russian language and history became required subjects at university; churches were built in a Russo-Byzantine style; a national anthem, "God Save the Tsar," was composed, under the emperor's supervision, as well as a national opera, *A Life for the Tsar*, by Mikhail Glinka, which incorporated folk music to tell the tale of a patriotic peasant, Ivan Susanin, who leads a band of Poles astray rather than reveal the hiding place of the future tsar.[111]

"Official Nationality" was an attempt to make an end run around the Western discourse of the nation and to resuture nation to state, to the monarch and the state religion at the moment when in Western Europe the political community known as nation was becoming separable from the state, at least conceptually, and was fast gaining an independent potency as the source of legitimacy.[112] In contrast to the discourse of the nation, tsarist ideology resisted the challenge to the ancien regime sense of political community (and sovereignty) being identified with the ruler or contained within the state. Generalizing from the Russian case, Benedict Anderson sees "official nationalisms" as a category of nationalisms that appear after popular linguistic-nationalisms, "*responses* by power-groups—primarily, but not exclusively, dynastic and aristocratic—threatened with exclusion from, or marginalization in, popular imagined communities." Official nationalism "concealed a discrepancy between nation and dynastic realm" and was connected to the efforts of aristocracies and monarchies to maintain their empires.[113] Certainly, the official tsarist view of what was national was deeply conservative in the sense of preserving a given state form that was being questioned by rival conceptions in the West. Looking back to an idealized past of harmony between people and ruler, Nicholas's notion of Holy Rus' was contrasted to godless, revolutionary Europe. At the same time, the monarchy, which was uneasily both Russian and European, resisted those domestic nationalists, like the Slavophile Konstantin Aksakov, who identified with the simple people (*narod*) by wearing a beard and Russian national dress. "In Nicholas' Western frame of mind, beards signified not Russians but Jews and radicals. The official view identified the nation with the ruling Western elite," and not with the mass of the people.[114] In the official scenario the people adored the tsar but did not sanction or legitimize his right to rule. That was conferred by God, by conquest, by hereditary right, the inherent superiority of the hereditary elite, and the natural affection of the Russian people for the autocratic foreigner whose rule benefited them.

In many ways, the appearance of the intelligentsia in the 1830s implied a social dialogue about what constituted "the nation." Made up of members from various classes, the intelligentsia lived apart from society and the people, isolated from and alien to official Russia, questioning fundamentals about the political order and religion, yet deeply desirous of becoming close to the people and serving it. As Alan Pollard suggests, "Herein lay the intelligentsia's dilemma. The elements which created consciousness tended to be products of the West, so that the very qualities which endowed the intelligentsia with understanding, and thus with its very essence, also alienated it from national life, to represent *which* was its vital function. Therefore, the intelligentsia's central problem was to establish a liaison with the people."[115] Young Russian intellectuals moved in the years from the 1830s to the 1860s, from contemplating the world to attempting to transform it through action. The opening event in the intelligentsia dialogue was the 1836 "Philosophical Letter" by Petr Chaadaev, which Aleksandr Herzen reported had an effect like "a pistol shot in the dark night." Radically antinationalist, the Letter proclaimed that Russia was unique in that it had no history or traditions, essentially making it a tabula rasa on which new ideas and forms could be written. This extreme Westernizer position was diametrically opposed to Official Nationality, which contrasted Russia's healthy wholeness to the rottenness of the West. After he was condemned as insane and placed under house arrest, Chaadaev published his *Apology of a Madman*, in which he argued that Russia's backwardness presented a unique opportunity for his country "to resolve the greater part of the social problems, to perfect the greater part of the ideas which have arisen in older societies."[116]

The ensuing discussion divided the intelligentsia into those who subscribed to a more rationalist, Enlightenment agenda for Russia—reform in a generally modernist European direction—and those who favored a more conservative reconstruction of what made up the Russian or Slavic tradition. While some liberals appeared to be indifferent or even hostile to issues of national identity, Ivan Kireevskii, Aleksei Khomiakov, and other Slavophiles followed the European Romantics and looked to the *narod*, which was largely identified with the peasantry, for *narodnost'*, the essential character of the Russian or Slav. National character was for Khomiakov contained in religion or a certain form of religiosity.[117] Slavs were the most highly spiritual, the most artistic and talented of the peoples of the Earth. Peace-loving and fraternal, spontaneous, loving, and valuing freedom, they realized their fullness in an organic unity of all in love and freedom, which he called *sobornost'*. Russians were the greatest of the Slavs and possessed an abundance of vital, organic energy, humility, and brotherly love. In the pre-Petrine past they had lived free and harmoniously, but Peter the Great had introduced alien Western notions of rationalism, legalism, and formalism to Russia and destroyed the organic harmony of the nation. For Konstantin Aksakov and other Slavophiles, not only was Orthodox Christianity the essential heart of Slavic nature, but the peasant commune was envisioned as "a union of the people who have renounced their egoism, their individuality, and who express their common accord." Critical of the newly triumphant capitalism of the West, they feared the depersonalization of human relations, the dominance of things over men, that came with private property. In Andrzej Walicki's telling analysis, Slavophilism was a "conservative utopianism" that defended community against the fragmenting effects of society.[118]

Both the state authorities and the Westernizer intellectuals rejected the Slavophile vision. For the autocracy, the repudiation of the Petrine reforms was an unacceptable challenge, while for the Westernizers the Slavophile reading of the Russian past was a narcissistic fiction. Though Slavophilism was in its origins primarily "a cultivation of the native and primarily Slavic elements in the social life and culture of ancient Russia," this conservative nationalism later blended into a larger concern with the whole of Slavdom (pan-Slavism), rather than a focused development of Russian national character.[119] In both official and unofficial presentations, Russia was submerged into an identification either with the state, the monarchy, and the empire or with Orthodoxy and Slavdom. "The Slavophiles," writes Bushkovitch, "though they moved in that direction, failed to fully establish a tradition of ethnic, rather than statist, identity for Russia."[120] Yet their contribution to Russian political and social thought was profound. From Herzen's "Russian socialism" and the celebration of the peasant commune to the revolutionary populism of the 1870s, ideas of Russian exceptionalism, of overcoming the burdens of Western capitalism and moving straight on to a new communitarianism, dominated the left wing of the Russian intelligentsia. Likewise, their influence was felt by more conservative figures like Dostoevskii and Solov'ev.

The Westernizer Vissarion Belinskii was critical both of the Slavophiles' celebration of the folk and the views of "humanist cosmopolitans," like Valerian Maikov, who believed that modernity would eliminate the specificities of nationality. Belinskii argued, instead, that nation must not be confused with the ethnic but was the result of a progressive civilizing development that came about when the people were raised to the level of society and not, as the Slavophiles suggested, when society was lowered to the level of the people.[121] Rather than condemn Peter's reforms for dividing people from society, Belinskii praised the tsar for turning Russians from a *narod* into a *natsiia* by breaking with instinctive nationality and allowing national consciousness to arise. Turning to literature, the critic claimed that national art was not to be confused with folk production but must refer to the new social and cultural amalgam that came with contact with universal values. For Russia, "truly national works should undoubtedly be sought among those depicting the social groups that emerged after the reforms of Peter the Great and adopted a civilized way of life."[122] Reflecting the early nineteenth-century discussions in Europe about nationality, Belinskii agreed that "nationalities are the individualities of mankind. Without nations mankind would be a lifeless abstraction, a word without content, a meaningless sound."[123]

Historians entered the debate over the nature of the Russian nation and the effects of Peter the Great's intervention, usually in opposition to the Slavophile interpretation. In a series of lectures in 1843-1844, Timofei Granovskii attacked the Slavophile idealization of the people. But more long-lasting was the work of the so-called statist school of Russian historians—Konstantin Kavelin, Boris Chicherin, and Sergei Solov'ev—who by proposing that the Russian state was the principal agent of progress in Russia's history ensured that state, rather than nation, would dominate the subsequent historical discussion. Russian "nationalist" thought, such as it was, usually centered either on the state or on a religious conception of identity and community and in the minds of its more conservative representatives included in that community all Slavs. The "nation," while always present as a palimpsest, was overlaid by other, more pressing social and political themes, and preoccupation with problems of the *narod* and its relationship to *obshchestvo* (society) indicates the conceptual difficulties of imagining a nation that cut across estate boundaries and included the whole of "national" community.

The tsarist empire tried at various times to extend official nationalism, to foster first bureaucratic, then cultural Russification, to suppress non-Russian nationalisms and separatisms, and to identify the dynasty and the monarchy with a Russian "nation." But these inconsistent nationalizing policies foundered before opposing tendencies, most significantly the powerful countervailing pull of supranational identifications of Russia with empire, Orthodoxy, and Slavdom. Even the conservative nationalist Mikhail Katkov (1818–1887) conceived of Russian identity as basically state centered. Since the state was not ethnically homogeneous, that condition had to be changed. Russification would provide the state with a loyal, ethnically homogeneous source of support. Though his newspaper, *Moskovskie Vedomosti*, was the most popular on the Right, his nationalist views had only limited appeal to the broader population. The idea of a pan-Slavic unity, perhaps headed by "the tsar of all the Slavs" and not just by Russia (an idea expressed by the poet Fedor Tiuchev, among others), was continually undermined by the resistance of other Slavic peoples, most importantly the Poles, who not only did not share Orthodoxy with the Russians but whose whole self-identity was bound up in resistance to Russian domination. Closer to home, both pan-Slavism and the more modest concept of the Russian people as including both "Little Russians," (Ukrainians) and "White Russians" (Belorussians), as well as "Great Russians," was dealt a severe blow by an emerging separate national identity among Ukrainians. After the government suppressed the Ukrainian Brotherhood of Cyril and Methodius, a radical pan-Slavic group, in 1847, it not only reversed its Ukrainophilic policy (directed against Polish influences) but officially condemned pan-Slavism as a dangerous and subversive doctrine.[124]

The articulation by intellectuals and government officials of a special character of the Russian people as something different from and inherently superior to the chaotic amoralism of the West provided Russian policymakers with motivation and justification for imperial expansion to the east and colonization of the "empty spaces" of Siberia and Central Asia. The voluminous writings of a conservative nationalist like Mikhail Pogodin, a historian who worshipped Karamzin and who held the first chair in Russian history at Moscow University, contained all of these themes—Russian exceptionalism, pan-Slavism, and a civilizing mission in the east.[125] Whereas in the West, Russia met resistance to its expansion—the Crimean War (1853–1856), the Treaty of Berlin (1878)—and rebellion (the Polish insurrections of 1831 and 1863), the East offered opportunities. With the defeat of Imam Shamil, battle-hardened troops were available to be deployed further east. While Russia's cautious foreign minister Prince A. M. Gorchakov opposed annexing the khanate of Khokand, even after General Cherniaev had seized Tashkent in 1865, the energetic general's policy of abolishing the khanate's autonomy eventually gained powerful supporters in the government. Russia's principal concern in Central Asia was neither economic nor religious but was largely strategic at first—

directed against the expansion of Bukhara and later of the British—and concerned with trade and settlement only later. After General Konstantin Von Kaufman defeated Bukhara and Khiva, they were made dependencies of the Russian tsar but allowed to keep their autonomy. Where Russians ruled directly, the military remained in charge, with all of its rigidity and authoritarianism. Even after civilians became more influential after 1886, the administration, manned by petty and ill-educated officials, was marked by callous and arbitrary treatment of the local peoples and by pervasive corruption. In Central Asia, a cultural and class chasm separated Russian administrators and settlers from the Muslim peoples. Educated Muslims either entered the Islamic clergy or accepted the benefits of European knowledge, mediated through Russian. The Muslim reformers, known as Jadidists (followers of the "new method"), attempted to bring Western learning to Central Asia but found themselves caught between suspicious Russians on one side and hostile Muslim clerics on the other.

Though tsarist Russia was not a "liberal bourgeois" empire, like the British, French, or Belgian empires, and did not have an inherent conflict between universal rights and liberties and the forms of its imperial rule, it nevertheless existed within a bourgeois European world and adopted a modernizing agenda in the late nineteenth century that undermined some of the earlier stabilities in the relationship of colonizer to colonized. Russian colonizers adopted the notion of "civility" (*grazhdanstvennost'*) as a way of expressing both the civilizing mission of the empire and a sense of the civic virtues that would bring "the other" into a multinational Russian world.[126] But even as they acculturated to imperial society, many educated, upwardly mobile, Russian-speaking non-Russian subjects found their access to the civil service and upper ranks of society blocked to a degree. One of the most telling arguments for the growth of nationalism among peripheral elites is precisely this frustrated mobility—what Benedict Anderson refers to as "cramped" or "vertically barred" "pilgrimages of Creole functionaries"[127]—that encourages them to consider reshaping the political and economic arena in which they can operate. In conditions of multinationality, nationalism often becomes an argument for privileged access, on the part of both majority peoples and minorities, to state positions.

As an imperial polity, engaged in both discriminating and nationalizing policies in the nineteenth century, the Russian state maintained vital distinctions between Russians and non-Russians, in their differential treatment of various non-Russian and non-Orthodox peoples, as well as between social estates. Whole peoples, designated *inorodtsy*, continued to be subject to special laws, among them Jews, peoples of the North Caucasus, Kalmyks, nomads, and Samoeds and other peoples of Siberia. The Great Reforms of the 1860s did not extend *zemstva* (local assemblies) to non-Russian areas. While distinctions and discriminations were maintained between parts of the empire and the constituent peoples, more concerted efforts were made to Russify some parts of the population. The government considered all Slavs potential or actual Russians, and officials restricted Polish higher education and the use of Ukrainian.[128] The Polish university in Vilno was closed after the rebellion of 1830–1831, only to be reopened later in Kiev as a Russian university. Alexander III's advisers, Dmitrii Tolstoi and Konstantin Pobedonostev equated Russianness and Orthodoxy and were particularly hostile to Catholics and Jews. All Orthodox students were to be educated in Russian, even if they considered themselves Ukrainian, Belorussian, Georgian, or Bessarabian. At the same time, however, the government was concerned that people have access to religious instruction in their own faith. Therefore, it permitted the establishment of Catholic, Protestant, Armenian, Muslim, and Jewish schools and occasionally allowed non-Orthodox education in languages other than Russian. Non-Christian confessional schools were also allowed to have instruction in other languages, while non-Christian state schools had to use Russian. The Church's own educational reformer, N. I. Il'minskii, argued persuasively that the heathen had to hear the Gospel in their own language, and in 1870 the so-called Il'minskii system, which established a network of missionary schools in local languages, became official policy.[129]

The most conventional image of late tsarism's "nationality policy" is that it was dedicated to Russification. But this image, in which every action from administrative systematization to repression of national movements is homogenized into a seemingly consistent program, is sorely deficient. In Russia, Russification had at least three distinct meanings. For Catherine the Great and Nicholas I, *obruset'* or *obrusevanie* was a state policy of unifying and making uniform the administrative practices of the empire. Second, there was a spontaneous process of self-adaptation of people to the norms of life and language in the Russian empire, an unplanned *obrusenie* (again the verb *obruset'* was employed) that was quite successful among the peoples of the Volga region and the western Slavic peoples and continued to be particularly powerful in the middle decades of the nineteenth century, when the empire was inclusive, relatively tolerant (except toward Poles and Ukrainians), and appealed to non-Russians as an available path to European enlightenment and progress. The third form of Russification is the one conventionally referred to, the effort to *obrusit'*, to make Russian in a cultural sense. Cultural Russification was a latecomer to the arsenal of tsarist state-building and was a reaction to the nationalisms of non-Russians that the governments of Alexander III and Nicholas II in their panic exaggerated beyond their actual strength.[130]

One of the fields where nationality began to emerge as a significant marker of difference in Russia was in education, and here as elsewhere this emergence of nationality as a politically salient category was the unintended consequence of state religious policy. As John Slocum suggests, "a state policy aimed at language rationalization, when pursued simultaneously with the implementation of a system of public education, induces a politics of nationality when the state encounters entrenched societal actors (in this case, non-Orthodox religious hierarchies) with a vested interest in upholding alternative world-views."[131] As elementary school enrollment in Russia increased fivefold from 1856 to 1885 and another fourfold by 1914, the issue of language of instruction became a major concern of the government. Non-Russianness was associated more and more with language, and the government intervened more frequently in favor of Russian education. In 1887, for example, elementary schools in the Baltic region, which were allowed to teach in Russian, Estonian, or Latvian for the first two years, were required to teach exclusively in Russian in the last year, except for religion and church singing. "By about 1910," Slocum argues, " 'nationality' had become a politically salient category within imperial Russia. . . . Language-based nationality achieved the status of the primary criterion for distinguishing Russians from non-Russians (and one group of non-Russians from another) by overturning an earlier official definition of the situation, according to which religion was the primary criterion for determining Russianness and non-Russianness."[132] From a politics of difference based primarily, but not entirely, on religion, Russia passed to a politics in which nationality counted as never before.

In the more open political arena in the period between the two revolutions, from 1905 to 1917, the "nationality question" became an issue of extraordinary interest both to the government and to the opposition. Very often, those Russians living in ethnically non-Russian areas, such as the western provinces, Ukraine, or Transcaucasia, were ferociously nationalist. They were represented in the Nationalist party, which flourished in the western provinces, and chauvinist publicists like Vasilii Velichko, with his anti-Armenian diatribes, became influential in Transcaucasia.[133] A widely read debate in the press between the "conservative liberal" Petr Stuve and the Ukrainian activist Bohdan Kistiakivs'kyi exposed the statism and assimilationist nationalism that underlay much Russian political thinking, even among those opposed to autocracy.[134] While Russian nationalists insisted that Ukrainians and Belorussians were lesser branches of a single Russian people, nationalists among Ukrainians claimed a nationhood based on a distinct culture. As a variety of ethnic nationalisms developed, among both conservative Russians and non-Russian peoples, the government held a series of conferences on nationality matters, one on pan-Turkism and another interdepartmental conference on the education of *inorodtsy*. The organizers of the latter conference hoped to attract *inorodtsy* into the general educational system of the Russian-language state schools, to develop the use of Russian "as the state language," though forcible Russification was to be avoided. This was clearly an abandonment of the "Il'minskii system," for now instruction, except in the first and possibly the second year of primary school, was ultimately to be in Russian. The goal no longer was the development of backward peoples within their own culture along with the Orthodox religion, but assimilation of non-Russians to the greatest extent possible. The conference opposed "artificial awakening of self-consciousness among separate *narodnosti* [peoples], which, according to their cultural development and numerical size, cannot create an independent culture."[135] As the conference report concluded. "The ideal school from the point of view of state unity would be a unified school for all the *narodnosti* of the Empire, with the state language of instruction, not striving for the repression of individual nationalities [*natsional'nosti*], but cultivating in them, as in native Russians, love of Russia and consciousness of her unity, wholeness [*tselost'*], and indivisibility."[136]

The state was prepared to use its resources to gain converts to Orthodoxy and the Russian language but also seemed to realize that "the majority of the empire's population was not and never would be truly Russian."[137] Religious boundaries were real and were to be enforced, while nationalism and separatism were to be repressed. While religion continued to be the primary distinction between Russians and non-Russians, language and nationality became highly relevant markers of difference in the last years of tsarism, and the shift from distinctiveness based on religion to one based on language, though never complete, was, in Slocum's words, "a transformation in the discursive regime, a revolutionary break in the political conversations between Russians and non-Russians."[138]

In the last years of tsarism the tsarist upper classes and state authorities were divided between those who no longer were willing to tamper with the traditional institutions of autocracy and nobility and those who sought to reform the state to represent the unrepresented, reduce or eliminate social and ethnic discriminations, and move toward forming a nation.[139] But the resistance to social egalitarianism or ethnic neutrality overwhelmed nation-making processes. The famous attempt to establish elective *zemstva* in the western provinces precipitated a political crisis. If the usual principle of representation by estate were observed, local power would pass into the hands of Polish landlords, but when a system of representation by ethnic curiae was proposed, the law was defeated in the conservative upper house of the duma because it compromised representation by estate. A law on municipal councils in Poland's cities collapsed before the resistance by anti-Semitic Poles, who feared Jewish domination of the municipal legislatures. Russian nationalists triumphed briefly in 1912 when the region of Kholm (Chelm), largely Ukrainian and Catholic in population, was removed from the historic Kingdom of Poland and made into a separate province.[140] In each of these three cases, particularistic distinctions about nationality and class dominated the discussion and divided the participants. Universalist principles about allegiance to a common nation were largely absent.

In his forced retirement, the former prime minister Sergei Witte, an exceptionally thoughtful analyst of the autocracy, perceptively noted the principal difficulties faced by traditional empires as they entered the twentieth century. In his *Zapiski* (Memoirs), Witte noted that the growing political consciousness of Russian society combined with the "not only inappropriate but fatally flawed" actions of the tsar were rendering autocracy untenable.[141] To the failures of the center and the mobilization of the masses, Witte added the threat presented by nationalism.

> The borderlands . . . began to avenge very real discrimination that had gone on for years, as well as measures which were entirely justified but unreconciled with the national feelings (*natsional'noe chuvstvo*) of conquered ethnic groups (*inorodtsy*) . . . The big mistake of our decades-long policy is that we still today do

not understand that there hasn't been a Russia from the time of Peter the Great and Catherine the Great. There has been a Russian Empire. When over 35 per cent of the population are ethnics, and Russians are divided among Great Russians, Little Russians, and White Russians, it is impossible, in the 19th and 20th centuries, to conduct a policy that ignores . . . the national tendencies (*natsional'nye svoistva*) of other nationalities who have entered the Russian Empire, their religion (s), their language (s), and so on. The motto of such an empire cannot be "I will make them all true Russians"–this is not an ideal that will inspire all subjects of the Russian Emperor, unify the population, create one political spirit.[142]

Tsarism never created a nation within the whole empire or even a sense of nation among the core Russian population, even though what looked to others like imperialism was for the country's rulers "part of larger state-building and nation-building projects."[143] Tsarist Russia managed only too well in building a state and creating an empire; it failed, however, to construct a multiethnic "Russian nation" within that empire. The history of tsarism is that of an empire that at times engaged in nation-making, but state practice was always in tension with the structures and discourses of empire. The imperial tended to thwart, if not subvert, the national, just as the national worked to erode the stability and legitimacy of the state. While Muscovy and imperial Russia were successful in integrating the core regions of its empire, often referred to as the *vnutrennie guberniia*, into a single nationality, diverse administrative practices, as well as the compactness of the local ethnicities and the effects of settlement policies, maintained and intensified differences between the Russian core and the non-Russian peripheries.[144] After relatively successfully conquering and assimilating the Orthodox Slavic population of central Russia (Vladimir, Novgorod, and other appanage states), Muscovy set out to "recover" lands with non-Slavic, non-Orthodox populations, such as Kazan. In some areas, the tsarist regime managed to create loyal subjects through the transformation of cultural identities, but its policies were inconsistent and varied enormously. It neither created an effective civic national identity nor succeeded in forging (or even tried very hard to forge) an ethnic nation, even among Russians. Localism, religious identity, and a pervasive concept of Russia as tied up with tsar and state, rather than with the people as a whole, hindered the imagining of a cross-class, cross-cultural nation within the empire. The tsarist government, it might be said, even failed to turn peasants into Russians.[145] There was no program, as there was in France, to educate and affiliate millions of people around an idea of the nation. Tsarist Russia's experience was one of incomplete nation-making. Here the parallels with England's success in integrating Britain and failing in Ireland or France's success in nationalizing the "hexagon" and failing in Algeria (as discussed by Ian Lustick) are suggestive in explicating the Russian case.[146]

Russia was a composite state with unequal relations between a "Russian" metropole, which itself was a multiethnic though culturally Russified ruling elite, and non-Russian populations. For all the haphazard nationalizing efforts of the ruling institution, both the programs of discrimination and inequity between metropole and periphery and the resistant cultures and counterdiscourses of nationalism of non-Russians prevented the homogenization and incorporation of the population into a single "imagined community" of a Russian nation. Though tsarist Russia's collapse occurred not because of nationalisms from the peripheries but because of the progressive weakening and disunity of the center, much of the legitimacy of the imperial enterprise had withered away by 1917. Elites withdrew support from the monarchy, and more broadly the regime was alienated from the intelligentsia and workers, strategically located in the largest cities, from the regime. Policies of industrialization and the limited reforms after 1905 had created new constituencies in tsarist society that demanded representation in the political order that the tsar refused to grant. In the new world in which discourses of civilization centered on the nation, constitutionalism, economic development (which tsarism was seen to be hindering), and (in some quarters) socialism and revolution, tsarism's political structure (autocracy) was increasingly understood to be a fetter on further advances.

In its last years, the dynasty appeared increasingly to be incompetent and even treacherous. As Russians suffered defeats and colossal losses in World War I, the fragile aura of legitimacy was stripped from the emperor and his wife, who were widely regarded as distant from, even foreign to, Russia. What the dynasty in the distant past had imagined was empowering, their difference from the people, now became a fatal liability. Elite patriotism, frustrated non-Russian nationalisms, and peasant weariness at intolerable sacrifices for a cause with which they did not identify combined lethally to undermine the monarchy. The principles of empire, of differentiation and hierarchy, were incompatible with modern ideas of democratic representation and egalitarian citizenship that gripped much of the intelligentsia and urban society. When the monarchy failed the test of war, its last sources of popular affection and legitimacy fell away, and in the crucial test of the February Days of 1917 Nicholas II was unable to find the military support to suppress the popular resistance to his rule in a single city.

Notes

This paper was originally given in a seminar at the Center for International Security and Arms Control at Stanford University, where I was an associate in 1995–1996, and as my inaugural address at the University of Chicago two years later. My gratitude to my colleagues at the Center, its codirector David Holloway, to colleagues at Chicago, with special thanks for comments and/or careful reading of various drafts to Lowell Barrington, Rogers Brubaker, Valerie Bunce, Prasenjit Duara, Lynn Eden, Barbara Engel, Matthew Evangelista, Ted Hopf, Michel Khodarkovsky, Jeremy King, Valerie Kivelson, David Laitin, Gail Lapidus, Stephen Pincus, Norman Naimark, Lewis Siegelbaum, and Katherine Verdery.

1. *Derzhava* is the name of General Aleksandr Rutskoi's political organization, the title of a book by Gennadii Zyuganov, head of the Communist party of the Russian Federation, and General Aleksandr Lebed, the presidential candidate of one of the nationalist parties, has written a book entitled *Za derzhavu obidna* (Shameful for a great power).

2. See, for example, G. P. Fedotov, "Sud'ba imperii," in *Novyi grad: Sbornik statei* (New York: Izdatel'stvo imeni Chekhova, 1952); Olaf Caroe, *Soviet Empire* (London: Macmillan, 1953, 1967); Albert Herling, *The Soviet Slave Empire* (New York: Funk, 1951); U.S. Library of Congress, Legislative Reference Service, *The Soviet Empire: Prison House of Nations and Races* (Washington, D.C.: U.S. Government Printing Office, 1958); Walter Kolarz, *Russia and Her Colonies* (London: George Philip and Son, 1952); George Gretton, ed., *Communism and Colonialism: Essays by Walter Kolarz* (London: Macmillan, 1964); Hélène Carrière d'Encausse, *Decline of an Empire* (New York: Newsweek Books, 1979); and Robert Conquest, ed., *The Last Empire: Nationality and the Soviet Future* (Stanford, Calif.: Hoover Institution Press, 1986).

3. A partial list would include: David Pryce-Jones, *The Strange Death of the Soviet Empire* (New York: Metropolitan, 1995); Kristian Gerner, *The Baltic States and the End of the Soviet Empire* (London: Routledge, 1993); David Remnick, *Lenin's Tomb: The Last Days of the Soviet Empire* (New York: Random House, 1993); Sanford R. Lieberman ed., *The Soviet Empire Reconsidered: Essays in Honor of Adam B. Ulam* (Boulder: Westview Press, 1994); Jack F. Matlock, *Autopsy on an Empire: American Ambassador* (New York: Random House, 1995); Robert Cullen, *Twilight of Empire: Inside the Crumbling Soviet Union* (New York: Atlantic Monthly Press, 1991); John B. Dunlop, *The Rise of Russia and the Fall of the Soviet Empire* (Princeton, N.J.: Princeton University Press, 1993); Neil Felshman, *Gorbachev, Yeltsin and the Last Days of the Soviet Empire* (New York: St. Martin's, 1992); Marco Buttino, ed., *In a Collapsing Empire: Underdevelopment, Ethnic Conflicts and Nationalisms in the Soviet Union* (Milano: Felltrinelli, 1993); G. R. Urban, *End of Empire: The Demise of the Soviet Union* (Washington, D.C.: American University Press, 1993); Richard L. Rudolph and David F. Good, eds., *Nationalism and Empire: The Habsburg Empire and the Soviet Union* (New York: St. Martin's, 1992); and Ryszard Kapuscinski, *Imperium* (New York: Knopf, 1994).

4. Mark R. Beissinger, "The Persisting Ambiguity of Empire," in *Post-Soviet Affairs* 11, no. 2 (April–June 1995): p. 155.

5. Ibid.

6. Among them were: "Great Power Ethnic Politics: The Habsburg Empire and the Soviet Union," held at the Center for Austrian Studies, University of Minnesota, April 26–28, 1990, which led to the Rudolph and Good volume cited in n. 3; an SSRC workshop, "The End of Empire: Causes and Consequences," at the Harriman Institute, Columbia University, November 20–21, 1994, and the subsequent publication, Karen Barkey and Mark von Hagen, eds., *After Empire: Multinational Societies and Nation-Building: The Soviet Union and the Russian, Ottoman, and Habsburg Empires* (Boulder, Colo.: Westview Press, 1997); and a conference, "The Disintegration and Reconstitution of Empires: The USSR and Russia in Comparative Perspective," held at the University of California, San Diego, January 10–12, 1996, which has appeared as Karen Dawisha and Bruce Parrott, eds., *The End of Empire? The Transformation of the USSR in Comparative Perspective* (Armonk, N.Y.: Sharpe, 1997). For debate, see Mark R. Beissinger, "The Persisting Ambiguity of Empire"; and the reply by Ronald Grigor Suny, "Ambiguous Categories: States, Empire and Nations," *Post-Soviet Affairs* 11, no.

2 (April–June 1995): 185–196. See also Dominic Lieven, *Empire: The Russian Empire and Its Rivals* (London: Murray, 2000).

7. Anthony Pagden, *Lords of All the World: Ideologies of Empire in Spain, Britain, and France, c. 1500–c. 1800* (New Haven, Conn.: Yale University Press, 1995), p. 12.

8. Ibid., p. 15.

9. Ibid.

10. Ibid., p. 16.

11. Ibid., p. 17.

12. Ibid., pp. 27–28.

13. Michael W. Doyle, *Empires* (Ithaca, N.Y.: Cornell University Press, 1986), p. 45.

14. Ibid., p. 12.

15. John A. Armstrong, *Nations before Nationalism* (Chapel Hill: University of North Carolina Press, 1982), p. 131.

16. Doyle, *Empires*, p. 45.

17. Ibid., p. 36.

18. As Alexander J. Motyl argues, the peripheries must be distinct by population—class, ethnicity, religion, or something else—have a distinct territory, and be either a distinct polity or a distinct society. "From Imperial Decay to Imperial Collapse: The Fall of the Soviet Empire in Comparative Perspective," in Rudolph and Good, eds., *Nationalism and Empire*, p. 18.

19. Of course, as an imperial metropole grows weaker and the peripheries stronger, as in the Habsburg Empire after 1848, it is forced to negotiate with powerful peripheries, as Vienna did with Budapest, and in time the empire may become a hybrid empire with various autonomous "kingdoms" and "principalities" that no longer respect the authority of the center as they did in the past.

20. Fatma Müge Göçek, "The Social Construction of an Empire: Ottoman State under Suleiman the Magnificent," in Halil Inalcik and Cemal Kafadar eds., *Suleiman II and His Time* (Istanbul: Isis Press, 1993), pp. 93–108.

21. Mark R. Beissinger, "Demise of an Empire-State: Identity, Legitimacy, and the Deconstruction of Soviet Politics," in Crawford Young ed., *The Rising Tide of Cultural Pluralism: The Nation-State at Bay?* (Madison: University of Wisconsin Press, 1993), pp. 98, 99.

22. A point made eloquently by Mark Beissinger.

23. Rogers Brubaker, *Citizenship and Nationhood in France and Germany* (Cambridge, Mass.: Harvard University Press, 1992), p. 22.

24. This process of internal political and cultural integration, developing urban centers, and consolidation of state forms has usually been limited by analysts to Western Europe, the traditional site of the first national states, but Victor Lieberman has convincingly argued that the whole of Eurasia, from Britain to Japan, underwent similar and connected process in the early modern period, from roughly 1450 to 1830. See his "Introduction" and "Transcending East-West Dichotomies: State and Culture Formation in Six Ostensibly Disparate Areas," *Modern Asian Studies* 31, no. 3 (1997): 449–461, 463–546.

25. Michael Hechter, *Internal Colonialism: The Celtic Fringe in British National Development, 1536–1966* (Berkeley: University of California Press, 1975), pp. 60–64.

26. The distinction between ethnic group and nationality/nation need not be territory but rather may be the discourse in which they operate. The discourse about ethnicity is primarily about culture, cultural rights, and some limited political recog-

nition, while the discourse of the nation is more often about popular sovereignty, state power, and control of a territorial homeland. But this is not necessarily or exclusively so, for one can conceive of nonterritorial nationalisms, like those of the Jews before Zionism, the Armenians in the nineteenth century, and the Gypsies. For another view on the problems of definitions, see Lowell W. Barrington, " 'Nation' and 'Nationalism': The Misuse of Key Concepts in Political Science," *PS: Political Science & Politics,* 30, no. 4 (December 1977): 712–716.

27. See, for example, Etienne Balibar, "The Nation Form: History and Ideology," in Etienne Balibar and Immanuel Wallerstein, *Race, Nation, Class: Ambiguous Identities* (London: Verso, 1991), pp. 86–106; Benedict Anderson, *Imagined Communities: Reflections on the Origin and Spread of Nationalism* (London: Verso, 1983; rev. ed., 1991).

28. Brubaker, *Citizenship and Nationhood in France and Germany,* pp. 22, 27.

29. Nation-states and empires can be seen as two poles in a continuum, but, rather than being fixed and stable, they may flow into each other, transforming over time into the other. A nation-state may appear stable, homogeneous, and coherent and yet, with the rise of ethnic, subethnic, or regionalist movements, be perceived by subaltern populations as imperial. For those who identify with the dominant population in Belgium, it is a nation-state, perhaps a multinational state, but for a Flemish militant who feels the oppression of the Walloon majority, Belgium is a kind of mini-empire. The term "empire" has been used polemically for small states like Belgium, Georgia, and Estonia, and it may seem anomalous to refer to such nationalizing states as empires. But it is precisely with the assimilating homogenizing, or discriminating practices of the nationalizing state that relationships of difference and subordination—here considered the ingredients of an imperial relationship—are exposed.

30. See Benedict Anderson's chapter on "Official Nationalism and Imperialism" in *Imagined Communities,* pp. 83–112; and Jane Burbank's unpublished essay, "The Imperial Construction of Nationality."

31. On the Ottoman case, see Ronald Grigor Suny, "Religion, Ethnicity, and Nationalism: Armenians, Turks, and the End of the Ottoman Empire," in Omer Bartov and Phyllis Mack, eds., *In God's Name: Genocide and Religion in the Twentieth Century* (Oxford: Berghahn Press, 2001).

32. See Frederick Cooper and Randall Packard, "Introduction," in Cooper and Packard, eds., *International Development and the Social Sciences: Essays on the History and Politics of Knowledge* (Berkeley: University of California Press, 1997), pp. 1–41.

33. Among the most familiar were Lenin's theory that the falling rate of profit in developed capitalist states propelled European states to build empires to absorb their surplus capital, and J. A. Hobson's, on which Lenin built, that the imbalanced distribution of wealth within capitalist societies leads to underconsumption by the masses, oversaving by the wealthy, and a need to find new markets in underdeveloped countries. Historians critical of economic explanations, such as Carleton J. H. Hayes, countered that, rather than the imperatives of capitalism, the metropole's national interests or nationalism drove states toward colonization of the non-European world.

34. Doyle, *Empires,* pp. 71–72.

35. Chris Tiffin and Alan Lawson, eds., *De-scribing Empire: Post-Colonialism and Textuality* (London: Routledge, 1994), p. 3.

36. Edward W. Said, *Orientalism* (New York: Pantheon, 1978); *Culture and Imperialism* (New York: Knopf, 1993).

37. Frederick Cooper and Ann Laura Stoler, "Between Metropole and Colony: Rethinking a Research Agenda," in their *Tensions of Empire: Colonial Cultures in a Bourgeois World* (Berkeley: University of California Press, 1997), p. 1.

38. Ibid.

39. Ibid., p. 9.

40. As Stoler and Cooper point out, "the most basic tension of empire" lies in the fact that "the otherness of colonized persons was neither inherent nor stable; his or her difference had to be defined and maintained. . . . Social boundaries that were at one point clear would not necessarily remain so" (ibid., p. 7).

41. One of these "inevitablists," Alexander J. Motyl, makes a useful distinction between imperial decay and imperial collapse and highlights the place of crisis in the final collapse. Decay occurs "when the absolute power of the center over the periphery can no longer be effectively maintained and the periphery can, and does, act contrary to the will of the center." A second form of decay, according to Motyl, involves the loss of the absolute quality of the emperor's rule. But, rather than accept Motyl's notion that "the power of emperors must be relatively absolute for their decision-making capacity to be considered imperial," which runs in the face of the experience of those nineteenth-century empires that were parliamentary monarchies or republics, it is enough to follow Doyle's formulation, that in order to remain effective the metropole must maintain internal political unity able to overcome the actual or potential resistance of the periphery. Shifts in metropolitan polities from absolutism to shared power arrangements do not necessarily lead to imperial decay, as long as elites remain united in their imperial policies.

42. Ibid., pp. 40, 36–37.

43. Jeremy King suggested to me that a similar process occurred in the Austro-Hungarian Empire where the German, Czech, and Hungarian urban bourgeoisies had withdrawn their support from the monarchy at the end of the nineteenth and beginning of the twentieth centuries.

44. Miles Kahler, "Empires, Neo-Empires, and Political Change: The British and French Experience," in Dawisha and Parrott, eds., *The End of Empire?*, p. 288. This delegitimatizing of empires seems to have occurred at several historical conjunctures, not only after the two world wars but, for example, in the second half of the eighteenth century, as the French, Spanish, and British empires in the Americas began to break down. See Pagden, *Lords of All the World*.

45. Ibid.

46. Paul Bushkovitch, "What Is Russia? Russian National Consciousness and the State, 1500–1917," unpublished paper, p. 3.

47. Richard Wortman, *Scenarios of Power: Myth and Ceremony in Russian Monarchy, Vol. I, From Peter the Great to the Death of Nicholas I* (Princeton, N.J.: Princeton University Press, 1995).

48. Ibid., p. 6.

49. This is a point well made by Andreas Kappeler, *Russland als Vielvolkerreich: Entstehung, Geschichte, Zerfall* (Munich: C. H. Beck'sche Verlagsbuchhandlung, 1992). I have used the French translation by Guy Imart, *La Russie, Empire multiethnique* (Paris: Institut d'Ètudes Slaves, 1994), pp. 25–30.

50. Nicholas V. Riasanovsky, "Historical Consciousness and National Identity: Some Considerations on the History of Russian Nationalism" (New Orleans: Graduate

School of Tulane University, 1991), pp. 2–3; Omeljan Pritsak, "The Origin of Rus',
Russian Review 36, no. 3 (July 1977): 249–273.

51. Valerie Kivelson, "Merciful Father, Impersonal State: Russian Autocracy in
Comparative Perspective," *Modern Asian Studies* 31, no. 3 (1997): 637–638.

52. Michael Cherniavsky, "Russia," in Orest Ranum, ed., *National Consciousness,
History, and Political Culture in Early-Modern Europe* (Baltimore: Johns Hopkins University
Press, 1975), pp. 119–121.

53. Gregory Guroff and Alexander Guroff, "The Paradox of Russian National
Identity," paper presented at the Russian Littoral Project Conference, "The Influence
of Ethnicity on Russian Foreign Policy," May 1993, no. 16, pp. 7–9.

54. Richard Hellie, *Slavery in Russia, 1450–1725* (Chicago: University of Chicago
Press, 1982), p. 392.

55. Ibid.

56. Kivelson, "Merciful Father, Impersonal State," p. 643.

57. Wortman, *Scenarios of Power,* p. 25.

58. Ibid., p. 28.

59. Cherniavsky, "Russia," p. 123; see also his "Khan or Basileus: An Aspect of
Russian Medieval Political Theory," *Journal of the History of Ideas* 20 (October–December 1959): pp. 459–476; reprinted in Cherniavsky ed., *The Structure of Russian History:
Interpretive Essays* (New York: Random House, 1970), pp. 65–79; and *Tsar and People:
Studies in Russian Myths* (New Haven, Conn.: Yale University Press, 1961).

60. Paul Bushkovitch, "The Formation of a National Consciousness in Early Modern Russia," *Harvard Ukrainian Studies* 10, no. 3–4 (December 1986): 363.

61. Michael Khodarkovsky, "From Frontier to Empire: The Concept of the Frontier in Russia, Sixteenth–Eighteenth Centuries," *Russian History,* 19, nos. 1–4 (1992):
115–128; *Where Two Worlds Met: The Russian State and the Kalmyk Nomads, 1600–1771*
(Ithaca, N.Y.: Cornell University Press, 1992); and "Of Christianity, Enlightenment
and Colonialism: Russia in the North Caucasus, 1550–1800," *Journal of Modern History*
71, no. 2 (June 1999): 394–430.

62. Marc Raeff, "Patterns of Russian Imperial Policy toward the Nationalities," in
Edward Allworth, ed., *Soviet Nationality Problems* (New York: Columbia University Press,
1971), pp. 22–42.

63. Yuri Slezkine, *Arctic Mirrors: Russia and the Small Peoples of the North* (Ithaca, N.Y.:
Cornell University Press, 1994), pp. 41–45.

64. Ibid., pp. 44–45.

65. Bushkovitch notes a little recognized development in the seventeenth century,
the arrival of what he calls "Renaissance slavism," the idea, developed in Poland,
Croatia, and elsewhere, that the Slavs in general have an ancient and distinguished
origin. Polish writers linked them back to the ancient Sarmatians, and scholars like
Simeon Polotskii brought the idea that Russians were a Sarmatian tribe into Russian
circles. In the eighteenth century, the idea found its way into the writings of Tatishchev
and Lomonosov, who attached it to their state-centered histories. But it died out with
the elevation of a more imperial ideology with the importation of Enlightenment ideas
and is not found in Karamzin's early nineteenth-century history. See Bushkovitch,
"What Is Russia?" pp. 4–7.

66. James Cracraft, "Empire versus Nation: Russian Political Theory under Peter
I," *Harvard Ukrainian Studies,* 10, no. 3–4 (December 1986): 524–540; reprinted in Cra-

craft, ed., *Major Problems in the History of Imperial Russia* (Lexington: Heath, 1994), pp. 224–234. Citations hereafter are from the latter publication.

67. Wortman, *Scenarios of Power*, p. 33.

68. Ibid., p. 38.

69. Ibid., p. 6.

70. Ibid., p. 41.

71. Ibid., p. 44.

72. Ibid., p. 61.

73. Ibid., p. 64.

74. Cherniavsky, "Russia," p. 141.

75. Ibid., p. 140.

76. Cracraft, "Empire versus Nation," p. 225.

77. Wortman, *Scenarios of Power,* p. 81.

78. Ibid., p. 82; for a discussion of the state as defender of noble interests, see Ronald Grigor Suny, "Rehabilitating Tsarism: The Imperial State and Its Historians," *Comparative Studies in Society and History* 31, no. 1 (January 1989): 168–179.

79. Wortman, *Scenarios of Power*, pp. 82–83.

80. Cynthia Hyla Whittaker, "The Idea of Autocracy among Eighteenth-Century Russian Historians," in Jane Burbank and David Ransel, eds., *Imperial Russia: New Histories for the Empire* (Bloomington: Indiana University Press, 1998), pp. 32–59.

81. Ibid., p. 41.

82. Wortman, *Scenarios of Power*, p. 136.

83. Raeff, "Patterns of Russian Imperial Policy toward the Nationalities"; "In the Imperial Manner," in Marc Raeff, ed., *Catherine the Great: A Profile* (New York: Hill & Wang, 1972), pp. 197–246; S. Frederick Starr, "Tsarist Government: The Imperial Dimension," in Jeremy Azrael, ed., *Soviet Nationality Policies and Practices* (New York: Praeger, 1978), pp. 3–38.

84. Michael Khodarkovsky, " 'Not by Word Alone': Missionary Policies and Religious Conversion in Early Modern Russia," *Comparative Study of Society and History*, 38, no. 2 (April 1996): 267–293.

85. Slezkine, *Arctic Mirrors*, pp. 47–71; Kappeler, *La Russie*, p. 47.

86. Quoted in Kappeler, *Russland als Vielvolkerreich*, p. 121; Wortman, *Scenarios of Power,* pp. 136–137.

87. Wortman, *Scenarios of Power*, p. 170.

88. Ibid., p. 217.

89. Ibid., p. 218.

90. Ibid., p. 221.

91. Ibid., p. 222.

92. Marc Szeftel, "The Form of Government of the Russian Empire Prior to the Constitutional Reforms of 1905–06," in John Shelton Curtiss, ed., *Essays in Russian and Soviet History in Honor of Geroid Tanquary Robinson* (New York: Columbia University Press, 1962), pp. 105–119.

93. Ibid., p. 230.

94. Victor Lieberman, "Transcending East-West Dichotomies."

95. For France, see Jonathan Dewald, *Pont-St.-Pierre 1398–1789: Lordship, Community, and Capitalism in Early Modern France* (Berkeley: University of California Press, 1987), p. 284.

96. William H. Sewell, Jr., "The French Revolution and the Emergence of the Nation Form," unpublished paper presented at the Purdue University conference on the Trans-Atlantic revolutionary tradition and at the Nations and Nationalism Workshop, University of Chicago, January 14, 1998, p. 13.

97. Jeffrey Brooks, *When Russia Learned to Read: Literacy and Popular Literature, 1861–1917* (Princeton, N.J.: Princeton University Press, 1985), p. 214.

98. Ibid., p. 215.

99. Note that the word "national," among its other meanings, can refer to the "whole political community." It is this sense of a broad, inclusive population that is often confused with the sense of the "national" that flows from the discourse of the nation, that is, a body of people who believe that they have the right to rule themselves by virtue of their common cultural characteristics.

100. To my mind, there is a serious methodological problem in reading popular literature as a window into the peasant mind, as if the willingness to buy a book implies agreement or identity with the views expressed in that book. Representations in print may reflect not the views of the authors but idealizations of what they conceived to be the desires of peasant readers. Artistry and skill in presentation, appeals to emotion, not to mention the constraints of form, genre, literary convention, and censorship, must be considered. The market should not be seen as a perfect medium through which sovereign consumers express their desires in an unmediated way by freely choosing among available choices.

101. *Memoir on Ancient and Modern Russia,* translated, edited, and introduced by Richard Pipes (Cambridge, Mass.: Harvard University Press, 1959).

102. See, for example, Susan Layton, *Russian Literature and Empire: Conquest of the Caucasus from Pushkin to Tolstoy* (Cambridge: Cambridge University Press, 1994); and Austin Jersild, *Colonizing the Caucasus: Muslims, Mountaineers, and Russification, 1845–1917* (forthcoming).

103. A point made to me by Kenneth Church and illustrated in his work on Russian rule in Western Georgia. See his unpublished paper, "Production of Culture in Georgia for a Culture of Production" (1996).

104. Quoted in Layton, *Russian Literature and Empire*, p. 108.

105. Ibid., p. 53.

106. Kenneth Church suggests that, while Susan Layton is certainly correct that the Russian image of the Georgian woman as a dangerous woman is suggested by the literary texts she explores, a wider acquaintaince with travel literature reveals a counterimage of Georgian women, seen not only as the quintessence of feminine beauty but also "as attractive victims in the history of Islamic conquests" and "victims to the categorically deceitful, lazy, and impotent Georgian male characters of these works" (p. 4). Rather than just being depicted as Oriental others, they were often seen "as fallen Christians, debauched and uncultivated to be sure, but redeemable" (p. 5) ("Conjuring 'the Most Beautiful Women in the World' in Nineteenth-Century Descriptions of Georgian Women," paper delivered at the AAASS annual convention, Boca Raton, Florida, September 26, 1998).

107. Layton, *Russian Literature and Empire,* p. 254.

108. S. Shevyrev, "Vzglad russkogo na sovremennoe obrazovanie Evropy," *Moskvitianin,* no. 1, p. 219 cited in Nicholas Riasanovsky, *Nicholas I and Official Nationality in Russia, 1825–1855* (Berkeley: University of California Press, 1967), p. 134.

109. Cited in Riasanovsky, *Nicholas I and Official Nationality*, p. 77.

110. Mikhail Pogodin, cited in ibid., pp. 118–119.

111. In Western Europe after the French Revolution, a new image of monarchy, one in which the ruler was less like a god and more like a human with conventional family values, developed. Monarchs "became exemplars of human conduct, of modest virtue, to be admired by their subjects." The idealization of the monarch's family elevated the ruling dynasty as the historical embodiment of the nation." This move toward family lessened the distance between monarch and his people, as now all were part of a common nation. This ideal of bourgeois monarchy took on a distinctive shape in tsarist Russia. Nicholas I identified his dynasty with the historical destinies of the Russian state and people. "His scenario . . . portrayed the emperor as exemplifying the attributes of Western monarchy, but now as a member of his family, as a human being elevated by heredity and his belonging to a ruling family that embodied the highest values of humanity. . . . The private life of the tsar was lavishly staged to portray a Western ideal before the Russian public" (Wortman, *Scenarios of Power*, p. 402; see also George Mosse, *Nationalism and Sexuality: Middle-Class Morality and Sexual Norms in Modern Europe* [Madison: University of Wisconsin Press, 1985], passim).

112. Anderson, *Imagined Communities*, pp. 86–87, 110.

113. Ibid., pp. 109–110.

114. Wortman, *Scenarios of Power*, p. 402.

115. Alan P. Pollard, "The Russian Intelligentsia: The Mind of Russia," *California Slavic Studies* 3 (1964): 15.

116. P. Chaadaev, *Philosophical Letters and Apology of a Madman*, trans. and introduced by Mary-Barbara Zeldin (Knoxville: University of Tennessee Press, 1969), p. 174.

117. See Austin Jersild's unpublished paper, "Khomiakov and Empire: Faith and Custom in the Borderlands," presented at the AAASS annual convention, Boca Raton, Florida, September 26, 1998.

118. Andrzej Walicki, *The Slavophile Controversy: History of a Conservative Utopia in Nineteenth-Century Russian Thought*, trans. Hilda Andrews-Rusiecka (Oxford: Oxford University Press, 1975).

119. Andrzej Walicki, *A History of Russian Thought from the Enlightenment to Marxism*, trans. Hilda Andrews-Rusiecka (Stanford: Stanford University Press, 1979), p. 92.

120. Bushkovitch, "What Is Russia?" p. 12.

121. Walicki, *A History of Russian Thought*, p. 137.

122. V. G. Belinskii, *Polnoe sobranie sochineniia* (Moscow, 1953–1959), vol. 7, p. 435; Walicki, *A History of Russian Thought*, p. 140.

123. Belinskii, *Polnoe sobranie sochineniia*, vol. 10, p. 29; Walicki, *A History of Russian Thought*, p. 143.

124. P. A. Zionchkovskii, *Kirilo-Mefodievskoe obshchestvo (1846–1847)* (Moscow: Izdatel'stvo Moskovskogo universiteta, 1959).

125. Pogodin's writings are scattered but can be sampled in N. Barsukov, *Zhizn' i trudy M. P. Pogodina*, 22 vols. (St. Petersburg, 1888–1910); *Bor'ba ne na zhivot, a na smert s novymi istoricheskimi eresiami* (Moscow, 1874); *Sobranie statei, pisem i rechei po povodu slavianskogo voprosa* (Moscow, 1978). Riasanovsky, *Nicholas I and Official Nationality*, passim, discusses Pogodin at length.

126. On *grazhdanstvennost'*, see the essays by Dov Yaroshevski and Austin Lee Jersild in Daniel R. Brower and Edward J. Lazzerini, eds., *Russia's Orient: Imperial Borderlands*

and Peoples, 1700–1917 (Bloomington: Indiana University Press, 1997), pp. 58–79, 101–114.

127. Anderson, *Imagined Communities*, p. 57.

128. Theodore R. Weeks, *Nation and State in Late Imperial Russia: Nationalism and Russification on the Western Frontier, 1863–1914* (De Kalb: Northern Illinois University Press, 1996), pp. 70–91.

129. Isabelle Kreindler, "A Neglected Source of Lenin's Nationality Policy," *Slavic Review* 36, no. 1 (March 1977): 86–100.

130. For a fascinating treatment of the varieties of Russification, see Edward C. Thaden, ed., *Russification in the Baltic Provinces and Finland, 1855–1914* (Princeton, N.J.: Princeton University Press, 1981), pp. 7–9, passim.

131. John Willard Slocum, "The Boundaries of National Identity: Religion, Language, and Nationality Politics in Late Imperial Russia" (Ph.D. diss., University of Chicago, 1993), p. 10.

132. Ibid., pp. 4–5.

133. Robert Edelman, *Gentry Politics on the Eve of the Russian Revolution: The Nationalist Party* (New Brunswick, N.J.: Rutgers University Press, 1980); Ronald Grigor Suny, *The Making of the Georgian Nation* (Bloomington: Indiana University Press in association with the Hoover Institution Press, 1988; 2d ed., Bloomington: Indiana University Press, 1994), p. 142.

134. Susan Heuman, *Kistiakovsky: The Struggle for National and Constitutional Rights in the Last Years of Tsarism* (Cambridge, Mass.: Harvard Ukrainian Research Institute, 1998), pp. 130–146.

135. Ibid., p. 214.

136. Ibid., p. 216.

137. Ibid., p. 256.

138. Ibid., p. 258.

139. This conflict between rival views of how to construct a modern Russian political community is worked out in Joshua A. Sanborn, "Drafting the Nation: Military Conscription and the Formation of a Modern Polity in Tsarist and Soviet Russia, 1905–1925" (Ph. D. diss., University of Chicago, 1998).

140. Weeks, *Nation and State*, pp. 131–192.

141. Francis C. Wcislo, "Witte, Memory, and the 1905 Revolution: A Reinterpretation of the Witte Memoirs," *Revolutionary Russia* 7, no. 2 (December 1995): 175.

142. Ibid., p. 176.

143. Beissinger, "The Persisting Ambiguity," p. 2.

144. This point particularly was a contribution by Kenneth Church, who gave a careful and critical reading to an earlier paper from which this essay is taken.

145. An idea suggested to me by Roman Szporluk.

146. Ian Lustick, *State-Building Failure in British Ireland and French Algeria* (Berkeley: Institute of International Studies, University of California at Berkeley, 1985).

An Affirmative Action Empire

The Soviet Union as the Highest Form
of Imperialism

RUSSIA'S NEW REVOLUTIONARY GOVERNMENT was the first of the old European multiethnic states to confront the rising tide of nationalism and respond by systematically promoting the national consciousness of its ethnic minorities and by establishing for them many of the characteristic institutional forms of the nation-state.[1] The Bolshevik strategy was to assume leadership over what now appeared to be the inevitable process of decolonization and to carry it out in a manner that would preserve the territorial integrity of the old Russian empire and enable the construction of a new centralized, socialist state. To that end, the Soviet state created not just a dozen large national republics but tens of thousands of national territories scattered across the entire expanse of the Soviet Union. New national elites were trained and promoted to leadership positions in the government, schools, and industrial enterprises of these newly formed territories. In each territory, the national language was declared the official language of government. In dozens of cases, this necessitated the creation of a written language where one did not yet exist. The Soviet state financed the mass production of books, journals, newspapers, movies, operas, museums, folk music ensembles, and other cultural output in the non-Russian languages. Nothing comparable to it had been attempted before, and, with the possible exception of India, no multiethnic state has subsequently matched the scope of Soviet affirmative action.[2]

Why did the Bolsheviks adopt this radical strategy? To answer this question, we must consider both their prerevolutionary analysis of nationalism and their experience with nationalist movements in the years directly following the revolution. When the Bolsheviks seized power in October 1917, they did not yet possess a coherent nationalities policy. They did have a powerful slogan, which they shared with Woodrow Wilson, celebrating the right of nations to self-determination.[3] This slogan, however, was designed to recruit ethnic support for the revolution, not to provide a model for governing a multiethnic state. While Lenin always took the nationalities question seriously, the unexpected strength of nationalism as a mobilizing force during the revolution and the subsequent civil war nevertheless greatly surprised and disturbed him. The Bolsheviks expected nationalism in Poland and Finland, but the numerous nationalist movements that sprang up across most of the former Russian empire were not expected, and the strength of the Ukrainian one was particularly unnerving.[4] It was this direct confrontation with nationalism that compelled the Bolsheviks to formulate a new nationalities policy.[5]

This process did not occur without contestation. On the one side were the nation-builders, led by Lenin and Stalin; on the other side were the internationalists, led by Georgii Piatakov and Nikolai Bukharin.[6] At the Eighth Party Congress, in March 1919, the two sides clashed over the question of the right of national self-determination. Piatakov argued that "during a sufficiently large and torturous experience in the borderlands, the slogan of the right of nations to self-determination has shown itself in practice, during the social revolution, as a slogan uniting all counter-revolutionary forces."[7] Once the proletariat had seized power, Piatakov maintained, national self-determination became irrelevant: "it's just a diplomatic game, or worse than a game if we take it seriously."[8] Piatakov was supported by Bukharin, who argued that the right to self-determination could be invested only in the proletariat, not in "some fictitious so-called 'national will.' "[9] Class, rather than nationality, they both argued, was the only politically relevant social identity in the postrevolutionary era.

Lenin, who had clashed with Piatakov and others on this issue before, answered this renewed challenge with characteristic vigor.[10] Nationalism had united all counterrevolutionary forces, Lenin readily agreed, but it had also attracted the Bolsheviks' class allies. The Finnish bourgeoisie had successfully "deceived the working masses that the Muscovites (*Moskvaly*), chauvinists, Great Russians want[ed] to oppress the Finns."[11] Arguments such as Piatakov's served to increase that fear and therefore to strengthen national resistance. It was only "thanks to our acknowledgement of [the Finns'] right to self-determination, that the process of [class] differentiation was eased there."[12] Nationalism was fueled by historic distrust: "the working masses of other nations are full of distrust (*nedoverie*) toward Great Russia, as a kulak and oppressor nation."[13] Only the right to self-determination could overcome that distrust, Lenin argued, but Piatakov's policy would instead make the party the heir to tsarist chauvinism: "scratch any Communist and you find a Great Russian chauvinist."[14] Class, Lenin argued, would become the politically dominant social identity only if national identity was given proper respect.

The Congress supported Lenin and retained a qualified right of national self-determination.[15] Of course, the majority of the former Russian empire's nationalities were forced to exercise that right within the confines of the Soviet Union.[16] The period from 1919 to 1923, therefore, was devoted to working out what exactly non-Russian "national self-determination" could mean in the context of a unitary Soviet state. The resulting policy was based on a diagnosis of nationalism worked out largely by Lenin and Stalin. Lenin had addressed the national question repeatedly from 1912 to 1916, when he formulated and defended the slogan of self-determination, and again from 1919 to 1922, after the alarming success of nationalist movements during the civil war.[17] Stalin was the Bolsheviks' acknowledged "master of the nationalities question": author of the standard prerevolutionary text, *Marxism and the Nationalities Question*, commissar of nationalities from 1917 to 1924, and official spokesman on the national question at party congresses.[18] Lenin and Stalin were in fundamental agreement on both the logical rationale and the essential aspects of this new policy, though they came into conflict in 1922 over important issues of implementation. Their diagnosis of the nationalities problem rested on three premises.

First, nationalism was a uniquely dangerous mobilizing ideology because it had the potential to forge an above-class alliance in pursuit of national goals. Lenin called nationalism a "bourgeois trick,"[19] but recognized that, like the hedgehog's, it was a good one. It worked because it presented legitimate social grievances in a national form. At the Twelfth Party Congress, in 1923, Bukharin, by then a fervid defender of the party's nationalities policy, noted that "when we tax [the non-Russian peasantry] their discontent takes on a national form, is given a national interpretation, which is then exploited by our opponents."[20] Ernest Gellner has parodied this argument as the "wrong-address theory" of nationalism: "Just as extreme Shi'ite Muslims hold that Archangel Gabriel made a mistake, delivering the Message to Mohammed when it was intended for Ali, so Marxists basically like to think that the spirit of history or human consciousness made a terrible boob. The wakening message was intended for *classes*, but by some terrible postal error was delivered to *nations*."[21]

The Bolsheviks, then, viewed nationalism as a masking ideology. Masking metaphors recur again and again in their discourse about nationality.[22] Stalin was particularly fond of them: "the national flag is sewn on only to deceive the masses, as a popular flag, a convenience for covering up the counter-revolutionary plans of the national bourgeoisie"[23]; "[i]f bourgeois circles attempt to give a national tint to [our] conflicts, then only because it is convenient to hide their battle for power behind a national costume."[24] This interpretation of nationalism as a masking ideology helps explain why the Bolsheviks remained highly suspicious of national self-expression, even after they adopted a policy explicitly designed to encourage it.

Bolshevik internationalists, such as Piatakov, saw this as an argument for attacking nationalism as a counterrevolutionary ideology and nationality itself as a reactionary remnant of the capitalist era. Lenin and Stalin, however, drew the exact opposite conclusion. They reasoned as follows. By granting the forms of nationhood, the Soviet state could split the above-class national alliance for statehood. Class divisions, then, would naturally emerge, which would allow the Soviet government to recruit proletarian and peasant support for their socialist agenda.[25]

Lenin argued that Finnish independence had intensified, not reduced, class conflict and that national self-determination would have the same consequences
within the Soviet Union.[26] Likewise, Stalin insisted it was "necessary to 'take'
autonomy away from [the national bourgeoisie], having first cleansed it of its
bourgeois filth and transformed it from bourgeois into Soviet autonomy."[27] A
belief gradually emerged, then, that the above-class appeal of nationalism could
be disarmed by granting the forms of nationhood.   *take away bourg. power*

This conclusion was buttressed by a second premise: national consciousness
was an unavoidable historic phase that all peoples must pass through on the way
to internationalism. In their pre-revolutionary writings, Lenin and Stalin argued
that nationality emerged only with the onset of capitalism and was itself a consequence of capitalist production.[28] It was not an essential or permanent attribute
of mankind. Bolshevik internationalists such as Piatakov understandably interpreted this as meaning that under socialism nationality would be irrelevant and
therefore should be granted no special status. However, both Lenin and Stalin
insisted that nationality would persist for a long time, even under socialism.[29] In
fact, national self-awareness would initially increase. Already in 1916, Lenin
stated that "mankind can proceed towards the inevitable fusion (*sliianie*) of
nations only through a transitional period of the complete freedom of all oppressed nations."[30] Stalin later explicated this paradox as follows: "We are un-
dertaking the maximum development of national culture, so that it will exhaust
itself completely and thereby create the base for the organization of international
socialist culture."[31]

Two factors appear to have combined to create this sense of the inevitability
of a national stage of development. First, the collapse of the Austro-Hungarian
empire and the surprisingly strong nationalist movements within the former Russian empire greatly increased the Bolsheviks' respect for the power and ubiquity
of nationalism.[32] Stalin was particularly impressed by the process of national succession in the formerly German cities of Austro-Hungary. At the 1921 Party Congress, he pointed out that, while just fifty years earlier all cities in Hungary had
been predominately German, they had now all become majority Hungarian. Likewise, he maintained, all Russian cities in Ukraine and Belorussia would "inevitably" be nationalized, even under socialism. Opposing this was futile: "it is impossible to go against history."[33]

Moreover, this national stage of development took on a more positive connotation as it became associated not only with capitalism but also with modernization in general. In his rebuttal of Piatakov and Bukharin, citing the example
of the Bashkirs, Lenin had stated that "one must wait the development of a given
nation, the differentiation of proletariat from bourgeois elements, which is unavoidable," and that "the path from the medieval to bourgeois democracy, or from
bourgeois to proletarian democracy . . . [is] an absolutely unavoidable path."[34] As
Lenin focused Bolshevik attention on the Soviet Union's eastern "backward" nationalities, the consolidation of nationhood became associated with historical developmental progress. This trend would reach its climax during the Cultural Rev-

olution of the late 1920s, when Soviet propaganda would boast that, in the Far North, the thousand-year process of national formation had been telescoped into a mere decade.[35] The formation of nations, then, came to be seen as both an unavoidable and a positive stage in the modernization of the Soviet Union.

A third and final premise asserted that non-Russian nationalism was primarily a response to tsarist oppression and was motivated by an historically justifiable distrust of the Great Russians. This argument was pressed most forcefully by Lenin, who already in 1914 had attacked Rosa Luxemburg's denial of the right of self-determination as "objectively aiding" reactionary Russian nationalists: "Absorbed by the fight with nationalism in Poland, Rosa Luxemburg forgot about the nationalism of the Great Russians, though it is exactly this nationalism that is the most dangerous of all."[36] The nationalism of the oppressed, Lenin maintained, had a "democratic content" that must be supported, while the nationalism of the oppressor had no redeeming value.[37] He ended his attack on Luxemburg with the slogan: "fight against all nationalisms and, first of all, against Great Russian nationalism."[38]

Bolshevik conduct between 1917 and 1919 convinced Lenin that the All-Russian Communist party had inherited the psychology of Great Power chauvinism from the tsarist regime. In non-Russian regions, the Bolshevik party initially relied almost exclusively on the minority Russian proletariat and agricultural colonists, who frequently adopted an overtly chauvinist attitude toward the local population.[39] This attitude alarmed Lenin and prompted his harsh words for Piatakov, who had conducted an anti-Ukrainian policy in Kiev.[40] Lenin's anger about such practices climaxed during the notorious Georgian affair of 1922, when he denounced Dzerzhinskii, Stalin, and Ordzhonikidze as Great Russian chauvinists (russified natives, he maintained, were often the worst chauvinists).[41] Such Bolshevik chauvinism inspired Lenin to coin the term *rusotiapstvo* (mindless Russian chauvinism), which then entered the Bolshevik lexicon and became an invaluable weapon in the national republics' rhetorical arsenals.[42]

Lenin's concern about Great Russian chauvinism led to the establishment of a crucial principle of the Soviet nationalities policy. In December 1922, he reiterated his 1914 attack on Great Russian chauvinism with the added admonition that one must "distinguish between the nationalism of oppressor nations and the nationalism of oppressed nations, the nationalism of large nations and the nationalism of small nations . . . in relation to the second nationalism, in almost all historical practice, we nationals of the large nations are guilty, because of an infinite amount of violence [committed]."[43] This distinction between offensive Great Power nationalism and defensive local nationalism, with the latter being viewed as a justifiable response to the former, then entered formulaic Bolshevik rhetoric. This belief in turn led to the establishment of the important "Greater Danger Principle," namely that Great Power (or sometimes Great Russian) chauvinism was a greater danger than local nationalism.[44]

Lenin's extreme formulation of this principle caused one of his two differences of opinion with Stalin over nationalities policy late in 1922.[45] Stalin had supported the Greater Danger Principle prior to 1922–23, reiterated his support in 1923, and supervised a nationalities policy based on that principle from April 1923 to December 1932 but was nevertheless uncomfortable with the idea that *all* local nationalism could be explained as a response to Great Power chauvinism.[46] On the basis of his experience in Georgia, Stalin insisted that Georgian nationalism was also characterized by Great Power exploitation of their Ossetine and Abkhaz minorities.[47] Stalin always paired his attacks on Great Russian chauvinism with a complementary attack on the lesser danger of local nationalism.[48] This difference of emphasis was also evident in Lenin and Stalin's terminology. Lenin typically referred to Russian nationalism as Great Power chauvinism, which distinguished it from other nationalisms, while Stalin preferred the term "Great Russian chauvinism." Despite these differences, however, Stalin consistently supported the Greater Danger Principle.

The intersection between nationalities and foreign policy was a fourth factor influencing the formation of the affirmative action empire. Already in November 1917, Lenin and Stalin issued an "Appeal to all Muslim Toilers of Russia and the East," which promised to end imperial exploitation within the former Russian empire and called on Muslims outside Russia to overthrow their colonial masters.[49] This linkage of domestic nationalities policy and foreign policy goals in the East was quite common during the civil war period.[50] After the 1921 peace treaty with Poland left millions of Ukrainians, and Belorussians in Poland, Soviet attention shifted westward. The Soviet Union's western border now cut through the ethnographic territory of Finns, Belorussians, Ukrainians and Romanians. It was hoped that an ostentatiously generous treatment of those nationalities within the Soviet Union would attract their ethnic brethren in Poland, Finland, and Romania. The eventual annexation of Poland's large Ukrainian population was the most important object of this strategy. It should be emphasized, however, that this foreign policy goal was never the primary motivation of the Soviet nationalities policy.[51] It was seen as an exploitable benefit of a domestically driven policy that affected the intensity of implementation in sensitive regions, but not the content of the policy itself.[52]

The analysis of nationalism outlined here implied Soviet state support for non-Russian national identities, but it did not yet specify precisely what this positive nationalities policy should include. How exactly can one support national consciousness without simultaneously encouraging nationalism? And how can one build a unitary state while encouraging potentially divisive substate identities? The reasoning that led from theory to practice can be summarized as follows. Nationalism is a masking ideology that leads legitimate class interests to be expressed, not in an appropriate class-based socialist movement but rather in the form of an above-class national movement. National identity is not an essential and permanent quality but rather an unavoidable by-product of the modern capitalist *and* early socialist world, which must be passed through before a mature internationalist socialist world can come into being. Since national identity *is* a real phenomenon in the modern world, the nationalism of the oppressed non-Russian

peoples expresses not only masked class protest but also legitimate national grievances against the oppressive Great Power chauvinism of the dominant Russian
nationality. Neither nationalism nor national identity, therefore, can be unequiv-
ocally condemned as reactionary. *Some* national claims—those confined to the
realm of national "form"—are in fact legitimate and must be granted in order
to split the above-class national alliance. Such a policy will speed the emergence
of class cleavages and so allow the party to recruit non-Russian proletarian and
peasant support for its socialist agenda. Nationalism will be disarmed by granting
the forms of nationhood.

An authoritative account of what forms of nationhood would be supported
was finally delineated in resolutions passed at the Twelfth Party Congress, in April
1923, and at a special Central Committee Conference on Nationalities Policy, in
June 1923.[53] These two resolutions, along with Stalin's speeches in defense of
them, became the standard Bolshevik proof texts for nationalities policy and remained so throughout the Stalinist era.[54] Prior to June 1923, nationalities policy
had been debated repeatedly at important party meetings. After these resolutions,
this public debate ceased.[55] The 1923 resolutions affirmed that the Soviet state
would maximally support those "forms" of nationhood that did not conflict with
a unitary central state, namely national territories, national languages, national
elites, and national cultures.

By June 1923, national territories had in fact already been formed for most of
the large Soviet nationalities.[56] The 1923 resolutions merely reaffirmed their existence and denounced all plans to abolish them.[57] There still remained, however,
the problem of territorially dispersed national minorities. Soviet policy opposed
their assimilation. It also opposed the Austro-Marxist solution of extraterritorial
national-cultural autonomy, whereby dispersed national minorities would be given
certain extraterritorial rights to govern their own cultural affairs.[58] Both were
considered likely to increase nationalism and to exacerbate ethnic conflict. The
solution hit upon by the Bolsheviks in the mid-1920s was characteristically radical.
Their national-territorial system would be extended downward into smaller and
smaller national territories (national districts, village soviets, collective farms) until
the system merged seamlessly with the personal nationality of each Soviet citizen.
The result was a grandiose pyramid of national soviets consisting of thousands of
national territories of varying size.[59]

The primary focus of the 1923 resolutions were the twin policies of promoting
national languages and creating national elites. In each national territory, the
language of the titular nationality was to be established as the official state language. National elites were to be trained and promoted into positions of leadership in the party, government, industry, and schools of each national territory.
While these policies had been articulated as early as 1920, and were officially
sanctioned at the 1921 Party Congress, virtually nothing had been done yet to
implement them.[60] The two 1923 decrees condemned this inactivity and demanded immediate action. These two policies were soon referred to as *korenizatsiia*
and became the centerpiece of the Soviet nationalities policy.

Korenizatsiia is best translated as "indigenization." It is derived directly not from the stem *koren-* ("root"—with the meaning "rooting") but from its adjectival form *korennoi* as used in the phrase *korennoi narod* (indigenous people). The coining of the word *korenizatsiia* was part of the Bolsheviks' decolonizing rhetoric, which systematically favored the claims of indigenous peoples over "newly arrived elements." In 1923, however, *korenizatsiia* was not yet in use. Instead, the term *natsionalizatsiia* was preferred, which emphasized the project of nation-building.[61] This emphasis was echoed in the national republics, where the policy was simply named after the titular nationality: *Ukrainizatsiia, Uzbekizatsiia, Oirotizatsiia*. The term *korenizatsiia* emerged later from the central nationalities policy bureaucracy, which serviced primarily extraterritorial national minorities and so preferred a term that referred to all indigenous (*korennye*) peoples, not just titular nationalities. *Korenizatsiia* gradually emerged as the preferred term to describe this policy, but it should be noted that Stalin always used *natsionalizatsiia*.[62]

The 1923 resolutions established *korenizatsiia* as the most urgent item on the Soviet nationalities policy agenda. In keeping with Lenin's and Stalin's highly psychological interpretation of nationalism, the subjective effects of *korenizatsiia* were emphasized. It would make Soviet power seem "native," "intimate," "popular," "comprehensible" (*poniatnaia*).[63] It would address the positive psychological needs of nationalism: "the [non-Russian] masses would see that Soviet power and her organs are the affair of their own efforts, the embodiment of their desires."[64] It would likewise disarm the negative psychological anxiety associated with the perception of foreign rule: "Soviet power, which up to the present time [April 1923] has remained Russian power, [would be made] not only Russian but international, and become native for the peasantry of the formerly oppressed nationalities."[65] Native languages would make Soviet power comprehensible. Native cadres, who understood "the way of life, customs, and habits of the local population," would make Soviet power seem indigenous rather than an external Russian imperial imposition.[66]

Finally, the 1923 resolutions also reiterated the party's recognition of distinct national cultures and pledged central state support for their maximum development.[67] Stalin famously defined Soviet national cultures as being "national in form, socialist in content" but did not elaborate on what exactly this meant.[68] The ambiguity was intentional, since Bolshevik plans for the social transformation of the country did not allow for any fundamentally distinctive religious, legal, ideological, or customary features.[69] The translation that best captures the meaning of Stalin's *natsional'naia kul'tura* is not "national culture" but "national identity" or "symbolic ethnicity."[70]

Soviet policy systematically promoted the distinctive national identity and national self-consciousness of its non-Russian populations. It did this not only through the formation of national territories staffed by national elites using their own national languages but also through the aggressive promotion of symbolic markers of national identity: national folklore, museums, dress, food, costumes, opera, poets, progressive historical events, and classic literary works. The long-

term goal was that distinctive national identities would co-exist peacefully with
an emerging all-union socialist culture that would supersede the pre-existing national cultures. National identity would be depoliticized through an ostentatious
show of respect for the national identities of the non-Russians.

It is also important to understand what the Soviet nationalities policy did
not involve. Above all, it did not involve federation, if this term means anything more than the mere formation of administrative territories along national
lines. At the April and June 1923 gatherings, the Ukrainian delegation, led by
Khristian Rakovskii, pressed very aggressively for the devolution of meaningful
federal powers to the national republics.[71] Stalin rebuffed Rakovskii's proposals
scornfully and mendaciously labeled his goal as confederation.[72] Although the
1922–1923 constitutional settlement was called a federation, it in fact concentrated all decision-making power in the center. National republics were granted
no more powers than Russian provinces.[73] Prior to June 1917, both Lenin and
Stalin denounced federation and advocated a unitary state with "oblast autonomy" for national regions. This meant the formation of national administrative
units and the selective use of national languages in government and education.[74] In June 1917, Lenin abruptly rehabilitated the term federation but used
it to describe what amounted to a much more ambitious version of "oblast autonomy." As Stalin noted coyly in 1924, federation "turned out to be not so
nearly in contradiction with the goal of economic unification as it might have
seemed earlier."[75] Soviet federation did not mean devolution of political or economic power.[76]

Economic equalization occupied a much more ambiguous place in the Soviet
nationalities policy. The 1923 nationalities policy decrees called for measures to
overcome "the real economic and cultural inequality of the Soviet Union's nationalities."[77] One economic measure proposed was transferring factories from
the Russian heartland to eastern national regions.[78] This policy was in fact
adopted but then almost immediately discontinued, a pattern that proved typical
of economic equalization programs. In contrast to the commitment to cultural
and national equalization, through affirmative action in education and hiring, the
Soviet commitment to economic equalization was never institutionalized. Attempts by the "culturally backward" republics to obtain an annual budget line
for a program designed to combat their "backwardness" failed.[79] The economic
commissariats were consistently hostile to the Soviet nationalities policy. On the
other hand, national republics could and often did use the 1923 resolutions and
their "backward" national status to lobby all-Union agencies for privileged economic investment.[80] However, they could make no absolute claim to investment
based on their national status. Gerhard Simon concludes, only a little too strongly,
that "Soviet economic policy has never made overcoming the rift between economically underdeveloped national territories a high-priority issue. Wherever economic equalization occurred, it was only a side effect of other planning priorities,
such as development of new resources, increasing regional economic specializa-
tion and primarily military-strategic conceptions."[81]

One issue that was not prominently discussed during the 1923 nationalities policy debates was control over migration into the non-Russian republics. The Soviet nationalities policy called for the formation of national territories. Did it also sanction measures to preserve (or create) national majorities in those republics? Initially the answer appeared to be yes. In Kazakhstan and Kirgizia, central authorities even sanctioned the expulsion of illegal Slavic agricultural settlers as a decolonization measure. In the early 1920s, the Soviet Union's eastern national territories were closed to agricultural colonization to prevent an influx of Slavic settlers. However, by 1927, all-Union economic interests had again prevailed over local national concerns, and all restrictions on migration were removed.[82] In the long run, this would have a dramatic Russificatory effect in many of the non-Russian republics.

The Soviet Union was not a federation, and it was certainly not a nation-state. Its distinctive feature was the systematic support of national forms: territory, culture, language, and elites. Of course, these were hardly novel choices. They are the primary domestic concerns of most newly formed nation-states. In Georgia and Armenia, for instance, the Soviet government did not repudiate the nation-building efforts of the Menshevik and *Dashnaktsutiun* governments that it deposed in 1920–1921 but rather boasted that Soviet power had deepened the national work begun by them.[83] Soviet policy was original in that it supported the national forms of minorities, rather than majorities. It decisively rejected the model of the nation-state and replaced it with a plurality of nation-like republics. The Bolsheviks attempted to fuse the nationalist's demand for national territory, culture, language, and elites with the socialist's demand for an economically and politically unitary state. In this sense, we might call the Bolsheviks internationalist nationalists, or better yet, affirmative action nationalists.

To develop this idea, I compare Soviet practice with Miroslav Hroch's famous three-phase model for the development of nationalism among the "small" stateless peoples of Eastern Europe: first, elite nonpolitical interest in folklore and popular culture (Phase A); second, the consolidation of a nationalist elite committed to the formation of a nation-state (Phase B); third, the emergence of a nationalist movement with mass popular support (Phase C).[84] Hroch largely ignored the existing multiethnic state, reflexively assuming it would oppose these developments. The Soviet state, instead, literally seized leadership over all three phases: the articulation of a national culture, the formation of national elites, and the propagation of mass national consciousness. It went still further and initiated even "Phase D" (my term now, not Hroch's) measures typical of newly formed nation-states: the establishment of a new language of state and a new governing elite. To use more familiar Bolshevik terminology, the party became the vanguard of non-Russian nationalism. Just as party leadership was needed to lead the proletariat beyond trade-union consciousness to revolution, the party could also guide national movements beyond bourgeois primordial nationalism to Soviet international nationalism.

This policy represented a dramatic shift from 1913, when Lenin had argued that the party should condemn all national discrimination but warned that "the proletariat cannot go further [than this] in the support of nationalism, for going further means the 'positive' (*pozitivnaia*) affirmative action (*polozhitel'naia deiatel'nost'*) of the bourgeoisie which aims at strengthening nationalism."[85] In the same spirit, the Bolshevik leader Zinovev told a Ukrainian audience in 1920 "that languages should develop freely. In the end, after a period of years, the language with the greater roots, greater life and greater culture will triumph."[86] Dmitrii Lebed, secretary of the Ukrainian Central Committee, called this theory "the battle of two cultures," in which, "given a party policy of neutrality, the victory of the Russian language will be guaranteed due to its historic role in the epoch of capitalism."[87]

By the 1923 Party Congress, neutrality had become anathema. Zinovev himself now stated: "We should first of all reject the 'theory' of neutralism. We cannot adopt the point of view of neutralism . . . , we should help [the non-Russians] create their own schools, should help them create their own administration in their native languages. . . . Communists [should not] stand to the side and think up the clever phrase 'neutrality.' " Neutrality, Zinovev insisted, was simply a cover for Great Russian chauvinism.[88] The 1923 resolutions supported this position.[89] Not only was Piatakov's call for a positive fight against nationalism denounced as Great Power chauvinism; so was Lenin's prerevolutionary policy of neutrality. Lebed's "battle of two cultures" was condemned in 1923, as was a similar "leftist" position in Tatarstan and Crimea.[90]

The Communist party had now embraced the "positive affirmative action of the bourgeoisie" that Lenin had criticized in 1913. However, as the Hroch comparison illustrates, Soviet affirmative action supported national minorities, not majorities. The Bolsheviks now scorned bourgeois governments for supporting only formal "legal equality" instead of taking positive action to achieve "actual equality."[91] This extreme suspicion of neutrality explains one of the most striking features of the Soviet nationalities policy: its resolute hostility to even voluntary assimilation. In this new model, neutrality would inevitably lead to voluntary assimilation because of the historic strength of Russian national culture. Positive action, therefore, was needed in order to defend non-Russian national culture against this unjust fate. No one denounced neutrality and assimilation more categorically than Stalin:[92]

> We are undertaking a policy of the maximum development of national culture. . . . It would be an error if anyone thought that in relation to the development of the national cultures of the backward nationalities, central workers should maintain a policy of neutrality—"O.K., fine, national culture is developing, let it develop, that's not our business." Such a point of view would be incorrect. We stand for a protective (*pokrovitel'stvennaia politika*) policy in relation to the development of the national cultures of the backward nationalities. I emphasize

this so that [it will] be understood that we are not indifferent, but actively protecting *(pokrovitel'stvuiushchie)* the development of national culture.

Of course, positive action on behalf of one nationality implies negative action toward others.

In the Soviet case, where all non-Russians were to be favored, Russians alone bore the brunt of positive discrimination. Bukharin stated this fact bluntly: "As the former Great Power nation, we should indulge the national aspirations [of the non-Russians] and place ourselves in an unequal position, in the sense of making still greater concessions to the national current. Only by such a policy, when we place ourselves artificially in a position lower in comparisons with others, only by such a price can we purchase for ourselves the trust of the formerly oppressed nations."[93] Stalin, who was more sensitive to Russian feelings, rebuked Bukharin for the crudeness of his statement but did not and could not dispute its content.[94] Soviet policy did indeed call for Russian sacrifice in the realm of nationalities policy: majority Russian territory was assigned to non-Russian republics; Russians had to accept ambitious affirmative action programs for non-Russians; they were asked to learn non-Russian languages; and traditional Russian culture was stigmatized as a culture of oppression.[95]

New phenomena merit new terminology. As a national entity, the early Soviet Union can best be described as an affirmative action empire. I am, of course, borrowing the contemporary American term for policies that give preference to members of ethnic groups that have suffered from past discrimination. Such policies are common internationally and go by various names: compensatory discrimination, preferential policies, positive action, affirmative discrimination.[96] They often accompany decolonization. I prefer the term "affirmative action" because it describes precisely the Soviet policy choice: affirmative action *(polozhitel'naia deiatel'nost')* instead of neutrality. The Soviet Union was the first country in world history to establish affirmative action programs for national minorities, and no country has yet approached the vast scale of Soviet affirmative action.[97] The Soviet Union also adopted even more extensive class-based affirmative action programs and considerably less assertive gender-based programs.[98] As a result, the vast majority of Soviet citizens were eligible for some sort of preferential treatment. Affirmative action permeated the early Soviet Union and was one of its defining features.

However, the existence of such programs alone does not justify calling the Soviet Union an affirmative action empire, since I am proposing this term as an ideal-type to distinguish the Soviet Union *as a national entity* from alternative ideal-types: nation-state, city-state, federation, confederation, empire. Affirmative action refers here not only to programs on behalf of members of a given ethnic group but primarily to Soviet state support for the national territories, languages, elites, and identities of those ethnic groups. As noted in the Hroch comparison, the Communist party assumed leadership over the usual process of national formation and took positive action to construct Soviet international nations (nations in form not content) that would accept the formation of a unitary, centralized Soviet state. Positive support of the forms of nationhood was the essence of Soviet nationalities policy. The formation of the Soviet Union in 1922–1923 established the territorial form of nationhood, not a federation of autonomous national territories.

Therefore, I refer to the affirmative action empire as the national constitution of the Soviet Union. I am using the word "constitution" here in the British sense of a set of fundamental rules that structure the political life of a state. I add the adjective "national," as I am concerned exclusively with how the Soviet Union was structured as a national or nation-like entity, that is with regard to the problem of nationality. It was not the Soviet Union's formal written constitution of December 1922 that constituted the Soviet Union as a national entity but rather the nationalities policy articulated in 1923. It was affirmative action, in the broad sense that I have defined it, that structured the Soviet Union as a multiethnic state.

The term "affirmative action empire" represents an attempt to capture the paradoxical nature of the multiethnic Soviet state: an extraordinarily invasive, centralized, and violent state formally structured as a federation of sovereign nations; the successor state to the collapsed Russian empire that successfully re-conquered most of its former national borderlands but then set out to systemat-ically build and strengthen its non-Russian nations, even where they barely existed. In 1967, Alec Nove and J. A. Newth puzzled over a state that seemed to privilege its eastern periphery while simultaneously holding it in subjection: "therefore, if we do not call the present relationship colonialism, we ought to invent a new name to describe something which represents subordination and yet is genuinely different from the imperialism of the past."[99]

The affirmative action empire was not a traditional empire. I am not aligning myself with those who now argue that the Soviet Union, because of its shared characteristics with other empires, can be classified in objective social science terms as an "empire."[100] On the contrary, I am emphasizing its novelty. Mark Beissinger has pointed out that, prior to the collapse of the Soviet Union, by and large only hostile observers called it an empire.[101] Supporters and neutral scholars called it a state. Beissinger likewise has noted the circularity of the currently popular argument that the Soviet Union collapsed, like the Habsburg and Ottoman empires before it, because it was an empire: in the modern world, empires collapse along national lines; the Soviet Union collapsed along national lines; therefore, the Soviet Union was an empire; therefore, as an empire, the Soviet Union was bound to collapse along national lines.[102] However, Beissinger goes on to argue that, because of the widespread assumption that in the modern world empires are doomed, empire is a very important subjective category. To the extent that citizens perceive their state as an empire (and themselves as subjects), its long-term viability is gravely compromised.

Lenin and Stalin understood very well the danger of being labeled an empire in the age of nationalism. In fact, here lies the real connection between the Soviet Union's national constitution and the collapse of the Habsburg and Ottoman empires. The nationalities crisis and final collapse of the Habsburg empire made an enormous impression on Lenin and Stalin, who viewed it as an object lesson in the danger of being perceived by their population as an empire. As a result, the Soviet Union became the first multiethnic state in world history to define itself as an anti-imperial state. They were not indifferent to the word "empire." They rejected it explicitly.

Indeed, the affirmative action empire was a strategy designed to avoid the perception of empire. The Greater Danger Principle was based on the belief that non-Russian nationalism was a defensive response to the experience of Russian Great Power or imperial chauvinism. Since the Bolsheviks intended to rule dictatorially and to promote major social transformation, their actions were likely to be perceived as Russian imperialism. To avoid this perception, the central state would not be identified as Russian. Russian national self-expression would be downplayed. Ironically, this preserved the national structure of the old empire. The Bolsheviks explicitly renounced the idea of a state-bearing people. Despite this fact, in an important sense the Russians did remain the Soviet Union's state-bearing people. Only the Russians were not granted their own territory and their own Communist party. Instead, the party asked the Russians to accept a formally unequal *national* status in order to further the cohesion of the multinational state. The hierarchical distinction between state-bearing and colonial peoples was thus reproduced, but reversed, as the new distinction between the formerly oppressed nationalities and the former Great Power nation.[103] As the state-bearing people, Russians were now literally asked to bear the burden of empire by suppressing their national interests and identifying with a non-national affirmative action empire. Had Lenin lived to write a theoretical account of his creation, he might have called it *The Soviet Union, as the Highest Stage of Imperialism.*[104]

In its ideal-typical form, the affirmative action empire persisted for a mere decade. In December 1932, in response both to the Soviet leadership's growing dissatisfaction with some of the unintended consequences of the affirmative action empire and to a short-term crisis in grain requisitions that was attributed to Ukrainian nationalism, the Soviet Politburo issued a series of resolutions that initiated a fundamental revision of the Soviet nationalities policy.[105] These changes have often been portrayed as the abolition of *korenizatsiia.*[106] This judgment is much too strong, but it is also symptomatic of the important subjective perceptual changes that followed as a consequence of these policy revisions.

Three of the four major policy components of the affirmative action empire survived the 1930s with only minor revisions. The commitment to training and promoting indigenous cadres, including the practice of affirmative action in university admissions and employment, continued throughout the 1930s and beyond. The principal change was that, in deference to Russian sensibilities, affirmative action was now carried out silently. It disappeared almost entirely from published Soviet sources, but not from bureaucratic archives or from real life.[107] The thousands of minute national territories established in the 1920s were either formally or informally abolished in the 1930s, but the remaining thirty-five larger national territories were actually strengthened in 1936, and most have remained an essential part of the Soviet and post-Soviet landscape to the present day.[108] The promotion of distinctive national identities actually intensified after December 1932, as the Soviet discourse of the nation shifted from an insistence that nations were modern constructs that emerged as a consequence of capitalist production to a primordial, essentialist conception of national identity that emphasized the deep historic roots of all Soviet nations.[109] The change in language policy was more substantial. By 1932, despite major efforts, the attempt to establish the non-Russian languages as the dominant language of government in the non-Russian republics had, with the exception of Georgia and Armenia, largely failed. After 1932, this policy was quietly abandoned, and Russian became the dominant (though not exclusive) language of the government, the party, large industrial enterprises, and higher technical education in the non-Russian territories. The national languages continued to be promoted in general education, in the press, and in cultural production.[110]

With respect to policy toward most non-Russians, then, the affirmative action empire continued with limited corrections throughout Stalin's rule.[111] There was, however, one policy change of the 1930s that struck at the heart of the affirmative action empire: the rehabilitation of the Russian nationality and traditional Russian national culture. In January 1934, Stalin officially announced the abandonment of the Greater Danger Principle that had stigmatized Russians as the former Great Power nationality.[112] Initially it seemed that Russians would acquire an equal national status, but by 1936 they had already been raised to the rank of "first among equals" in the Soviet family of nations.[113] The new policy did not involve forced cultural or linguistic russification, but it did involve an aggressive promotion of bilingualism and a re-engineering of non-Russian languages and cultures to accentuate their proximity and openness to Russian linguistic and cultural influence.[114] There were two main reasons for this dramatic policy shift. First, the aggressive affirmative action of the 1920s had provoked high levels of resentment among Russian party members. Second, and more important, the Bolshevik leadership increasingly felt that the affirmative action empire had led to an unacceptably high level of national Communist assertiveness among non-Russian cultural and political elites and so provided an inadequate principle of Soviet unity.[115] In the 1920s, the voluntary invisibility of the Russian nationality was meant to unify the multiethnic state (by disarming non-Russian distrust of their former oppressor); in the 1930s, the visibility and centrality of the Russians would serve the same function. This new principle of Soviet unity was represented by the metaphor of the Friendship of the Peoples, a friendship that was said to have been forged by the Russians and to have existed already for many centuries.[116] The Friendship was propagandized as a kind of supranational imagined community for the multiethnic Soviet people.[117]

The affirmative action empire was a logically coherent but highly utopian strategy. The reform of that strategy in the mid-1930s moved it in a more pragmatic direction but in doing so introduced a contradiction that would persist

throughout Stalin's rule and beyond. The affirmative action empire had preserved, indeed accentuated, the imperial structure of a state-bearing imperial nation and colonial nations but reversed its valence by promoting the national
"forms" of the former colonial nations and downplaying the expression of Russian national identity. The first half of this formula persisted in a revised form
beyond 1932 because Stalin continued to believe that the promotion of non-
Russian national "forms," if properly supervised, did reduce non-Russian resentment and so forestalled the growth of non-Russian nationalism.[118] In the
short run, this was probably correct. However, in the long run, the simultaneous
promotion of non-Russian identities and the re-establishment of the Russians as
the much-praised and highly visible state-bearing nationality of a centralized
state proved a recipe for the subjective perception of empire. As the non-Russian
nations modernized and developed a sizable literary intelligentsia under Khrushchev and Brezhnev, the subjective perception that they were living in a Russian empire slowly spread. With the advent of Gorbachev's political reforms, this
perception would suddenly explode and fatally undermine Lenin's affirmative action empire.

Notes

1. The Austro-Hungarian Empire was the first of the old European empires to see
its existence threatened by separatist nationalism. Its nationalities policy was therefore
followed closely by Russian intellectuals, including Lenin and Stalin, both of whom
polemicized with the Austro-Marxists over the nationalities question. The Austrian
half of the empire pioneered many of the strategies adopted by the Soviet Union, but
theirs was primarily a defensive strategy of granting concessions to nationalist demands, whereas the Soviets pursued an active, prophylactic strategy of promoting non-
Russian nation-building to prevent the growth of nationalism. See Adam Wandruszka
and Peter Urbanitsch, eds., *Die Habsburgermonarchie, 1848–1918. Band III. Die Völker des
Reiches* (Vienna: Verl. d. Osterr. Alad. d. Wiss., 1980).

2. The standard work on Indian affirmative action is Marc Galanter, *Competing
Equalities: Law and the Backward Classes in India* (Delhi: Oxford University Press, 1984).
See also Sumita Parikh, *The Politics of Preference: Democratic Institutions and Affirmative Action
in the United States and India* (Ann Arbor: University of Michigan Press, 1997). India's
version of *korenizatsiia*, the formation of language-based territories shortly after independence, was influenced by the Soviet model. See *Report of the States Reorganisation
Commission* (New Delhi: Management of Publications, 1955), pp. 40–43.

3. This embarrassing fact was pointed out by Georgii Chicherin, "Protiv tezisov
tov. Stalina," *Pravda*, no. 50, March 6, 1921, p. 2.

4. Richard Pipes, *The Formation of the Soviet Union: Communism and Nationalism* (rev.
ed., Cambridge, Mass.: Harvard University Press, 1964); Ronald Grigor Suny, *The
Revenge of the Past: Nationalism, Revolution and the Collapse of the Soviet Union* (Stanford,
Calif.: Stanford University Press, 1993), pp. 20–83; Andrea Graziosi, *Bol'sheviki i
krest'iane na Ukraine, 1918–1919 gody. Ocherk o bol'shevizmakh, natsional-sotsializmakh i
krest'ianskikh dvizheniiakh* (Moscow: Airo-xx, 1997).

5. Jeremy Smith, *The Bolsheviks and the National Question, 1917–1923* (Basingstoke: Macmillan, 1999); Yuri Slezkine, "The USSR as a Communal Apartment, or How a Socialist State Promoted Ethnic Particularism," *Slavic Review* 53 (Summer 1994): 414–452; Suny, *The Revenge of the Past*, pp. 84–106; Hélène Carrère d'Encausse, *The Great Challenge: Nationalities and the Bolshevik State, 1917–1930* (New York: Holmes & Meier, 1992).

6. For a good background discussion, see Smith, *The Bolsheviks and the National Question*, pp. 7–28.

7. *Vosmoi s"ezd RKP/b/. 18–23 marta 1919 g. Protokoly* (Moscow, 1933), pp. 79–80.

8. Ibid., p. 82.

9. Ibid., pp. 48–49. This position was briefly supported by Stalin as well in December 1917 and January 1918. I. V. Stalin, "Otvet tovarishcham Ukraintsam v tylu i na fronte," *Sochineniia*, vol. 4 (Moscow: Gosudaestvennoe izoatelstvo politicheskoi literatury, 1953–1955), p 8; "Vystupleniia na III vserossiiskom s"ezde sovetov R., S. i K. D.," vol. 4, pp. 31–32.

10. Lenin's two major prerevolutionary attacks on Piatakov's position, whose major exponent was Rosa Luxemburg, were "O prave natsii na samoopredelenie" (1914) in V. I. Lenin, *Polnoe sobranie sochinenii* (hereafter PSS), vol. 25 (Moscow, 1975–1977), pp. 255–320, and "Sotsialisticheskaia revoliutsiia i pravo natsii na samoopredelenie" (1916), PSS, vol. 27, pp. 151–166. He also debated Piatakov at the Party's Seventh Conference in April 1917; see *Natsional'nyi vopros na perekrestke mnenii. 20-e gody. Dokumenty i materialy* (Moscow: Nauka, 1992), pp. 11–27.

11. *Vosmoi s"ezd*, p. 55.

12. Ibid., pp. 54–55.

13. Ibid., p. 107.

14. Ibid., p. 108.

15. Ibid., p. 387. Smith, *The Bolsheviks and the Nationalities Question*, p. 21.

16. On the Bolsheviks' reconquest of the Imperial Russian borderlands, see Pipes, *The Formation of the Soviet Union*.

17. For the period 1912–1916, in addition to the works already cited, see "Tezisy po natsional'nomu voprosu" (1913), PSS, vol. 23, pp. 314–322; "Kriticheskie zametki po natsional'nomu voprosu" (1913), PSS, vol. 24, pp. 113–150; "Itogi diskussii o samoopredelenii" (1916), PSS, vol. 30, pp. 17–58. For the period 1919–1922, besides his speeches at party congresses, see "Pis'mo k rabochim i krest'ianam Ukrainy . . ." (1919), PSS, vol. 40, pp. 41–47; "Ob obrazovanii SSSR" (1922), PSS, vol. 45, pp. 211–213; "K voprosu o natsional'nostiakh ili ob 'avtonomizatsii' " (1922), PSS, vol. 45, pp. 356–362.

18. Iz istorii obrazovaniia SSSR. Stenogramma zasedaniia sektsii 12 s"ezda RKP/b/ po natsional'nomu voprosu 25.04.23," *Izvestiia TsK KPSS* no. 3 (1991): 169. Stalin's articles and speeches are collected in I. Stalin, *Marksizm i natsional'no-kolonial'nyi vopros* (Moscow: Partizdat, 1934).

19. Lenin, "Kak Episkop Nikon zashchishchaet Ukraintsev?" (1913), PSS, vol. 24, p. 9.

20. *Dvenadtsatyi s"ezd RKP/b/. 17–15 aprelia 1923 goda. Stenograficheskii otchet* (Moscow: Izadtel'stvo politicheskoi literatury, 1968), p. 612.

21. Ernest Gellner, *Nations and Nationalism* (Ithaca, N.Y.: Cornell University, 1983), p. 129.

22. In addition to the examples given from Stalin, see Lenin's "Kriticheskie zametki," pp. 119–120.

23. Stalin, "Politika sovetskoi vlasti po natsional'nomu voprosu v Rossii" (1918), in *Marksizm*, p. 54.

24. Stalin, "Vystupleniia na III vserossiiskom s"ezde," p. 31.

25. For a good early statement of this position, see S. Dimanshtein, "Narodnyi kommissariat po dele natsional'nostei," *Zhizn' nastional'nostei*, no. 41, December 26, 1919, p. 2.

26. In his prerevolutionary writings, Lenin repeatedly cited Sweden's granting Norway independence in 1905 as having sped up the emergence of class conflict in both countries. Lenin, "O prave natsii," p. 289; "Sotsialisticheskaia revoliutsiia," p. 253.

27. Stalin, "Odna iz ocherednykh zadach" (1918) *Sochineniia* vol. 4, p. 75.

28. Stalin, *Marksizm*, 4–15; Lenin, "O prave natsii," pp. 255–271.

29. On Lenin, see *Tainy natsional'noi politiki TsK RKP. Stenograficheskii otchet sekretnogo IV soveshchaniia TsK RKP, 1923 g.* (Moscow, 1992), pp. 30–31; on Stalin, see *Marksizm*, pp. 155–165.

30. Lenin, "Sotsialisticheskaia revoliutsiia," p. 256.

31. *Rossiiskii Tsentr Khraneniia i Izucheniia Dokumentov Noveishei Istorii* (RTsKhIDNI) 558/1/4490 (1929): 9.

32. Expressions of Bolshevik surprise at the strength of nationalism in the former Russian empire were common. For an example, see Zatonskyi's comments at the Tenth Party Congress. N. N. Popov, ed., *Desiatyi s"ezd RKP/b/. Mart 1921 g.* (Moscow: Partiinoe Izdatel'stvo, Moscow, 1933), pp. 205–209.

33. Ibid., p. 216.

34. *Vos'moi s"ezd*, p. 55.

35. *II sessiia VTsIK XV sozyva. Stenograficheskii otchet* (Moscow, 1931), p. 16. For a sophisticated analysis of Soviet developmentalist ideology, see Yuri Slezkine, *Arctic Mirrors. Russia and the Small Peoples of the North* (Ithaca, N.Y.: Cornell University Press, 1994).

36. Lenin, "O prave natsii," p. 277.

37. Ibid., pp. 275–276.

38. Ibid., p. 319.

39. Popov, *Desiatyi s"ezd*, pp. 195–209. Pipes, *The Formation*, pp. 126–154; 172–183; Alexander G. Park, *Bolshevism in Turkestan, 1917–1927* (New York, 1957), pp. 3–58; V. L. Genis, "Deportatsiia russkikh iz Turkestana v 1921 godu ('Delo Safarova')," *Voprosy istorii*, no. 1 (1998): 44–58.

40. Andrea Graziosi, "G. L. Piatakov (1890–1937): A Mirror of Soviet History," *Harvard Ukrainian Studies* 16 (June 1992): 102–166.

41. Lenin, "K voprosu o natsional'nostiakh," pp. 356–362. The Georgian Affair has drawn an enormous amount of attention because of its link to Lenin's "testament." See Smith, *The Bolsheviks and the National Question*, pp. 172–212; Pipes, *The Formation*, pp. 276–293; Richard Pipes, *Russia under the Bolshevik Regime* (New York: Knopf, 1993), pp. 471–480; Moshe Lewin, *Lenin's Last Struggle* (New York: Pantheon, 1968), pp. 43–64. For documents on the affair, see "Iz istorii obrazovaniia SSSR," no. 9 (1989): 191–218; Yuri Buranov, ed., *Lenin's Will: Falsified and Forbidden* (Amherst, N.Y.: Prometheus, 1994).

42. At the 1921 Party Congress, Zatonskyi attributes this term to Lenin. Popov, *Desiatyi s"ezd*, p. 207.

43. Lenin, "K voprosu o natsional'nostiakh," p. 359.

44. *Dvenadtsatyi s"ezd*, pp. 693–695.

45. Their second difference of opinion came over the structure of the Soviet Union and in particular the place of Russia within the Soviet Union. Stalin strongly opposed the formation of a separate Russian republic with its own separate government (TsIK) in Moscow, as this would provide a potent center for Russian separatism. Lenin insisted on this as a consequence of making the RSFSR, Belorussia, Ukraine, and the Transcaucasus formally equal, and Stalin reluctantly agreed. See Terry Martin, "The Russification of the RSFSR," *Cahiers du monde russe* 39 (1998): 99–118.

46. Popov, *Desiatyi s"ezd*, p. 188; *Dvenadtsatyi s"ezd*, pp. 486–487.

47. *Dvenadtsatyi s"ezd*, pp. 487–490.

48. Ibid., pp. 487–488. This tendency led the Ukrainian National Communist, Mykola Skrypnyk, to attack Stalin's constant "double bookkeeping," p. 572.

49. I. Lazovskii and I. Bibin, *Sovetskaia politika za 10 let po natsional'nomu voprosu v RSFSR* (Moscow-Leningrad: Gosudanstvennoe Izdatel'stvo, 1928), pp. 2–3.

50. Suny, *Revenge of the Past*, pp. 83–97; Edward Hallet Carr, *The Bolshevik Revolution, 1917–1923*, vol. 1 (London: Macmillan, 1950), pp. 314–339; Pipes, *Formation*, pp. 155–192.

51. Bolsheviks hostile to the affirmative action empire often interpreted it as no more than a foreign policy ploy. See *Tainy natsional'noi politiki*, pp. 79, 221.

52. For a fuller discussion, see Terry Martin, "The Origins of Soviet Ethnic Cleansing," *Journal of Modern History* 70 (1998): 813–861.

53. *Dvenadtsatyi s"ezd*, pp. 691–697; *Tainy natsional'noi politiki*, pp. 282–286.

54. These proof texts were collected in periodic editions of Stalin's *Marksizm i natsional'no-kolonialnyi vopros*.

55. As already mentioned, nationalities policy was discussed at the 1917, 1919, 1921, and 1923 party congresses. It was also discussed separately at the June 1923 TsK conference on nationalities policy, at several TsK plenums in 1923, and at numerous TsIK and VTsIK sessions. After June 1923, the content of nationalities policy was not discussed again in higher party bodies, with one exception: Kalinin's Politburo Commission on RSFSR Affairs in 1926–1927. On this commission, see Martin, "The Russification of the RSFSR." Issues of implementation were discussed, but nevertheless, from 1924 to 1938, nationalities policy was never an agenda point at a party congress and was only twice an agenda point at a TsK plenum: in 1924 on the national delimitation of Central Asia and in 1937 on the study of the Russian language. RTsKhIDNI 17/2/153 (1924): 123–132; 17/2/628 (1937): 120–123.

56. By June 1923, there were already two federal republics, five union republics, twelve autonomous republics, and eleven autonomous oblasts. The delimitation of Central Asia in 1924 would complete the process of forming national territories. For an overview of the establishment of national territories in this period, see the special issue of *Zhizn natsional'nostei*, no. 1 (1923); also Smith, *The Bolsheviks and the National Question*, pp. 29–107. For the best case study we have of territorialization, see Daniel E. Schafer's essay in this volume and his dissertation, "Building Nations and Building States: The Tatar-Bashkir Question in Revolutionary Russia, 1917–1920" (Ph.D. diss., University of Michigan, 1995).

57. *Dvenadtsatyi s"ezd*, pp. 693–694; *Tainy natsional'noi politiki*, pp. 283–284.

58. Tim Bottomore and Patrick Goode, eds., *Austro-Marxism* (Oxford: Clarendon Press, 1978).

59. On this policy, see Terry Martin, "Borders and Ethnic Conflict: The Soviet Experiment in Ethno-Territorial Proliferation," *Jahrbucher fur Geshchicte Osteuropas* 47 (September 1999): 538–555.

60. This policy was not yet articulated in the 1919 Party Congress resolution. For early statements, see S. Dimanshtein, "Eshche malo opyta," *Zhizn natsional'nostei*, no. 33 August 31, 1919, p. 1; Stalin, "Politika sovetskoi vlasti po natsional'nomu voprosu v Rossii," in *Marksizm*, pp. 58–64.

61. *Tainy natsional'noi politiki*, p. 284.

62. For instance, see Stalin's remarks at the Sixteenth Party Congress in 1930. *XVI s"ezd vsesoiuznoi kommunisticheskoi partii/b/. Stenograficheskii otchet* (Moscow, 1930), p. 54.

63. Stalin, *Marksizm*, p. 62; *Tainy natsional'noi politiki*, p. 102; *Dvenadtsatyi s"ezd*, pp. 481–482.

64. Stalin, *Marksizm*, p. 62.

65. *Dvenadtsatyi s"ezd*, p. 482.

66. Stalin, *Marksizm*, p. 62.

67. The more important statement on national culture, however, was a 1925 speech by Stalin. Stalin, "O politicheskikh zadachakh universiteta narodov vostoka," in *Marksizm*, pp. 155–165.

68. Ibid., 158. Stalin's original formulation was actually "proletarian in content." It appears that the shift to the canonical "socialist in content" occurred after Stalin's use of the phrase at the June 1930 Party Congress. *Marksizm*, p. 194.

69. For an account of Soviet attacks on such customs, see Douglas Northrop's essay in this volume and his dissertation, "Uzbek Women and the Veil: Gender and Power in Stalinist Central Asia" (Ph.D. diss., Stanford University, 1999). See also Gregory J. Massell, *The Surrogate Proletariat: Moslem Women and Revolutionary Strategies in Soviet Central Asia, 1919–1929* (Princeton, N.J.: Princeton University Press, 1974); Jörg Baberowski, "Stalinismus als imperiales Phänomen: die islamischen Regionen der Sowjetunion, 1920–1941," in Stefan Plaggenborg, ed., *Stalinismus: neue Forschungen und Konzepe* (Berlin, 1998), pp. 113–150; Shoshana Keller, "The Struggle against Islam in Uzbekistan, 1921–1941: Policy, Bureaucracy and Reality" (Ph.D. diss., Indiana University, 1995).

70. Herbert Gans, "Symbolic Ethnicity: The Future of Ethnic Groups and Cultures in America," *Ethnic and Racial Studies* 2 (1979): 9–17. On the relationship of national culture and national identity, see the sophisticated analysis in K. Anthony Appiah, "Race, Culture, Identity: Misunderstood Connections" in K. Anthony Appiah and Amy Gutmann, *Color Conscious: The Political Morality of Race* (Princeton: Princeton University Press, 1996), pp. 30–107.

71. "Iz istorii obrazovaniia SSSR," *Izvestiia TsK KPSS*, no. 9 (1989): 18–19; "Iz istorii obrazovaniia SSSR. Stenogramma," no. 3 (1991): 170–172; no. 5 (1991): 154–176; *Dvenadtsatyi s"ezd*, pp. 576–582; *Tainy natsional'noi politiki*, pp. 107–110; *Natsional'nyi vopros na perekrestke mnenii*, pp. 86–91, 97–100.

72. "Iz istorii obrazovaniia SSSR. Stenogramma," no. 4 (1991): 169–176; no. 5 (1991): 154–176; *Dvenadtsatyi s"ezd*, pp. 649–661; *Tainy natsional'noi politiki*, pp. 260–272.

73. However, they were granted different governmental structures, including their

own sovnarkom, several independent commissariats, and in Ukraine even their own Politburo. After Stalin's death, this would prove important.

74. Stalin, *Marksizm*, pp. 42–43, 48–49; "Protiv federatsii" (1917), *Sochineniia*, vol. 3, pp. 23–28; Lenin, "Proekt platformy k 4 s"ezdu sots-dem latyshskogo kraia" (1913), PSS, vol. 23, pp. 209–210; "Tezisy po natsional'nomu voprosu," pp. 317–320.

75. "Protiv federatsii," p. 31.

76. Stalin's associates often joked about the "autonomy" of their national territories. Voroshilov began his letter to Stalin about the formation of the Chechen autonomous oblast in January 1923 with jocular congratulations: "I congratulate you on the formation of yet another autonomous territory!" The letter's editor sees this as evidence of an ironic attitude toward the Soviet nationalities policy as a whole, but Voroshilov goes on to express his concern that the local Communists did not understand the importance of promoting Chechen national cadres. Autonomy was a joke, but *korenizatsiia* was not. " 'Chechentsy, kak vse gortsy, ne khuzhe, ne luchshe'. Pis'mo K. E. Voroshilova I. V. Stalinu," *Istochnik*, no. 1 (1999): 66–67.

77. *Dvenadtsatyi s"ezd*, p. 694.

78. Ibid., p. 694; *Tainy natsional'noi politiki*, p. 285; "Iz istorii obrazovanii SSSR. Stenogramma," no. 3 (1991): 178–179.

79. These attempts are discussed in chapter 4 of Terry Martin, *The Affirmative Action Empire: Nations and Nationalism in the Soviet Union, 1923–1939* (Ithaca, N.Y.: Cornell University Press, 2001).

80. For an excellent case study, see the successful lobbying efforts of the Kazakh government to get central approval for the construction of the Turkestano-Siberian railway. Matthew Payne, "Turksib: The Building of the Turkestano-Siberian Railroad and the Politics of Production during the Cultural Revolution, 1926–1931" (Ph.D. diss, University of Chicago, 1995). See also R. W. Davies, *Crisis and Progress in the Soviet Economy, 1931–1933* (London: Macmillan, 1996), pp. 485–487.

81. Gerhard Simon, *Nationalism and Policy toward the Nationalities in the Soviet Union* (Boulder, Colo.: Westview, 1991), p. 297. On this issue, see Alec Nove and J. A. Newth, *The Soviet Middle East: A Model for Development?* (London: Allen and Unwin, 1967); Donna Bahry, *Outside Moscow: Power, Politics and Budgetary Policy in the Soviet Republics* (New York: Columbia University Press, 1987); Donna Bahry and Carol Nechemias, "Half Full or Half Empty? The Debate over Soviet Regional Equality," *Slavic Review* 40 (1981): 366–383; Gertrude Schroeder, "Nationalities and the Soviet Economy" in Lubomyr Hajda and Mark Beissinger, eds., *The Nationalities Factor in Soviet Politics and Society* (Boulder Colo.: Westview, 1990), pp. 43–72; I. S. Koropeckyj, *Location Problems in Soviet Industry before World War II* (Chapel Hill, N.C.: University of North Carolina Press, 1971).

82. See Martin, "Borders and Ethnic Conflict."

83. *Tainy natsional'noi politiki*, pp. 141–156. *Natsional'nyi vopros na perekrestke mnenii*, pp. 141–150.

84. Miroslav Hroch, *Social Preconditions of National Revival in Europe* (Cambridge: Cambridge University Press, 1985). Hroch's paradigm has been utilized extensively by Andreas Kappeler, "The Ukrainians of the Russian Empire, 1860–1914," in Andreas Kappeler, ed., *The Formation of National Elites* (New York: New York University Press, 1991), pp. 105–132; Kappeler, *Russland als Vielvoelkerreich: Entstehung, Geschichte, Zerfall* (Munich: Beck, 1992): pp. 183–191. See also Robert J. Kaiser, *The Geography of Nationalism in Russian and the USSR* (Princeton, N.J.: Princeton University Press, 1994), pp. 33–93.

85. Lenin, "Kriticheskie zametki," p. 132.

86. RTsKhIDNI 374/27s/1709 (1929): 50. See also D. Lebed, *Sovetskaia Ukraina i natsional'nyi vopros za piat' let* (Kharkov: Derzhavne Vyd-vo Ukrainy, 1924).

87. Lebed, *Sovetskain Ukraina*, p. 50.

88. *Dvenadtsatyi s"ezd*, p. 604.

89. Ibid., pp. 693–694. See also "Zanozy v nashei natsional'noi politike," *Zhizn natsional'nostei*, nos. 6–7 (1922): 1–2.

90. See Stalin's comments on the "leftists," *Tainy natsional'noi politiki*, pp. 83–84.

91. *Dvenadtsatyi s"ezd*, p. 694.

92. RTsKhIDNI 558/1/4490 (1929): 9.

93. *Dvenadtsatyi s"ezd*, p. 613. Presumably Bukharin also authored the Pravda editorial that appeared the same day as his speech (April 24, 1923), which called for "the greatest concessions and self-sacrifice on the part of the former Great Power nation—even at this price we must purchase the fullest trust, support and brotherly solidarity from the formerly oppressed nations." *Natsional'nyi vopros na perekrestke mnenii*, p. 178.

94. Ibid., p. 651.

95. This does not mean Russians were discriminated against in any other aspect or that their life opportunities were worse than those of non-Russians. All nationalities had equal legal rights. The expression of national hatred was punished. Moreover, as individuals, Russians were often in a better position, since the central government worked in Russians as did the best universities.

96. Galanter, *Competing Equalities*; Thomas Sowell, *Preferential Policies: An International Perspective* (New York: Morrow, 1990); Nathan Glazer, *Affirmative Discrimination: Ethnic Inequality and Public Policy* (Cambridge: Cambridge University Press, 1987; 1st ed, 1975); Donald Horowitz, *Ethnic Groups in Conflict* (Berkeley: University of California Press, 1985), pp. 653–680.

97. India is usually credited with having invented affirmative action, but Indian affirmative action programs for national minorities (The Scheduled Tribes) began in 1951. Galanter, *Competing Inequalities*, pp. 18–40.

98. Affirmative action for workers is discussed in Sheila Fitzpatrick, *Education and Social Mobility in the Soviet Union, 1921–1934* (Cambridge: Cambridge University Press, 1979); and Fitzpatrick, "Stalin and the Making of a New Elite," in *The Cultural Front: Power and Culture in Revolutionary Russia* (Ithaca, N.Y.: Cornell University Press, 1992), pp. 149–182. Labor policies toward women are discussed briefly in Wendy Z. Goldman, *Women, the State & Revolution: Soviet Family Policy and Social Life, 1917–1936* (Cambridge: Cambridge University Press, 1993), pp. 109–118. These Soviet programs were established at the same time as the first caste-based affirmative action programs in pre-independence India, which were adopted in the 1920s and 1930s. Galanter, *Competing Inequalities*, pp. 18–40.

99. A. Nove and J. A. Newth, *The Soviet Middle East: A Model for Development?* (London: Praeger, 1967), p. 122.

100. Karen Dawisha and Bruce Parrot, eds., *The End of Empire? The Transformation of the USSR in Comparative Perspective* (Armonk, N.Y.: Sharpe, 1997). Karen Barkey and Mark Von Hagen, eds., *After Empire. Multiethnic Societies and Nation-Building: The Soviet Union and the Russian, Ottoman and Habsburg Empires* (Boulder, Colo.: Westview, 1997).

101. Mark Beissinger, "The Persisting Ambiguity of Empire," *Post-Soviet Affairs* 11 (1995): 149–151.

102. Ibid., pp. 154–158.

103. Prerevolutionary class identities were likewise preserved as Soviet categories with their valence likewise reversed; see Sheila Fitzpatrick, "Ascribing Class: The Construction of Social Identity in Soviet Russia," *Journal of Modern History* 65 (December 1993): 745–770.

104. Lenin, "Imperializm, kak vysshaia stadiia kapitalisma" (1916), PSS, vol. 27, pp. 299–426.

105. The key resolution blaming the grain requisitions crisis in Ukraine and Kuban on the implementation of Ukrainization was passed on December 14, 1932. Two further resolutions followed on the next two days. *Holod 1932–1933 rokiv na Ukraini. Ochyma istorykiv, movoiu dokumentiv* (Kyiv: 1990), pp. 291–294. RTsKhIDNI 17/3/911 (16.12.32): protokol 126, punkt 1; 17/3/911 (15.12.31): protokol 126, punkt 50. For a detailed analysis of the origins and causes of this abrupt policy shift, see Martin, *The Affirmative Action Empire*, particularly chapter 7.

106. For instance, Bohdan Nahaylo and Victor Swoboda, *Soviet Disunion: A History of the Nationalities Problem in the USSR* (New York: Hamilton, 1990), pp. 60–80.

107. The evidence for this claim can be found in Martin, *The Affirmative Action Empire*, chapter 9.

108. Martin, "The Russification of the RSFSR." The number thirty-five includes the union and autonomous republics and autonomous oblasts as of 1938. Several of these (Kalmyk, Chechen-Ingush, Kalmyk, Crimean) were abolished in 1944 when their indigenous inhabitants were deported. With the exception of the Crimean ASSR, they were restored shortly after Stalin's death.

109. See Terry Martin, "Modernization or Neo-Traditionalism? Ascribed Nationality and Soviet Primordialism," in David Hoffman and Yanni Kotsonis, eds., *Russian Modernity: Politics, Practices, Knowledge* (New York: St. Martin's, 2000). See also Mark Saroyan, *Minorities, Mullahs, and Modernity: Reshaping Community in the Former Soviet Union* (Berkeley: International and Area Studies, University of California at Berkeley, 1997), pp. 135–166.

110. Georgia and Armenia are exceptions where the native language lost some ground to Russian but remained dominant. Otherwise, these generalizations summarize a complex reality that varied from republic to republic. For more detail, see Martin, *The Affirmative Action Empire*, chapter 9.

111. I say "most" non-Russians, since the 1930s also witnessed the emergence of the category of "enemy nations" who were targeted for deportation, arrest, and, in 1937–1938, mass execution. Prior to World War II, this category embraced "diaspora" nationalities, and during World War II it spread to other "indigenous" nationalities, such as the Chechen, Ingush, Kalmyks, Crimeans, Kabardinians and several other small nationalities. Martin, "The Origins of Ethnic Cleansing"; N. F. Bugai, *L. Beriia– I. Stalinu: "Soglasno vashemu ukazaniiu . . ."* (Moscow: Airo-xx, 1995).

112. *XVII s"ezd*, p. 32.

113. The phrase "first among equals" is used in Peredovaia, "RSFSR," *Pravda*, no. 31 February 1, 1936, p. 1. On the growing promotion of a "russocentric" ideology in the 1930s and after, see David Brandenberger's essay in this volume and his dissertation, "The 'Short Course' to Modernity: Stalinist History Textbooks, Mass Culture and the Formation of Popular Russian National Identity, 1934–1956" (Ph.D. diss., Harvard University, 1999).

114. On the question of linguistic russification, see Peter Blitstein's essay in this volume.

115. For a more detailed discussion of the causes of the rehabilitation of the Russian nationality, see Martin, *The Affirmative Action Empire,* chapters 7, 10, 11.

116. Martin, *The Affirmative Action Empire,* chapter 11; Lowell Tillett, *The Great Friendship: Soviet Historians on the Non-Russian Nationalities* (Chapel Hill, N.C.: University of North Carolina Press, 1969).

117. On the precursors to the Friendship in late imperial Russia and the early Soviet Union, see Joshua Sanborn's essay in this volume.

118. For evidence that Stalin did believe this and intervened to preserve Soviet affirmative action, see Martin, *The Affirmative Action Empire,* chapter 9.

PART II

The Revolutionary Conjuncture

Family, Fraternity, and Nation-Building in Russia, 1905–1925

T HE TERM "NATION" HAS CARRIED tremendous emotional and political force throughout the modern era. The domestic and international power of the word has been such that virtually all politicians who have supported programs that seek to establish civic equality, social solidarity, and the political sovereignty of a specific historical territorialized community have tried to appropriate the term for their own projects. Historians of the nation around the globe have therefore focused their attention on movements and individuals that declared themselves to be national. This approach of limiting the study of the nation to those that carry the name has the signal advantage of combining considerable theoretical strength with a much-desired limitation to the object of study.

Scholars of modern Russia have adopted this approach nearly universally.[1] Since many influential political figures in modern Russia (most prominently the early Bolshevik leadership) tended to conflate nationalism and ethnonationalism, it is not surprising that the lion's share of research has been centered on ethnicity and ethnic policies, as the contributions to this volume suggest. The problem with this approach is that it eliminates from scholarly consideration one of the strongest and most forcefully articulated positions regarding political community in the first half of the twentieth century, a position that supported the building and culti-vation of a multiethnic nation. Indeed, some scholars have not only ignored the development of such a "civic" nationalist position but have also declared it im-possible in a country that did not have a civil society on the Western model. As a result, the tendency of scholars of both tsarist and Soviet Russia has been to equate ethnic with national and multiethnic with imperial.[2] My goal in this essay is to challenge these easy conflations, to argue that ethnicity, though often a crucial factor in the imagining of political community, should not be seen as the sole factor in determining national stances. What marks the nation is not membership in a particular community whose members believe that they are bound by distant ties of blood or a shared native language but the desire for a particular type of social and political cohesion based on belonging to a historical, territorialized community that is politically sovereign. More succinctly, I argue that nations generally work on the principle of metaphoric kinship rather than actual kinship. With this point of departure, it becomes clearer that studying nationalism requires just as much attention to *family* policy and rhetoric as it does attention to *ethnic* policy and rhetoric.

In Russia, the most important and influential institution that attempted to build a multiethnic nation based on metaphoric kinship was the army. Both before and after the revolutions of 1917, military planners placed themselves at the center of the debate over what shape the political community should assume in the modern era. At the heart of their concern and their political program was the problem of social cohesion. Continuously concerned with having large numbers of men tied by affinitive bonds and convinced that the differential policies of the tsarist and Soviet states had thwarted cohesion by creating divisions and distinctions among various subsections of their recruit base, these men adopted a national stance of promoting civic equality throughout the first quarter of the twentieth century.

Military intellectuals under the last tsars fully understood the difficulties this reform program faced. As Peter Holquist points out in his contribution to this volume, army staffers had been at the forefront of population studies throughout the second half of the nineteenth century. The upshot of all this research was a general conviction on the part of the army brass that the Russian empire was ethnically diverse, socially stratified, and devoid of a strong sense of community. To make matters worse, they were fully aware that the autocratic political system was antinational. The state lacked mechanisms that tied it meaningfully to the populace, and conservative officials distrusted any attempts by would-be citizens to become active in building and sustaining a sense of political community.

These social and political incongruities were serious and potentially fatal military weaknesses in the eyes of modernizing reformers, who quite clearly understood that modern wars were massive and total, requiring not only military effort but also social mobilization. Their goal, therefore, was to build a nation by creating a sense of community and unity among the populace and by overcoming the conservative elite's fear of mass mobilization.

The first task was complicated by the empire's ethnic diversity. Proponents of nation building believed either that they had to walk away from the empire, retaining only "Russian" territories, or that they had to build a nation without relying on ethnicity as a cohesive factor. Military nation-builders overwhelmingly chose the latter path and became civic nationalists.

The second task was equally daunting. Defenders of the old regime lurked everywhere in St. Petersburg, not least in the person of the tsar himself. As the struggle to build a nation developed, so too did it acquire an institutional form.

The Ministry of War sought ways to create a unified political community that included the many ethnicities and social strata that populated the empire. This "modern" military urge was one of the many legacies of the French Revolution and the Napoleonic Wars. Ever since 1812, Russian military leaders had understood the power of the nation in mobilizing men, resources, and morale. When the time seemed right to do so, as it did both in the Great Reform era and in the post-1905 era, they pressed civilian officials to assist them in creating a "nation-in-arms." Civilian officials, especially those in the Ministry of Internal Affairs (MVD), were understandably reluctant to do so. Mobilization as a regular feature of political and social life was the last thing that the besieged autocracy wanted. By definition, autocracy does not rest upon a base of popular support, much less active public participation in politics, and the attempts of the last tsars to appropriate the beneficial aspects of Western polities, while trying to avoid the negative aspects of the West's "dual revolution," failed miserably.[3] In the tense, revolutionary atmosphere that dominated Nicholas II's reign, MVD officials assumed that any group of mobilized men was dangerous. Even after the tide had clearly shifted in favor of a mobilized society during World War I, agents of the MVD conducted surveillance not only on clearly subversive revolutionary groups and potentially subversive liberal political groupings but also on staunchly monarchist associations.[4]

The problem of nation building therefore revolved not only around the question of identity but also around the question of mobilization. The effort to develop mobilized or mobilizable identities promised to bring about powerful but volatile results, and the autocracy accordingly dithered in response to military demands. In the end, Russia ended up a bizarre hybrid, with a military system (since the institution of universal conscription in 1874) based on the premise that the army would be composed of mobilized citizen soldiers fulfilling a duty to state and nation and a police system structured to stem the tide of actual public mobilization itself. The autocracy's dilemma became even more acute after 1905, as the military struggled with the aftermath of its defeat in the Russo-Japanese War at the hands of a fully mobilized Japanese army and the MVD struggled with the aftermath of the Revolution. Not surprisingly, the lessons each bureaucracy learned were quite different. The military's lesson from 1905 was that Russia had lost the war because it had failed to mobilize as well as Japan had.[5] The lesson drawn by the MVD was that mass political mobilization had almost toppled the autocracy and had to be hindered at all costs.

World War I gave the final answer to the dilemma of mobilization and should be seen as a central turning point in Russian political history for that reason. From 1914 on, the state played mass politics in order to achieve mass mobilization. For the first time, the nation-state eclipsed the police state.[6] The result was disastrous for the autocracy. The tsarist government discovered that even the latitude offered leaders in a wartime state of emergency proved insufficient to stabilize the volatile combination of mass politics and minority rule. Within three years, the regime was dead. The Provisional Government that followed encountered similar difficulties in keeping the proliferation of mobilized movements under control and was discredited and ruined in a mere eight months. The Bolsheviks, on coming to power, faced the same problems; indeed, the Russian civil war may legitimately be seen as a violent confrontation between the mobilized movements that were born in the late imperial era and that matured in World War I. The Bolsheviks were therefore immediately forced to address the dilemma posed by the necessity of mass mobilization and the centrifugal tendencies of mass politics.

Combining grass-roots participation with centralized authority is a common modern political problem, but it was particularly acute for the tsarist and soviet states. Political leaders in modern Russia quickly came to understand that appeals to defend minority regimes with shaky legitimacy were unpersuasive. Thus, they attempted to mobilize their populations by appealing to feelings of devotion to the sovereign political community and to appropriate those feelings by making the strongest claim to be the best mortal representatives of these immortal communities. In other words, they became nationalists.

But most political elites did not become *ethnic* nationalists. Though they believed, with most of their educated compatriots, that factors such as ethnicity, culture, and language were "natural" cohesive mechanisms, they also understood that none of those mechanisms could be consistently and reliably used in a vast multicultural state. So they had to go deeper to find a powerful common denominator around which they could mobilize. They found it in a nation defined in familial terms, rather than by ethnicity, culture, or language.

The use of familial affinities as the prototype for national affinities was common throughout the first quarter of the twentieth century. Family imagery was intended to inspire feelings of loyalty, closeness, and, above all, unity. When Mikhail Rodzianko opened one crucial wartime Duma session in January 1915, for instance, he appealed to potentially fractious delegates to maintain political unity in the midst of war by using the rhetoric of kinship. "The Russian tsar," he proclaimed to thunderous applause, "with his sensitive heart, divined the feelings of the people, and he has heard here the response of a united, harmonious, Russian family. . . . And presently, after a half of a year of unprecedented bloodshed, Russia stands . . . indivisible, firm in will, and strong in spirit."[7]

The use of the family metaphor to promote unity and cohesion did not stop with the Bolshevik rise to power in 1917. In the very first oath given to Red Army volunteers in April 1918, men promised before their "brothers in arms" and the laboring masses that they would fight for the great cause of soviet power and the triumph of socialism, "for which the best children of the worker-peasant family have given their lives."[8] In 1925, the family image still dominated. In a textbook for military schools, future commanders and soldiers learned that "the leader is required to show respect to his subordinates, because they are both equal citizens of a united Republic, because they are comrades serving in a united army, because both of them, finally, are members of a united worker-peasant family, as a result of which respect cannot fail to be mutual."[9]

The family metaphor was used not only to build affinitive bonds between conationals but between soldiers as well. The nation was like a family, as was the army, as indeed was the primary battle group to which the soldier belonged. The attempt to utilize kinship bonds as a model for new social relations was intentional and was part of the military's repertoire throughout the twentieth century. The only real disagreement was whether officers should try to *replace* blood kinship affinities in the unit or try to *extend* those original family ties to a broader set of men. Those who sought transference argued that soldiers had to "forget temporarily his old hometown interests, had to devote himself completely to service, had to merge with his company, had to look at it as his new family" in order for real soldier bonding to occur. Young soldiers had to leave their "hearth and home," since soldiers stationed near their homes only "strengthen their feeling of belonging to their own family and love for it, and never develop a feeling of belonging to their company or regiment."[10] The uniting of men from all over the realm required a corresponding weakening of family ties.

Most leaders, in both the tsarist and the Soviet eras, did not perceive a need to weaken blood kinship ties, however. In fact, the stronger those were, the better, since young soldiers were told that their units and the nation were *like* their families, not that they would *replace* their families. Recruitment slogans regularly made this analogy, telling young men that both the army and the citizenry were just like "one tight family."[11] In many cases, the imagery stuck. Even when conditions in the Red Army were worsening in 1919, soldiers and commanders tried to keep faith in their family. "Almost all the guys are barefoot . . ." one soldier wrote, "[but] the relationship between [members of the unit and their commanders] is comradely, like a single family."[12]

That the crucial task was to build on familial affections, rather than to replace them, is underscored by the fact that one of the key recruiting maneuvers during both World War I and the civil war was to convince potential soldiers (or potential deserters) that, regardless of their feelings for the particular regime that was appealing to them, the defense of the country was first and foremost the defense of their blood family. The very first draft of the civil war was explained in this fashion by the mobilization department, which claimed that, proletarian revolution notwithstanding, military conscription targeted peasants "no less than workers," since they too were "interested in the defense of the Republic and their own familial hearths from enemy attack."[13] The ability to link the danger to the Republic to the direct danger to a man's family was crucial, and enlistments went up where this case could be effectively made. Throughout the civil war, peasants were far more likely to respond to mobilizational appeals when enemy armies approached their home province.[14]

The second component of this system was to enact concrete family policies for soldiers and their families. If military service was justified within the rhetoric of the nation because it protected families, then it was incumbent upon the state that claimed to represent the nation not to build up the army at the expense of soldiers' relatives. The most direct way that the state showed its concern was by giving cash payments to soldier families. The law establishing the payment of state rations for soldiers' wives and children out of the state treasury in wartime was passed in 1912.[15] As Russia's first welfare entitlement program, this law marked a real shift in the concept of state-citizen relations from one under which the state demanded obligations from its citizens as a matter of tradition or duty to one in which citizens could also demand obligations from the state. Crucially, it was the family that served as the nexus around which this new power relationship was structured.

Given the national mobilizational tactics used by both states, there was a logic to supporting soldiers' families that went beyond the obvious *Realpolitik* realization that states have to take care of the citizens with guns in their hands before they have to take care of those who are unarmed. If soldiers were to defend the state in order to defend their blood families, then the state had a moral obligation to protect the families of those who were away. Because the state expected soldiers to treasure kinship feelings and asked soldiers to extend those affinities to conationals, it had to expect that family misfortunes would tempt men to forgo their duty to their imagined family when their duty to their blood family became obvious and pressing.

It was therefore predictable that the policy of linking family welfare with military service, undertaken in a positive fashion in 1912, would acquire a punitive character, as well. This it did in 1915, when officials decided that, in order to stem the tide of desertion (of which the most popular form was surrendering to the enemy), they would stop providing rations to the family of any soldier who was suspected of giving himself up voluntarily. At the beginning of the war, only one article in the disciplinary code touched on voluntary surrender, and that article mandated the death penalty, a difficult punishment to enact when the soldier in question was in a POW camp and when the crime was so ubiquitous.[16] Over the first couple of months of the war, several commanders noted their frustration with the situation, but the best solution they came up with was to promise Siberian exile after the war for soldiers who surrendered, thus avoiding the Scylla of letting traitors escape unscathed and the Charybdis of mass executions of returning POWs.[17]

The first person to hit upon the idea of punishing families for the crimes of soldiers appears to have been the commander of the First Army. He was enraged by an officer and several soldiers who went over to the German trenches during a Christmas fraternization episode in 1914 and ended up getting captured, and he decided that, in addition to sentencing the officer (but not the soldiers) to death in absentia, he would at the same time "issue a decree concerning the immediate announcement of the names of the surrendered soldiers to their home region *(rodina)*, so that they can cease issuing the ration to their families in their villages at once, and so that all there would know that they betrayed their motherland *(rodina)*." He was also quite clear that punishing families was not a violation of legal principles, for "in view of the fact that the law undoubtedly intended the provisioning of families only of loyal defenders of the state, it is necessary to realize that families of enlisted men who surrendered to the enemy voluntarily, and in this fashion betrayed their *rodina*, should be deprived of their food ration."[18] This argument that state aid to families was not a supplement for people deprived of breadwinners but an entitlement given to families of citizen-soldiers won the day. The Council of Ministers approved cutting off the ration to the families of deserters on March 27, 1915, and Nicholas agreed on April 15 of the same year. For the rest of the war, commanders dutifully notified local officials of the names of deserters and requested that their families be taken off the welfare rolls. Judging by the volume of petitions from soldiers' wives who claimed they had been unfairly deprived of sustenance, these requests were assiduously fulfilled.[19]

The Red Army also recognized the value of the ration and acknowledged the need to provide for the families of their soldiers.[20] During the brief volunteer period in 1918, though the state assumed no formal responsibilities for soldiers' families, army organizers were told to inform potential volunteers that their families would receive preferential treatment for food, clothing, and medical treatment.[21] With each successive crisis, the state responded with increased professions of concern for families. In August 1918, one of the dark months of the civil war for the Bolsheviks, the state decreed a raise not only in soldier salaries but also in the welfare benefits given to the families of soldiers.[22] In December 1918, the state once again proclaimed its intention to provide for the families of soldiers, a declaration that pointed out both the continued commitment of the center to support soldier families and its inability to do so.

This failure to make good their promises to soldiers and their families nearly cost the Bolsheviks the revolution. As families starved, soldiers deserted, which in turn forced the state to target families ever more directly. On the one hand, in cases where citizen-soldiers failed to fulfill their duty to the state, their families were punished. The kin of deserters were subject to punishments ranging from fines to being struck from the rolls of the local labor exchange, not to mention the by then well-established practice of cutting off rations.[23] On the other hand, in the frequent cases where the state failed to fulfill its duty toward the families of citizen soldiers, deserters were treated with much greater compassion. Indeed, the single greatest factor in determining whether a deserter was declared a deserter with a "weak will" or one with "evil intent," a distinction that often meant the difference between life and death, was the condition in which the deserter's family was living. This was official policy:

It is necessary for commissions to distinguish between the desertion brought about by family circumstances, such as the death or illness of a loved one, difficult material conditions, or the general lack of development of the accused, and the desertion of those with evil intent. . . . In the first case, in view of the mitigating circumstances of guilt, much milder punishment should be given to deserters, in most cases just send them to the front, in cases where evil intent is unearthed, punish desertion with all the severity of revolutionary law.[24]

Family problems were both the most acceptable and the most common reason for desertion in the eyes of Bolshevik officials. Thus, family policy was the key to stemming the tide of desertion and, as was patently clear in 1919, to winning the civil war. Nearly every official, later analyst, or later historian who examined the question of civil war desertion came to this same conclusion.[25]

The Bolsheviks, as a result, took family welfare very seriously, not only in their propaganda, where their claims of being more family-friendly than the Whites were important both for raising Red morale and for lowering White morale, but in practice as well.[26] Even the hated "sweep" detachments that surrounded villages, threatened civilians, and drove away livestock in their desperate attempts to flush out deserters were specifically ordered to determine whether the families of deserters had been getting the payments and privileges the state had promised them.[27]

In June 1919, Bolshevik family policy was even more closely linked with military service, as a new policy was implemented whereby property of the families of deserters was to be confiscated and redistributed to the families of "honorably serving" soldiers.[28] The dynamic created was powerful: it allowed for economic redistribution within villages on a massive scale from families of deserters to families of soldiers still in the Red Army.[29] In conditions of widespread famine and disease, soldiers fought not just for the Revolution, or for Russia, or even for themselves, but primarily for their families.

The family rhetoric rather quickly percolated down to regular soldiers. Not surprisingly, given the policy and practice of the regime, the claim that one's family was in dire trouble was often used by soldiers as an excuse for desertion. Sob stories about family circumstances were ubiquitous. Iosif Drozhzhin was one such soldier whose last-ditch effort in October 1919 to save his life included an appeal to the ideal of the family:

> I lived as a deserter . . . for seven months, and all that time I did agricultural work, since I'm the only worker at home, and there are seven mouths to feed. I showed up voluntarily, although I deserted because of extreme necessity, but this doesn't justify me, I realize my guilt, but I didn't expect such severe punishment. I beg the Appeals Court to lessen my punishment for the sake of my little children . . . and send me to the front.[30]

The ideal of the family was the pivot of the power relationship among citizen, soldier, army, and state.[31]

At the same time, that ideal of the proper family was in the midst of a dramatic change, a change that was also driven by the increasing militarization of Russian society and Russian politics. The familial imagery of the old regime prior to the turn of the twentieth century had been fully patriarchal, and political power was legitimated in this way. As one traditional author explained to young recruits, "a family can live happily only when all its members subordinate themselves to the eldest [man] in the house. Russia is the same kind of family, the eldest is the

Emperor."[32] This patriarchal imagery extended to the familial rhetoric within the army. Officers were the patriarchs of the family, noncommissioned officers were the older brothers, and the enlisted men were younger brothers. The chapbook written by top training expert M. I. Dragomirov and given to soldiers in the late nineteenth century included the following advice: "Look at the unit as your family, at the commander as your father, at your comrades as your blood brothers, and at subordinates as your little brothers; then everybody will be happy and friendly."[33]

During the last years of tsarist rule, however, military reformers became increasingly concerned about the "younger brothers." Success in modern warfare depended less on the wisdom, courage, and brilliance of the elders and more on common soldiers. Reformers wanted to increase cohesion, raise the competence of enlisted men, and create a real esprit de corps. The obvious way to do this was to stress the need for junior officers and noncommissioned officers to spend more and more "quality time" with enlisted men, teaching them, training them, and inspiring them. Not surprisingly, the model for this interaction was familial. More specifically, it was fraternal.

Forming a "band of brothers"[34] within combat units was the explicit goal of young staff officers throughout the early twentieth century. This generation of military intellectuals, which included such important future Soviet "military specialists" as Mikhail Bonch-Bruevich, Pavel Lebedev, Aleksandr Svechin, and Aleksandr Neznamov, first emerged as a powerful force in military politics and military training circles in the aftermath of the Russo-Japanese War.[35] In the widely read army newspaper *Russkii invalid*, in 1906, Neznamov advised officers that

> earlier, when a soldier served for almost his whole life, questions of moral training were solved by themselves: the military family itself, in the person of the veteran soldier . . . trained the young ones, absorbed them. Now training has become the job of the officer; now the latter has been transformed from an exacting commander into a strict father, an elder brother. Life demanded from the commander, as a substitute for the earlier fear . . . that the commander and his subordinates become linked through mutual trust and love.[36]

In 1906, Neznamov was straddling the line, telling commanders to be strict fathers *and* elder brothers, but, as he was to make clear later in the same article, the primary task of the officer was to be an "elder comrade"[37] who was essentially equal before the nation. That is, he was to try to build fraternal relations with his soldiers.

By the time of World War I, the ambiguity within mass mobilization tracts had disappeared. One appeal to deserters reminded them that they all "swore an oath to be loyal to tsar and motherland" and that breaking that oath meant becoming "unworthy to your fellow brothers and sons of Russia."[38] Russia was the mother, and all officers and soldiers were "fellow brothers."

The idea propagandized by the military leadership that fellow soldiers were brothers caught on. Well before the February Revolution put the word "fraternity" on everyone's lips, men across the empire used the concept when speaking about affinitive ties between fellow soldiers or fellow nationals. Reservists in the wilds of the Priamur district told military officials in 1915 that "each of us . . . willingly showed up when we were mobilized, being sure that we were going to help our brothers smash the enemy."[39] Another letter, complaining about the draft exemption for policemen, recommended sending all 300,000 of them into "the ranks of our fighting brothers."[40] The ubiquity of the image extended even to men who had never served in the army. When Kirgiz representatives petitioned the Duma for a deferral of their labor draft in 1916, they also stressed that they felt that the eventual imposition of conscription not only was just but was also their "civic duty." "We Kirgiz," they proudly proclaimed, "consider ourselves the equal sons of a unified Russia and sincerely hope that the victorious war will serve as a stimulus for the introduction of a rule of law for our motherland, for the passage of reforms necessary for the good of the fatherland, and for the establishment of fraternity between the tribally variegated sons of the fatherland."[41]

This widespread use of fraternity as a metaphor in the late imperial period is not only surprising given the overwhelmingly patriarchal imagery usually propagandized by the autocratic regime but is also indicative of the beginnings of a basic shift in the imagining of the political community. Fratriarchal political communities are radically different from patriarchal ones. Traditional hierarchies are disrupted. The unquestioned authority of father over son disappears, and authority between brothers must be renegotiated. It is thus no accident that fraternity appears on banners alongside equality. The basis of social solidarity is also transformed. Rather than fear, affinity must provide cohesiveness.

Ironically, given the embrace of fraternity by many army ideologues, it was in the military that the most immediate disruption was felt when the tsar's abdication in 1917 removed the linchpin of the patriarchal system of power. The basic reason for the crisis of authority in the army was that, despite the vocal support of reformers for the idea of building fraternal bonds between officers and soldiers, many officers simply had not bothered to establish authority on any basis other than the traditional, unquestioning command-obedience model. In those units where reform-minded officers had sought to create a fraternal bond and had succeeded, the shift of models of authority was less traumatic than it was elsewhere in the army. The soldier deputies of the Kiev garrison joyously informed the Provisional Government about the

> unprecedented upsurge in the fraternization of soldiers, officers, doctors, staffers, and junkers which has seized all the military men in the garrison and has never been seen to this point in Russia. There are no words to express the stupendous grandeur of the spectacle as the prejudices of the old military life are destroyed and exposed for the mutual understanding and respect of the hearts of soldiers and officers and out from under the ruins of the old grows a united will bonded with a united heart, a new powerful Russian army of citizen-soldiers.[42]

In the same vein, where officers proved willing to engage in "mutual understanding and respect," they fared relatively well. According to Allan Wildman, after the February Revolution, "[o]fficers could easily maintain their popularity by relaxing discipline and displaying their enthusiasm for the new order, but they could no longer overawe by the threat of punishment."[43]

The Provisional Government, to its great detriment, chose the wrong side of this issue and wound up aligned in opposition to the revolutionary slogan of fraternity. Preempted by the Petrograd Soviet's explicitly fraternal Order No. 1, which gave power to the "band of brothers" by instituting soldier committees, and predisposed to seeing a change in authority relations in the army as a breakdown in authority itself, the Provisional Government soon found itself associated with patriarchal officers, a fact that neither new proposals for fraternity-based "Revolutionary-Volunteer" units nor Kerensky's rise to power proved able to overcome.[44]

The loss of the Provisional Government was the gain of the Petrograd Soviet and, increasingly, the Bolshevik Party.[45] It was hardly surprising, then, that the Bolsheviks, when they took power, reaffirmed their support of fraternity. Indeed, given the long history of fraternal metaphors within the European socialist movement, it would have been shocking if the Bolsheviks had abandoned fraternal rhetoric. As a result, whether a given individual was used to the language of brotherhood from his army days or from his revolutionary days (or for that matter from his church days) mattered little. "Brother" was on everyone's lips.[46]

Again, the keys here were the proclamation of "equality"[47] and the creation of mutual affinitive bonds. Hence the initial reaffirmation of the soldier committees, which would determine the "general will" that the unit would be bound to follow, and the repeated assertions of equality in the army, including the forbidding of the wearing of any decorations or medals save St. George crosses (which were achievement based). Discipline, as with the Provisional Government's limited attempt to institute fraternal relations, was to be based on "comradely influence, the authority of committees, and comrade's courts," that is, on the decisions of the band of brothers.[48]

Soldier committees died with the old army, as part of the conscious strategy by the Bolshevik leadership (more specifically, Lenin and Trotsky) to step back from unfettered revolutionary idealism in military affairs. The institutional form of fraternity therefore changed, but the ideals and functions of brotherhood did not disappear. To the contrary, the aspect of equality inherent in fraternity remained prominent. If anything, soldiers became even more adamant that the "defense of the motherland and the revolution" should be "mandatory in an identical fashion both for command staff and for soldiers." Soldier protests were frequently centered around perceptions of injustice, as one group of soldiers noted in early 1918: "we are achieving fraternity and equality, but nevertheless, we see a distinction in salaries, and there should be no difference in the salaries between command staff and rank and file soldiers."[49] Two and a half years later, a peasant from Altai province complained about draft exemptions for Kalmyks, using the same fraternal rhetoric that had been used throughout the twentieth century. "Three and a half years ago the tsarist throne was overthrown, and now our beloved Soviet power, which was won with our blood, exists. It would be desirable to be a family with all fully equal brothers equally fulfilling their military duty. [But] for some reason, Kalmyks aren't drafted. Now everything has become offensive. [Among] . . . brothers one goes to defend the Soviet Republic, another stays home."[50]

So too did the theme of brotherhood provide solidarity visible in the Soviet era. Commanders and soldiers, being from the same "family" of laborers and being equal citizens, were bound by moral ties, political workers argued, in sharp contrast to the bonds of fear instituted under the tsars.

> In the old days . . . they forced the new recruit to forget about his native family and home while in the barracks. For him "I'm listening," "Exactly so," and "Sir, no sir" became law. In response, he got "don't argue, you brute."
> Now the Red Army is composed of workers and peasants. The soldier and the commander come from the same family of laborers—they are blood brothers.
> The Red Army is welded together with conscious revolutionary discipline. The discipline of the stick and of punches in the mouth has no place in the Red Army. When on duty, the commander is the leader. When off duty, he's a comrade.[51]

Needless to say, even had the political workers not mentioned the ideal of brotherhood explicitly, the model here was fraternal. Commanders and soldiers were equal in status ("comrades") and were cohesive by virtue of their "familial" connections as workers and peasants.[52]

Rank-and-file soldiers were just as likely to use fraternal rhetoric as were their commanders. One such soldier, Pavel Tsymbal, pleaded in his 1918 appeal to have his death sentence for desertion overturned: "I swear upon my honor as a citizen that it won't happen again. If I run away a second time, shoot me on the spot. I fervently request once again that you give me the opportunity to blot out my guilt and provide if only a little use to Soviet Russia alongside my brothers and comrades at the front rather than die with this shameful stigma in prison."[53] Though appeals to brotherhood could be effective for deserters seeking leniency, the concept of fraternity itself was more often used to prevent desertion in the first place. Political workers were quite clear that deserters not only were traitors to the Soviet Republic but were also the "enemy of his own soldier brother."[54]

Solidarity, equality, loyalty—these were the bases of fraternity. No wonder, then, that fraternity was the model chosen very early on to describe not only the kind of interaction that separate individuals in the nation should have but also the type of interaction that ethnic groups should have within the nation. State actors during the civil war regularly referred to different ethnic groups as "brother peoples."[55] By late 1918, the idea that ethnic relations would be understood in fraternal terms had percolated down to regular soldiers. "Long live the World Revolution!" cheered the soldiers of one regiment. "Long live the fraternity of peoples!"[56] The use of the fraternal metaphor continued, even multiplied, as the 1920s wore on.[57]

Nor should the later phenomenon of a loss of enthusiasm for fraternity as a slogan and concept blind us to the very real and emotional connotation that this word had in the first decade of Soviet power.[58] Its very overuse by propaganda officials (which no doubt contributed to the increasing staleness of fraternal rhetoric) is indicative of the power that those officials ascribed to it. Fraternity was a wonderfully useful concept, incorporating all the aspects of nation that state officials desired and reinforcing the popular slogan of equality without significantly lessening maneuvers of power and domination. After all, as Ukrainian nationalists (and Russian peasants) would soon grow tired of hearing, within any fraternal system there is room for older brothers and younger brothers, leaders and followers. It was not until the 1930s that the fraternal revolution "retreated" under Stalin's paternalistic pressure.[59]

Unable to use purely ethnic or class identities as "natural" cohesive mechanisms when forming military and political communities, army ideologues instead relied on the image of the family as their major "natural" cohesive force, and as a result they committed themselves to family in action as well as rhetoric. It was a savvy decision to try to appropriate those powerful local emotions and to transfer them to the multiethnic nation, rather than to a single ethnicity. Ideals of fraternity and family were understood, and, though they were occasionally cynically manipulated by regular conscripts, they just as often seem to have been genuinely treasured (and no doubt these two stances coexisted easily).

Not only did the strongest and most consistent efforts to build the multiethnic nation come from the military, but it was also the military that latched upon family and fraternity as effective techniques to do so. Well before the Great War, indeed, even well before the Great Reforms, the army had trained its men to envision an obviously "constructed" community (the agglomeration of strangers that composed a regiment or platoon) in terms of family and fraternity. When army intellectuals became convinced that a much broader community had to be constructed, therefore, they had the experience, the language, and the methods ready at hand.

This multiethnic stance often clashed with ethnic national stances, but the result was not total victory for the ethnic vision. Despite the fact that the multiethnic identity propagated by military intellectuals was not always, perhaps not even often, adopted by the individuals they were trying to mobilize, ethnic national identity was weaker still. The problem of much subsequent narrowly ethnic nationalist historiography is that it assumes that the battle taking place was between "true" nations and the bastardized regimes that were either "Russifying" or "breakers of nations." Actually, the main struggle was between personal concerns and those of the larger political community. Local concerns were connected with the broader nation through both coercive measures and welfare programs.

Punishing the families of bad soldiers while rewarding the families of good soldiers was the key to maintaining the triangular relationship among state, nation, and citizen, and this relationship developed in response to total war. Ethnic nationalists, deprived of the resources and punitive organs of the state, struggled to establish the same sort of nexus of power.

Made urgent by total war, state-sponsored nation-building gradually developed from 1874 to 1904 and became an issue of tremendous significance in the final decade before World War I. Beginning in 1914, the state had no choice but to conduct mass mobilizations around mobilizable identities, and the population was literally saturated with appeals to an expansive, integrated multiethnic political community and programs that made the nation a tangible force. When the seven years of total war came to an end, this national identity was new and shaky, but it was stronger than any other nonlocal appeal.

Notes

1. A notable exception to this rule is Frederick C. Barghoorn, *Soviet Russian Nationalism* (New York: Oxford University Press, 1956). I would like to thank Prasenjit Duara and the other members of the conference from which this volume sprang for their useful comments. In addition, I thank Rafe Blaufarb, Troy Davis, and the reviewers for Oxford University Press for their advice in the final stages of revision.

2. Geoffrey Hosking acknowledged that there were concerted attempts made to build a multiethnic nation in modern Russia, but his definitional framework (in which ethnic Russians are the "people" and the multiethnic community is the "empire") made it difficult for him to treat the question effectively. Geoffrey Hosking, *Russia: People and Empire* (Cambridge, Mass.: Harvard University Press, 1997). For Soviet-era examples, see the unanimous declarations of our most prominent scholars of the nation, who claim that there was never an attempt to build a "Soviet nation." Ronald Grigor Suny, "Ambiguous Categories: States, Empires and Nations," *Post-Soviet Affairs* 11, no. 2 (1995): 190; Yuri Slezkine, "The USSR as a Communal Apartment, or How a Socialist State Promoted Ethnic Particularism," *Slavic Review* 53, no. 2 (Summer 1994): 435; Rogers Brubaker, *Nationalism Reframed: Nationhood and the National Question in the New Europe* (Cambridge: Cambridge University Press, 1996), p. 28.

3. The term "dual revolution" refers to the combined impact of the industrial revolution and the French revolution. See Eric Hobsbawm, *The Age of Revolution, 1789–1848* (London: Mentor, 1962), p. xv.

4. See for instance the letter from General N. von Kol'ts (Chief of Tula Gendarmes Administration) to S. P. Beletskii (Minister of Internal Affairs). January 9, 1916. Included in "Perepiska pravykh i drugie materialy ob ikh deiatel'nosti v 1914–1917 godakh," *Voprosy istorii*, no. 3 (1996): 159.

5. See for instance General [A. N.] Kuropatkin, *The Russian Army and the Japanese War*, trans. A. B. Lindsay (London: Murray, 1909).

6. On the mass mobilizations of the populace in the economic sphere during World War I, see Lewis H. Siegelbaum, *The Politics of Industrial Mobilization in Russia, 1914–17: A Study of the War-Industries Committees* (New York: St. Martin's, 1983), esp. pp. 49–53. On public mobilization more broadly, see Raymond Pearson, *The Russian*

Moderates and the Crisis of Tsarism, 1914–1917 (London: Macmillan, 1977), p. 21; Peter Gatrell, *A Whole Empire Walking: Refugees in Russia during World War I* (Bloomington: Indiana University Press, 1999).

7. Speech of Rodzianko (chairman) to first meeting of third session of Fourth State Duma. January 27, 1915. RGIA f. 1278, op. 5, d. 201, l. 3.

8. Text of the first oath. Reprinted in Iu. I. Korablev and M. I. Loginov, eds., *KPSS i stroitel'stvo vooruzhennykh sil SSSR (1918–iiun' 1941)* (Moscow: Voenizdat, 1959), p. 75.

9. N. P. Vishniakov and F. I. Arkhipov, *Ustroistvo vooruzhennykh sil SSSR,* 2d ed. (Moscow: Voennyi vestnik, 1926), p. 142.

10. "Neskol'ko slov o komplektovanii armii molodymi soldatami." n/a. November 1912. RGVIA f. 2000, op. 3, d. 1114, l. 47.

11. "Spisok lozungov otpravliaemykh na agitpunkty PVO i chastiam." 1922. RGVA f. 9, op. 28s, d. 403, l. 64ob.

12. Report from the military censor of the Third Army, compiled from correspondence from the Red Army examined June 1–15 1919. RGVA f. 16, op. 6, d. 3, l. 59ob.

13. "Otchet o deiatel'nosti Mobilizatsionnogo Upravleniia Vserossiiskogo Glavnogo Shtaba s 25 oktiabria 1917 goda po 15-e avgusta 1920 goda." Secret. RGVA f. 11, op. 8, d. 36, l. 15ob.

14. Orlando Figes, *Peasant Russia, Civil War: The Volga Countryside in Revolution, 1917–1921* (Oxford: Oxford University Press, 1989), pp. 178, 309. Likewise, bands of local peasants often attacked any army entering their territory as a purely defensive maneuver. Vladimir N. Brovkin, *Behind the Front Lines of the Civil War: Political Parties and Social Movements in Russia, 1918–1922* (Princeton, N.J.: Princeton University Press, 1994), pp. 148–149.

15. For more on the implementation of the ration system, see Emily E. Pyle, "Village Social Relations and the Reception of Soldiers' Family Aid Policy in Russia, 1912–1921" (Ph.D. diss., University of Chicago, 1997).

16. *Svod voennykh postanovlenii 1869 g.* kn. 22, st. 248. Version in force during war printed in D. F. Ognev, comp., *Voinskii ustav o nakazaniiakh (S.V.P. 1869 g., XXII, izd. 3)* (St. Petersburg: Berezovskii, 1912), pp. 298–299.

17. Report from the Chief of Staff of the Main Commander of Armies of the Southwest Front to Stavka. March 6, 1915. RGVIA f. 2003, op. 2, d. 784, l. 9.

18. Report of the Pension Department to the Stavka. March 16, 1915. RGVIA f. 2003, op. 2, d. 784, l. 13–14.

19. "Osobyi zhurnal soveta ministrov." March 27, 1915, with notation of Emperor's agreement attached. Ibid., l. 17, 33, 34, passim.

20. See for instance M. D. Bonch-Bruevich report to Lenin. Secret. March 15, 1918. RTsKhIDNI f. 5, op. 1, d. 2415, l. 5.

21. "Instruktsiia po organizatsii RKKA." February 18, 1918. RGVA f. 2, op. 1, d. 8, l. 193; Copy of contract given to volunteers to sign. April 1918. RGVA f. 11, op. 8, d. 53, l. 122.

22. Circular to all Military District Commanders from Lenin and Trotskii. August 5, 1918. RGVA f. 2, op 1, d. 33, l. 198.

23. In Kostroma province alone, sixty-three families were fined for a total of more than 97,000 rubles over a two-week period in 1919. "Svodka deiatel'nosti tsentral'noi (*sic*) i mestnykh komitetov po bor'be s dezertirstvom." September 1–15, 1919. RTs-

KhIDNI f. 5, op. 1 d. 2452, l. 17; telegram from Central Desertion Committee to Lenin. January 4, 1919. Ibid., l. 10b.

24. Decree of the Central Desertion Committee to provincial commissions. April 10, 1919. RGVA f. 11, op. 15s, d. 49s, l. 50b.

25. See for instance, the telegram from Rattel (Vseroglavshtab) to all district, provincial, and local military committees. June 13, 1920. RGVA f. 11, op. 8, d. 48, l. 41–46; S. Olikov, *Dezertirstvo v krasnoi armii i bor'ba s nim* (Moscow: Izd. NKVM, 1926), p. 48; Mark von Hagen, *Soldiers in the Proletarian Dictatorship: The Red Army and the Soviet Socialist State, 1917–1930* (Ithaca, N.Y.: Cornell University Press, 1990), pp. 73, 78.

26. Von Hagen, *Soldiers in the Proletarian Dictatorship*, p. 78.

27. "Organizatsiia oblav." Signed by Timofeev (Chairman of the Moscow District Desertion Committee). n/d but probably 1919. RGVA f. 25883, op. 1, d. 271, l. 6020b.

28. This argument is forwarded in Pyle, "Village Social Relations." For concrete evidence that the property taken from deserters was actually given to soldier families, see esp. pp. 334–343.

29. In the month of January 1921 alone, *after the end of the Civil War proper,* property was confiscated from 20,739 deserter families and 2,254 concealers. In addition, families and concealers paid 217,414,918 rubles in fines. Report from Central Desertion Commission. Completely secret. March 11, 1921. RTsKhIDNI f. 5, op. 1, d. 2452, l. 41.

30. Appeal of Iosif Sergeevich Drozhzhin to Appeals Court of Supreme Court of RSFSR. October 19, 1919. GARF f. r-1005, op. 2, d. 11, l. 19b.

31. For more on the importance of the family ideal in the Red Army, see von Hagen, *Soldiers in the Proletarian Dictatorship*, pp. 78, 282.

32. V. Akulinin, *Znachenie voennoi sluzhby i obiazannosti soldata: molodym liudiam, prizyvaemym na sluzhbu tsariu i otechestvu,* 2d ed. (Kherson: Gub. tip., 1913), pp. 28–29.

33. M. I. Dragomirov, "Iz soldatskoi pamiatki," in M. I. Dragomirov, *Izbrannye trudy: voprosy vospitaniia i obucheniia voisk,* ed. L. G. Beskrovnyi (Moscow: Voenizdat, 1956), p. 43.

34. This is the terminology (borrowed in turn from Freud) used by Lynn Hunt, *The Family Romance of the French Revolution* (Berkeley: University of California Press, 1992). See also Elizabeth Jones Hemenway, "Mother Russia and the Crisis of the Russian National Family: The Puzzle of Gender in Revolutionary Russia," *Nationalities Papers* 25, no. 1 (1997): 103–121.

35. The indispensable source for biographical details on military specialists is A. G. Kavtaradze's lovingly detailed *Voennye spetsialisty na sluzhbe respubliki sovetov, 1917–1920 g.g.* (Moscow: Nauka, 1988).

36. A. Neznamov, "K nachalu zimnikh zaniatii [1906]," in A. Neznamov, *Tekushchie voennye voprosy (sbornik statei)* (St. Petersburg: Khudozhestvennaia pechat', 1909), pp. 105–106.

37. Ibid., p. 106.

38. "Ob"iavlenie voiny doblestnoi i velikoi russkoi armii." Circular from Stepanov (Duty General of the Staff of Armies on the Northern Front). January 18, 1916. RGVIA f. 2003, op. 2, d. 784, l. 261.

39. Petition from reservists stationed in the city of Nikolsk-Ussurite. n/d but after the September 1915 reservist mobilization. RGVIA f. 2000, op. 3, d. 2694, l. 73.

40. "Zemnaia pros'ba krest'ianstva." Sent to State Duma. August 5, 1915. RGIA f. 1278, op. 5, d. 1193, l. 106.

41. Telegram from representatives of fifteen counties near Karkaralov to the Chair of the State Duma. August 30, 1916. RGIA f. 1278, op. 5, d. 1234, l. 41, 42.

42. Telegram from Kiev Garrison committee (Lt. Col Ottskii and Private Task) to Rodzianko (Duma). March 15, 1917. RGIA f. 1278, op. 5, d. 1257, l. 82.

43. Allan Wildman, *The End of the Russian Imperial Army: The Old Army and the Soldiers' Revolt (March-April 1917)* (Princeton, N.J.: Princeton University Press, 1980), p. 225.

44. On fraternal ideas in new volunteer units, see "Plan formirovaniia revoliutsionnykh batalionov iz volonterov tyla." Approved by Brusilov May 23, 1917. RGVIA f. 400, op. 19, d. 182, l. 6.

45. Wildman, *End of Russian Imperial Army*, pp. 279, 379–380.

46. See for instance the congratulatory telegram from Poznanskii (Moscow Soviet) to Podvoiskii (RVSR) sending the Red Army a "fraternal socialist greeting" on the taking of Kazan'. September 12, 1918. RGVA f. 3, op. 1, d. 92, l. 33.

47. "Equality" in the army context, of course, never meant the absence of leaders or of orders but meant an equality before the nation and hence the need for equality of respect and for mutual relations.

48. All these included in "Polozhenie o demokratizatsii armii." Order signed by Supreme Commander N. Krylenko. December 3, 1917. RTsKhIDNI f. 5, op. 1, d. 2, l. 27–28.

49. Instruction to the delegate of the transport division of the 136th infantry division in Petrograd and to the comrade people's commissar for the explanation of questions raised by a general meeting of citizens in the transport division of the 136th infantry division. January 23, 1918. GARF f. r-1235, op. 79, d. 27, l. 125.

50. Letter from Ivan Kuzmin (peasant in Altai province) to Trotskii. August 22, 1920. RGVA f. 11, op. 8, d. 692, l. 262.

51. "Pervyi den' iavki," n/a. In newspaper *Krasnyi novobranets* (one-day newspaper published by the political department of the Saratov Rifle Division and the political secretary of the Provincial Military Commissariat). May 3, 1924. In RGVA f. 9, op. 28s, d. 865, l. 229.

52. From very early on in the revolution, peasants used fraternal rhetoric. See declarations cited by Figes, *Peasant Russia*, pp. 154, 175.

53. Appeal from Pavel Tsymbal to Kalinin. August 1918. GARF f. r-1005, op. 2, d. 11, l. 6.

54. "Pochemu dezertir vrag trudiashchikhsia?" Discussion topic #4 sent out to political workers by PUR in 1922 for use with new recruits. RGVA f. 9, op. 28s, d. 403, l. 43.

55. See for instance "Otchet o deiatel'nosti voennogo komissariata goroda Moskvy s 9 marta 1918 po 1 oktobria 1919." RGVA f. 33988, op. 1 d. 25, l. 61; also see appeal to all officials in the "free and independent soviet republic of Latvia." n/d but late 1918 or early 1919. GARF f. r-393, op. 1, d. 37, l. 80b.

56. Resolution of the 148th Rifle Regiment in the 17th Rifle Division. December 6, 1918. GARF f. r-1235, op. 79, d. 2, l. 137.

57. For examples of the use of brotherhood as a model for ethnic relations, see PUR's urging to train soldiers of "laborers of all nations and ethnicities in a fraternal spirit," more specifically to "reinforce the agitation and propaganda work in the army

to strengthen the idea of fraternity and the solidarity of the peoples of the USSR . . . that the RKKA is not a Great Russian or a Russian army, but the army of the USSR." Resolutions on national question in Red Army affirmed at a conference of leading political workers of the Caucasian Red-banner Army. October 13, 1923. RGVA f. 9, op. 28s, d. 324, l. 205–2050b.

58. Terry Martin sees the fraternal metaphor as much weaker than the "friendship" metaphor that would replace it. Terry Martin, "An Affirmative Action Empire: Ethnicity and the Soviet State, 1923–1938" (Ph.D. diss., University of Chicago, 1996), p. 919.

59. Indeed, it is a sign of just how pervasive the fraternal rhetoric was that as late as 1927 a group of Pioneers wrote, "Dear brother I. V. Stalin, we send you *(tebe)* our fraternal Pioneer greeting and wish you success in your work." Letter from the Poltava detachment of Young Pioneers to Stalin. n/d but received in Moscow on May 30, 1927. RTsKhIDNI f. 17, op. 85, d. 504, l. 17.

To Count, to Extract, and to Exterminate

Population Statistics and Population Politics in Late Imperial and Soviet Russia

IN THE LATE SUMMER AND EARLY FALL OF 1925, Soviet forces conducted a massive military operation throughout the Chechen autonomous republic, employing more than seven thousand troops, two dozen artillery pieces, and eight airplanes. In the course of the campaign, they subjected 101 of the region's 242 communities to artillery and machine-gun fire and bombed a further sixteen from the air. One, Urus-Martan aul, the very same settlement at which the Chechen autonomous republic had been declared in 1923, was hit by nine hundred artillery shells, as well as by air bombardment. One might present this campaign as Russian imperialism in a Soviet guise or, alternately, as a specifically Soviet form of ethnic repression. But the explicit goal of all this violence was "the extraction of the bandit element," which, according to the campaign's operational summary, was concluded with satisfaction.[1]

The purpose of this chapter is to examine how Soviet officials came to think in terms of "extracting elements" from the population and to analyze the sciences and techniques that made this goal possible. This story is not simply a Russian or Soviet one but is rather a trans-European one.[2] The idea of extracting "elements" of the population first became conceptually and practically possible only with the rising concern throughout the nineteenth century for a realm termed "the social" and with the emergence of technologies for measuring and acting upon this realm. The rise of military statistics, in Russia and throughout Europe, was a critical link in this more general process. Experience in Europe's colonies provided a crucial testing ground for ideas about manipulating populations as social aggregates, in the process transforming these technologies from abstract to applied disciplines. And, finally, the First World War brought many of these measures back from the colonies to their European home and, in doing so, removed previous geographic and conceptual limits on the use of violence.[3]

In seeking to extract "bandit elements" from the Chechen population, the Soviet state was explicitly engaging in "population politics." Of course, states had always acted on the people they ruled over. But the nineteenth century saw an increasingly self-conscious attention to the "population" as an object of policy, reflected in the emergence of the concept of "population politics." New disciplines first constituted and then typed collectivities within the population as component parts of a social field, with each being ascribed distinct qualitative features. One corollary to this mapping was the desire to excise and expunge those segments typed as somehow "harmful" or "unreliable." States now sought to know and to categorize their subjects, in the belief that knowing "the population" would make it possible to ameliorate their conditions, diminish their restlessness, and strengthen their character. Statistics were thus not a descriptive endeavor but were intended as a tool for acting on society. Ian Hacking, a leading historian of statistics as a discipline, notes that the era of statistical enthusiasm, 1830–1848, was bracketed by two revolutions.[4] The mid–nineteenth century thus saw the emergence of both the population as a discrete aggregate and the social realm as a sphere for intervention. In addition to redefining the object of governance and state intervention, this social field also explicitly related the individual to the larger social body. New disciplines such as statistics and economics, and later anthropology and criminology, shifted from the traditional metaphoric relationship between the individual and the body politic to an argument that there now existed an actual and explicit correlation between the individual and the social body. Thus, the health or sickness of individuals represented a threat to the larger body social in a way it had not for the body politic.[5]

In Russia, as throughout Europe, the nineteenth century witnessed the rise of population politics and the disciplines and technologies predicated on it. The critical discipline of statistics, adhering to standards laid down by international statistical congresses, came to define "social processes" as the preeminent object of inquiry for Russian state actors. Transposing Western sociological paradigms and ideas of state intervention, Russian officials and administrators came to believe that the observation of the social ought to guide political decisions, and statistics became the preeminent means of political intervention in this emerging social sphere.[6] In the years leading up to 1917, textbooks on subjects such as law and statistics noted their fields' shift toward a greater emphasis on the social.[7] By 1909, a Russian encyclopedia forthrightly defined "population politics," a term originally derived from the German, "which is engaged in solving those problems of social life which flow from [statistical] facts and their regularity, and in particular, relating to questions of government intervention in that sphere."[8] The Soviet state, in a guidebook published in 1920 for establishing statistics courses at the local level, declared bluntly that statistics were "a tool for governing and organizing the state" and that the primary object of statistical analysis was to be the "social mass."[9]

The specialized discipline of military geography and statistics played a critical role in constituting the social field in late imperial Russia, shaping how both administrators and the educated public viewed the population.[10] Through a decades-long, ongoing series of empire-wide and local studies of the empire's inhabitants, military statistics transformed them from a hitherto amorphous "people" into a well-defined "population." Military statistics played a major role both in the rise of ethnography and in the administrative categorization of people according to ethnicity. It also widely disseminated the idea that "the population" comprised discrete "elements" that could be manipulated for reasons of state. But the discipline was significant beyond being one of the earliest and most influential representations of "the population." Military statistics, a required subject at the General Staff Academy, taught generations of Russian administrators and military men that the empire's population comprised different component elements and that these elements represented a state resource.

New social disciplines such as statistics certainly did not produce reality out of thin air. Statistics and concerns about the newly conceived "social realm" served as a type of feedback loop. Emerging concerns about certain social issues, such as poverty and urban living conditions, led people to employ statistics to understand the underlying dynamic of these problems. Statistics then focused the attention of state officials on particular developments, freezing these processes into a form state officials believed they could then manipulate and act on. Of course, statistical representation often did not correspond neatly with the reality it purported to describe. However, by claiming to "scientifically" portray various social processes, statistics contributed to officials' belief that they could grasp and manipulate such processes. In this sense, military statistics in Russia solidified and gave content to an understanding of "ethnicity" in a manner anologous to what state officials and public activists did for "class" within European cities or what colonial administrations did for caste in India.[11]

Military statistics were one of the first attempts by the imperial state to catalogue its population. As writers in the late nineteenth century pointed out tirelessly, earlier imperial census "revisions" were concerned more with fiscal issues, namely taxable units ("souls") than with all individuals who constituted the population. In contrast, imperial military statistics, informed by the rise of statistics throughout the rest of Europe, focused on the population itself as the object of inquiry. Between 1837 and 1854 (Hacking's "age of statistical enthusiasm," 1830–1848), officers of the imperial General Staff compiled three editions of military-statistical overviews on each of the sixty-nine provinces and territories of European Russia. The founder of this new discipline was Dmitrii Alekseevich Miliutin. Having graduated from the imperial military academy (the future Nicholas General Staff Academy) and after serving a long tour of duty in the Caucasus, he had taken a tour of Europe in 1845. Miliutin then took over the teaching of military geography at the imperial General Staff Academy, where he developed the discipline of "military statistics."[12] Inspired by impressions gained in his travels and in his study of the Prussian army, Miliutin insisted on the significance of statistics as a discipline and the need for a specialized offshoot, to be termed military statistics. He looked to the newly emerging social sciences as the foundations of this new discipline. Henceforth, military statistics and geography (which encompassed the population) would occupy a prominent place in the curriculum of the General Staff Academy, with fully one-quarter of the students' coursework devoted to this subject. As one of the five primary subjects of study, military statistics took precedence over such secondary subjects as tactics and foreign languages.[13] General Staff officers, having had military statistics drilled into their heads, graduated and took up key military and administrative posts.

Military statistics arose alongside, and in dialogue with, an entire spectrum of new "social disciplines," such as ethnography, anthropology, and public health.[14] Many scholars and ethnographers were themselves imperial administrators or military men, and it was the "administrative distinctions of the tsarist regime [that] accounted for ethnicity."[15] Indeed, nearly all the leading ethnographers of the empire's western provinces were military men, as would later also be the case in Central Asia.[16] But, whereas ethnography evolved as a preeminently literary pursuit, statistics conceived of itself as a science and set about constructing the Russian empire as an edifice of numbers.[17]

Military statistics established a grid of ethnicity for the Russian empire and disaggregated the population into ethnic categories. In addition to tabulating the population by estate and occupation, the overviews of each province included extensive ethnographic descriptions of the local population's lifestyles and customs. The volumes also tabulated the population by ethnicity, with several including ethnographic maps. At this stage, of course, ethnicity was not a standardized administrative term, but military statistics first began to give quantitative content to this category.

As many administrators noted, the significance of military statistics became all the greater with the 1874 military reforms, which were orchestrated by the erstwhile theorist and professor of military statistics Dmitrii Miliutin. Miliutin, having disaggregated the population through the discipline of military statistics, now, as minister of war, sought to employ this knowledge to transform this newly delineated object, "the population." The military reforms were intended not only to strengthen the army but equally to use the army as a tool for intervening in the social domain. Contemporaries wrote worriedly about the lack of statistical data required for properly managing this process of social engineering. Several studies in this period invoked the same passage in the tsar's 1874 manifest introducing universal conscription: "the power of states is found not only in the number of forces, but preeminently in their moral and intellectual qualities." Proponents of more and better statistics interpreted the tsar's words to mean that one had first to know how such qualities were distributed among the population before they could be used effectively. Statistics—military and otherwise—were essential to this project.[18] Indeed, issues related to universal military conscription, introduced in 1874, were a driving force behind the first "universal" census of the Russian empire in 1897, which was explicitly contrasted to the essentially fiscal goals of the earlier revisions.[19] Even after the universal census, officers of the General Staff diligently continued to catalog the empire's population and disaggregate it into its requisite elements.

In the final years of the empire, military statistics ceased to be a discipline narrowly restricted to General Staff officers. From 1903, military statistics and geography became a mandatory subject in all cadet schools, and in 1907 their instruction was extended to all secondary military schools. Thus, in the decade before the First World War, an entire generation of students in military schools studied military statistics and geography from a welter of new textbooks, authored primarily by General Staff officers serving in various military schools.[20] These textbooks held that "Man was, is, and will remain the primary instrument of warfare. . . . *The population, then, which makes up the armed forces and provides its replacements, is the essential geographic datum for determining [military] might.*"[21] But how to evaluate this datum? According to military statistics, "The ethnic composition of the population has primary significance among the factors conditioning the categories of a country's population in a military sense. . . . An ideal population is a monoethnic population, with one language."[22] From these principles, military statisticians deduced that the empire's ethnic Russian core was healthy and reliable but that the composition of the empire's peripheries was "undesirable" and "unreliable." One textbook author, V. R. Kannenberg, cited the racial theorist Ernest Renan as an authority on the tendency of the Jewish population to separateness and pointed with displeasure to the distribution of ethnicities on the empire's peripheries:

> The further we move from the central Russian core to the peripheries, the population density decreases and its ethnic composition becomes more and more diverse, and the percentage of the Russian element [*sic*] in it decreases. . . . It is evident that such a composition of the population on the peripheries is impossible to consider advantageous in a political or in a military sense. Without even speaking of cases of military conflicts on the territory of these peripheries, [the composition of the population] is unfavorable even in peacetime.[23]

As military statisticians disaggregated the "population" into its component "elements," they increasingly ascribed qualitative traits to each. Unsurprisingly, Russians were deemed patriotic and loyal; Jews were described as unpatriotic, greedy, and selfish, Poles and Muslims, as alien and unreliable.[24] In studies of the Far East, Russian military statisticians, public activists, and government officials all singled out Chinese, both imperial subjects and aliens alike, as a particular threat. In addition to their growing numbers, the military men identified Chinese, like Jews, with commerce and the market, thereby conflating ethnic stereotypes with apprehension about the modern world.[25] In short, by the turn of the twentieth century, and especially after 1905, ethnicity increasingly became the preeminent category by which military statistics determined the quality and reliability of the population's various elements.[26] Ominous in this development was the statisticians' manifest preference for homogeneity and their tendency to essentialize these "elements" as having innate features.

In classrooms, military statistics was an abstract science. General Staff officers made it an applied science when they went forth to campaign and rule, especially in the Russian empire's expanding colonial territories. Like their European counterparts, Russia's administrators in the colonies—especially in regard to the Caucasus and Central Asia—enjoyed far greater latitude and powers than officials in the metropole. Colonial officials could therefore act to an unparalled degree to implement their social imaginary. Military statistics, for Russia as well as for other colonial powers, proved to be one of the key devices for projecting nineteenth-century European modelings of "society" on non-European reality. All European powers engaged in extensive military statistical studies of their own colonies: the English in India and Central Asia;[27] the French in North Africa and Indochina;[28] and the United States in Cuba and even China.[29] Officers of one power read and learned from the work of fellow officer-statisticians, thereby making military statistics a cross-fertilized hybrid of European sociomilitary thinking. Russian military journals explicitly compared the British experience in India and the French experience in Algeria with their own campaigns in the Caucasus. Indeed, the terms the Russians employed for the Algerian Kabyles [*gortsy*] and for their mountain communities [*auly*] were the identical to the terms for the Caucasian mountaineers and their communities.[30] One officer-participant in the 1860–1864 campaigns in the Northern Caucasus described Algeria as "a miniature of the Caucasus. In our Algeria, everything—the nature and the people—far exceeded the size of French Algeria," an observation highlighted by the book's reviewer in *Voennyi sbornik*.[31]

When Soviet forces shelled Chechen auls (mountain communities) in 1925 to extract the "bandit element," they were returning to a region that had already served as a testing ground for population politics. Dmitrii Alekseevich Miliutin, the founder of the discipline of military statistics in Russia, left his post as professor at the General Staff Academy in 1856 to return to the Caucasus, this time as chief of staff to Alexander II's close friend Prince Alexander Ivanovich Bariatinskii, newly appointed viceroy of the Caucasus and commander-in-chief of the Caucasian theater. There, as Bariatinskii's chief of staff, he orchestrated a systematic operation to finally subjugate the Caucasus after several decades of warfare.[32] One of the measures he championed was the expulsion of the native inhabitants and their replacement by a Russian population through the systematic and state-sponsored establishment of Cossack settlements. In an 1857 memorandum, Miliutin wrote: "The Europeans' colonization of America brought in its wake the extermination of almost all of the original inhabitants there; but in our age, obligations to humanity require that we take measures in advance for securing the existence even of those tribes hostile to us, which for reasons of state we force from their lands." Defending his proposal against critics, Miliutin described the aims of his policy: "resettling [the mountaineers] is proposed not as a *means* towards clearing lands which allegedly are insufficient for new Cossack settlements; on the contrary, it is the *goal*, to which end the territories presently occupied by our foe will be settled by [Cossacks], by which means the numerical force of the hostile native population will be reduced." Russian forces were not to clear land in order to settle Cossacks; rather, they were to settle Cossacks so as to clear the land of the native population.[33] In 1858, Alexander II approved the plan for deporting hostile mountain tribes to the Kuban plains and colonizing both sides of the Caucasus chain with Cossack settlements, which Miliutin described in an 1862 report as the "Russian element."[34] Over the next six years, Russian forces would conduct a systematic effort, planned and overseen by Miliutin, to pursue this state policy.

The campaigns of Graf Nikolai Ivanovich Evdokimov, commander of one of the columns under Bariatinskii's command, were a watershed in the emerging imperial policy of demographic conquest. Following the capture of Shamil in 1859, Russian planners feared that Western powers would seek to agitate among the mountain tribes, as they had done during the Crimean War. With Russian naval strength in the Black Sea limited by treaty to several revenue cutters, Russian planners discussed plans for the total subjugation of the Caucasus, and especially for clearing the Black Sea littoral. In late August 1860, Prince Bariatinskii chaired a staff meeting to discuss the goals for future operations and how to achieve them. Evdokimov, who declared that fear was the only possible way to deal with the mountain tribesmen, proposed a plan to drive all the mountain tribesmen in the Western Caucasus theater from their homes, either to the plains of Kuban' and Stavropol or to Turkey, and then to settle the region with Russians. The war council approved these measures without dissension. Miliutin departed directly from this meeting for St. Petersburg, where as war minister he would oversee the conduct of operations in this theater.[35] In a report on the last stage of military operations, Evdokimov declared that he had achieved his goal: by early June 1864, "the expulsion of natives of the Western Caucasus had been completed."[36]

While the Russian empire had earlier practiced "demographic warfare," contemporaries saw this campaign's breadth and systematic nature as marking a new departure. These measures aimed, one participant wrote, to subjugate the Caucasus "to such a finality of result as had never previously been seen."[37] Such goals did not rule out humanitarian considerations, if they contributed to the final end. In early April 1862, Miliutin, now minister of war, proposed that the impoverished Russian treasury help fund the emigration of mountain tribesmen from the Caucasus to their coreligionists in the Ottoman Empire. The "Commission for resettling the mountaineers to Turkey," in its concluding report, fastidiously tabulated that between 1862 and 1865 the Russian treasury had expended "289,678 rubles, 17 kopeks" to facilitate the transfer.[38] Miliutin had written in 1857 about taking humanitarian "measures for securing the existence even of tribes hostile to us," but his "resettlement" proposal was intended to induce as many mountain tribesmen as possible to leave the Western Caucasus. Evdokimov and other field commanders heartily approved of the measure.[39] For purely tactical reasons, Miliutin continued to prefer the "voluntary resettlement" of mountain tribesmen (induced, of course, by merciless military operations) to forced deportation, but he sanctioned forced deportations whenever the situation required it.[40]

The 1860–1864 campaigns in the Western Caucasus, which Miliutin conceived and supervised, represented a major departure in "population politics." The campaign's violence was not simply the by-product of military operations. To "cleanse" undesirable populations in the Caucasus, Russian forces employed violence in an instrumental manner. Contemporaries and participants conceded as much. At the August 1860 war council, Evdokimov stated outright that "terror" was the only way to influence these tribes. Instructions issued to field units (the following is from July 1864) were quite explicit on this point: "The advance ought to be conducted as decisively as possible, in order from the very first to produce terror among the mountaineers and to demonstrate to them the impossibility of resistance; to reduce their homes to ashes; to treat the inhabitants like prisoners; and to take prisoner only those who give themselves up."[41] Rostislav Fadeev, an officer-participant in the Western Caucasus campaign under Evdokimov, explained the methods of the campaign equally frankly in an 1865 article published in *The Moscow Gazette*. Fearing that the local population would side with Russia's foes in a future war, the state's goal had been to "cleanse" the region and turn it into Russian land. "Of course," Fadeev continues, "a war conducted to this end would cause desperate resistance, and thus demanded from our side redoubled energy; *it was necessary to exterminate a significant portion of the Trans-Kuban population, in order to bring the other portion to lay down its arms unconditionally*" [my emphasis—P.H.].[42]

To carry out these goals, Russian forces descended on mountain communities, or auls, in order to burn them to the ground, regardless of whether they had offered resistance. One participant recalled that during such operations, "on clear days, the sun often disappeared on account of numerous fires." This same officer noted that Russian forces accomplished their task with little trouble because the inhabitants offered absolutely no resistance, and hence soldiers could devote themselves fully to burning houses.[43] If the community's inhabitants had not taken to flight, they were either taken prisoner or, at times, simply slaughtered. One British diplomatic report described how a Russian detachment captured the village Toobeh, along with about one hundred inhabitants. "After these had surrendered themselves prisoners," the report claims, "they were almost all massacred by the Russian troops. Among the victims were two women in an advanced state of pregnancy and five children. The detachment in question belongs to Count Evdokimoff's army."[44] Participants freely admitted that women and children formed the vast majority of those taken prisoner.[45]

However, in the words of one British observer, Russia's policy, "though unrelenting, has not been deliberately sanguinary. There was no desire to exterminate the people; the object was to remove them." Geins, who participated in the operations, frankly described their goal to be "depopulation,"[46] not extermination. In this the Russian forces were successful. "The newly conquered region offered an unusual sight at the end of May [1864], in June, and later," recalled one observer.[47]

> One could look down from the very highest peak on all sides: one saw numerous beautiful valleys, chains of mountains, rivers and streams; among the old fruit gardens, which resembled the forest, there were remnants of former dwellings. But it was all dead, there was not a soul to be seen anywhere. . . . One didn't want to believe that throughout this immense territory, as far as the eye could see from the great peak, there was no one around; but that was indeed the case.

An official report on the resettlement operation concluded that "[i]n this year, 1864, a fact was achieved that has almost no precedent in history: a huge mountaineer population . . . suddenly disappears from this land; a striking transformation proceeds in these lands—not one of those mountaineer inhabitants remains on their previous place of settlement, they all seek to abandon the region so as to surrender it to the new Russian settlement."[48]

Russian officials conducted a series of statistical studies in 1864 and 1865 to determine how many mountaineers now inhabited the region. From these studies, and from reports of the resettlement commission, Russian officials estimated that, out of an original population of roughly 505,000, between 400,000 and 480,000 mountaineers had departed.[49] Scholars have subsequently estimated the total number of mountaineers who either were deported or who "emigrated" under compulsion during the 1860–1864 operations at between 500,000 and 700,000. In all, between 1859 and 1879, two million native inhabitants left the Caucasus. It is estimated that one-quarter of them perished in the process.[50]

Having cleansed the region, Russian officials then planned to settle it with Russians. As Fadeev expressed it, "The Russian population was meant not just to crown the region's subjugation; it was to serve as one of the main means of conquest."[51] Clearly, it is not anachronistic to speak of the imperial regime's "population politics" in the Caucasus. In the aftermath of the Crimean War, the Russian state pursued a similar, if less systematic, expulsion policy in the Crimea.[52]

Following the conquest of the Caucasus, Central Asia became the next arena for the development of colonial techniques. Here, as well, Russians drew parallels with other European colonial measures, such as the French conquest of Algeria. One of the executors of Russian imperial conquest in Central Asia was Aleksei Nikolaevich Kuropatkin, who served the Russian empire for nearly forty years in a variety of high posts. Having begun his career in Central Asia, Kuropatkin then entered the General Staff academy.[53] In 1874 he finished first in his class and for this performance was awarded a study tour in 1875. On that tour he spent an extensive period in Algeria, where the French had just four years previously suppressed the great Kabyle insurrection in Algeria, confiscating vast tracts of the best land.[54] From Algeria, Kuropatkin contributed a series of reports to the Russian journal *Military Courier* and later published several works on French operations in Algeria, including a "military-statistical overview" of Algeria. This exchange, however, was not entirely in one direction. French officers, such as France's leading theorist of colonial warfare, Hubert Lyautey, devoted particular attention to the Russian conquest of both the Caucasus and Central Asia, including the exploits of Kuropatkin's mentor, General Skobelev.[55]

Despite their indisputable orientalist fascination with Central Asia, Russian military men did not approve of the region's population in a military sense. Not surprisingly, both specialized military-statistical studies and the more general textbooks decried the local population's heterogeneity and the lack of a firm Russian element.[56] One study of the Semirech'e region in Turkestan concluded dryly that "one cannot term the [composition of the population] favorable, since the Russian element comprises less than fifty percent . . . from a military point of view, one must recognize the composition [of the population] to be unfavorable." This study then counseled that "the question of colonizing the Semirech'e region with a Russian element is most important in a military sense" and suggested that officials pursue an "intensified colonization of the region by the Russian ethnicity, even if at the expense of the natives."[57] This proposal echoed the proposals of M. I. Veniukov, who was one of Russia's leading specialists on Central Asia and, typically, also a General Staff graduate and former participant in the 1860–1864 Russian campaigns in the Caucasus. From the 1870s on, Veniukov wrote in official publications about the need to think about the future "ethnographic physiognomy of Central Asia . . . and of strengthening our own ethnic predominance in that vast country." Veniukov's program was quite concrete: he offered specific recommendations for achieving the quasi-scientific management of the population's component elements. By strengthening the "Russian element" through colonization, it would be possible, he claimed, "to influence strongly the transformation of the physiognomy of the entire country."[58]

And these views extended far beyond the offices of imperial administrators. The volume on Turkestan in V. P. Tian-Shanskii's popular *Full Description of Our Fatherland,* relying in no small part on military-statistical studies, fully shared the conceptual categories of military statisticians. This ostensible "description" of Turkestan contained a veritable program for state manipulation of the region's population. It was desirable, commented the author, "to strengthen the Russian element" by pursuing a coordinated policy of colonization.[59] The imperial state pursued precisely these measures. The government sponsored a series of studies to determine how best to direct a "Russian element" into these regions, and in 1905 it formed a settlement region in Semirech'e. One imperial inspector described colonization officials here as "fanatics" who were often at odds with local administrators and who were "intent on flooding the country with emigrants. . . . Here at last [colonization officials] were in a land which seemed to them to offer unlimited scope for applying their ideals." When these colonization officials needed to calculate how to parcel out the population upon the land, they simply reached for a map prepared by General Staff officers.[60]

But military statistics did not just describe the population to officials. They also suggested measures for operating upon it. The second volume of the 1910 military-statistical description of the Semirech'e region was the secret strategic overview. It contained guidelines for various potential military contingencies, including "attributes of the region in case of a popular uprising." With great foresight, the volume predicted that "if military units are dispatched to face a foreign foe, a rebellion might rapidly spread." In this event, Russian officers were explicitly directed to rely on the Russian settlers and to anticipate partisan warfare from the native insurgents. In that case, the guidebook suggested Russian forces take hostages from the among the insurgents' families. Hostage taking, it counseled, would separate the more moderate "elements" from the incorrigible ones and would "compel the more moderate elements of the population to return to a peaceful life. The remaining incorrigible element," it continued, "would either have to be exterminated [*sic*] or driven across the border." The volume concluded with the predictable suggestion that the surest way to improve the region's strategic situation was to colonize it with "the Russian element."[61]

It was precisely in accordance with these prewar guidelines that Russian forces operated in suppressing the 1916 rebellion.[62] The rebellion was touched off when the imperial regime, facing a manpower shortage in the First World War, attempted to draft previously exempt local inhabitants for service in labor battalions, thereby exacerbating existing tensions over the regime's colonial policy. The man appointed to to suppress the rebellion was Aleksei Kuropatkin.[63] As suggested by the 1910 guidelines, Russian commanders formed volunteer detachments from among the recently arrived "Russian element" and extensively employed "punitive detachments." Superiors left these detachments with no doubts as to how they should operate. General M. A. Fol'dbaum, military governor of Semirech'e, directed his subordintates to employ the measures he himself had sanctioned: exterminate insurgent settlements to the last man, burn the nomadic camps, and drive off the livestock.[64] Fol'dbaum similarly ordered Police Sergeant Bakurevish's detachment "to eliminate all the Kirghiz you come across, and burn their auls," which it then did. The commander of the Pishpek garrison mobilized all European inhabitants and formed them into punitive detachments, "the purpose of which will be to instill terror in the native population. How you do that will be explained to you, but for now it is a military secret."[65] Meanwhile, flying detachments were instructed "to drive the Kirghiz into the mountains and to destroy them there."[66]

This violence led to an official Duma investigation, headed by Alexander Kerensky.[67] After touring the region, Kerensky reported that Russian punitive detachments had burned native settlements to the ground and had killed the local population without regard for age or sex. He testified that "nursing babies were eliminated, as were old women and old men." Kerensky concluded that local inhabitants were "exterminated, by the tens of thousands, in an organized and systematic manner."[68] One local newspaper had reported that "all the insurgents have been driven into the kind of mountainous regions where they will soon, on account of hunger and exposure, feel the full consequences of their insane rebellion. Reports are already coming in about their suffering and illness among them, but the forces have been ordered to offer no mercy." As a result of such measures, by January 1917 the native population of Semirech'e had fallen by more than 20 percent, with certain districts experiencing a drop of 66 percent.[69]

Russian authorities did not seek simply to reimpose order upon the insurgent regions. In the aftermath of the rebellion, they sought to eliminate the cause of unrest. Relying on their science of society, they sought to uproot what they believed were the rebellion's social preconditions. Kuropatkin, overseeing the suppression as military governor of Turkestan, confided to his diary on October 12, 1916, that "I am thinking all the time over how to settle affairs in Semirech'e, how to reestablish a peaceful life in that rich region, how to reconcile Russians with the Kirghiz. I am coming to the conclusion that it will be necessary to separate, where possible, these ethnicities for a long time to come." He then indicated the regions he thought needed to be made Russian. Four days later, Kuropatkin held a meeting to formulate plans for expelling the Kirghiz from certain districts of Semirech'e and for placing Russian settlers on their lands, in order to form districts "with a purely Russian population." Kuropatkin himself indicated that the goal was to create a space inhabited by a homogeneous and reliable "element." Instead of expelling Kirghiz and resettling Russians wherever unrest had occurred, he adjusted the boundaries of areas subject to deportation so as "to create a territory with a Russian population isolated from the Kirghiz not only within ethnographic but also geographic boundaries." In his final report to Nicholas II, in late February 1917, Kuropatkin noted that plans had already been completed and sent to the war minister for confiscating native land in Semirech'e "for the purposes of strengthening the Russian element in the Turkestan area" and forming homogeneous and purely Russian regions.[70] It seemed as if the long-standing program for consolidating the region through population management was about to be realized. Only the 1917 revolution prevented implementation of Kuropatkin's plan to expel all Kirghiz from broad stretches of the Chu valley and from the area around the Issyk-Kul lake.[71]

While it is certainly true that the Russian empire's self-perception regarding its colonial holdings differed in general terms from the "character and ideology" of other Western colonial powers,[72] Russian colonial *practices* must be seen within the spectrum of other European colonial measures. Miliutin, Kuropatkin, and other leading Russian military men studied the colonial practices of other European powers, with special attention to the French experience in Algeria. Russians remained well informed regarding early-twentieth-century developments in colonial military practices. Many of the patterns and methods of violence we commonly identify with the twentieth century in fact were first widely employed during the nineteenth and early twentieth centuries in colonial spaces. Machine guns, barbed wire, certain forms of administrative domination, concentration camps— all emerged or were first employed in the colonial peripheries. Concentration camps for civilians, for instance, were systematically employed for the first time in Cuba by General Valeriano Weyler in 1896–1897.[73] The Russian military observer with Spanish forces, General Staff Colonel I. G. Zhilinskii (subsequently commander of the northwest front in the opening phase of the First World War), reported in great detail on these measures, including the fact that mortality rates among the *reconcentrados* reached 25 to 30 percent. He described such practices as "measures for terrifying the population."[74] The Russian military and the public at large were even better informed regarding the more well-known British use of concentration camps during the Boer War. (Britain's policies became so notorious, however, not because they were unique but, rather, because they received extensive critical attention in the British press and among the public.)[75] The Russian observer to South African forces during the war, Vasilii Gurko, would later serve as Russian commander in chief in 1916, and his report covered British antiinsurgency measures.[76] The Russian press also extensively covered the British camps. The *Courier of Europe,* for instance, described both general British antiinsurgency measures in South Africa and, specifically, British reliance on what were first described as "special closed camps." Transposing the English word, these camps soon came to be known instead as "concentration camps." The *Courier of Europe* opined that "it was as if the war's aim was the extermination of the Boers."[77]

Hannah Arendt has suggested that imperialism served as "a preparatory phase for coming catastrophes." Yet, Arendt insists, the horrors of imperialism "were still marked by a certain moderation and controlled by respectability."[78] Colonial violence was geographically circumscribed within colonial territories. All the violence described thus far took place in areas under direct military rule, either in the course of military operations or in colonial regions governed directly by the military.[79] The Revolution of 1905–1907 marked an important intrusion of this targeted state violence into civilian spheres.[80] Yet, before 1914, a conceptual distinction still remained between the military-colonial realms on the one hand and the civilian public sphere on the other.

The First World War re-imported colonial practices of violence back to their homeland, Europe. In the process, however, the war transformed the nature and extent of this violence. The emergence of total war mobilization, breaking down the traditional barrier between the military and the civilian realms, vastly extended preexisting practices of violence into domestic civilian spheres.[81] In Russia, the First World War marked the watershed when the imperial state massively expelled large segments of its own population that had been quasi-scientifically typed over the previous decades as "unreliable." These expulsions were hardly the result of military exigency or local excesses. Throughout Europe, the shift from professional armies to a reserve system—the "nation in arms"—caused all European states increasingly to view any working-age male "enemy alien" as a potential foe. Prewar military guidelines granted Russian military authorities the power, in areas under martial law, to deport individuals to the empire's interior provinces.[82] For decades military statistics had assiduously catalogued "suspect" populations among the empire's own subjects, particularly those of Jewish and

German ethnicity. With the outbreak of hostilities, the Russian military officially sanctioned the taking of civilian hostages from among its own population, both to secure collective loyalty and to ensure prompt compliance with military requisitioning.[83]

From the very first days of the war, Russian imperial authorities engaged in a massive program of compulsory deportations from regions of the front, translating into policy what military statistics had been preaching for decades about the population of these areas.[84] Military authorities oversaw the compulsory deportation of nearly one million of their own subjects from the western provinces and Caucasian borderlands. As the deportations began virtually at the war's outbreak, the ferocity and unexpected length of the conflict cannot explain such policies.

Military statistics undoubtedly incorporated existing anti-Polish, anti-Muslim, and anti-Jewish prejudices. But they then recast these existing prejudices in a new register. Deportation measures toward Jewish subjects during the First World War were not simply the enactment of old-style anti-Judaism. Instead, they reflected the shift from traditional religious stereotypes—anti-Judaism—into a new form of civic anti-Semitism, one not derived primarily from religion and not focusing exclusively on Jews. The Council of Ministers and the General Staff repeatedly disagreed throughout 1915 over the Jewish deportations.[85] The dispute arose precisely out of a clash between the old-style anti-Judaism of traditional bureaucrats, seeking to keep Jews isolated in the Pale of Settlement, and the new-style anti-Semitism of "progressive" military men, identifying whole segments of the population as *politically* and *militarily* unreliable. It was *this* anti-Semitism, and not the supposedly congenital Russian peasant anti-Judaism (as manifested, say, in pogroms), that framed the violence against Jews in the succeeding revolutionary convulsions.

Nor did Russian authorities limit such measures to the territory of their own empire. Relying on Austro-Hungarian censuses, among other sources, Russian military statistics in both specialized, secret analyses and equally in general textbooks had long paid particular attention to the ethnic composition of Austrian Galicia.[86] Austro-Hungarian military statistics had, in fact, come to analogous conclusions and drew up preparatory lists of supposedly unreliable "Russophile" subjects.[87] With the outbreak of the war, both Austro-Hungarian and Russian military authorities then sought preemptively to isolate, remove, or execute outright those portions of the Galician population each considered "unreliable" (Ruthenians for the Austro-Hungarians, Germans and Jews for the Russians).[88]

These measures cannot be justified simply by military necessity. They make sense only if one takes seriously the concept of transforming the population by either injecting elements into it or eliminating certain elements from it. Increasingly, threats to the state were defined in prophylactic terms, as threats to health of the social body. Russian authorities deported "unreliable" populations from the Western border region because they were purported to be an "element" that was "pernicious" and "harmful and dangerous to the Russian people," terminology nearly identical to that later employed to justify Soviet "mass operations" in the 1930s. The goal of such measures was to affect the composition of the population, to "cleanse" regions of specific elements.[89] In the course of the Great War, deportation of "unreliable and harmful elements" simply became part of the conceptual landscape, a landscape that had been mapped by military statistics. On the floor of the Duma, deputies called for the total deportation of Germans, even those who were Russian subjects. In the aftermath of the May 1915 anti-German pogrom in Moscow, the city's appointed head expressed regret that there were simply too many imperial subjects of German descent for them all to fit in a "concentration camp" in the middle of the Volga river.[90] Instead, the Council of Ministers directed military commanders to dispatch deportees to a specified set of interior provinces reserved for each category of deportee (e.g., German colonists, Jewish hostages, and enemy aliens).[91] Of course, the problem then became that this "unreliable element" risked polluting the previously homogeneous and reliable interior provinces. In 1915 Major General M. D. Bonch-Bruevich, chief of staff of the northwestern front, wrote to the *Stavka* chief of staff Ianushkevich that "purely Russian provinces are being completely defiled by elements hostile to us, and therefore the question arises in and of itself of the exact registration of all deported enemy subjects, in order to liquidate without a trace this entire alien element at the end of the war."[92] When the Bolsheviks came to power in October 1917, Bonch-Bruevich became army chief of staff, and played a major role in establishing the Red Army.

Thus, "colonization" policies for injecting "reliable elements" into regions— or, more precisely, policies for deporting certain populations while simultaneously introducing others—were hardly limited to the Caucasus or Central Asia, nor were they a Bolshevik innovation. The imperial state, in its total-war manifestation, extended to the entire political space of the empire practices that had previously been confined to either colonial territories or the "dangerous spaces" of cities. The Russian imperial state's total-war regime had thus elaborated a whole repertoire of practices for operating upon the population in its entirety, practices that were to be carried across the revolutionary divide.[93] While the Provisional Government initially inclined toward a general lifting of restrictions on those Russian subjects who had been deported to distant interior regions, it soon decreed that only military authorities could grant exemptions, and only on a case-by-case basis.[94]

Such punitive policies predicated on population politics, however, were no Russian anomaly but represented instead a particular inflection of a more general European phenomenon. In the decades preceding 1914, Germany also pursued "a state policy, very definitely self-conscious and planned, directed towards changing the population composition by nationality of certain areas of the Prussian kingdom." To this end, it expelled tens of thousands of Jews and Poles as an "unwanted element."[95] German authorities carried over these perceptions and practices to the vast tracts of territory they occupied in the First World War.[96] Pursuing a program to dismember the Russian empire by establishing proxy states, German authorities engaged in extensive ethnographic and statistical studies of the local population, hoping to use the East as a reservoir for dumping displaced populations.[97] To wall off this space, German planners discussed establishing an ethnically cleansed border strip in Poland, cleared of all Slavs and settled by ethnic Germans.[98] *Ober Ost* officials deported large segments of the local population and prevented hundreds of thousands of refugees from returning from Russia.[99] The Hamburg banker Max Warburg argued in 1916 for the establishment of German "colonies" in the Baltic:

> The Latvians would easily be evacuated. In Russia, resettlement is not regarded as cruel in itself. The people are used to it. . . . Those alien [i.e., non-Russian] peoples who are of German descent and are currently so ill-treated can be allowed to move into this area and found colonies. [These] do not need to be integrated into Germany, but must merely be affiliated, albeit with cement, so that their slipping back to the Russian side is ruled out.[100]

There was a clear continuum in German thinking between colonial policies in Africa and plans for the East.[101] *Ober Ost* was staffed by several men who had knowledge of the colonial order in Africa, such as Dr. George Escherich, who had been a colonial administrator in the German Cameroons and who later would head the Freikorps *Organisation Escherich,* which crushed the Bavarian Communist government in Munich in 1919.[102]

During the course of the war, Austria-Hungary also interned and deported hundreds of thousands of its own subjects whom it considered suspect.[103] From occupied Serbia, Austro-Hungarian military officials expelled and interned up to 180,000 inhabitants.[104] Analogous to Germany's proposed border strip in Poland, the Austro-Hungarian Supreme Army Command "requested that a 15-mile zone be established along the borders with Russia, Romania, Serbia, Montenegro, and Italy, and that resident 'foreigners' and politically unreliable inhabitants be removed forcefully. The lands thus depopulated could be settled with invalids and veterans." (As with so much else, Hungary vetoed the proposal.)[105] In its attempt to deal with its suspect Armenian population, Ottoman Turkey went further: it proceeded on a systematized slaughter of those subjects it deemed to be unreliable.[106]

Thus, while significant variations in practice existed, such measures were not anomalies of any one nation, nor did they emerge merely from the exigencies of war. Deportation and "elimination" of those segments of the population deemed unreliable were the application, to varying degrees and in nationally specific ways, of "population politics" as elaborated in the decades before 1914 and first employed, in a circumscribed manner, in the colonies. The First World War then re-imported these practices, and the violence associated with them, back home to Europe and significantly expanded their scope and breadth. The Soviet commanders in charge of the 1925 antibandit operation in Chechnia operated with a set of practices that had first been widely employed in the colonial context. Yet the commanders themselves were all products of the First World War. M. A. Alafuzo, the officer responsible for drawing up plans for the Soviet 1925 antibandit operation in Chechnia, had received his training in the Russian Imperial Army and had graduated from expedited General Staff courses during the First World War. The four subordinates upon whom he relied to carry out the operation had likewise all become officers in the course of the First World War.[107] Their life trajectories underscore William Rosenberg's contention that Bolshevik policies "represented essentially a radical extension, rather than a revolutionary break, with the past."[108]

The First World War did not end neatly on November 11, 1918, or the following summer at Versailles but wound down in a paroxysm of revolutions and a series of civil wars throughout central and eastern Europe. In these civil wars, methods forged for external war over the preceding four years were turned to domestic conflicts. In this light, Russia's civil war might be seen as only the most developed instance of a more extended "European civil war" stretching through and beyond the Great War. The violence of the Russian civil war has often been portrayed simply as the result of the brutal circumstances of the period, or of some violence intrinsic to Russian life. Instead of viewing the violence of the Russian civil war not as something sui generis, however, one might see it instead as the extension of state practices conceived in the nineteenth century and massively implemented in the course of the Great War. Indeed, one early Cheka study of its struggle against banditism in Siberia from 1920 through 1922 noted that "the seven-year experience of war [1914–1921] had a marked impact upon the insurgent movement."[109] Emerging from the experience of total war and sharing a common conceptual matrix for population politics, Whites just as much as Reds reflexively disaggregated the population into "elements" of varying reliability. In 1918, the anti-Soviet government of the Don Territory, a Cossack region, actually passed a decree legally sanctioning the deportation of individuals who opposed its agenda. In the neighboring Kuban' Territory, the anti-Soviet legislature (Rada) went so far as to debate measures to expel all non-Cossacks. One delegate proposed simply killing them all off, instead.[110]

As this Cossack deputy's comment suggests, the Whites, too, practiced a prophylactics of violence on those elements deemed malignant or harmful. Jews were "microbes" or "bacilli," Bolshevism, "a social disease." *Pace* many existing treatments, White application of violence was not "wild" but very well structured. To be sure, anti-Soviet movements invested much less effort than their Soviet counterparts in attempting to articulate the meaning of their actions through textual formulations. Nevertheless, it is quite clear that the use of violence was not arbitrary or incidental, but quite purposeful. One might suggest here an analogy with the German *Freikorps,* who also emerged out of the chaos of the war's end. The ideology of the *Freikorps* was much more an ethos and a style than a coherent doctrine, but it was no less an ideology for that.[111] It is hard to imagine that the slaughter of Jews during the Russian civil wars, totaling 150,000 dead by some estimates, could have occurred *without* some form of ideology—and particularly the virulent linkage drawn between Jews and Communists.[112] Anti-Soviet commanders and foot soldiers believed they knew who their enemies were, and they equally believed they knew what they had to do with such foes. White commanders sifted their POWs, selecting out those they deemed undesirable and incorrigible (Bolsheviks, Jews, Balts, Chinese) and executed these individuals in groups later, a process the Whites described as "filtering."[113] One official of the White counterintelligence agency explained why his agency resorted so frequently to execution: "that which is harmful can never become useful," and, in such cases, "surgery is the best cure." Of course, he counted Jews prominently among those who required such "surgical" excision.[114] This official understood his task in terms of population politics: he believed he was protecting the social body from those individuals who might infect it.

White commanders believed equally in the positive corollary to population politics. Wrangel's chief of staff, Major General Makhrov, a graduate of the General Staff academy, advised him, in April 1920, that the only way to recover the Don region was to return to it the "most active element," meaning those Cossacks who had been evacuated to the Crimea. In proposing to recolonize, as it were, the Don Territory with a reliable and active Cossack element, Makhrov thus proposed an inversion of the Soviet "de-Cossackization" program (discussed later).[115]

Thus, the preconditions and tools for operating on the social body through techniques of violence long predated the Bolshevik regime. Continuity, in disciplinary fields and in personnel, ensured that the template of population politics was carried over into the Soviet period. General Staff officers from the imperial army, for instance, continued to teach the discipline of military statistics at the Soviet General Staff academy.[116] But the Soviets then employed "violence as technique" to fashion the population to a model now refracted through a Marxist lens. Soviet policies, so often portrayed as original and unique in their criminality and ruthlessness, merely shifted preexisting practices from an ethnocultural axis to a class one. Indeed, the conceptual grid of population politics became so prevalent in the Soviet period that the idea of "element" to mean a discrete and qualitatively distinct component of the social realm passed from purely administrative terminology to common usage.[117]

Soviet power, however, set new ends for employing practices drawn from a common European repertoire. Russia's revolution occurred in the midst of total-war mobilization. Institutions and practices of total mobilization were incorporated into the societies and governments of other combatants, but they were dispensed with or subordinated to the existing order once the war was over. In revolutionary Russia, the institutions and practices of total mobilization became the building blocks of a new state and socioeconomic order. Because of both its particular moment of emergence and the nature of Bolshevik ideology, the centralized Soviet state for the duration of its existence would have very few institutional checks in formulating and implementing policy. The revolution, therefore, provided a new matrix for practices that were emerging out of total war. Whereas these tools had originally been devised for use against external foes and intended for use only during the extraordinary period of wartime, the Soviet state transformed the ends to which these practices were deployed. A state committed to the cause of revolution could extend the total-war practices from their previously limited goal of waging war against external enemies to a new, more all-encompassing—and open-ended—goal: the forging of a revolutionary society.

The Bolshevik revolutionary project provided a powerful and original organizing principle for political authority and its techniques of social intervention. From the very first, the Soviet regime sought to practice a science of society, with all that entailed. In 1919, in the midst of a civil war for its very existence, the Soviet state engaged in a policy of "de-Cossackization." This attempt to remove an entire "element" of the population was not some defensive reaction to a hostile group but instead a preemptive attempt to secure Cossack regions for Soviet power by excising putatively counterrevolutionary elements. The party decree laying down this policy explicitly called for the instrumental use of "mass terror" and the outright and "total extermination" of the Cossack elite.[118] A local Soviet official in this period suggested that "until we slaughter all [the Cossacks] and resettle the Don with an external element, there will be no Soviet power."[119] In a policy review, one senior party member expressed as the goal of de-Cossackization "to make the Don healthy" by "exterminating, simply physically destroying the vast portion of Cossacks." And one prong of this officially proclaimed policy of population management was to conduct an "agrarian-resettlement policy."[120] As a direct consequence of this decree, upward of ten thousand people were judicially executed.

However, the regime abjured de-Cossackization within several months and normalized Cossacks as a regular part of the Soviet population. This abrupt shift suggests that what was critical was not the *particular* category itself. Depending on the moment, the category could be Cossacks, officers, bandits, kulaks, or Trotskyite-Japanese agents. Rather, the key feature was the perceptual template that sought to identify particular "elements" as malignancies that needed to be removed, in order both to secure society's health and to refashion it in some idealized image. De-Cossackization thus was simply one instance of a more overarching Soviet propensity for fashioning visions of society by subtraction, as much as by addition.[121]

Soviet officials, in fact, went about reversing the population profile of certain regions by resorting to the very same measures that the tsarist regime had employed to create that profile in the first place. In 1920–1921 the Soviet state sought to reverse the demographic composition in the Caucasus, which itself had been established fifty years earlier by the imperial regime's program to push out the mountaineers. An October 1920 Politburo resolution now decreed the expulsion of thousands of Cossack families as "counterrevolutionaries" and ordered the settlement of mountaineers in their place. While some Cossack communities in the region had recently rebelled against Soviet power, Stalin reported to Lenin in October 1920 that this rebellion merely made the deportation easier by providing "a fitting occasion." In words strikingly similar to Kuropatkin's musings in 1916, Stalin argued that "the cohabitation of Cossacks and mountaineers in one administrative unit has become harmful and dangerous." In the course of the operation, Soviet forces burned Kalinovskaia stanitsa to the ground, entirely "cleansed" Ermolovskaia stanitsa, and deported the entire male population of five stanitsas to the North for forced labor. In all, nine thousand families were subjected to deportation.[122]

Just as in the Caucasus, Soviet policies in Turkestan exhibited a symmetry with earlier imperial colonial measures.[123] Whereas the tsarist regime had proposed deporting native inhabitants of Semirech'e to make room for Russian settlers in 1916–1917, the Soviet state moved to deport the Russian settlers and replace them with native inhabitants. A Politburo decree of June 29, 1920, set forth a policy of "land reform," to be realized through "punitive means of deportation" and the "deportation of the kulak element." However, just as the proposed expulsion of Kirghiz was preempted by the 1917 revolution, an August 1922 Politburo resolution likewise put an end to the systematic deportation of the "Russian element" from Semirech'e.[124]

Whereas the imperial regime had employed such measures largely in colonial spaces and imperial peripheries, total war and civil conflict extended them throughout the Soviet polity, where such practices were employed by Red and White alike. In the course of the civil war, the Soviet state came increasingly to use the term "banditism" as a catch-all category to criminalize and pathologize political action. By conflating political opposition and criminal deviance, this concept suggested that resistance was merely antisocial behavior from which society must be protected. Banditism was defined less as an act than as a social phenomenon. Rather than merely seek to reimpose order, Soviet authorities understood the goal of their struggle against banditism as "removing and exterminating the bandit element." Soviet officials thus viewed banditism (variously described as "a dangerous epidemic" and "a psychological illness") as a symptom pointing to the presence of a deeper problem: the existence of malignant and dangerous elements. Once the symptom of banditism revealed the presence of dangerous elements, cleansing was required, whether or not the insurgency itself had continued. Military operations were therefore conducted explicitly "to remove and eliminate the bandit element" and "to cleanse those regions infected with banditism."[125] The Cheka plan of operations submitted to the Central Committee for the second half of 1921 included a section "on cleansing Samara, Saratov, and Tambov provinces and the Territory of the Volga Germans." The Cheka believed it was essential "to extract all active participants in rebellions from the above-named regions and dispatch them to distant provinces."[126]

The leading theorist and practitioner of antibandit operations was Mikhail Tukhachevskii, whose operation against the Antonov movement in Tambov provided the blueprint for future "antibandit" campaigns. His goal for the campaign, according to a whole welter of official decrees and orders, was first to occupy a space and then to remove, uproot, and exterminate the "bandit element."[127] The microtechniques of coercion—"immediate physical extermination," concentration camps, the taking of hostages—were all employed. The most harmful of the "bandit element" were slated for execution by special troikas. The remaining bandits and their families, as well as anyone suspected of banditism and their families, were "subject to expulsion to the heart of Russia for detention in concentration camps." By August 1921, Soviet authorities in Tambov had imprisoned or deported 100,000 people and shot fifteen thousand.[128] Tukhachevskii's most infamous measure in these operations was his use of poison gas, an invention of the First World War, against insurgent villages.[129] Tukhachevskii's techniques have traditionally been presented as military expression of Bolshevik ruthlessness. Yet he had received a military education under the old regime, where he would have studied military statistics, and had then passed through the First World War. Tukhachevskii's chief of staff at the height of the operation in Tambov, as well as his direct military superiors in planning the antibandit operations, were all products of an imperial General Staff education.

Once the Antonov movement had been crushed, Soviet forces were dispatched to other regions to combat banditism. They took with them their successful techniques. In order to combat the endemic banditism that flared on the Don in 1921, party officials in July 1921 established the Don territorial military assembly for combating banditism, subordinate to the all-union commission for combating banditism. After a policy of amnesty had failed, and with bandits reported to control 30 percent of the territory, the Don military assembly, in September 1921, embarked on punitive measures, meaning executions and hostage taking.[130] The chairman of the Don military assembly's northern sector described his task in the following words: "to totally destroy banditism's manpower, and all forces that aid and abet it. . . . In order to accomplish this [task], we must strive by all means at our disposal: (1) to capture all individuals who have participated directly in bands, as well as all those who have offered any aid to individual bands, and (2) then, to eliminate mercilessly a portion of them, and to resettle the remainder beyond the boundaries of the Don Territory."[131]

In 1926, Tukhachevskii summarized the lessons of his anti-insurgency operations in a series of articles.[132] He insisted that commanders should operate on both the political and military fronts. But "in regions where rebellion has firmly taken root, one must conduct not battles and operations, but an entire war, [one] which should conclude with the firm occupation of the insurgent region . . . liquidating the very possibility of the population forming bandit detachments. In a word, the struggle must be essentially conducted not against the bands, but against the entire civil population." Prior to occupation, "Cheka and GPU organs should compile lists, as complete as possible, of both bandits . . . and the families they come from."[133] (One list from the 1921 Tambov operation had more than ten thousand such names.)[134] People so identified were to be either deported or detained in concentration camps. Tukhachevskii ended his overview by providing his "general conclusions":

> among [forms of] repression, the most effective are: the deportation of bandits' families who are hiding their members, the confiscation of their property, and its distribution to pro-Soviet peasants. If deportation cannot be organized immediately, then one should establish a wide set of concentration camps. . . . In carrying out these measures, the cleansing of the population will proceed in full coordination with the actions of the Red Army against this or that band. The bands will be exterminated either on the fields of battle, or will be extracted from their territorial regions during cleansing.[135]

It was neither a Russian nor a Bolshevik anomaly to view military operations through such a social lens. Many of Tukhachevskii's proposals, including his insistence on the interdependence of military activity and political initiatives, had been foreshadowed more than two decades before by Hubert Lyautey, the leading theorist and practitioner of French colonial warfare in Algeria, Indochina, Madagascar, and, most notably, Morocco.[136] Lyautey, too, argued that one must not simply combat bandit formations but must transform the social milieu so as to make it inhospitable to them. In suppressing a tenacious insurgency in Morocco, Lyautey, in 1924, even requested that his superiors grant him permission to employ poison gas against the rebels. (Paris refused. Spanish forces showed no such qualms and resorted to gas against Moroccan rebels in their zone.)[137]

As the experience of total war and revolution had expanded the breadth of practices previously employed in limited ways in colonial contexts, Soviet power then re-exported these more expansive practices back out again to the peripheries. Soviet campaigns throughout the 1920s in Chechnia and in Central Asia were not simply colonial policies, campaigns specific to "Russian" expansionism or a socialist attempt to eradicate Islam. When reporting on the successful completion of the 1925 antibandit operation in Chechnia, the head of the USSR's military-revolutionary council explicitly credited lessons Soviet forces had learned in earlier campaigns during the civil wars and against "bandits" in Ukraine and Tambov.[138]

Soviet power continued to compile population statistics and to practice population politics well into the Stalin period. In this light, the better known and much more profligate applications of Soviet state violence in the ensuing decades operated within a conceptual framework that posited the possibility of constituting a socialist society by excising those malignant elements that threatened to pollute it. Both the belief in the possibility of creating a pristine socialist society through political intervention and the specific techniques employed to secure this society predated the Great Terror. The state violence of the 1930s, then, was a radical extension and expansion of preexisting aspirations. Dekulakization, often identified as the opening salvo of a campaign that could have been orchestrated only by Stalin, bore striking similarities to the de-Cossackization campaign that preceded it by ten years. Indeed, one fruitful way of understanding dekulakization is to see it as a preemptive, Union-wide antibandit campaign, an attempt to excise a "pernicious" element, rather than as a war on the peasantry in toto. Soviet operational orders for dekulakization described their goal as "to cleanse the collective farms of kulak and other counterrevolutionary elements."[139] The Great Terror was similarly directed at eliminating "elements," this time those that were "anti-Soviet," "counterrevolutionary," and "socially alien." The February–March 1937 Party Plenum, a crucial moment in the unfolding of the Terror, discussed with much concern the supposed presence of a great number of "anti-Soviet elements" in Soviet society. The now infamous NKVD order #00447 "Concerning Anti-Soviet Elements" then ordered the execution of the "most hostile . . . elements" and ten-year exile to camps for the less hostile. With macabre precision, the Soviet state indicated region-by-region target figures for the total number of this "anti-Soviet element" (259,450 people), as well as the precise number of those who belonged to the first, "most hostile" category that was subject to execution (72,950)—a number equaling roughly 10 percent of the total executions in 1937–1938.[140] The following decades, up until Stalin's death in 1953, saw the Soviet state continue to excise various "elements" from the population and to introduce others.

In looking at state-sponsored violence against various social and ethnic groups from 1917 to Stalin's death, one discerns not a regime zig-zagging from one unrelated repression to the next. Rather, one sees a state continually seeking to sculpt and mold its population according to an applied science of society. To be sure, the intensity and extent of Soviet violence as technique varied greatly, and the particular categories of persecution did shift. Yet the Soviet state proved remarkably consistent in operating with a particular template of population politics, a template suggesting that certain "elements" could be identified within the population and that the population's general well-being required either the removal or the extermination of harmful elements.

However, the practices and disciplines for population politics in the Soviet Union were a particular variation of more generalized trends. Key moments in the crystallization of such practices were, first, the rise of new ways of conceiving of society that arose in the nineteenth century; second, the late nineteenth-century colonial administrative and military experience; and, third, the catalytic impact of the First World War. From the vantage point of European colonial experience, as well as the conduct of war in the East during the Great War, the Bolshevik state seems much less an exception to European norms. Hannah Arendt rightly suggests that key strands of the horrors of the twentieth century, in important respects, reach back to the nineteenth century. Alexis de Tocqueville's observations on the French Revolution, then, would seem almost prescient for the Russian case: "A great many of the practices we associate with the Revolution had precedents in the treatment of the people by the government in the last two centuries of the monarchy. The old régime provided the Revolution with many of its methods; all the Revolution added was a savagery peculiar to itself."[141]

Notes

I wish to thank Omer Bartov, Nathaniel Knight, Charles Steinwedel, Eric Lohr, Fran Hirsch, and Terry Martin for their comments on an earlier draft of this article.

1. "Vtoroe pokorenie Kavkaza: bol'sheviki i chechenskie povstantsy," *Rodina* (1995), no. 6: 43–48; " 'Stalin dal lichnoe soglasie': dokumenty o sobytiiakh v Chechne," *Vestnik Staroi Plosmchadi* (1995), no. 5: 140–151. All citations are from documents in these publications.

2. David Hoffmann and I pursue this argument for understanding Soviet history overall in *Cultivating the Masses: The Modern Social State in Russia, 1914–1941* (Ithaca, N.Y.: Cornell University Press, forthcoming).

3. Rogers Brubaker, "Aftermaths of Empire and the Unmixing of Peoples," in Karen Barkey and Mark von Hagen eds., *After Empire* (Boulder, Colo.: Westview, 1997).

4. Ian Hacking, "Biopower and the Avalanche of Printed Numbers," *Humanities in Society* 5, nos. 3–4 (1982): 279–295, here at p. 281.

5. Ian Hacking, *Taming of Chance* (Cambridge: Cambridge University Press, 1990); and John Horn, *Social Bodies* (Princeton, N.J.: Princeton University Press, 1994).

6. Alain Blum, "Oublier l'état pour comprendre la Russie," *Revue des Études slaves* 66, no. 1 (1994): 140–141.

7. V. F. Deriuzhinskii, *Politseiskoe pravo: posobie dlia studentov*, 3d ed. (St. Petersburg: Senatskaia tipografiia, 1911), pp. 14–16; M. V. Ptukha, *Ocherki gosudarstvennoi statistiki naseleniia i moral'noi* (Petrograd: Tip. Frolovoi, 1916).

8. *Bol'shaia entsiklopediia Iuzhakova* (St. Petersburg: Prosveshchenie, 1904–1909), s.v. "naselenie."

9. Ts. S. U., *Programmy statisticheskikh kursov, raionnykh i gubernskikh* (Moscow: Ts. S. U., 1920), pp. 9–11.

10. David Rich, *The Tsar's Colonels* (Cambridge, Mass.: Harvard University Press, 1998), and Rich, "Imperialism, Reform, and Strategy: Russian Military Statistics, 1840–1880," *Slavonic and East European Review* 74, no. 4 (1996): 621–639. For the broader impact of military statistics, see A. N. Pypin's *Istoriia russkoi etnografii*, 4 vols. (St. Petersburg: Tip. Stasiulevicha, 1892), 2:305–309 and 4:79–80.

11. I am indebted to Reginald Zelnik for suggesting many of the ideas in this paragraph.

12. *Stoletie voennogo ministerstva, 1802–1902*, tom 3, otd. 6 *Voennye ministry* (St. Petersburg: Tip. M. O. Vol'fa, 1911), pp. 240–43. Miliutin laid down the principles of the new discipline in D. Miliutin, *Pervye opyty voennoi statistiki*, 2 vols. (St. Petersburg: tipografiia voenno-uchebnykh zavedenii, 1847–1848), 1:38–39, 44–45, 54, 56, 58.

13. E. F. Morozov, "Poslednii Fel'dmarshal," *Russkii geopoliticheskii sbornik*, 1997, no. 2: 33–38; Carl Van Dyke, *Russian Imperial Military Doctrine and Education* (New York: Greenwood, 1990), pp. 20–21; N. A. Mashkin, *Vysshaia voennaia shkola rossiiskoi imperii* (Moscow: Academia, 1997), pp. 225–232.

14. Yuri Slezkine, *Arctic Mirrors: Russia and the Small Peoples of the North* (Ithaca, N.Y.: Cornell University Press, 1994); Nathaniel Knight, "Grigor'ev in Orenburg," *Slavic Review* 58, no. 4 (1999), and "Ethnicity, Nationality and the Masses: *Narodnost'* and Modernity in Pre-Emancipation Russia," in David Hoffmann and Yanni Kotsonis, eds., *Russian Modernity: Politics, Knowledge, Practices* (New York: Macmillan, 2000), pp. 41–64.

15. Austin Lee Jersild, "Ethnic Modernity and the Russian Empire," *Nationality Papers* 24, no. 4 (1996): 641–1648, here at pp. 643, 645.

16. S. A. Tokarev, *Istoriia russkoi etnografii* (Moscow: Nauka, 1966), p. 316.

17. This paragraph, and particularly this last observation, owes much to Professor Knight's suggestions.

18. Iu. E. Ianson, "Ustroistvo pravil'noi perepisi naseleniia v Rossii," pts. 1–2 in *Sbornik gosudarstvennykh znanii,* vols. 1–2 (St. Petersburg: D. E. Kozhanchikov, 1874–75). Also see A. F. Rittikh, *Plemennoi sostav kontingentov russkoi armii i muzhskogo naseleniia evropeiskoi rossii* (St. Petersburg: A. A. Il'in, 1875); Ia. A. Grebenshchikov, "Voennaia organizatsiia i statistika," in *Sbornik gosudarstvennykh znanii,* vol. 7 (1879).

19. *Ocherk razvitiia voprosa o vseobshchei narodnoi perepisi v Rossii* (St. Petersburg, 1890), pp. 1, 8–11, 31–40; for the results, see *Obshchii svod po imperii rezul'tatov razrabotki dannykh pervoi vseobshchei perepisi naseleniia,* 2 vols. (St. Petersburg: Tip. N. L. Nyrkina, 1905). Both these works insist that the new "universal" census differed fundamentally from the earlier revisions, which had been compiled strictly for "reasons of a fiscal-financial character" (*Obshchii svod,* 1:1).

20. For a General Staff textbook, see A. M. Zolotarëv, *Zapiski voennoi statistiki,* 2 vols. (St. Petersburg: A. E. Landau, 1885). Textbooks for cadet and military schools include A. M. Zolotarëv, *Voenno-geograficheskii ocherk okrain Rossii: kurs voennykh i iunkerskykh uchilichsh* (St. Petersburg: Tip. M. P. Frolovoi, 1903); V. R. Kannenberg (instructor at the Corps of Pages), *Voennaia geografiia: kurs voennykh uchilishch primenitel'no k programme 1907 g.* (St. Petersburg: Berezovskii, 1909); Captain E. Zavadskii (instructor at the Nicolas Cavalry School), *Voennaia geografiia: obshchii obzor Rossii i kratkie obzory Germanii i Avstro-Vengrii* (St. Petersburg: [n.p.], 1909); General Staff Colonel Gisser and Lieutenant Colonel Markov (instructors at the Pavlov and Vladimir military schools, respectively), *Voennaia geografiia Rossii,* 2d, enlarged ed. (St. Petersburg: Typography of the Guards Staff and the Petersburg Military District, 1910); General Staff Colonel Gisser and Lieutenant Colonel Markov, *Voennaia geografiia: voennaia organizatsii Germanii, Avstro-Vengrii, Rumynii, Turtsii, Kitaia i Iaponii; Kratkii obzor inostrannykh pogranichnykh teatrov* (St. Petersburg: Typography of the Guards Staff and the Petersburg Military District, 1911).

21. Zavadskii, *Voennaia geografiia,* p. 1 [emphasis in original]; similar formulations at pp. 2, 34; similarly, Gisser and Markov, *Voennaia geografiia Rossii,* p. 5.

22. Kannenberg, *Voennaia geografiia,* p. 16; for similar formulations, see Zavadskii, *Voennaia geografiia,* p. 38; Zolotarëv, *Zapiski voennoi statistiki,* 1:120.

23. Kannenberg, *Voennaia geografiia,* pp. 19–20; analogous statements can be found in virtually all military-statistical studies.

24. Earlier studies had cataloged the population's various component "elements" but did not ascribe any qualitative traits to them. Zolotarëv's 1885 textbook provides descriptive typologies for various "elements": Zolotarëv, *Zapiski,* 2:31, 92, 163, 275; also Zolotarëv, *Voenno-statisticheskii ocherk,* p. 18. Kannenberg, Gisser and Markov, and Zavadskii all share Zolotarëv's template.

25. General Staff Colonel Nadezhnyi and General Staff Lieutenant Colonel Iu. Romanovskii, *Dal'nii vostok,* 3 vols. (St. Petersburg: Benke, 1911 [confidential; each copy individually numbered]), 3:131–138. See also A. Panov, "Zheltyi vopros v Priamur'e: istoriko-statisticheskii ocherk," *Voprosy kolonizatsii* no. 7 (1910): 53–117.

26. For this trend in other spheres, see Charles Steinwedel, "The Making of Dif-

ference: The Construction of the Category of Ethnicity in Late Imperial Russian Politics," in Hoffmann and Kotsonis, eds., *Russian Modernity*, pp. 67–86.

27. E.g., Lieutenant Colonel C. M. MacGregor, *Central Asia: A Contribution towards the Better Knowledge of the Topography, Ethnogoraphy, Statistics and History, Compiled for Military and Political Reference* [confidential] (Calcutta: Superintendent of Government Printing, 1871–1873); S. R. Townshend Mayer and John Paget, *Afghanistan: Its Political and Military History, Geography and Ethnology* (London: Routledge, 1879).

28. Infantry Captain and Professor of Geoegraphy at Saint-Cyr Recoing, *Géographie militaire et maritime des colonies françaises, suivi d'un aperçu sur la géographie militaire et maritime des colonies anglaises* (Paris: Libraire militaire de L. Baudoin, 1884); Marcel Dubois, *Précis de géographie à l'usage des candidats à l'École spéciale militaire de Saint-Cyr* (Paris: Masson, 1895); on the role of French army ethnographers in shaping policies, see William Hoisington, *Lyautey and the French Conquest of Morocco* (New York: St. Martin's, 1995), pp. 12, 64.

29. U.S. War Department, *Notes on China* (Washington: Government Printing Office, 1900); U.S. War Department, *Military Notes on Cuba, 1909* (Washington: Government Printing Office, 1909).

30. A. Berens, "Kabyliia v 1857 godu," *Voennyi sbornik* (1858), no. 2: 247–274, no. 3: 121–172, 449–86; "Ocherk vosmushcheniia Sipaev v Ost-Indii," *Voennyi sbornik* (1858), no. 2: 107–138.

31. R. A. Fadeev, "Pis'ma s Kavkaza," *Sobranie sochinenii R. A. Fadeeva* (St. Petersburg: V. V. Komarov, 1889), t. 1, ch. 1, pp. 118–120. The review of Fadeev's "Pis'ma s Kavkaza" is found in *Voennyi Sbornik* 47 (1866), pt. 3, pp. 1–16.

32. Marc Pinson, "Demographic Warfare: An Aspect of Russian and Ottoman Policy, 1854–1856" (Ph.D. diss., Harvard University, 1970).

33. Miliutin's original report to the War Minister (November 29, 1857), and subsequent correspondence responding to General Adjutant Kochubei's criticism, in *Akty sobrannye kavkazskoiu arkheograpficheskoiu kommissieiu*, vol. 12, ed. E. Felitsyn (Tiflis: Kantseliariia glanvonachal'stvuiushchego grazhdanskoi chast'iu, 1904), pp. 757–763, citations at pp. 763, 761 (emphasis in original). On the widespread European rhetoric and practice of exterminating native peoples, see Sven Lindqvist, *"Exterminate All the Brutes!"* (New York: New Press, 1996).

34. Miliutin's memorandum on settling the Western Caucasus with the Russian element (April 3, 1862), *Akty* 12:981–983.

35. "Graf Nikolai Ivanovich Evdokimov," *Russkaia starina* (August 1889): 395–398; for Prince Bariatinskii's plan of operations, see *Akty* 12:664–666 (letter to war minister, December 29, 1860); for Miliutin's oversight of these operations while war minister, see his *Vospominaniia: 1860–1862* (Moscow: Rossiiskii arkhiv, 1999).

36. "Otchet gr. Evdokimova o voennykh deistviiakh, ispolnennykh v Kubanskoi oblasti v period vremeni s 1-go iiulia 1863 goda po 1-e iiulia 1864 goda," reproduced in T. Kh. Kumykov, *Vyselenie adygov v Turtsiiu—posledstvie kavkazkoi voiny* (Nal'chik: El'brus, 1994), pp. 47–76, here at 75.

37. R. A. Fadeev, "Pis'ma s Kavkaza," t. 1, ch. 1, quote at pp. 148–149 (Fadeev participated in the operations as an officer; his "Letters" were originally published in *Moskovskie vedomosti* during 1864–1865); see also Fadeev, "Delo o vyselenii gortsev," *Sobranie sochenenii*, t. 1, ch. 2, pp. 61–76. Other contemporaries shared Fadeev's sense that these campaigns were a new departure: "Graf Evdokimov," p. 399; A. P. Berzhe,

"Vyselenie gortsev s Kavkaza," *Russkaia starina* (February 1882): 337–339; K. Geins, "Pshekhskii otriad," *Voennyi sbornik* (1866), no. 1 (t. 47): 3, 4, 6 and no. 5 (t. 49): 38.

38. "Doklad komissii po delu pereseleniia gortsev v Turtsiiu, 18 fevrelia 1865, g. Tiflis," reproduced in T. Kh. Kumykov, *Vyselenie adygov v Turtsiiu*, pp. 21–41, estimate at p. 40.

39. Miliutin, Memorandum (April 3, 1862); Evdokimov, Report (July 25, 1862); letter from Kartsov, chief of staff for the Caucasus Army, to Evdokimov (August 9–10, 1862); Evdokimov to Kartsov (September 5, 1862), in *Akty* 12:983, 1006–1007, 1009–1010; also Pinson, "Demographic Warfare," p. 115.

40. Miliutin's report to commander of the Caucasus Army (November 3, 1864), in *Pereselenie gortsev v Turtsiiu*, ed. G. A. Dzagurov (Rostov-on-Don: Sevkavkniga, 1925), pp. 36–37; other documents reflecting Miliutin's continued involvement in this campaign, pp. 28–29, 40–46.

41. Geins, "Pshekhskii otriad," *Voennyi sbornik* (1866), no. 5 (t. 49): 18; earlier, Geins had described the goal of these military operations as "to cause terror in the foe" ("Pshekhskii otriad," no. 4 [t. 48]: 238).

42. Fadeev, "Pis'ma s Kavkaza," t. 1, ch. 1, p. 150.

43. Geins, "Pshekhskii otriad," no. 1, p. 29.

44. Consul Dickson to Earl Russell, March 17, (1864), in House of Commons, *Accounts and Papers* (1864), vol. 63: 583.

45. Geins, no. 3, pp. 41–44; A. Lilov, "Poslednie gody bor'by russkikh s gortsami na zapadnom kavkaze," *Kavkaz*, (1867), no. 11: 62.

46. Lord Napier to Earl Russell, May 23, (1864), in House of Commons, *Accounts and Papers* (1864), vol. 63: 589; Geins, "Pshekhskii otriad," no. 5 (t. 49): 38.

47. Dukhovskii, as cited in Lilov, "Poslednie gody bor'by russkikh s gortsami na zapadnom kavkaze," *Kavkaz* (1867), no. 19: 110.

48. "Pereselenie tuzemtsev Kubanskoi oblasti v Turtsiiu i na ukazannye im mesta v predelakh oblasti," reproduced in Kumykov, *Vyselenie adygov v Turtsiiu*, pp. 88–112, here at p. 88.

49. These figures from three separate documents reproduced in Kumykov, *Vyselenie adygov v Turtsiiu*, pp. 39, 46, and esp. 105. See also "Chislovye dannye o kavkazskom gorskom naselenii," *Voennyi sbornik*, no. 4 (1866), citing material from *Russkii invalid*, no. 56 (1866).

50. G. A. Dzidzariia, *Makhadzhirstvo* (Sukhumi: Alashara, 1982), pp. 210–212, for evaluations of various estimates for 1859–1864; Kemal Karpat, *Ottoman Population, 1830–1914* (Madison: University of Wisconsin Press, 1985), pp. 65–70, estimate for 1859–1879 at p. 68.

51. Fadeev, "Pis'ma s Kavkaza," p. 150.

52. Pinson, "Demographic Warfare," ch. 1; "O vyselenii tatar iz Kryma v 1860 godu: zapiska generala-ad"iutanta E. I. Totlebena," *Russkaia starina* (June 1893): 531–550; "Pereselenie tatar iz Kryma v Turtsiiu: iz zapisok G. P. Levitskogo," *Vestnik Evropy* (1882), t. 5: 596–639.

53. David Schimmelpenninck, "The Yellow Peril: Aleksei Kuropatkin," in "Oriental Dreams: Russian Ideologies of Empire in Asia," (unpublished manuscript); *Stoletie voennogo ministerstva, 1802–1902*, tom 3, otd. 6, *Voennye ministry* (St. Petersburg: Tip. M. O. Vol'fa, 1911), pp. 280–282. I am indebted to Professor Schimmelpenninck for sharing his work prior to publication.

54. Stephen Roberts, *The History of French Colonial Policy, 1870–1925* (London: Frank Cass, 1963; first published, 1929), pp. 179–81. On French colonial military techniques, see Douglas Porch, "Bugeaud, Galliéni, Lyautey: The Development of French Colonial Warfare," in Peter Paret, ed., *Makers of Modern Strategy* (Princeton N.J.: Princeton University Press, 1986).

55. Jean Gottmann, "Bugeuad, Galliéni, Lyautey: The Development of French Colonial Warfare," in Edward Mead Earle, ed., *Makers of Modern Strategy* (Princeton, N.J.: Princeton University Press, 1971), p. 246.

56. Zolotarëv, *Venno-geograficheskii ocherk okrain Rossii*, pp. 176–177; Gisser and Markov, *Voennaia geografiia Rossiia*, pp. 99–100; Kannenberg, *Voennaia geografiia*, p. 89; Zavadskii, *Voennaia geografiia*, pp. 41–42, 144; General Staff Captain Tikhmenev, *Voennoe obozrenie vostochnoi pogranichnoi polosy semirechenskoi oblasti* (St. Petersburg: Transhel', 1883); General Staff Colonel Fedorov, *Voenno-statisticheskoe opisanie turkestanskogo voennogo okruga: chzhungarsko-semirechenskoi prigranichnyi raion*, 2 vols. (Tashkent: Tipografiia shtaba Turkestana Voennogo Okruga, 1910; vol. 1 with imprint "confidential"; vol. 2 with imprint "secret"), 1:98, 76, 163, 2:32; General Staff Colonel Prince Stokasimov, *Voenno-statisticheskoe opisanie turkestanskogo voennogo okruga: Ferganskii raion* (Tashkent: Shtab Turkestanskogo voennogo okruga, 1912), pp. 113–114.

57. Fedorov, *Chzhungarsko-semirechenskoi prigranichnyi raion*, 1:98, 76, 163; also 2:32.

58. M. I. Veniukov, "Postupitel'noe dvizhenie Rossii v srednei azii" and "Ocherk politicheskoi etnografii stran lezhashchikh mezhdu Rossieiu i Indeiu," *Sbornik gosudarstvennykh znanii*, 3 (1877): 58–106 and 5 (1878): 58–106, quotes at 3: 61, 64–65. Veniukov recounted his service in the Caucasus in "Kavkazskie vospominaniia (1861–1863)" *Russkii arkhiv* 1880 (t. 18), no. 1: 400–448.

59. Prince V. I. Masal'skii, ed., *Turkestanskii krai* (St. Petersburg: Devrien, 1913) [= vol. 19 of V. P. Semenov Tian-Shanskii, ed., *Rossiia: polnoe opisanie nashego otechestva*]; for "strengthening the Russian element," see pp. 322–333, 358, 365. Among other military-statistical studies, the volume's bibliography includes Zolotarëv's 1903 *Voenno-geograficheskii ocherk okrain*.

60. Count K. K. Pahlen, *Mission to Turkestan*, ed. Richard Pierce (London: Oxford University Press, 1964), pp. 196, 191; on the colonization officials' enthusiasm for statistics, see also pp. 181, 189.

61. Fedorov, *Voenno-statisticheskoe opisanie turkestanskogo voennogo okruga*, 2:28–29.

62. Dan Brower, "Kyrgyz Nomads and Russian Pioneers: Colonization and Ethnic Conflict in the Turkestan Revolt of 1916," *Jahrbücher für Geschichte Osteuropas* 44, no.1 (1996): 41–53; Edward Sokol, *The Revolt of 1916 in Russian Central Asia* (Baltimore: Johns Hopkins University Press, 1954); Richard Pierce, *Russian Central Asia, 1867–1917* (Berkeley: University of California Press, 1960). On the rebellion's suppression, see K. Usenbaev, *Vosstanie 1916 goda v Kirgizii* (Frunze: Ilim, 1967) and G. Sapargaliev, *Karatel'naia politika tsarizma v Kazakhstane* (Alma-Ata: Nauka, 1966).

63. See the relevant portions from Kuropatkin's diary for this period in "Vosstanie 1916 g. v Srednei Azii: iz dnevnika Kuropatkina," *Krasnyi arkhiv* 3, no. 34 (1929): 39–94.

64. A. V. Piaskovskii et al., eds., *Vosstanie 1916 goda v srednei azii i kazakhstane* (Moscow: Izd. Akademii nauk, 1960), pp. 662–663.

65. G. I. Broido, "Materialy k istorii vosstaniia kirgiz v 1916 godu," *Novyi vostok*, 1924, no. 6: 407–434, citations at pp. 428–431.

66. *Vosstanie 1916 goda*, pp. 662–663, 668, 673, 662, 675.

67. " 'Takoe upravlenie gosudarstvom—nedopustimo': Doklad A. Kerenskogo na zakrytom zasedanii Gosudarstvennoi dumy dekabr' 1916,"*Istoricheskii arkhiv* 1997, no. 2: 4–22. All citations taken from this source. The Duma's right to inquire into such military operations differed markedly from the situation in Germany, where such activities were beyond civilian inquiry: see Isabel Hull, "German Final Solutions in Wilhelmine Germany" (unpublished manuscript).

68. The aide to the Turkestan governor-general likewise reported that punitive detachments "methodically and systematically exterminated women and children" (as cited in Usenbaev, *Vosstanie 1916 goda v Kirgizii*, p. 222).

69. Pierce, *Russian Central Asia*, p. 293.

70. "Iz dnevnika," p. 60; *Vosstanie 1916 goda*, pp. 684–687, 99–100. For analogous instructions by the military governor of Semirech'e to his forces in the field to expel natives in order to transform certain districts into "purely Russian regions," see Usenbaev, *Vosstanie 1916 goda*, pp. 676–677.

71. Brower, "Kyrgyz Nomads," p. 52.

72. Leopold Haimson, "Summary," in V. Iu. Cherniaev *et al.*, eds., *Anatomiia revoliutsii*, (St. Petersburg: Glagol, 1994), pp. 424–426.

73. S. B. Spies, *Methods of Barbarism: Roberts and Kitchener and Civilians in the Boer Republics, January 1900–May 1902* (Cape Town: Human and Rousseau, 1977), pp. 148–149, 214–216, 265–266.

74. General Staff Colonel [Iak. Grig.] Zhilinskii, *Ispano-Amerikanskaia voina: otchet komandirovannogo po vysochaishemu poveleniiuk ispanskim voiskam na ostrove Kuby* (St. Petersburg: Ekonomicheskaia tipo-litografiia, 1899), pp. 52, 66. The number of deaths caused by these measures is now estimated at 100,000.

75. Spies, *Methods of Barbarism*.

76. Vasilii Iosifovich Gurko, *Voina Anglii s iuzhno-afrikanskimi respublikami, 1899–1901 gg.: Otchet komandirovannogo po vysochaishimu poveleniiuk voiskam iuzhno-afrikanskikh respublik V. I. Gurko* (St. Petersburg: Voennaia tipographiia-izd. Voenno-uchennogo komiteta Glavnogo shtaba, 1901 [confidential]).

77. "Inostrannoe obozrenie," *Vestnik Evropy* (1901), no. 9: 398–399 (Kitchener's September 1901 deportation order for Boers serving in commando bands); "Inostrannoe obozrenie," *Vestnik Evropy* (1902), no. 1: 379–381 ("a special system for concentrating [*sosredotocheniia*] Boer women and children under the guard of British forces. The establishment of special closed camps for many thousand Boer families has hurt the British in public opinion"); "Inostrannoe obozrenie," *Vestnik Evropy* (1902), no. 7: 364–372 ("women and children were driven into concentration camps" [*kontsentratsionnye lageri*]), citation at p. 368. Note also formulation that "the British element [*sic*] has now achieved numerical preponderance over the Boers" (no. 7, p. 368).

78. Hannah Arendt, *Origins of Totalitarianism* (New York: Harvest, 1973), pt. 2, citations at p. 123; also Lindqvist, *"Exterminate All the Brutes!"*; Isabel Hull, "German Final Solutions."

79. I thank Eric Lohr for suggesting this point.

80. Stephen Wheatcroft, "The Tsarist Prison System in the Perspective of Stalinist and Other Prison Systems" (unpublished ms.).

81. My thinking on the role of World War I in redirecting social organization toward total war and destruction has been much influenced by Omer Bartov, *Murder*

in Our Midst (New York: Oxford University Press, 1996), and Michael Geyer, "The Militarization of Europe," in John Gillis, ed., *The Militarization of the Western World* (New Brunswick University Press, N.J.: Rutgers, 1989).

82. Eric Lohr, "Enemy Alien Politics in the Russian Empire during World War One" (Ph.D. diss., Harvard University, 1999); the guidelines can be found in *Zakony i rasporiazheniia voennogo vremeni* (St. Petersburg: N. N. Klobukov, 1905), p. 11.

83. For the August 3, 1914, instruction sanctioning hostage taking in order to facilitate requisitioning in the war zone, see *Evakuatsiia i rekvizitsiia: spravochnik deistvuiushchikh uzakonenii i rasporezhenii* (Petrograd: Tsentral'nyi voenno-promyshlennyi komitet, 1916), pp. 99–102; for the taking of hostages from Jewish communities to protect imperial forces "from harmful threats from the Jewish population," see "Dokumenty o presledovanii evreev," *Arkhiv Russkoi Revoliutsii*, vol. 19 (1928): 245–284, here at pp. 248, 250–251, 256–258. For the taking of hostages from German colonists (that is, imperial subjects), see S. G. Nelipovich, " 'Nemetskuiu pakost' uvolit', i bez nezhnostei,' " *Voenno-istoricheskii zhurnal*, no. 1 (1997): 42–52, here at pp. 48–49.

84. Lohr, "Enemy Alien Politics"; S. G. Nelipovich, "Repressii protiv poddannykh 'tsentral'nykh derzhav': deportatsii v Rossii, 1914–1918," *Voenno-istoricheskii zhurnal*, no. 6 (1996): 32–42; Nelipovich, " 'Nemetskuiu pakost' uvolit' "; Mark von Hagen, "The Great War and the Mobilization of Ethnicity," in Barnett Rubin and Jack Snyder, eds., *Post-Soviet Political Order* (New York: Routledge, 1998). For documents on treatment of Jewish subjects, see "Iz 'cheroi knigi' rossiiskogo evreistva: materialy dlia istorii voiny 1914–1915 g.,"*Evreiskaia starina* 10 (1918): 195–296, and "Dokumenty o presledovanii evreev."

85. For discussion in the Council of Ministers on the military's measures, see Michael Cherniavsky, ed., *Prologue to Revolution: Notes of A. N. Iakhontov on the Secret Meetings of the Council of Ministers, 1915* (Englewood Cliffs: Prentice Hall, 1967); *Sovet ministrov Rossiiskoi Imperii v gody pervoi mirovoi voiny* (St. Petersburg: Sankt-Peterburgskii filial Instituta Rossiiskoi istorii Rossiiskoi Akademii Nauk, 1999), pp. 163–164. Overall, see the excellent treatment in Lohr, "Enemy Alien Politics."

86. Specialized studies include G. G. Khristiani, *Voennyi obzor vostochnykh oblastei Germanii i Avstro-Vengrii* (St. Petersburg: A. G. Rozen, 1906); General Staff General Major G. G. Khristiani, *Voennyi obzor Galitskogo teatra* (St. Petersburg: Skachko, 1910: with imprint "confidential"), pp. 96–102; General Staff Lieutenant Colonel S. Pototskii, *Avstro-Vengerskaia armiia: spravochnik sovremennogo ustroistva vooruzhennykh sil Avstro-Vengrii* (St. Petersburg: Rittikh, 1911); General Staff Colonel Pototskii, under the general editorship of General Staff Colonel Samoilo, *Avstro-Vengriia: voenno-statisticheskoe opisanie*, part 1: *Vostochno-Galitskii raion* (St. Petersburg: Military Typography, 1912), pp. 149–155, appendix 16; General Staff Colonel Kulzhinskii, *Sopredel'naia s Podoliei polosa Galitsii* (Kiev: District Typography, 1914). General textbooks include Zavadskii, *Voennaia geografiia*, pp. 178–184, esp. 182; Gisser and Markov, *Voennaia geografiia*, p. 93.

87. Tellingly, Austro-Hungarian military statistics frequently combined studies of Galicia with those of Western Russia. See General Staff Major Ferdinand Fiedler, *Militär-Geographie: Galizien und das westliche Russland* (Vienna: Seidel, 1878), pp. 231–243, esp. p. 235; *Militär-Geographie: Galizien und westliche Russland* (Vienna: Die K. K. Hof- und Staatsdruckerei, 1883); Captain Emil Pramberger, *Behelf zum Studium der Militär-Geographie von Mittel-Europa*, 3d ed. (Vienna: Seidel und Sohn, K. u. K. Hof-Buchhändler, 1899), p. 142. By 1910, Franz Conrad von Hötzendorf, the Austro-Hungarian chief of staff, had indicated the risks of Russian agitation in the region

(Christoph Führ, *Das K.u.K. Armeeoberkommando und die Innenpolitik in Österreich, 1914–1917* [Graz: Hermann Böhlaus, 1968], p. 63). For Austro-Hungarian prewar lists and surveillance of Russophile suspects, see *Voennye prestupleniia Gabsburgskoi monarkhii* (Trumball, Conn.: Peter Hardy, 1964; first published in 4 vols., L'vov, 1924–1932).

88. On Austro-Hungarian policy, see Führ, *Das K.u.K. Armeeoberkommando und die Innenpolitik in Österreich, 1914–1917*, pp. 63–74; *Voennye prestupleniia Gabsburgskoi monarkhii*; Joseph Redlich, *Austrian War Government* (New Haven, Conn.: Yale University Press, 1929), pp. 85, 103. On the Russian occupation of Galicia, see von Hagen, "Great War and Mobilization of Ethnicity," and A. Iu. Bakhturina, *Politika rossiiskoi imperii v vostochnoi Galitsii v gody pervoi mirovoi voine* (Moscow: AIRO, 2000).

89. For the characterization of the Jews as a "pernicious element," see "Dokumenty o presledovanii evreev," *Arkhiv Russkoi Revoliutsii* vol. 19 (1928): 275; for decrees explicitly employing the term "cleanse," see Nelipovich, "Repressii," pp. 37–38, and "Nemetskuiu pakost'," p. 49.

90. Robert Coonrod, "The Duma's Attitude toward War-Time Problems of Minority Groups," *American Slavic and East European Review* 13 (1954): 34; Nikolai Kharlamov, "Izbienie v pervoprestolnoi: nemetskii pogrom v Moskve v mae 1915," *Rodina*, no. 8–9 (1993): 127–132.

91. *Osobyi zhurnal soveta ministrov*, 1915, no. 46 (January 23, 1915); no. 448 (June 12, 1915); 1916, no. 31 (April 5, 1916).

92. As cited in Eric Lohr, "Deportation, Nationality and Citizenship: Enemy Aliens within Russia during World War I," paper presented to AAASS, Seattle, November 1997, p. 11.

93. Peter Holquist, " 'Information Is the Alpha and Omega of Our Work: Bolshevik Surveillance in Its Pan-European Context," *Journal of Modern History* 69, no. 3 (1997): 415–450.

94. GARF, f. 1791, op. 2, d. 496 (interior ministry circular to all provincial commissars, April 21, 1917); *Zhurnaly zasedanii vremennogo pravitel'stva* no. 43 (April 5, 1917) and no. 114, point 7b (June 21, 1917).

95. Robert Lewis Koehl, "Colonialism inside Germany: 1886–1918," *Journal of Modern History* 25, no. 3 (1953): 255–272, here at pp. 261–262; Jack Wertheimer, " 'The Unwanted Element': East European Jews in Imperial Germany," *Leo Baeck Institute Yearbook* 26 (1981).

96. For German explanations of their goals in the East, see *Das Land Ober Ost: Deutsche Arbeit in den Verwaltungsgebieten Kurland, Litauen, und Bialowstok-Grodno* (Stuttgart-Berlin: Verlag der Pressabteilung Ober Ost, 1917); Rudolf Häpke, "Die geschichtliche und landeskundliche Forschung in Litauen und Baltenland, 1915–1918," *Hansische Geschichtsblätter* Band 25 (1920): 17–33. For studies of this administration, see Vejas Liulevicius, "Warland: Peoples, Lands and National Identity on the Eastern Front in World War One" (Ph.D. diss., University of Pennsylvania, 1994); Aba Strazhas, *Deutsche Ostpolitik im Ersten Weltkrieg: Der Fall Ober Ost, 1915–1917* (Wiesbaden: Harrossowitz, 1993); Michael Burleigh, *Germany Turns Eastwards: A Study of* Ostforschung *in the Third Reich* (Cambridge: Cambridge, 1988).

97. Burleigh, *Germany Turns Eastwards*, p. 21.

98. "Memorandum of the Supreme Command on the Polish Border Strip, July 5, 1918," in Gerald Feldman, ed., *German Imperialism, 1914–1918* (New York: Wiley, 1972), pp. 133–137; Fischer, *Germany's Aims*, pp. 111, 115–116, 276–279; Immanuel Geiss, *Der polnische Grenzstreifen, 1914–1918* (Lübeck-Hamburg: Matthiesen, 1960).

99. Aba Strazhas, "The *Land Oberost* and Its Place in Germany's *Ostpolitik*, 1915–1918," in V. Stanley Vardys and Romuald Misiunas, eds., *The Baltic States in Peace and War*, (University Park: University of Maryland, 1978), pp. 51, 58.

100. Niall Ferguson, *The Pity of War* (New York: Basic Books, 1999), p. 144.

101. Woodruff Smith, *The Ideological Origins of Nazi Imperialism* (New York: Oxford University Press 1986); and Lindqvist, *"Exterminate All the Brutes!"*

102. Strazhas, "The *Land Oberost*," pp. 51–52.

103. Mark Cornwall, "Morale and Patriotism in the Austro-Hungarian Army," in John Horne, ed., *State, Society and Mobilization* (Cambridge: Cambridge University Press, 1997), pp. 175–76; Holger Herwig, *The First World War: Germany and Austria-Hungary* (New York: Arnold, 1997), p. 160.

104. Herwig, *The First World War*, p. 160; Iu. A. Pisarev, *Serbiia i Chernogoriia v pervoi mirovoi voine* (Moscow: Nauka, 1968), pp. 182–98, deportees estimated at p. 190; Dragan Zivojinovic, "Serbia and Montenegro: The Home Front, 1914–1918," in Béla Kiraly and Nándor Dreisziger eds., *East Central European Society in World War I* (Boulder, Colo.: Social Science Monographs, 1985), p. 252 for figure of 180,000.

105. Herwig, *The First World War*, p. 232.

106. James J. Reid, "Total War, the Annihilation Ethic and the Armenian Genocide, 1870–1918" in Richard G. Hovannisian, ed., *The Armenian Genocide: History, Politics, Ethics*, (New York: St. Martin's, 1992); see also Hull, "German Final Solutions."

107. See biographical information in "Vtoroe pokorenie Kavkaza," p. 48.

108. William Rosenberg, "Social Mediation and State Construction(s) in Revolutionary Russia," *Social History* 19, no. 2 (1994): 168–188, citation at p. 188.

109. *Obzor banditskogo dvizheniia v Sibiri s dekiabria 1920 po ianvar' 1922* (Novonikolaevsk: Tipografiia predstavitel'stva V.Ch.K. v Sibiri, 1922), p. 18.

110. Orlando Figes, *A People's Tragedy: The Russian Revolution* (New York: Penguin, 1998), p. 570 (Kuban delegate); "Zakon o priniatii v donskie kazaki, ob izkliuchenii iz donskogo kazachestva i vyselenii iz predelov Donskogo voiska" (passed September 19, 1918), in *Sbornik zakonov priniatykh Bol'shim voiskovym krugom Vsevelikogo voiska Donskogo chetvertogo sozyva, v pervuiu sessiiu, 15-e avgusta po 20-e sentiabria 1918* (Novocherkassk: Donskoi pechatnik, 1918).

111. Liulevicius, "War-Land," chapter 7; Waite, *Vanguard of Nazism*; Klaus Theweleit, *Male Phantasies*, 2 vols. (Minneapolis: University of Minnesota Press, 1987).

112. Peter Kenez, "Pogroms and White Ideology in the Russian Civil War," in John Klier and Shlomo Lambroza, eds., *Pogroms and Anti-Jewish Violence in Modern Russian History* (New York: Cambridge University Press, 1992); Figes, *A People's Tragedy*, pp. 676–679; Richard Pipes, *Russia under the Bolshevik Regime* (New York: Vintage, 1994), pp. 99–114.

113. Kenez, "Pogroms and White Ideology"; A. L. Litvin, "Krasnyi i belyi terror v Rossii, 1917–1922," *Otechestvennaia istoriia* (1993), no. 6: 46–62; E. I. Dostovalov, "O belykh i belom terrore," *Rossiiskii arkhiv*, vol. 6 (1995): 637–697, "filtering" at p. 678.

114. "Nashi agenty ot millionera do Narkoma," *Rodina* (1990), no. 10: 64–68.

115. "Dokladnaia zapiska" in P. S. Makhrov, *V beloi armii generala Denikina* (Saint-Petersburg: Logos, 1994), p. 288.

116. E.g., A. E. Snesarev, *Avganistan* (Moscow: Gosizdatel'stvo, 1921); N. S. Elizarov, *Rumyniia: voenno-geograficheskoe opisanie* (Moscow: Razvedyvatel'noe upravlenie shtaba Raboche-krest'ianskoi armii, 1925; with imprint "confidential"). Both authors were graduates of the Imperial General Staff Academy. For the subsequent careers of

imperial General Staff officers in the Red Army, see A. G. Kavtaradze, *Voennye spetsialisty na sluzhbe respubliki sovetov, 1917–1920 gg.* (Moscow: Nauka, 1988).

117. E. Polivanov, "Revoliutsiia i literaturnye iazyki soiuza SSR," *Revoliutsionnyi vostok* no. 1 (1927): 41, and A. M. Selishchev, *Iazyk revoliutsionnoi epokhi* (Moscow: Rabotnik prosveshcheniia, 1928), p. 85.

118. Peter Holquist, "Conduct Merciless, Mass Terror," *Cahiers du Monde russe* 38, no. 1–2 (1997): 127–162.

119. GARF, f. 1235, op. 82, d. 15, l. 311 (report on collapse of Soviet power in Khoper region to CEC Cossack section, 1919).

120. I. I. Reingol'd to the CC, "Dokladnaia zapiska" in Oleg Khlevniuk et al., eds., *Bol'shevistkoe rukovodstvo: perepiska, 1912–1927,* (Moscow: Rosspen, 1997), pp. 107–110.

121. My argument here has been much influenced by Detlev Peukert, "The Genesis of the 'Final Solution' from the Spirit of Science," in Thomas Childers and Jane Caplan, eds., *Reevaluating the Third Reich* (New York: Holmes and Meier, 1993).

122. Stalin to Lenin (October 30, 1920), in "Repressirovannye narody: Kazaki," *Shpion* 1994, no. 1 (3): 38–68, here at pp. 51–52; see also I. V. Kosior's telegram to G. Ordzhonikidze (November 13, 1920) on the course of the operation *Bol'shevistkoe rukovodstvo: perepiska*, pp. 164–165. For overviews, see N. F. Bugai, "20–40-e gody: deportatsiia naseleniia s territorii evropeiskoi rossii," *Otechestvennaia istoriia* 1992, no. 4: 37–41; and Terry Martin, "The Origins of Soviet Ethnic Cleansing," *Journal of Modern History* 70, no. 4 (1998): 813–861, for this and the further Soviet policies.

123. See Francine Hirsch, "Empire of Nations" (Ph.D. diss., Princeton University, 1998), for a more extensive discussion of the Soviet state's employment of colonial techniques.

124. B. L. Genis, "Deportatsiia russkikh iz Turkestana v 1921 godu," *Voprosy istorii* 1998, no. 1: 44–58, quotes at pp. 44, 47; decree ending "deportation of Russian population" in Semirech'e (August 10, 1922) in "Repressirovannye Narody: kazaki," p. 55.

125. The following citations are taken from operational decrees, orders, and directives found in Viktor Danilov, ed., *Antonovshchina: dokumenty i materialy,* (Tambov: Redaktsionno-izdatel'skii otdel, 1994). See esp. documents 174–177, 179–181, 189, 200, 212, 221, 259, 272, 275.

126. V. P. Naumov and A. A. Kosakovskii, eds., *Kronshtadt, 1921* (Moscow: Demokratiia, 1997), pp. 355–360, citation at p. 359.

127. The Tambov campaign was held up a model for other operations: A. S. Kazakov, "Obshchie princhiny vozniknoveniia banditizma i krest'ianskikh vosstanii," *Krasnaia armiia* (1921), no. 9: 21–39; I. Trutko, "Razgrom bandy Antonova," *Krasnaia armiia* (1921), no. 7–8: 20–25; N. Kakurin, "Organizatsiia bor'by s banditizmom po opytu tambovskogo i vitebskogo komandovanii," *Voennaia nauka i revoliutsiia* (1922), no. 1: 82–102.

128. *Antonovshchina*, documents 207, 258, 290 (listing children held in ten concentration camps); Figes, *A People's Tragedy*, p. 768.

129. *Antonovshchina*, documents 199, 204.

130. Rossiiskii gosudarstvennyi voennyi arkhiv [RGVA], f. 25896, op. 1, d. 8, ll. 2–12 ("Report on the Activity of the Don Territorial Military Assembly for Combating Banditism from Its Formation (12 July) to 1 December 1921").

131. RGVA, f. 25896, op. 6, d. 65, ll. 38–44 (report of commander of northern sector to chairman of Don military assembly).

132. M. Tukhachevskii, "Bor'ba s kontrrevoliutsionnymi vosstaniiami," *Voina i re-voliutsiia* (1926), nos. 7–9.

133. Tukhachevskii, "Bor'ba," 6:9, 16; similarly, 7:11–13.

134. Antonov-Ovseenko's report on the campaign against the insurgent movement (July 20, 1921), in *Antonovshchina*, p. 234.

135. Tukhachevskii, "Bor'ba," 9:15–16.

136. See Porch, "Bugeaud, Galliéni, Lyautey"; Gottmann, "Bugeaud, Galliéni, Lyautey."

137. Hoisington, *Lyautey*, pp. 196, 198, 450 n. 45.

138. Note from I. Unshlikht to CC, 8 September 1925, in "Stalin dal lichnoe soglasie," pp. 145–147.

139. On collectivization, see Lynne Viola, *Peasant Rebels under Stalin* (New York: Oxford University Press, 1996); citations from the Smolensk Archive, WKP 166, ll. 3–5, 30–38.

140. Tsentr khraneniia sovremennoi dokumentatsii [TsKhSD], f. 89, perechen' 73, documents 10, 41, 49, 50, 75, 78, 86, 95, 99, 102, 103, 107, 115, 120, 121, 136, 144, 155. For an overview of this operation, see Oleg Khlevniuk, "Les mécanismes de la 'Grande Terreur' des années 1937–1938 au Turkménistan," *Cahiers du monde russe* 39, no. 1–2 (1998): 197–208.

141. Alexis de Tocqueville, *The Old Régime and the French Revolution* (New York: Vintage, 1983), p. 192.

Nationalizing the Revolution in Central Asia

The Transformation of Jadidism, 1917–1920

IN 1917, RUSSIAN CENTRAL ASIA CONSISTED of the province of Turkestan, the product of two decades of Russian conquests in the late nineteenth century, and the two rump khanates of Bukhara and Khiva, dynastic states under Russian protectorate. By 1924, the old boundaries had been replaced by two (and ultimately five) soviet socialist republics, each bearing the name of a nation. The process through which this came about has received little serious attention. Conventional views ascribe the national delimitation of Central Asia, carried out in 1924, to Russian machinations, in which the imperial center, reborn under a new name, imposed its will on the colonial periphery in a classic display of divide and rule.[1] Slightly more nuanced views recount abortive cooperation between "nationalists" and Bolsheviks but end by emphasizing the betrayal of the former by the Bolsheviks as soon as their goals of conquering power had been achieved.[2] In either case, the political contest in revolutionary Central Asia is seen as a binary struggle in which the two sides are well defined and stable.

There are several problems with this analysis. It imputes ideological stability to both sides during a period of massive upheaval, when, indeed, actions of both sides were governed by emergency responses to unforeseen contingencies. It also implies the existence of internal homogeneity in the two camps that vanishes on closer inspection. But, most important, such an analysis is blind to the massive transformation in notions of identity that took place in these years in Central Asia. The triumph of ethnic nationalism over dynastic, territorial, or confessional forms of identity needs to be explained. Seeing the national delimitation simply as a divide-and-conquer strategy of the Soviets transforms Central Asians into passive victims of imperial intrigue. Equally, seeing the creation of national boundaries as a transparent application of ethnographic knowledge blinds us to the fact that the ethnographic knowledge that attached unequivocal national labels to every individual in the new Soviet state itself was the product of a complex politics involving the drawing of boundaries both of inclusion and of exclusion. The Soviet state was only one actor in this politics.

I propose to draw a more complicated picture of the politics of Central Asia to show that Russian/native or Bolshevik/nationalist dichotomies cannot explain the transformation of Central Asia in the early Soviet period. Conflict between Russian settlers and the government in Moscow was a central feature of this period. But neither were the "nationalists" securely in command of their society. Indeed, the very definition of the nation that the nationalists represented was in flux. The various sides in the conflict were therefore neither united nor in possession of fully formed ideologies. As the various actors negotiated the uncertainties of revolution and war, their political agendas were transformed, often in unexpected ways.

My primary focus is on the intellectual and political trajectory of Central Asian intellectuals, the "Jadids," in the years of the civil war. Through a close reading of several key texts by Abdurrauf Fitrat (1886–1938), easily the most influential Jadid of the period, I seek to outline the Jadids' shift from reform to revolution in this period. Between autumn 1917 and summer 1920, two fundamental transformations took place in Jadid rhetoric: their already profoundly secularized Muslim identity gave way to a much more stridently "nationalist" vision (although they never entirely abandoned their Muslim identity), and previous Jadid exhortations to seek admonition from the "civilized" nations of Europe gave way to a bitter anti-imperialism. This anti-imperialism had its own revolutionary logic, one in which class was replaced by nation and which shared fully in the iconoclastic mood of the moment. The Jadids found much to admire in the Bolsheviks and their methods.

Yet, empire refused to die. From the moment of the collapse of the tsarist order, Russian settlers had worked to preserve their privileged position in the region. By autumn 1917, with famine looming, maintaining this privileged position had become, quite literally, a matter of life and death. The assumption of power by the Tashkent soviet was motivated by the food supply crisis. In its first months in power, the Tashkent soviet found all sorts of reasons to deny the local population any share in the power it had acquired through force of arms. Russian settlers, largely concentrated in Semirech'e, had been in conflict with the indigenous population since the uprising of 1916; armed by the state, they continued to wreak vengeance throughout 1917. In the winter of 1917–1918, with famine a reality, the revolutionary slogan of *vlast' na mestakh* ("power to the localities") provided a convenient mask for continuing the bloodletting.[3] There were divisions within the Russian community, to be sure—Russian peasants in Semirech'e acted to protect their grain as much from the requisitioning proclaimed by urban Russians as from the famine-stricken native population—but both sides were united in seeking to exclude the indigenous Muslim population from power. In this chaotic situation, ideology and political labels were of little consequence as various actors sought to protect their interests in a series of often bewildering alliances.[4] This was not how the central Bolshevik leadership in Moscow wanted to see Turkestan, however, and as early as spring 1918 it sought to intervene in Turkestani affairs, although Moscow's ability to enforce its will remained greatly circumscribed until Central Asia was subdued by the Red Army in 1920. Driven by its own visions of revolutionizing the East, the Bolshevik leadership saw in Turkestan the gateway to India and beyond. Thus, Moscow became an ally of Central Asian nationalists against local (settler) Russians. Anticolonialism worked in curious ways to bring the center closer to nationalist intellectuals on the periphery. The de facto alliance between the two was unequal and temporary, but it nevertheless left a deep mark on the course of events.

Attention to this politics allows us to locate the conjuncture of anticolonial struggle, global revolution, and the breakdown of imperial order at which modern Central Asia was forged. The transformation of the Jadids' view of identity merits closer attention because it allows us to question facile views of Central Asian history as being simply a record of victimization by the Russians and, even more important, because the Jadids were instrumental in articulating many of the identities that came to be entrenched in institutions of Soviet power. More broadly speaking, we need to pay attention to voices from the "periphery," especially those speaking in languages other than Russian, to appreciate the full extent of the social and intellectual transformations wrought by the collapse of the Russian autocracy.

A Contested Revolution

Conventional views of the national delimitation as Russian machination pay little heed to the extremely fluid political situation that obtained in Central Asia from autumn 1917 through summer 1920. The revolution had effectively redefined the geopolitical situation in Central Asia. Although the Russian civil war did not officially begin until May 1918, the military situation in the empire had been uncertain at least since autumn 1917 and had seriously undermined the apparatus of colonial power established half a century earlier. The blockade of Orenburg by Cossack forces had cut Turkestan off from European Russia; Cossacks also controlled Semirech'e for long periods. In Transcaspia, moderate Russian socialists succeeded in ousting the soviet and formed a government that actively sought assistance from the British in Iran. Bukhara remained under the control of the amir, whose power was only strengthened by the breakdown of order in Russia and whose independence was recognized de facto by the Soviet regime in Tashkent. The Ferghana valley was the scene of widespread rural disorders, as armed Russian settlers terrorized the native population, which in turn sought protection from armed bands (the so-called Basmachi). The southern border of the empire was porous for the first time since the conquest. The British, worried about the effect the absence of political control in Central Asia might have on their position in India, made three halfhearted attempts at intervention in the Russian civil war in Central Asia and the Caucasus. Spring 1918 also witnessed a string of victories for Ottoman armies in the Caucasus, while, in 1919, the third Anglo-Afghan war threw the situation open even further. Soviet power was established in a militarily meaningful way only in 1920; until then, the Soviet regime in Tashkent remained vulnerable. When the Tashkent soviet decided to send a diplomatic mission to Iran, with the unrevolutionary goals of reviving commerce, its representatives thought it prudent to take along a letter of introduction from F. M. Bailey, the British agent who had arrived by way of Kashgar to monitor matters of concern to the British.[5] The letter proved to be of no use, for the mission was promptly arrested by British troops after entering Iranian territory and its members sent off to detention camps in India. Similarly, in 1919, the Soviet regime in Tashkent established diplomatic relations with Afghanistan, only to have the Afghan government start opening unauthorized diplomatic missions all over Central Asia, much to the consternation of both the Soviets and the British.[6]

This geopolitical uncertainty was accompanied by a profound economic crisis. By 1918, the cotton economy was in utter ruin, while the famine of 1917 had assumed disastrous proportions. Over the next three years, the famine, its accompanying epidemics, and armed conflict with Russian settlers devastated the local population of Central Asia. Marco Buttino has estimated that the indigenous rural population of Central Asia declined by 23 percent between 1917 and 1920, mostly due to hunger and war.[7]

These traumatic events produced a profound change in the worldview of the Jadids. They had welcomed the fall of the autocracy as a moment of liberation and an opportunity to achieve national salvation. Their assumption, however, that their vision for the future would be widely shared by their society were quickly dashed, as opposition from within their society mounted during the course of the year. By the end of the year, a certain desperation had built up among the Jadids, for clearly the nation needed more than exhortation to heed their call for reform. At the same time, the collapse of the constitutional order on which they had pinned their hopes added to the desperation, just as the triumph of radicalism throughout Russia provided them with new models of change. The transformation of the geopolitical order as a result of World War I (and the Russian withdrawal from it) also allowed them to imagine change on a grander scale than had hitherto been possible. By spring 1918, the Jadid mood was quite different.[8]

The confrontation with the old order was nowhere more direct than in Bukhara. The February revolution in Russia brought the hope to Bukharan Jadids that the new liberal democratic regime in Russia would force the amir to promulgate reforms they had advocated for years. But the amir turned the issue into a question of Bukharan sovereignty and cast the Jadids as traitors to Islam and Bukhara. After a bloody confrontation in April, many Jadids fled to Kagan, the Russian enclave outside Bukhara. This marked a major turning point in Jadid attitudes in Bukhara. Persecution radicalized the Jadids, who now came to be called Young Bukharans and took on the form of a political party. Their realization that reform could not expected from the amir brought them closer to the Soviets. Over the next three years, the Young Bukharans were to travel an immense distance in their political odyssey.

These setbacks only convinced the Jadids of the necessity of a change in tactics. They put the fact of their electoral defeat down to the ignorance of their society and its need for education and enlightenment. But their inability to influence society had also brought home to them the importance of the state as an agent of change. Prerevolutionary Jadidism, excluded from the political realm, had existed as a discourse of reform and self-help in which the state played little part. This changed dramatically after 1917, and from summer 1918, many Jadids flocked to the new organs of government being built by the Soviet regime and opened to them under pressure from Moscow. Their aim was both to use the power of these organs to defend the local population against settler violence and to bring about radical change in that society. The Jadids negotiated a complex balance among Russian settlers, the regime in Moscow, and conservative forces in Muslim society itself.

The Turn to Anti-Imperialism

The radicalization of the Jadids as a result of the revolution affected also their outlook on the rest of the world. To a surprising extent, Jadid rhetoric before 1917 held out a highly positive view of Europe (or "the West"). Fitrat had even used a fictional European as his mouthpiece in what was perhaps the most influential piece of reformist writing of the period. For the Jadids, Europe and Europeans were exemplary sources of inspiration, a standard against which Central Asian society was to measure its shortcomings and its achievements.[9] Much of this admiration survived three years of war, in which most Jadids supported the Russian war effort, even after the Ottoman empire entered the war against Russia. By autumn 1917, however, the mood had begun to change, and it was to change dramatically over the next two years, as the hopes of radical change produced by the revolution coincided with anguish over Ottoman defeat and British victory in the heartlands of the Muslim world. In 1919, Fitrat, who eight years earlier had appropriated a fictional European as his mouthpiece, wrote a bitter denunciation of Europe and its civilization in a pamphlet entitled *The Eastern Question*.[10] The pamphlet provides an interesting look at how the new geopolitics appeared to a Central Asian intellectual at the high point of Muslim defeat, when the Ottoman empire had capitulated, when Muslim agitation in India seemed not to bear any fruit, and before the nationalist resistance in Anatolia had really begun.

The tract reverses many stereotypes of the East. For Fitrat, the East was a font of knowledge and enlightenment when Europe "wandered in the deserts of ignorance and barbarism."[11] But "unlike European imperialism, the East attempted not to drink the blood of its friends or to rob the house of its neighbors, but to raise the level of humanity in the world."[12] Ultimately, however, the East lost interest in learning and education, while its rulers became concerned only with filling their own bellies. As a result, "European imperialists" descended on the East. In order to hide their private interest in this exploitation, European imperialists proclaimed the savagery and ignorance of the Orientals and proclaimed for themselves a civilizing mission. The exploitation of the East was merciless: Fitrat claims that the British extracted 450 million rubles in revenue from India every year, while 3 percent of the Indian population died of hunger annually.[13] But the greatest damage was done at the moral level:

> It is a lie that Europe gave civilization to the East. European imperialists never allowed any progress or civilization in the countries they conquered in the East. The things given to us by Europe are well known: dissipation, immorality, gambling, drinking. Brothels, which are completely incompatible with the religion and customs of the East, were opened in our land by European imperialists. Liquor stores, which despoil the life and society of all humanity, were founded in our country through the efforts of European imperialists. The frightening disease called "syphilis" also came to the East along with the conquests of European imperialists. In short: to this day, European imperialists have not given the East anything but immorality and destruction. . . . One wonders whether European imperialists did such things knowingly or unknowingly? Of course they did [so] knowingly, intentionally. They desired not to civilize us, disseminate knowledge among us, [or] to help us progress; [they desired, rather] to open all sorts of brothels and taverns, and [thus] to destroy our morals, ruin our health, to weaken our race, to ruin our commerce, and to make us dependent on themselves.[14]

Fitrat here reverses the usual essentialist stereotypes of the East, but his argument remains, of course, essentialist. Fitrat speaks of "European imperialists" exploiting their own peasants ("the 'hungry hawks' of Europe . . . sent their own ignorant and illiterate workers and peasants to the East, who understanding nothing, attacked the workers and peasants in the East"),[15] and he describes in some detail the economic aspect of colonial exploitation, but, beyond that, he sees Europe's animosity to the East as driven entirely by an innate cultural flaw. The explanation for the change in the East's fortunes is given solely in terms of knowledge and morals. As I argue later in this chapter, this was the only diagnosis that a radicalized and politicized cultural elite living through a tumultuous period could arrive at. The answer to the misfortunes of the East lay in enlightenment and astute leadership, both of which the Jadids claimed to provide.

Writing in summer 1919, it appeared to Fitrat that the long-term offensive of European imperialism was nearing a culmination: the Ottoman empire, the most powerful Muslim state and symbolic of much more than a dynasty, lay prone (the nationalist resistance led by Mustafa Kemal had not yet emerged), and the British occupied vast tracts of land in the heartland of the Muslim world and were preparing to establish an Arab caliphate as a puppet regime. The answer lay in an alliance with the only force that was anti-imperialist: Soviet Russia. In October 1917, Fitrat had been less than enthusiastic about the Bolshevik seizure of power in Petrograd, but by 1919 things had changed, and he proposed a strategic alliance between the Muslim world and Soviet Russia. "The government of Soviet Russia has struggled with European imperialists. Its motto is 'Victory or Death.' This is exactly the kind of effort, and exactly this kind of nobility required to unite the East."[16] Fitrat noted that "Comrade Lenin, the leader of Soviet Russia, is a great man, who has already begun the attempt at awakening and uniting the East," but that these efforts had been less than successful: "In order to unify the East, it was necessary to take the Orientals into confidence and to make [the Soviets] known to them. In order to gain the trust of the Orientals, it was necessary to not paint the East in the colors of Communism by force, but to take account of the point of view of the East, and its own intuition."[17] Russian communists in Turkestan had balked at the prospect of forging a nonideological alliance with the East. At the same time, given that the European and American proletariat had failed to rise to the Soviets' support, the Soviets had no choice but to form an alliance with the East.[18]

This optimistic estimate of mutual need explains why there is nary a mention of Russian imperialism in *The Eastern Question*. While the British bear the burden of the bulk of Fitrat's wrath and the French come in for scathing comment, Russian imperialism attracts only a single comment: "Our oppression by the Russian imperial government was no less than the oppression of India by the British."[19] With settler violence at its height in 1919, it is striking that Fitrat does not even mention it. Imperialism was connected, for Fitrat, with state policies, and, therefore, settler violence did not qualify. Moreover, Fitrat had attached his hopes to the regime in Moscow, not to Russian communists in Turkestan. The distinction between what Moscow stood for and what Central Asian Soviets did was accepted by many Jadids, who sought to fight the latter with the help of the former.

The shift in Jadid rhetoric to anti-imperialism had several sources. World War I, with the Ottomans fighting against the Russians, had tested the loyalties of the Russian empire's Muslim population from the beginning. Russian officialdom feared all along that Russia's Muslims would act as a fifth column for the Ottomans. At the height of the age of empire, the Ottoman empire was the only independent Muslim state in the world, and its travails over the previous decade had attracted a great deal of sympathy among the Muslims of the Russian empire. Yet, ultimately, officialdom's fears were based in an essentialist view of Muslim opinion that had little connection with political realities. Russia's Muslims remained loyal through three years of war. Muslim troops had fought on the front lines, and the rest of the Muslim population had remained calm. In Central Asia, the secret police lived in constant fear of native rebellion under the influence of Ottoman propaganda, but none transpired until the revolt of the Kazakh and

Kyrgyz nomads provoked by a decree mobilizing them for work in the rear in 1916. That revolt, while anti-Russian and antiwar, had little to do with Ottoman machinations. Central Asian Jadids had indeed opposed the revolt and cooperated with the authorities in making conscription work smoothly.[20]

The revolution changed all that. As the war effort melted away in 1917, old Russia's enemies began to appear as friends, while the Bolsheviks' anticapitalist rhetoric aimed at Russia's erstwhile allies found resonance, for slightly different reasons, with the Jadids. By autumn 1917, it was permissible to openly sympathize with the Ottomans. If capitalism, so to speak, was the highest form of imperialism, then Britain and France were the champions of imperialism; alongside the world's proletariat and the entire colonial world, the Ottoman empire (and hence the entire Muslim world) was among the victims of imperialism. The publication by the Bolsheviks of the secret treaties signed by imperial Russia with Britain and France during the war, most of them at the expense of the Ottoman empire, touched a raw nerve among the Jadids. Fitrat, who knew the Ottoman empire more intimately than any other Central Asian Jadid, having spent four formative years as a student in Istanbul, wrote that "it had now become clear who the real enemies of the Muslim, and especially the Turkic, world are."[21] The defeat of the Ottoman empire in 1918 further fueled anti-Entente (and especially anti-British) sentiment, especially as the British emerged as the biggest victors in the Near East. Europe was now synonymous with imperialism, and the British were its worst perpetrators.

While sympathy with the plight of the Ottomans was the most important factor in the transformation of Jadid attitudes, it was hardly the only one. The revolution had radicalized Jadid thought in general. Before February 1917, the Jadids had worked in a precarious public space allowed by the autocracy, and their aims had been correspondingly modest. Moreover, at the height of the age of empire, the imperial order had seemed "natural." Knowledge was the key to progress and happiness; ignorance brought death and extinction or, at the very least, conquest and colonization. The Russian revolution had brought an empire to its knees and allowed many to imagine a world in which empire was not a fundamental fact of political life. The turn to anti-imperialism among the Jadids in 1917–1918 was part of a broader shift to a more systemic critique of the modern world.

That anti-imperialism was more than a surrogate for pan-Turkist sympathies becomes clear from the popularity of India and anti-British struggles in India as a theme in Jadid writing in this period. In 1920 Fitrat wrote two plays, both of which played very successfully in Turkestan, that bear directly on India. In *Chin sevish* (True Love), he portrayed the love of Zulaikha for Nuruddin, a patriotic, revolutionary poet, which is foiled by Rahmatullah, an Anglophile who desires Zulaikha as he has desired many young maidens before. In the traditions of Jadid theater established before the revolution, the play ends in a bloodbath, as a secret meeting of an Indian revolutionary committee, attended by both Zulaikha and Nuruddin, is ambushed by the police (who are led it to it by Rahmatullah). But the linkage among love, patriotism, and revolution is firmly established. True love is inextricable from patriotism, while the failure to support patriotic revolution is synonymous with treason. In *Hind ixtilolchilari* (Indian Revolutionaries), which also portrays the struggle of Indian patriots for independence, Fitrat repeated these themes, but in a more overtly political manner. Rahim Bakhsh is an educated young man in love with Dilnavoz, both of them afire with patriotic love. After the police arrest Dilnavoz, Rahim Bakhsh has to overcome his earlier ambivalence, and he joins a clandestine group of "revolutionaries" in a mountainous redoubt on the Afghan frontier. The plot is similar in its tragic ending, but love for country is again equated with love for a woman and protection of her honor. Anti-imperialism, patriotism, and revolutionary action are inextricably intertwined.

Nation and Revolution

Revolution was comprehensible to the Jadids only as national salvation. When Jadid authors wrote of oppression and exploitation, they tended to refer to that of colonial nations by imperial nations and their lackeys, rather than that of classes. But the revolution was also to revolutionize the nation itself, for only revolutionary change could ensure the salvation of the nation. For years, the Jadids had argued that nothing less than the survival of their nation was stake if the nation did not heed their call for change.[22] The mayhem of civil war and famine seemed to them to have confirmed their worst fears. The Jadids had seen the path to salvation to lie through enlightenment, education, and moral rectitude, things that only a cultural elite could provide. This basic prescription did not change after 1917, although the methods that the Jadids could contemplate to bring this about changed dramatically. The Jadids' propensity to see in the revolution a national allegory was a direct result of their status as a *cultural*, rather than a political, elite.

Yet, this culturalist and anti-imperialist reading of the revolution fit very well with Bolshevik practice of the moment. For Stalin, people's commissar for nationalities affairs, the Muslim areas of the Russian empire were inhabited by "culturally backward peoples"; the tasks of the Soviet regime in these areas were to "raise the cultural level of the backward peoples, . . . to enlist the toiling masses . . . in the building of the Soviet state, [and] to do away with all disabilities . . . that prevent the peoples of the East from . . . emancipating themselves from the survivals of medievalism and national oppression."[23] The Jadids could have found little in this prognosis with which to disagree. Similarly, from their first moments in power, the Bolsheviks had conflated their ideological and their strategic goals. Their list of the oppressed of the planet ranged from the European proletariat, through the (non-Russian) peoples of Russia, to the entire colonial world. Revolutionizing the East thus early became an important foreign policy concern for the Bolsheviks. Lenin had issued a proclamation to the "Toiling Muslims of Russia and the East" as early as November 1917, and in the ensuing years Moscow and other Soviet cities became centers where colonial intellectuals and radicals congregated. The Bolsheviks expended considerable organizational energy on the matter. A Central Bureau of Muslim Communist Organizations of the RKP(b) had been organized in November 1918, with responsibility for revolutionary work among the Muslims of the Russian empire and its neighbors. The Bolsheviks also ceaselessly claimed to be the champions of all "oppressed peoples of the East," but especially of the Muslim world. When Amir Amanullah Khan of Afghanistan declared his country independent of the British, he was widely hailed, both by the Bolsheviks and the Jadids, as a hero. The unfolding struggle against foreign occupation in Anatolia similarly aroused great interest in both Russia and Central Asia. Numerous groups of "Indian revolutionaries"—nationalists who sought to bring down British rule in India by armed force—converged on Soviet Russia and were favorably received.[24]

Bolshevik support for anti-imperialist movements in "the East" was based on the same conflation of anticolonialism, Islam, and revolution that Fitrat wrote about. Sometimes it made for strange bedfellows, as when Enver Pasha, the erstwhile Ottoman war minister, received moral and material support from the Soviet regime in 1919 and 1920.[25] Other, less well-known cases of cooperation were of more significance to Central Asia. As Amanullah readied to take on the British in the third Afghan war, he sent a personal mission to Moscow to seek Soviet support for his actions. The mission was headed by Muhammad Barkatullah, a veteran "Indian revolutionary" who had spent the war years in Kabul attempting to persuade Amanullah's predecessor to declare war on the British by invading India. Now Barkatullah's long-held anticolonialism turned naturally into support for the Soviet regime. On his way to Moscow, he passed through Tashkent, where he was widely quoted in the Muslim press. Having fulfilled his mission, which included a meeting with Lenin, Barkatullah spent the rest of the year roaming the Muslim areas of the Russian empire, exhorting Muslims to support the Bolsheviks. With official blessings, he published in Persian (a language understood by most educated Central Asians) a pamphlet called *Bolshevism and Islam*, in which he argued for a great affinity between the two.[26]

The hope of using anti-imperialist sentiment to destabilize capitalist regimes in Europe played a significant role in bringing Moscow closer to Central Asian Jadids. The policies of the Tashkent Soviet in the winter of 1917–1918 were completely reckless from Moscow's point of view. In February 1918, therefore, the newly formed people's commissariat for nationality affairs sent a mission with plenipotentiary powers to Turkestan to assert its will. The mission, composed of P. A. Kobozev and two Tatars, Y. Ibrahimov and Arif Klevleev, was largely successful in attracting Muslims into Soviet and Party organs. While archival research on the recruitment of Muslims into the party in its first years is still not possible, all evidence suggests that large numbers of Jadids joined it as soon as it was possible. Existing organizations adopted new, revolutionary names: the Samarqand Labor Union turned itself into the Muslim Soviet of Workers' and

Peasants' Deputies of Samarqand *uezd* (district), while the Tatar Union in Tashkent became the Tatar Socialist Workers' Committee, and eventually the Tatar section of the Communist Party of Turkestan (KPT). The Samarqand Jadid newspaper *Hurriyat* (Liberty) was adopted by the education section of the Samarqand Soviet as its organ and was soon renamed *Mehnatkashlar tovushi* (Toilers' Voice).[27] Radicalized Jadids became Muslim communists.

The Young Bukharans similarly entered into ever-closer cooperation with the Soviet regime. Before the end of 1917, several Young Bukharans were members of the executive committee of the Kagan soviet, and many others found refuge in Turkestan. Fayzullah Kho'jaev, future president of Uzbekistan, spent much of 1918 in Moscow, where an office of the Young Bukharan party was supported by the Central Bureau of Muslim Communist Organizations. The identification of the Jadids with revolution and the convergence of their interests with those of Soviet power were quite unequivocal. When the Red Army stormed first Khiva and then Bukhara in 1920, it was accompanied by the Jadids, who proceeded to form their own governments there. These so-called People's Republics proved short-lived, but that should not hide from view the fact of the very real identity of interests that then existed between two different kinds of revolution.

The conflation of class and nation allowed by anti-imperialism could, of course, be used against Russian settlers in Turkestan just as easily as against the British. Fitrat had avoided any mention of Russian settlers in *The Eastern Question*, but conferences of Muslim communists routinely criticized them. Food supply committees, subordinated to the soviets by early 1918, became the most significant arena of political conflict, but the conflict soon spread to the highest organs of the party itself. A Central Committee decree in July 1919 demanding that the indigenous population of Turkestan enjoy proportional representation in all state organs provided an opportunity for Muslims in the party to act. New party and Soviet congresses were hurriedly convened, and both elected new executive committees dominated by Muslims. Turar Rïsqulov, future head of government in Turkestan and author of one of the most important books on the revolution in Central Asia, was elected president of both committees. This burst of activity culminated in January 1920 at the Fifth Regional Conference of the KPT, where Muslim communists succeeded in passing a resolution changing the name of the KPT to the "Communist Party of the Turkic Peoples" and that of the Turkestan Republic to the "Turkic Republic." Another resolution demanded wide-ranging autonomy for Turkestan.[28]

The juxtaposition of nationalist and communist language was used again when a plenipotentiary delegation from Turkestan traveled to Moscow in May 1920 to present the Muslim communist case to the highest party authorities after the January resolutions had been overridden, after some vacillation, by the recently appointed Special Commission on Turkestan Affairs of the RKP(b) (Turkkomissiia). In a presentation to the Central Committee, the delegation argued that there were only two basic groups in Turkestan, "the oppressed and exploited colonial natives and European capital."[29] The delegation went on to demand the transfer of all authority in Turkestan to the Central Executive Committee of Turkestan, the abolition of the Turkkomissiia, and the establishment of a Muslim army subordinate to the autonomous government of Turkestan.[30] These demands were couched in the language of revolution, but class had been replaced by nation; national liberation of the Muslim community could be achieved through communist means and in the soviet context.

Defining the Nation

The exact constitution of the nation remained a matter of contestation, both among Central Asians and between them and various Russian actors, for several years to come. For Fitrat, the nation clearly extended to the entire "Muslim world," an expression that he uses repeatedly. Much of the rhetoric of the Young Bukharans appealed, instead, to a Bukharan nation defined territorially. Yet, Jadid rhetoric from 1917 on was also marked by an often strident pride in Jadidists' Turkic origins. Islam, patriotism, and nationalism provided three interlinked visions of identity that coexisted in considerable tension in Jadid thought in this period.

The Eastern Question was by far the most stridently pan-Islamic text to be penned by a Jadid author. Appeals to Muslim unity on a pan-Islamic basis were always coupled with an insistence that Muslim society reform itself and its culture in order to be able to cope with the needs of the new age. Pan-Islamists were modernists, just as pan-Islam was a modern sentiment, reflecting a community ("the Muslim world") imagined for the first time in the late nineteenth century. In official Soviet parlance, too, "Muslim" designated a nationality in the same way that "Jewish" did, and the creation of Musbiuro indicated that such designations created their own realities. "Muslim" in Central Asia thus became an entity more closely circumscribed than the entirety of the Muslim world, a designation of the Muslims of Central Asia, a convenient marker for distinguishing the indigenous population from European settlers of various sorts.

The Bukharan nation evoked by the Young Bukharans was primarily territorial. Yet, Islam, as the religious and cultural marker of identity of the vast majority of Bukhara's population, could never be extricated from definitions of Bukharan nationhood. Patriotism loomed large in Jadid thought, both before and after 1917. For Fitrat, patriotic duty such as driving the English out of India was a great duty, "as great as saving the pages of the Qur'an from being trampled by an animal . . . a worry as great as that of driving a pig out of a mosque."[31] Indeed, the demands of patriotism and anti-imperial struggle seemed to outweigh Islam as a node of solidarity. In *Indian Revolutionaries*, Fitrat took great pains to make this point. His revolutionaries include both Muslims and Hindus. When Dilnavoz expresses reservations about the appropriateness of sharing the sentiments of the Hindu Lala Hardayal, Rahim Bakhsh replies, "Humanity does not depend of paganism or Islam. Lala Hardayal is a human being."[32] Later in the play, Maulavi Nu'man, a tribal leader on the Afghan frontier and a traditional Muslim scholar, objects similarly to cooperating with Hindu patriots. Abdussu-buh, a Muslim revolutionary leader, harangues him thus:

> You mullahs always say this. For many years, you have filled India with disputes over tribes and nations. You have divided the people into seventy-four groups and set them against one another. You have filled our land with internal squab-bles and thus brought the English upon our heads. After a hundred years, we have [finally] begun to unify in order to liberate ourselves. Again you want to block our path with squabbles over religions and sects! . . . We will struggle [for our freedom] hand in hand. Neither you, nor religion can keep us from this path.[33]

But patriotism was also connected to nationalism. Beginning in 1917, Jadid rhet-oric turned more and more to a radical form of Turkism. For the Jadids, the new conditions pushed to the fore the romantic notions of Turkicness that had been present in their rhetoric before the revolution. All through the year, Jadid writers evoked Genghis Khan, Timur, and Ulugh-bek as Central Asian heroes. Fitrat wrote in July 1917: "O great Turan, the land of lions! What happened to you? What bad days have you fallen into? What happened to the brave Turks who once ruled the world? Why did they pass? Why did they go away?"[34] Other assertions of Turkicness were legion. In spring 1918, a newspaper, *Turk so'zi* (Turkic Word), was being published in Tashkent by an organization called Turk O'rtoqlig'i (Turkic Friendship). More significant was the claim, now asserted for the first time, that Central Asia was the homeland of the Turks and that Turks had a claim to ownership of the territory. Central Asian Jadids now commonly claimed that all inhabitants of Central Asia were "really" Turks; if they did not speak Turkic, it was because they had forgotten it.[35] The targets of this claim were, of course, the large numbers of Persian speakers who inhabited the cities of Bukhara, Samarqand, and Khujand, as well as the large rural areas surround-ing them. The revolution, as we have seen, meant national salvation, which was to be achieved through the enlightenment of the nation and the development of a national literature in *the* national language. Revolution thus became synonymous with Turkicizing the Persian-speaking population of Central Asia. One of the first acts of the Young Bukharans after assuming power in 1920 was to replace Persian with Turkic as the official language of the new republic. The ensuing politics constituted, over the next several years, the national entity called "Tajik," which in 1924 emerged as an autonomous republic within Uzbekistan, upgraded to a union republic in 1929. The Turkic nationalists managed, however, to make sure that Bukhara and Samarqand remained in Uzbekistan.

The assertion of Turkicness was itself complex. Conceptions of Turkic nation-alism in the romantic mold had moved Turkic intellectuals in both the Ottoman and the Russian empires since the late nineteenth century. The discourse of Turkic nationalism remained differentiated and polyphonic, as Ottoman, Tatar,

Azerbaijani, and Central Asian intellectuals produced different visions of Turk-icness. Pan-Turkism, the project of uniting all Turkic peoples of the world in one political entity, was the most extreme assertion of the Turkist vision, and, although it became official policy in the last years of the Ottoman empire, it was never synonymous with Turkic nationalism. The emphasis on Turkism in Central Asia from 1917 on stemmed from the radical mood among the Jadids, rather than from any direct Ottoman influence, and it remained limited to Central Asia itself. In 1918, Fitrat was the moving force behind the creation of the Chig'atoy Gurungi (Chaghatay Conversation), a literary circle that brought together many leading political and literary activists. Its members were concerned with the reform of the Central Asian Turkic literary language and script, as they sought to define an identity for the people of Central Asia rooted in ethnicity, as well as in history.[36] "Chaghatayism" sought to create a common national identity for Turkic Central Asia. The term "Chaghatay" referred to the name of the Eastern Turkic literary language around which the fifteenth-century efflorescence of Central Asia had taken place. It also evoked the Genghisid heritage of the region, although the central role in the Chaghatayid tradition was played by Timur (Tamerlane), the Turkic Muslim conqueror of the fourteenth century. The realm of Chaghatay was also an eastern counterpart to the western Turkic empire of the Ottomans. As such, Chaghatayism was clearly not pan-Turkic, since it asserted the existence of local group boundaries within the Turkic world. Rather, Central Asia was the heart of a distinct Turkic realm, an Eastern counterpart of the now vanquished Ottoman empire.

The jump from Chaghatay to Uzbek was made quite easily. Jadid writers had argued, though not very insistently, that the entire Turkic population of Central Asia was Uzbek. This argument was primarily directed at the label "Sart," the designation for the local turcophone population preferred by Russian administrators and scholars and, after their fashion, even by Tatar intellectuals.[37] Jadid writers routinely used Turkic (*Turk, turkcha*) synonymously with Uzbek (*O'zbek, o'zbekcha*) even before 1917. With the assertion of ethnic nationalism after 1917, the usage of the term "Uzbek" became very widespread, as is clearly evident from the vernacular press of the period. Hymns to the Uzbek nation were common-place in periodicals published by organs of the Soviet regime. Chaghatayism was to provide the historical inheritance of the modern Uzbek nation, which encom-passed all the Muslim inhabitants of Central Asia. Ultimately, this maximalist vision of Uzbekness lost out to a slightly more circumscribed vision, which ex-cluded the Persian-speaking population of the region (who came to constitute the Tajik nation), as well as various nomadic groups (Türkmen, Kazakh, Kyrgyz, Karakalpak), which could be easily marked off from the sedentary Turkic pop-ulation of the region. In a sense, the Uzbek nation that emerged in 1924 at the time of the national delimitation was residual, but it could therefore claim the entire inheritance of urban Central Asia. Uzbek nationalism developed, therefore, as a regionally hegemonic ideology, since it represented what it saw as the main-stream Turkic, Muslim, urban—and revolutionary—tradition of Central Asia.

The political uncertainty born of the revolution and the civil war began to ebb by late 1920, when, having secured victory in the civil war, the party could effectively assert its will in the borderlands. The Turkkomissiia began by subduing the Muslim communists led by Rïsqulov. In July 1920, it dissolved the nationalist-dominated *Kraikom* of the KPT and replaced it with a provisional committee, which held new party and soviet congresses in September. These accepted Central Committee resolutions calling for stricter control by the center over affairs in Turkestan.[38] This defeat for Rïsqulov and his followers did not, however, spell the end of the alliance between the center and local nationalists. Members of the Turkkomissiia were very enthusiastic about revolutionizing the East, which in 1920 came to be synonymous with Red Army action. During that year, the Red Army helped install Soviet republics in Khiva, Bukhara, and Gilan, all under Soviet overlordship but run by local activists.[39] It was only in spring 1921 that improving relations with Britain forced authorities in Moscow to rein in the Turk-komissiia. The ouster of Muslim communists from control of the KPT also has to be considered alongside the Turkkomissiia's actions against Russian settlers, thousands of whom were deported to central Russia in 1921 for having opposed Soviet power and especially its nationality policies.[40]

Soviet power, moreover, came with a vision of the world divided into nations that could be objectively defined and demarcated.[41] This view of the ontological reality of nations had a great deal in common with the nationalism espoused by Central Asian intellectuals. The regime also placed a high priority on matters of enlightenment and on overcoming backwardness, issues that had long been dear to the Jadids. The grounds for cooperation between Moscow and the Jadids were substantial. The vernacular press from the early 1920s had a marked Jadid flavor, as writers celebrated the great national awakening then under way and the progress the nation was making by the day. The one difference was over defining national boundaries: the Jadids hoped to retain the unity of Turkestan and Bu-khara as homelands for a single Turkic Muslim nation, while Soviet ethnographers insisted on narrower definitions. The latter triumphed in 1924, although Uzbekness retains many of the characteristics of the Turkic Muslim nation imagined by the Jadids. The revolution had succeeded rather well for the Jadids.

In Central Asia, the revolution was effectively nationalized by a radicalized cultural elite bent on revolutionizing the nation. This nationalization of the revolution benefited from an alliance of the nationalists with the Bolsheviks, who found common cause with the nationalists against local manifestations of empire in the form of settler violence. The alliance was short lived, to be sure, but it was instrumental in shaping new identities and in setting the agenda for social and cultural transformation in the first decade of Soviet rule. It reminds us that Soviet nation building in Central Asia was a deeply contested process that cannot be adequately explained in terms of simple dichotomies of empire versus nation or center versus periphery.

Notes

1. See, e.g., Edward Allworth, *The Modern Uzbeks: A Cultural History* (Stanford: Stanford University Press, 1990), pp. 176–188.

2. The classic expression of this view is Richard Pipes, *The Formation of the Soviet Union: Communism and Nationalism, 1917–1923* (Cambridge, Mass.: Harvard University Press, 1954). From a different point on the political spectrum, essentially the same argument is made by R. Vaidyanath, *The Formation of the Soviet Central Asian Republics: A Study in Nationalities Policy, 1917–1936* (New Delhi: People's Publishing House, 1967). As far as Soviet scholarship was concerned, there was nothing to this problem other than the Solomonic division of the land between several objectively existing nationalities, a task successfully carried out by the party. For a classic statement of this view, see R. Tuzmuhamedov, *How the National Question Was Solved in Soviet Central Asia* (Moscow: Progress, 1973).

3. Marco Buttino has analyzed this period in a series of articles; see his " 'La terra a chi la lavora': la politica coloniale russa in Turkestan tra la crisi dello Zarismo e le rivoluzioni del 1917," in Alberto Masoero and Antonello Venturi, eds., *Russica: Studi e ricerche sulla Russia contemporanea* (Milan: Franco Angeli, 1990); Buttino, "Politics and Social Conflict during a Famine: Turkestan Immediately after the Revolution," in Buttino, ed., *In a Collapsing Empire: Underdevelopment, Ethnic Conflicts and Nationalisms in the Soviet Union* (Milan: Fondazione Giangiaconio Feltainelli, 1993).

4. Jeff Sahadeo, "Creating a Russian Colonial Community: Urbanization, Nationality, and Empire in Tashkent, 1865–1924" (Ph.D. diss., University of Illinois at Urbana-Champaign, 2000), ch. 6; Buttino, "Ethnicité et politique dans la guerre civile: à propos du *basmačestvo* au Fergana," *Cahiers du monde russe* 38 (1997): 195–222.

5. M. V. Popov, *Missiia E. A. Babushkina v Irane (maloizvestnaia stranitsa istorii sovetskoi diplomatii)* (Moscow: Nauka, 1974), pp. 35–36.

6. Ludwig Adamec, *Afghanistan, 1900–1923: A Diplomatic History* (Berkeley: University of California Press, 1967).

7. Marco Buttino, "Study of the Economic Crisis and Depopulation in Turkestan, 1917–1920," *Central Asian Survey* 9, no. 4 (1990): 64–69.

8. Adeeb Khalid, *The Politics of Muslim Cultural Reform: Jadidism in Central Asia* (Berkeley: University of California Press, 1998), chapter 8.

9. See my "Representations of Russia in Central Asian Jadid Discourse," in Daniel R. Brower and Edward J. Lazzerini, eds., *Russia's Orient: Imperial Borderlands and Peoples, 1700–1917* (Bloomington: Indiana University Press, 1997), pp. 188–202.

10. [Abdurauf] Fitrat, *Sharq siyosati* (n.p., n.d. [1919]).

11. Ibid., p. 1.

12. Ibid., p. 7.

13. Ibid., p. 16.

14. Ibid., pp. 12–13.

15. Ibid., p. 10.

16. Ibid., p. 40.

17. Ibid., pp. 40–41.

18. Ibid., p. 43.

19. Ibid., p. 22.

20. Khalid, *The Politics of Muslim Cultural Reform*, pp. 241–242.

21. Abdurauf Fitrat, "Yoshurun muohidalari," *Hurriyat* (Samarqand), November 28, 1917.

22. Khalid, *The Politics of Muslim Cultural Reform*, chapter 4.

23. I. V. Stalin, "Nashi zadachi na Vostoke," *Pravda*, March 2, 1919.

24. M. A. Persits, *Revoliutsionery Indii v strane sovetov, 1918–1921* (Moscow: Nauka, 1973); Tilak Raj Sareen, *The Russian Revolution and India* (New Delhi: Sterling, 1978); Khizar Humayun Ansari, *The Emergence of Socialist Thought among North Indian Muslims (1917–1947)* (Lahore: Book Traders, 1990), chapter 1.

25. On Enver's career in Soviet Russia, see Masayuki Yamauchi, *The Green Crescent under the Red Star: Enver Pasha in Soviet Russia, 1919–1922* (Tokyo: Institute for the Study of Languages and Cultures of Asia and Africa, 1991); V. M. Gilensen, "Sotrudni-chestvo krasnoi Moskvy s Enver-Pashoi i Dzhemal'-Pashoi," *Vostok* (1996), no. 3: 45–63.

26. I have not yet been able to locate a copy of the original, but a typescript English translation is in India Office Library and Records, London, L/P&S/10/836, 52–63. On Barkatullah, see Sayyid Abid Ali Vajdi al-Husaini, *Maulana Barkatullah Bhopali: inqilabi savanih* (Bhopal, 1986).

27. *Pobeda Oktiabr'skoi revoliutsii v Uzbekistane: sbornik dokumentov*, 2 vols. (Tashkent: Fan, 1963–1972), 2:235, 289, 303, 420–421.

28. Gosudarstvennyi arkhiv Rossiiskoi Federatsii, Moscow, f. 130, op. 4, d. 786, ll. 3–30b; see also *Rezoliutsii i postanovleniia s"ezdov Kommunisticheskoi partii Turkestana (1918–1924 gg.)* (Tashkent: Uzbekistan, 1968), p. 70.

29. T. R. Ryskulov, "Doklad polnomochnoi delegatsii Turkestanskoi respubliki V. I. Leninu," *Sobranie sochinenii v trekh tomakh* (Almaty: Qazaqstan, 1998), 3:175.

30. Ibid., pp. 180–181.

31. Abdurauf Fitrat, "Hind ixtilolchilari," in Sherali Turdiev, ed. *Sharq yulduzi* (1990), no. 6: 37.

32. Ibid., 38. Lala Hardayal was a historical figure, a veteran leader of the Indian revolutionary movement in exile. Yet, there is considerable irony in Fitrat's spirited defense of Hardayal's right to lead Indian revolutionaries, for Hardayal's passion for revolution ran out by 1920. Desperate to return home, he sought to ingratiate himself with the British by writing a craven denunciation of his own past. See Har Dayal, *Forty-four Months in Germany and Turkey: A Record of Personal Impressions* (London: P. S. King & Dayal, 1920).

33. Fitrat, "Hind ixtilolchilari," p. 45.

34. [Abdurauf] Fitrat, "Yurt qoyg'usi," *Hurriyat*, July 28, 1917.

35. This claim was first made before the war by Turkists in the Ottoman empire (see, e.g., "Buhara-yi serif Gazetesi," *Türk Yurdu* 1 [1912], 376) but seldom put in print in Central Asia itself. The Bukharan Jadid Abdulvohid Munzim, who later opted for a Tajik identity, recalled in some autobiographical notes that Fitrat, a fellow Bukharan, had returned from Istanbul in 1914 deeply convinced that all Bukharans were Turks who had, over the generations, forgotten their "real" language; see Sohib Tabarov, *Munzim* (Dushanbe: Irfon, 1992), p. 40. Fitrat, however, continued to write almost exclusively in Persian until 1917, after which he almost never wrote in it.

36. Hisao Komatsu, "The Evolution of Group Identity among Bukharan Intellectuals in 1911–1928: An Overview," *Memoirs of the Research Department of the Toyo Bunko*, no. 47 (1989): 115–144.

37. The debate over Sart is described in Khalid, *The Politics of Muslim Cultural Reform*, pp. 199–208.

38. *Ocherki istorii Kommunisticheskoi Partii Turkestana*, 5 vols. (Tashkent: Uzbekistan, 1958–1964), 3:152–156.

39. Soviet actions in Central Asia have received substantial scholarly attention recently; see V. L. Genis, "Razgrom Bukharskogo emirata v 1920 godu," *Voprosy istorii*, (1993), no. 7: 39–53; Genis, *Krasnaia Persiia* (Moscow: MNPI, 2000); M. A. Persits, *Zastenchivaia interventsiia: o sovetskom vtorzhenii v Iran i Bukharu v 1920–1921 gg.* (Moscow: Muravei Nuravei-Gaid, 1999).

40. V. L. Genis, "Deportatsiia russkikh iz Turkestana v 1921 godu ('Delo Safarova')," *Voprosy istorii* (1998), no. 1: 44–58.

41. This point has been made in excellent fashion by Yuri Slezkine, "The USSR as a Communal Apartment, or How a Socialist State Promoted Ethnic Particularism," *Slavic Review* 53 (1994): 414–452; see also Rogers Brubaker, *Nationalism Reframed: Nationhood and the National Question in the New Europe* (Cambridge: Cambridge University Press, 1996), chapter 2.

PART III

Forging "Nations"

Local Politics and the Birth of the Republic of Bashkortostan, 1919–1920

IN EARLY 1919, AMONG THE DARKEST DAYS of the Russian civil war, the Soviet government began a collaboration with a small group of Bashkir politicians and military officers who had previously fought against Soviet power alongside the troops of Admiral Alexander Kolchak, the tsarist naval officer who commanded anti-Bolshevik forces in Siberia. The two sides reached an agreement whereby the Bashkirs would end their anti-Soviet activities and turn their weapons against Kolchak; in return, the Soviet government recognized Bashkortostan, a land of rugged hills and broad plains straddling the Ural mountains, as an autonomous part of the Russian Soviet Federated Socialist Republic (RSFSR). There followed some sixteen months of increasingly difficult collaboration between the Bashkir nationalists and the Russian Bolsheviks, ending when the foremost figure in the Bashkir movement, Ahmed Zeki Validov, and his closest aides abandoned the effort and fled to join the Basmachi guerrillas in Central Asia.

Why should this episode command our attention? The dramatic defection of Bashkir troops weakened Kolchak's front on the eve of his 1919 spring offensive, dramatically revealed the discontent among his non-Russian allies, and may have marked a significant turning point in the military campaign on the eastern front. Historian Richard Pipes viewed the Bolshevik-Bashkir collaboration as the "first experiment in Soviet nationality policy," by which he meant the emerging Soviet practice of granting territorial autonomy to non-Russian nationalities. For Pipes, the failure of the Bashkir experiment prefigured the failure of Soviet nationality policy in general, as non-Russian hopes for autonomy were crushed by both the inherent tendency of the Soviet regime toward centralization and its affinity with Russian nationalism. Finally, we can see the formation of a Bashkir republic as a critical moment in the history of the emerging Bashkir nation, for it created the framework within which Bashkir national identity has been nurtured up to the present.[1]

This chapter focuses on the Bolshevik-Bashkir collaboration as an example of the relationship during the Russian civil war between centralized decision making on nationality affairs and the messy world of local political life in the provinces, with its opportunistic alliances and awkward coalitions, its sudden shifts in political fortunes and possibilities. As Terry Martin and Ron Suny have argued elsewhere in this volume, the premier makers of Soviet nationality policy, specifically the head of party and state Vladimir Lenin and the commissar for nationality affairs Iosif Stalin, shared a firm commitment to the creation of national republics outfitted with a small set of guaranteed national rights. However, this overall conceptual framework leaves many questions of vital strategic and tactical significance wide open. Which "nations" would be recognized as deserving of a territorial republic? When and under what circumstances would their recognition bring maximum political benefit? With which nationalist groups should the regime negotiate? How could this nationality policy be implemented in the chaos of civil war? At this level, Soviet nationality policy was a great act of improvisation. Moreover, these decisions were not always carefully planned out in Moscow but were shaped in critical ways by local actors and conditions, frequently in directions that policymakers like Lenin and Stalin did not expect or intend.[2] Examining the vagaries of local political life will help us answer several specific questions. Why did the Bolshevik leadership recognize Bashkir autonomy in 1919? Was there a deliberate Soviet effort to divide Bashkirs from their fellow Turkic-speaking Muslims, in particular the neighboring Tatars? What factors conditioned the Bashkir-Soviet collaboration and contributed to its collapse?

Our examination of the local must begin by probing the nature of the Bashkir movement. The Bashkirs were a historically nomadic people who had undergone a significant degree of sedentarization since the eighteenth century but remained predominantly nomadic or seminomadic in the Ural mountains and in the steppe to the south. Like several other nomadic or otherwise "primitive" peoples in the Russian empire before 1917, the Bashkirs formed a distinct, hereditary, corporate group within the empire's complex hierarchy of orders, ranks, and estates. This status marked Bashkirs with several peculiar features, among them the legal right to hereditary communal possession of their land and the obligation to provide military service in the form of an irregular Cossack-like force, the Bashkir Host. This Host had existed from 1798 and involved the Bashkirs in a certain degree of self-administration, the Bashkirs being divided into a number of cantons, each of which supported a part of the Host. The second half of the nineteenth century, however, saw an erosion of this corporate identity. First of all, the Bashkir Host was abolished as militarily superfluous during the Great Reforms of the 1860s and 1870s. Meanwhile, land-hungry Russian peasants increasingly migrated to eastern parts of the empire to seek their fortune, some of them settling on Bashkir land in Orenburg and Ufa provinces. Traditional Bashkir rights to nomadize on large tracts of land disintegrated as Russian officials permitted entrepreneurs to buy up Bashkir communal land for resale to peasant colonists from central and western Russia. These political and economic challenges to Bashkir distinctiveness and well-being were highlighted by an emerging Turkic nationalism among the Volga Tatars, the wealthiest, most highly educated, and most urbanized of all the empire's Muslim nationalities. Toward the end of the nineteenth century, Tatar intellectuals began to elaborate new nationalist conceptions of their community. Some imagined that most, if not all, of the Muslim Turkic peoples residing in Russia's empire should form a single cultural and national entity under Tatar leadership, while even those who shied away from such an ambitious pan-Turkic project hoped to see some sort of political and social union between Tatars and Bashkirs because of the close religious, linguistic, and cultural affinities between the two groups. Since Tatars significantly outnumbered the Bashkirs, the threat of Tatar assimilation appeared as a serious threat to an emerging Bashkir intellectual elite already concerned about Russian colonization and the erosion of Bashkir corporate rights.[3]

In 1917, a small Bashkir nationalist movement emerged under the leadership of Ahmed Zeki Validov, a young Orientalist scholar and moderate socialist who championed Bashkir particularism and campaigned against Tatar efforts to subsume the Bashkirs. By the end of the year, a Bashkir Kurultai (assembly or legislature) had met in Orenburg and elected a "Bashkir government." Validov and his associates pressed forward with optimistic plans to recreate the Bashkir Host and to establish territorial autonomy in the largely nomadic region of eastern Bashkortostan known as Little Bashkiria.[4] The anti-imperialist nature of this movement is highlighted by one of its most radical goals: gradual elimination of the Russian presence in Bashkortostan by forcing Russians to return the land illegally seized from Bashkirs before the revolution and eventually inducing them leave entirely and exchange their land with Muslims from outside the republic.[5]

The specific ethnic-political circumstances in the Volga-Ural region complicated efforts of the new Soviet regime to forge relationships with Bashkirs and other local Muslims. National identities were fluid and not yet well established, while rival political movements espoused conflicting visions of the nation. In 1917, the main division among the Muslim Turks of the Volga-Ural region was between two increasingly irreconcilable groups: a diverse conglomeration of Turkic intellectuals, primarily Volga Tatars, who saw a basic affinity among Muslim Turkic-speaking peoples of the region and sought nationhood for them—and here the terms they used varied—as Muslims, Turko-Tatars, or Tatar-Bashkirs on one side and Validov and the defenders of Bashkir particularism on the other. In these conditions, the Soviet decision to recognize a particular "nation" and its right to national self-determination meant taking a position in this Tatar-Bashkir dispute, with its complex mixture of politics and ethnography, as a result of which possibilities for flexible alliances with other local political movements would be constrained. The opposite was also true: decisions to forge partnerships with particular local actors and movements, decisions reached in response to local political needs, could commit the Soviet authorities to supporting the nationalist vision of their protégés.

Such a dynamic played out during 1918. Stalin and his commissariat of nationality affairs (Narkomnats) initially sought to cooperate with both Tatar and Bashkir leftists but learned that the two groups would not cooperate. Instead, the Soviet government found itself taking sides in the Tatar-Bashkir dispute, almost entirely in reaction to local conflicts and initiatives. First of all, in March 1918 Soviet authorities chose to promulgate a Tatar-Bashkir Soviet Republic that would have incorporated Bashkortostan. This step was taken in response to a rebellion in Kazan' by Tatar politicians and military officers who intended to declare an autonomous and potentially anti-Bolshevik Idel-Ural (i.e., Volga-Ural) state in early 1918. Local left-leaning Tatar nationalists, collaborating with Narkomnats, convinced Stalin to co-opt the Idel-Ural scheme by promulgating a nearly identical Tatar-Bashkir republic under Soviet auspices. This decision alienated Bashkir autonomists, as did a series of repressions against Bashkirs in Orenburg province instigated by local Russian Bolsheviks and Tatar activists who allied with the Socialist Revolutionary party. Validov and other government members were arrested in February 1918, and several were executed, although Validov escaped jail during a midnight Cossack raid on Orenburg. This occurred at a time when Stalin seemed to be seeking an accommodation with Validov and his movement, yet Moscow feebly accepted these local actions as a fait accompli. After general civil war broke out in the spring of 1918, virtually every Bashkir of note either abandoned politics or joined the Whites; Validov's group supported the anti-Bolshevik Committee of Members of the Constituent Assembly (Komuch), formed their own military forces, and strove to implement Bashkir autonomy on White territory. By summer 1918, Soviet "Bashkir policy" was limited to distributing propaganda leaflets on the Tatar-Bashkir Soviet Republic, a project to which Stalin and Lenin remained committed.[6]

By early 1919, conditions in the region had changed. The civil war raged in full force, and Russia's political climate was increasingly polarized, with the "democratic counterrevolution" that Validov had joined in defeat and more conservative forces in control of the White movement. After Admiral Kolchak overthrew the socialist-dominated Komuch and assumed supreme control over anti-Bolshevik forces in eastern Russia in November 1918, he ordered the abolition of Bashkir territorial autonomy and the dissolution of Bashkir military forces.[7] By early 1919, Validov and his men were prepared to shift sides again and to reach agreement with the Bolsheviks. The Bashkir leaders hoped that, despite their quite reasonable skepticism on this point, Bolshevik promises of national self-determination for all peoples held out more for the Bashkir nationalists than did a political future dominated by Russian military officers. Before we examine the Bashkir-Bolshevik collaboration itself, let us turn to the important question of Soviet motivations in 1919.

The motives behind Soviet recognition of separate Bashkir autonomy, a decision apparently reached by Lenin and Stalin personally, have yet to be fully elucidated. Military considerations are often cited: the defection of Validov brought six thousand soldiers to the Soviet side at a crucial moment in the civil war, just before the Kolchak offensive of spring 1919. The decision was at least partly an opportunistic effort to weaken Kolchak's southern flank and to strengthen Soviet forces on the eastern front. Reports of disorganized Muslim units in the Red Army suggest that the Soviets could certainly have profited from the expertise and discipline of Bashkir officers and soldiers.[8] Communist party politics also played a significant role in the recognition of Bashkir autonomy. Initial negotiations with the Bashkirs began less than two months before the Eighth Communist Party Congress of March 18–23, 1919, where Lenin was to defend his nationality policy in a bitter confrontation with the "internationalist" wing led by Bukharin and Piatakov, both of whom saw national-territorial federalism as a needless and dangerous concession to the bourgeoisie. Lenin certainly anticipated opposition to his position and must have wanted a practical example of its benefits; defection of two complete Bashkir divisions from Kolchak and the loyalty of the "Bashkir masses" certainly fit the bill. The final Soviet-Bashkir treaty was signed on the third day of the party congress, and there is evidence that the Soviet leadership hoped to complete the treaty even before the congress began. Lenin brought up the Bashkir question twice during the party congress, both times to justify the creation of Soviet national republics.[9]

Yuri Slezkine and other historians have written about Lenin's peculiar and paradoxical enthusiasm for nation building, particularly among the "small nations" of the Russian East.[10] However, the creation of a separate Bashkir republic was not simply the next logical step in Soviet nationality policy; it represented a significant shift in that policy, for it contradicted the earlier commitment to a united Tatar-Bashkir republic. Tatar communists were soon hopping mad about the decision, and one is left wondering why Lenin and Stalin broke their promise and exactly how they intended to reconcile one state-building project with the other. Several hypotheses suggest themselves.

The original decree on the Tatar-Bashkir republic contained a provision that Bashkortostan might form a separate administrative district within the larger unit; quite possibly Lenin and Stalin thought Bashkir autonomy did not in fact exclude a joint republic at some point in the future. In practice, however, it did, since Validov and other Bashkir leaders firmly rejected incorporation in the Tatar-Bashkir republic and requested that the March 1918 decree promulgating the republic be repealed. After much Tatar resistance, Lenin complied in December 1919.[11] By the next spring, Lenin's government had announced the formation of a Tatar republic to the west of Bashkortostan. Soviet recognition of Bashkir autonomy thus meant the division of the joint state into two separate republics, one Tatar and one Bashkir.

Another possibility is that, far from stumbling into it, Lenin and Stalin intended to break up the Tatar-Bashkir republic all along and simply used Validov's movement as a handy tool for the job. Scholars in the West, Tatar émigrés, and Tatar national activists in the Russian Federation have rightly pointed out that the creation of a separate Bashkir republic helped solidify the cultural and linguistic distinctions between the Tatars and Bashkirs over the following decades. Writing for the émigré journal *East Turkic Review* in the late 1950s, Validov Grishko echoed Tatar arguments of 1919 that creating two republics "separated the Tatars and Bashkirs, although they spoke the same language, had the same religion, enjoyed a common culture, and were united by blood and history and customs."[12] For the late French scholar Alexandre Bennigsen and his American coauthor S. Enders Wimbush, Soviet efforts to foster a separate Bashkir national identity after 1919 had an important political motive: "to weaken any potential Tatar national movement."[13] Professor Azade-Ayse Rorlich of the University of California at Los Angeles argued in her comprehensive English-language history of the Tatars that the Bashkir republic served as "the key to erecting administrative, and even cultural, barriers between the Tatars and the Bashkirs, whose cultures and historical paths had always been closely intertwined." Like Bennigsen and Wimbush, she concluded that fear of Tatar nationalism and Turkic unity lay behind the decision.

> The Idel-Ural or the Tatar-Bashkir state had been divided up before it ever came into existence because its existence would have become a danger too real to be overlooked by the Soviet government, which was already weary of the nationalism of its Muslim minorities. A Tatar-Bashkir republic with the capital at Kazan would have further enhanced the role of that city as the political and cultural center of the Muslims of Russia. To prevent Turkic unity and the emergence of a dynamic republic in the Middle Volga, the Soviet government chose to sponsor the formation of smaller republics; by doing so, it also fostered isolation and even nourished old jealousies and rivalries, thus facilitating its control over the peoples of the area.[14]

At root of these assessments is the assumption that, before 1917, the Bashkirs were on the path of assimilation into the Tatar ethnos in a natural process artificially interrupted by the Soviet state. Bashkir identity was weak and likely to grow weaker without Soviet intervention. In this view, the Bashkir national movement headed by Validov was a transient phenomenon, a historical accident, brilliantly exploited by Lenin and Stalin in 1919.

We can take issue, first of all, with the notion that Bashkir identity was an artificial creation of the Soviet state. This dismissive attitude toward Bashkir identity and Validov's movement seems rooted in a conception of national identity as exclusively linguistic or cultural. The various Bashkir and Tatar dialects were similar, Bashkir was unwritten, many facets of material and spiritual culture were shared, including Islamic faith—therefore, goes this argument, they were in essence one people. Social and economic differences between the Tatars and the Bashkirs may have existed but could not in the end overcome their basic cultural unity.[15] However, theoretical works on nationalism and national identity, new and old, demonstrate that this distinction is arbitrary and that many "social and economic" factors may serve to differentiate nations, nationalities, and ethnic groups.[16] Validov made such a successful case for Bashkir identity precisely because it did *not* rely on slight linguistic differences; Bashkir identity was based on those features that clearly distinguished Bashkirs from their western Tatar neighbors: a nomadic past, a history of rebellion against Russian authority, corporate rights to land, the semi-autonomous canton system, the Bashkir Host. If these elements of Bashkir particularism were in decline due to changes in tsarist policies, Russian colonization, or Tatar assimilation, this only convinced the Bashkir separatists that their nation was in danger. The emphasis that Validov put on the features that sharply distinguished Bashkir from Tatars is in keeping with Fredrik Barth's observations on the importance of "boundary markers" in defining ethnic and national identity. Emphasizing slight differences with closely related groups is often much more important to the nationalist than belaboring the chasms that divide the insider from the obvious foreigner.

Beyond the ethnographic issues, it should be noted that evidence of a Soviet plan to use the Bashkir movement as a means to weaken Tatar nationalism in 1919 is at this point largely circumstantial. Prerevolutionary tsarist officials were indeed concerned about Tatar assimilation and Islamification of neighboring peoples, while the Soviet regime developed an even more pronounced fear of pan-Turkism and pan-Islamism in the late 1920s and 1930s.[17] Therefore, one might argue, it is not unreasonable to suspect that concerns about Tatar expansionism and hegemony lay behind Soviet policy in 1918 and 1919. Unfortunately, suspicion does not constitute proof. While historians may someday find documents to demonstrate that Soviet leaders indeed planned to break up the Tatar-Bashkir republic throughout 1918–1919, my research suggests that improvisation, rather than careful planning, typically characterized decision making during the civil war, so for now this supposed plan remains in the realm of speculation. I argue that the declarations of a Tatar-Bashkir republic and later of a separate Bashkir republic did indeed represent policy of *divide et impera* but that the enemy that Lenin and Stalin sought to divide was not a Turkic nation-in-formation (be it Muslim, Turko-Tatar, or Tatar-Bashkir) but the anti-Bolshevik movement as a whole. In 1918, Soviet leaders hoped that a Tatar-Bashkir republic would free Tatar workers and radicals from the domination of anti-Bolshevik forces in the Muslim Turko-Tatar movement. In 1919, they used a similar strategy to coax Validov and other Bashkir leaders into leaving the camp of Kolchak. In the year between these decisions, policy on Tatar-Bashkir affairs drifted: Soviet leaders did not seem interested in "dividing" the Tatars and Bashkirs by attracting Bashkir national leaders into the Soviet fold, and, indeed, Stalin permitted Tatars in his nationality commissariat to alienate those few Bashkirs who had joined the Soviet cause. Throughout 1918, Stalin's support for the Tatar-Bashkir project seemed complete; a joint republic would have been implemented had not the civil war intervened. If Lenin and Stalin deliberately forged a plan to betray their own Tatar allies and torpedo the Tatar-Bashkir republic in the winter of 1918–1919, it left no trace in the historical record.[18]

The initial conditions of Bashkir-Soviet collaboration reflect two features, both of which suggest that misunderstandings, poor planning, and local initiatives lay at the heart of the Bashkir-Soviet relationship in 1918 and in 1919. First of all, from the beginning, the two sides could not reach a coherent statement of the terms of their collaboration and papered over their differences in the agreement they signed in March 1919. A second factor was the continuing inability of Soviet authorities in Moscow to control events on the ground, where local actors who were not direct parties to the evolving relationship between Soviet leaders and Validov's group nevertheless structured the conditions of that collaboration, in this case through outright pogroms that Red Army soldiers and local Russians inflicted on the Bashkirs in connection with their defection in 1919.

In January 1919, a Bashkir envoy named Mullaian Khalikov made contact with Soviet leaders in Ufa's provincial revolutionary committee (*gubernskii revoliutsionnyi komitet*, or Gubrevkom). He presented six conditions under which the Bashkir government would be willing to switch sides in the civil war: Soviet recognition of Bashkir autonomy, Bashkir control of Bashkortostan's administrative and police functions, Soviet assistance in forming a Bashkir corps for the struggle against Kolchak, political amnesty for Bashkir leaders, expulsion of "Siberian reactionaries" from Bashkortostan, and a halt on all immigration into the Bashkir republic except by "Turko-Tatars" (this reference to the Bashkir concern with Russian colonization of their land proved too sensitive and was dropped as an issue in later negotiations). The Ufa Bolsheviks made no promises but indicated a willingness to continue talks after consultation with Moscow.[19] Within a week or so, instructions arrived from the center, although only of the most general sort. Stalin and Lenin discussed the situation (no other members of the leadership seem to have been consulted) and sent the Ufa Gubrevkom a message that reflects the predominance of military priorities in their thinking on the matter:

> We propose not to antagonize Khalikov, to agree to an amnesty on the condition that we establish a single front against Kolchak with the Bashkir regiments. Soviet power's guarantee of Bashkir national freedom is complete. Of course, along with this one must cut off [*otsech'*] the counterrevolutionary elements of the Bashkir population in the severest possible manner and achieve de facto control over the proletarian trustworthiness of the Bashkir troops.[20]

Military issues were of great concern to Bashkir leaders as well, though from a different perspective. As negotiations progressed during February, it became clear that the Bashkirs sought broad—if, in retrospect, unrealistic—autonomous powers, particularly in military matters. They proposed first of all that Soviet forces halt all military activity within Bashkortostan. Their own military forces, five infantry and two cavalry regiments, would defend the front where it ran through the republic. Soviet troops would *not* have the right to routinely cross Bashkir territory but would be called in by the Bashkirs if needed. The Bashkirs did agree to subordinate their forces to a single high command but insisted that individual Bashkir military units be commanded by Bashkirs.[21]

Meanwhile the Bashkir government elected at the Bashkir Kurultai of December 1917 was dissolved, its powers assumed by a Bashkir revolutionary committee (Bashrevkom) elected by Bashkir officers and soldiers on February 21, 1919.[22] By agreement with Moscow, this body was to govern Soviet Bashkortostan until its first Congress of Soviets selected a new government. All of its members were close associates of Validov and strongly dedicated to his image of autonomous Bashkortostan; none had ever been a communist, and all had fought Soviet power until three days before the Bashrevkom was formed. That Soviet Bashkortostan was to be ruled by former White Guards was the great paradox of the Soviet-Bashkir agreement, and it was a constant source of trouble. Members of the Bashrevkom were not subject to Communist party discipline or any other form of influence from Moscow, and they had notions about the scope and nature of Bashkir autonomy that brought them into direct conflict with Bolshevik figures locally and at the center.

On March 20, 1919, representatives of the Bashkir and Soviet governments signed a definitive treaty recognizing the Autonomous Bashkir Soviet Republic as a federal part of the RSFSR.[23] The greater part of the treaty was dedicated to enumerating the territories that would comprise Little Bashkiria. In this matter the Soviet government essentially accepted the plans sketched out by Validov and his associates in 1917–1918. The republic was to include some 130 townships from the provinces of Ufa, Orenburg, Samara, and Perm. Townships were selected in such a manner as to maximize the Bashkir element in the republic and minimize the size of its Russian population; indeed, two areas with large Russian populations were to remain provisionally in RSFSR control until plebiscites could be held.[24] Little Bashkiria was internally divided among thirteen cantons; ten cantons formed a reasonably compact territory, but three were enclaves, Bashkir islands in the middle of Russian territory to the northeast and southwest. Unfortunately, the March treaty failed to lay out the procedure for transferring land from existing provinces to the new republic, creating fertile ground for argument.

Having laid out Bashkir territory in great detail, the remainder of the treaty gave only the barest outline of how the republic would actually be governed. In theory, the Soviet constitution of July 1918 applied in Little Bashkiria, but, until the first Congress of Soviets, "absolute power" would be held by the Bashrevkom, a body dominated by Validov and his closest associates. Moscow obtained a provision that railroads, factories, and mines on Bashkir territory would remain under its direct jurisdiction, while the Bashkirs received guarantees that they could form a "separate Bashkir army" under overall Red Army command. The RSFSR agreed to arm and supply Bashkir troops and to provide financial support to cultural and educational programs in the new republic. Public order in Bashkortostan would be upheld "by the armed proletariat of the republic." This was all. More than a year after national-territorial federalism had become a fundamental principle of the Soviet state system, formal delineation of powers between federal and local authorities was still rudimentary and sketchy.[25] Nor was it clear how the theoretically highest authority in Bashkortostan, the Bashrevkom, was supposed to relate to the local Communist party. The domination of one by Bashkirs and the other by Russians gave a strong ethnic flavor to the inevitable state-party conflicts, while relative lack of overlapping personnel guaranteed that such conflicts would occur. The ambiguity about the nature and the extent of Bashkir autonomy would give rise to endless disputes and quarrels, which raged all the fiercer since the treaty seemed to grant vast political, military, and police authorities to the Bashkir nationalists, who believed they now had a free hand to pursue their goals.

Another obstacle to Bashkir autonomy in 1919 and 1920 was hostility on the part of local Communists and much of the region's Russian population. This animosity had already torpedoed Bolshevik-Bashkir cooperation in 1918 and nearly did so again in early 1919, as defecting Bashkir soldiers and the general Bashkir population were victimized by Red Army soldiers and Russian settlers. Concerned about their deteriorating military circumstances, the Bashkir government had resolved on February 16, 1919, to begin the defection two days later without waiting for the conclusion of negotiations with Moscow.[26] However, it rapidly became clear that the defection was not going as the Bashkir leadership had planned. They thought that they had reached an understanding with Soviet authorities that Bashkir soldiers could simply walk across the front lines with guns in hand, maintain the integrity of their Bashkir-speaking regiments, and simply turn their weapons against Kolchak's forces. And, indeed, the official Soviet policy, sanctioned by Lenin on February 19 but apparently in place earlier, *did* order that Bashkir soldiers would not be disarmed if they began immediate military action against Kolchak. However, Red Army commanders on the scene saw the situation differently. They either did not know what Moscow had ordered—quite likely, since most belonged to the First Army, based in Orenburg, and not the Fifth Army, in Ufa, with whom the Bashkirs had negotiated—or they did not care. Whatever the politicians might say, local commanders saw the operation as a simple surrender by Bashkir troops. As one divisional commander argued, how could Soviet troops allow an "armed mass" in their rear that was permeated by a national spirit and uninterested in the defense of the proletariat? Defecting Bashkir soldiers were disarmed and held as prisoners of war; those who resisted were stripped, beaten, and, in some instances, shot. Bashkir regiments that surrendered their weapons were dissolved, their soldiers transferred to existing Red Army units where Russian, not Bashkir, was the language of command. The remaining Bashkir soldiers were understandably reluctant to cross the front. The experiment in Soviet-Bashkir collaboration seemed to have ended before it had even begun.[27]

When Validov asked local and divisional commanders to change the policy of disarming and disbanding Bashkir units, his proposal met with hostility. Commander Gai of the Soviet First Army was more sympathetic but nevertheless insisted that the Bashkirs join existing Red Army units if they wished to keep their weapons. Finally, Validov presented his case to Stalin by direct wire on February 26. The Soviet promise to create a Bashkir Soviet republic and to preserve the Bashkir corps as single unit under general Soviet command had, he said, been broken. For Validov, placing Bashkirs in Russian-speaking units was not merely an inconvenience created by the foreign language of command. It was a direct assault on the Bashkir people and their autonomy, for "a Bashkir republic without armed force is a fiction." Dissolving the Bashkir units could only encourage the Russian "tsarist settlers" and "kulaks," who were joining the rampaging Red Army specifically to take revenge on the Bashkir "poor."[28]

While Validov tried to prick the revolutionary conscience of the Soviet leadership with his class analysis of the nature of imperialist oppression in Bashkortostan, Soviet soldiers in Bashkortostan—whether they were local "settlers" or not is difficult to determine—indeed acted like a conquering army. Bashkir soldiers and officers were disarmed, insulted, beaten, stripped of their clothes, and otherwise treated as prisoners. Local peasants joined in the degradations and insults, pelting captured Bashkir soldiers with horse manure while they were marched through Russian villages. Red Army soldiers made off with property and moneys of the Bashrevkom and various canton administrations. Reports soon told of executions. Bashkir military mullahs, a Bashkir brigade commander, and soldiers fell before Red firing squads, and forty-seven Bashkir police officers were shot by the Red Army International Regiment. Red soldiers broke open beehives in a Bashkir village and took the honey; several Bashkirs who complained about this pillaging were tried and executed. Bashkir military units that remained intact were plagued by desertion as soldiers fled to their home villages or returned to the Whites. Indeed, the entire Bashkir First Cavalry Regiment reverted its allegiance to Kolchak in late March and stayed with the Whites for five more months. Anti-Bashkir activity was not limited to Red Army units; with the rout of the Bashkir authorities and military units, local Russians formed revolutionary committees in several Urals factory towns, apparently encouraged by the Orenburg Soviet Executive Committee, which recognized neither the Bashrevkom nor Bashkir autonomy. The Preobrazhensk committee formed its own military detachment, which arrested local Bashkir officials and executed forty Bashkir soldiers.[29]

The most complete account of this shameful episode was compiled by Validov himself from his own observations and reports from Bashrevkom agents sent to investigate Red Army atrocities. He describes dozens of cases of murder, pillage, and rape, often including names of both perpetrators and victims. Validov blamed the atrocities on the duplicity of local Red Army commanders and on the influx of local settlers into Red Army units, the latter a "wealthy immigrant class" who wanted only to settle scores with the Bashkirs. Many Bashkir villages were compelled to pay an exorbitant tribute to the conquering Russian soldiers, anywhere from five thousand to thirty thousand rubles, or were plundered. Kharis Iumagulov, another Bashkir autonomist, suggested that wealthy Russian kulaks had deliberately adopted Bolshevik rhetoric in order to justify their atrocities as "expropriation of the Bashkir bourgeoisie."[30]

A member of the Central Committee who visited the region tersely confirmed the scope of the disaster: "I report that one of the Bashkir regiments has gone over to the enemy. The feeling of the population is hostile towards us. Desertion among Bashkir troops has reached colossal proportions. We must send workers [*rabotniki*] there. Forces at the front are inadequate." Commander Gai of the Soviet First Army tried to regain control of his men, warning that those committing "unauthorized actions" against Bashkir soldiers and civilians would be executed. Nevertheless, the Red Army's pillaging of Bashkortostan continued for many weeks, stopping only when the White advance in March and April 1919 forced the Red Army to withdraw. When Kolchak's forces fell back that summer and the Red Army occupied the region for the third and final time of the civil war, advancing Soviet troops again took revenge on local Bashkirs. Bashkir fear and suspicion of Soviet institutions was clearly reflected in an odd phenomenon that occurred as officials of Validov's government attempted to recruit men for a Bashkir brigade in areas recently freed from the Whites in July 1919. When the Bashkir recruiters and their Soviet military advisors questioned Muslim peasants about their nationality, known Bashkir villages produced only one or two recruits; the rest denied that they were Bashkir. As it turned out, rumors had swept through the region that the Red Army was again rounding up Bashkirs for execution. Extra public relations work was required to persuade Bashkirs to identify with "their" Soviet Bashkir republic.[31] The Red Army's rampage through Bashkortostan in 1919 had clearly left a bitter legacy.

These depressing events were reminiscent of the anti-Bashkir repressions of early 1918, but they differed in several ways. They were first of all much more violent, in keeping with the general escalation of atrocities on all sides of the civil war over the previous year. However, in 1919 the central authorities were willing and able to assert their authority over local actors in a much more direct way than they had a year earlier and would not permit marauding soldiers to define Soviet policy in Bashkortostan. Perhaps most important from a political perspective, the events of 1919 illuminated the shrinking options open to the Bashkir leadership. When Bolshevik repressions struck the Bashkir movement in 1918, Validov and his associates soon found a democratic alternative to Bolshevism in Komuch—but, by 1919, that alternative had vanished, and the choice was more difficult: either Kolchak or Lenin. Bashkir leaders had little confidence in either man, and their hostility toward Bolshevism had only increased in the weeks since the defection. Yet Validov saw little sense in returning to the White camp to face a likely death sentence as a Bolshevik traitor. For the moment, he and his colleagues chose to remain with the Soviets and try to make the best of it.

In August 1919, as the last White troops were expelled from the Volga-Ural region, Validov and his Bashkir autonomists arrived in Bashkortostan with plans to realize their cherished state-building projects and to begin overcoming the legacies of Russian imperialism.[32] Despite Moscow's official endorsement of Bashkir autonomy, its own anti-imperialist rhetoric, and the surreal and sometimes warm personal relationship that had developed between Validov and Stalin, Bashkir leaders faced serious obstacles. The most immediate and critical was the hostility of local Soviet and Communist party authorities toward Bashkir autonomy. To this must be added a series of sharp policy differences that emerged between the Bashkir leadership and their local rivals and, increasingly, between the Bashkirs and the central authorities. Issues were muddied by the ambiguity of the March 1919 agreement, while economic collapse, shortages, social breakdown, and the general dislocation of civil war exacerbated every conflict at the local level in Bashkortostan. Growing Bashkir disillusionment with their Soviet experiment was matched by increasing concern in Moscow that their Bashkir allies were getting out of hand.

Since early in 1918, most Russian communists in the provinces of Ufa and Orenburg had remained unconvinced that national republics, and the Bashkir republic in particular, had anything at all to recommend them. This proved true as well of many communists within Little Bashkiria itself, whose Urals mines and foundries still boasted significant party organizations, particularly in Beloretsk and Sterlitamak. Communist forces in the Bashkir capital were bolstered by a series of official representatives of the Central Committee, most notably Fedor Samoilov, "Artem" (the veteran Old Bolshevik from Ukraine), and Evgenii Preobrazhenskii, whom the Politburo dispatched to Bashkortostan after he and Bukharin finished their famous commentary on the party program.[33] None of these men shared Lenin and Stalin's enthusiasm for nation building among small peoples such as the Bashkirs. The regional party committee (*oblastnoi komitet*, or Obkom) that took shape in Little Bashkiria in November 1919 was led by the representatives from Moscow and dominated by Russian and Tatar figures. A major figure in the Obkom was the Bashkir autonomists' old nemesis, Gali Shamigulov, who had participated in the arrests of Validov and other Bashkir leaders in early 1918. Trotsky commented on local Russian attitudes in a telegram to the Central Committee: "In determining relations with the Bashkir republic one must consider the harmful feelings in Ufa. There they openly speak of the Bashkir republic as a temporary charitable gift, which annoys the Bashkirs extremely. Preobrazhenskii spoke at the party meeting about the need to review the nationality program at the party congress and blamed the Central Committee for offering Ufa's workers as a sacrifice to its Eastern policy. The narrow-mindedness of [Ufa party leader] El'tsin, the hysteria of Artem, the philosophy of Preobrazhenskii will soon turn our Bashkir policy into its opposite."[34]

Political life in Little Bashkiria quickly became an extended power struggle between the nationalists in the Bashrevkom and the largely Russian communists in the Obkom and the Soviet administration of neighboring provinces. Throughout Bashkortostan, local state bodies (the canton administration, dominated by Bashkirs) clashed with largely Russian party committees.

Quarrels began first with authorities in Ufa. Large parts of that province were supposed to join Little Bashkiria according to the March 1919 treaty. Yet the Ufa Gubrevkom insisted that transfer of territories to Bashkortostan be gradual so as not to disrupt grain requisitioning. In frustration, the Bashrevkom forced matters with its Decree No. 1 (August 26, 1919), by which it assumed "direct administration" of Bashkortostan. The decree in effect annulled all previous Soviet laws in Little Bashkiria and halted requisition of grain, lumber, and other resources. It was clear that the Bashkir leadership took their autonomy very seriously, particularly in the sensitive area of food supply. Within weeks, the Ufa Gubrevkom had assembled a long list of the Bashrevkom's more controversial actions: banning the export of foodstuffs and other resources from the Bashkir republic and proposing armed detachments to enforce the ban; obstructing efforts by the Ufa province food commissariat to requisition grain and extract food reserves; expelling Ufa's agents from Bashkir territory.[35]

Differences over wartime requisitioning grew into virtual economic blockades between Bashkortostan and its neighbors. In December 1919, Ishmurzin, the commander of Sterlitamak's Bashkir garrison, forbade anyone to take leather or other raw materials out of the city (there was a large tannery in Sterlitamak). Orenburg authorities retaliated by holding up textiles and other manufactured goods destined for Bashkortostan and distributing them to inhabitants of their own province. Bashkir food supply officials complained to Moscow that Orenburg had blocked textile shipments "with a counterrevolutionary goal, wishing to arouse the Bashkirs against Soviet power," while two Bashkir cantons that Orenburg had jilted out of their textiles simply halted grain deliveries in March 1920. Orenburg communists blamed the Bashkir republic for triggering economic collapse by depriving the region of raw material and fuel.[36]

Food and resource policy was just one point of conflict. Another was the definition of borders between Bashkortostan and its neighbors. Bashkir territory had been delineated in the March 1919 treaty, itself based on Validov's "Regulation on the Autonomous Administration of Little Bashkiria" of 1918. Both documents had several inadequacies. First, they relied on zemstvo data collected over the years from 1906 to 1913, and since that time many of the townships had fragmented, reorganized, or been renamed. It was unclear which of the townships existing in 1919 were meant to join Little Bashkiria. Second, the authors of the original "Regulation" focused on border townships and sometimes carelessly omitted the names of those well within Bashkir territory. For these reasons, the Bashrevkom wanted to revise the March 1919 document. In this matter they received little cooperation from the authorities of Ufa and Orenburg provinces, who tended to interpret the March 1919 agreement literally and to their own advantage. Thus, Bashkir officials complained to Moscow that Ufa authorities blocked the transfer of territories already allocated to Bashkortostan, while Ufa charged the Bashrevkom with illegal annexation of lands not mentioned in the March 1919 treaty.[37]

The liberal economic policies of autonomous Bashkortostan earned it a certain popularity among the peasants of neighboring provinces, particularly in the densely populated Muslim regions to the west. In the fall of 1919, villages and entire townships began sending petitions to the Bashkir government requesting incorporation in Little Bashkiria. The Bashkir Obkom denounced the petitions as nationalist and counterrevolutionary, though Ufa authorities rather honestly concluded that the flood of peasant petitions arose from a desire to avoid their own grain requisitioning. The Bashrevkom, however, welcomed the petitions, seeing in them an opportunity to create the Greater Bashkiria that Validov and the Bashkir Kurultai had envisioned in 1917, and raised with Moscow the possibility of annexing these lands to Bashkortostan. Indeed, there is evidence that the Bashkir government encouraged and even instigated such petitions. In early January 1920, Soviet authorities in Belebei learned that agents from Bashkortostan were encouraging peasants of the nearby Dëma river basin to join Little Bashkiria, even though that region had not been allocated to the republic. The agitators supposedly promised that "in Bashkortostan there will be free trade, and there will be no grain monopoly or cattle requisitioning as there is in the Soviet republic of Russia." Villages that joined Bashkortostan were promised additional land allotments. Rumors that communists were being expelled from Bashkortostan only made the autonomous republic more attractive to villagers weary of endless requisitioning and repressions.[38]

Another issue was the disposition of Sterlitamak. This small town was officially part of Ufa province but, because of the lack of suitable facilities elsewhere, the Bashrevkom had chosen it as its seat of government. Russian officials in Sterlitamak proved to be extremely hostile to Bashkir autonomy in general and to the Bashrevkom in particular; Bashkir leaders reciprocated these feelings, and quarrels multiplied. The shortage of public buildings served as a catalyst for conflict, as when the Bashrevkom seized the prison and post office from local Soviet authorities, who appealed all the way to the Politburo. The Bashrevkom requested that Sterlitamak be placed under its jurisdiction, but the Politburo left the issue unresolved throughout the winter. Meanwhile, the Bashrevkom and the Sterlitamak district Soviet uneasily shared the city.[39]

In February 1920, Trotsky spoke somewhat sarcastically about the "hysteria" that Russian communists felt about the Bashkir autonomists. Yet this hysteria was not entirely unprovoked. In Russian memoirs about Little Bashkiria during 1919 and 1920, references to arrests of communists by the Bashrevkom and canton agents are commonplace.[40] Occasionally, matters took a more serious turn, as when a Bashkir platoon executed four Red Army soldiers near Sterlitamak in September 1919. This quickly brought the Bashrevkom into conflict with Soviet Russia's chief instrument of terror and repression, the Cheka, which sent an agent out from Ufa to investigate the executions. This agent was then assaulted by Bashkir soldiers, according to an Ufa Cheka report filed with Moscow. Later that same month, the Cheka in Sterlitamak arrested three employees of the Bashkir military commissariat for counterrevolutionary activities, which may have included the four executions. Ishmurzin, commander of the Bashkir garrison, surrounded the prison with a detachment of seventy armed men and eleven machine guns and forced the Cheka to hand over his men. Soviet authorities in Sterlitamak and Ufa handled this crisis with caution and did not take immediate military action, primarily because their forces in Sterlitamak were inadequate in the face of the four thousand Bashkir troops in the town.[41] The atmosphere in Sterlitamak remained extremely tense and likely to break into armed conflict.

During the troubled fall of 1919 the Politburo—and Lenin personally—began to pay special attention to the situation in Bashkortostan. Frustrated by its inability to control events in the autonomous republic, particularly in the sensitive area of grain requisitioning, the Politburo reminded the Bashrevkom of the need to fulfill its obligations to the Soviet state. There must be "a single policy, not only military but economic, for the entire [Russian] republic."[42] In September 1919, the Soviet government began to transfer Bashkir troops from Little Bashkiria to other fronts; some went to Ukraine to fight off Denikin's advance, while others defended Petrograd from Iudenich. Clearly, the troops were of better service at the front than sitting around in liberated Bashkortostan, but the Politburo also saw their removal as a means to weaken the troublesome Bashrevkom and to limit its future options.[43] At about this time, Lenin began collecting names of "reliable Bashkir communists or honest sympathizers in Bashkiria."[44]

Soon after the New Year, disputes over Bashkir autonomy brought on yet another crisis in Sterlitamak. This time, the pretext was a Bashrevkom initiative to form a "department of external relations" to handle its growing conflicts with Moscow and other provinces. The Obkom perceived this department as nothing less than a ministry of foreign affairs, declared it incompatible with Soviet autonomy, and declared its abolition. In response, Kharis Iumagulov, then head of the Bashrevkom, arrested several members of the Obkom and Bashkir Cheka on 16 January 1920 on charges of a counterrevolutionary conspiracy against Soviet Bashkortostan.[45] Rapid intervention by Mikhail Frunze, commander of the Turkestan front, soon convinced Iumagulov to release the captives. The gambit had achieved little, and the Bashrevkom's position deteriorated over the following months. Communists of neighboring provinces were quick to judge the arrests as an unjustified provocation arranged to discredit the Communist party in Little Bashkiria. Soviet leaders in Orenburg even scolded the Central Committee for ignoring their warnings and for placing so much trust in "adventurists of Iumagulov's type." Petitions from communists inside Little Bashkiria told tales of "counterrevolution" and domination of the Soviet apparatus by "nationalists."[46] After January 1920, the Bashkir question came up repeatedly in the Politburo. Trotsky paid a great deal of attention to the matter; he formulated instructions for Frunze on Bashkir affairs and hosted a meeting with Bashrevkom and other local figures in Ufa in March 1920 that failed to ease tensions. Felix Dzerzhinskii, head of the all-Russian Cheka, suspected that former counterrevolutionaries in the Bashrevkom, in league with the SR Viktor Chernov, had inspired the massive peasant rebellion in Ufa province in February 1920; the Politburo accordingly gave him authority to arrest any Bashkir leader with connections to Chernov.[47]

The collaboration between Soviet authorities and Validov's Bashkir autonomy movement ended as abruptly as it had begun. In April 1920, the Politburo appointed Stalin head of a special commission on the Bashkir situation; this group proposed to resolve the endless crises by imposing strict and well-defined restrictions on Bashkir autonomy, promulgated by government decree on May 19, 1920.[48] The republic's departments for military affairs, supply, finance, worker-peasant inspection, labor, post and telegraph, and the economy would be fully subordinated to the corresponding organs of the RSFSR government. These were the most critical areas from Moscow's perspective, and ones not to be left in the hands of the uncommunist and erratic Bashkir national leadership. Only the departments of education, justice, health, agriculture, social security, and internal affairs were autonomous and responsible directly to the Bashkir government.[49] Significantly, this decree was part of a larger effort to regularize the relations of the central authorities with the autonomous republics. The republic of Tatarstan, created in mid-1920, received an identical statute.[50] Moscow's unilateral revision of the rights granted to the Bashkir republic finally convinced Validov of the futility of further collaboration with the Soviet regime. In June 1920, he and the majority of Bashrevkom members quietly slipped away from their offices in Sterlitamak and Moscow and joined either the Basmachi guerrillas in Turkestan or a new Bashkir partisan movement in the Ural mountains. Thus ended sixteen months of collaboration between the Soviet government and the chief founder of twentieth-century Bashkir political nationalism.[51]

After Validov's flight in June 1920, the adversarial relationship among the Bashkir Obkom, the Bashrevkom, and agents from Moscow largely evaporated. Tatars, Russians, and a few token Bashkirs with strong Communist credentials and a general commitment to the Obkom's policy of centralization henceforth dominated the Bashkir government.[52] Tensions between the Bashkir government and Obkom certainly arose from time to time, particularly over strategies for suppressing the new rebellions in Bashkir villages that arose later in 1920 and again in 1921.[53] The Politburo intervened in Bashkir affairs repeatedly during the months and years after Validov's departure, particularly to facilitate repression of the rebellion, maintain order, requisition grain and other foodstuffs, coordinate famine relief, and manage the transition to the New Economic Policy. Yet, never again did the central authorities have to deal with such a force as Validov and his movement.

One must agree with Terry Martin, Ronald Grigor Suny, and other contributors to this volume that, even during the darkest days of the civil war, the premier formulators of Soviet nationality policy, specifically Lenin and Stalin, demonstrated an extraordinary commitment to the creation of national republics, the forging of partnerships with non-Russian elites, and the establishment frameworks for the future growth of national cultures. Both men took a major political risk in recognizing Bashkir autonomy, a step that had opponents at every level of party and government, from the smallest Russian township in the Urals all the way up to the Politburo—not to mention among important cadres of Tatar communists—and they intervened in Bashkir affairs throughout 1919 and 1920 to keep this project alive. This conclusion must, however, be qualified, since the collaboration with Validov did indeed fail. Five factors were critical elements of this failure, and all of them could have been foreseen in early 1919: fundamental differences of opinion over the meaning of autonomy, the improvised nature of Soviet nationality policy, the reliance of Moscow on local leaders to implement policies, the inherent conflict between autonomy and other vital priorities of the Bolshevik regime, and the escalating climate of violence during the civil war.

The vast political and ideological gulf separating the two sides on the question of autonomy was perhaps the most critical issue. Validov and his followers saw themselves as the vanguard of a Muslim Turkic struggle against European imperialism or, more specifically, Russian imperial domination of Bashkortostan, and since 1917 their struggle had been to reverse the consequences of that domination. They believed that land taken from Bashkirs should be returned; Russian peasant immigrants, or at least the most recent ones, should leave; Bashkir corporate rights to a self-governing region with its own military units must be restored, although recast as a national republic with an independent armed force; and Bashkirs should be able to control all land, food, and other resources on "their" territory. Once the Bolshevik leadership came to a definitive conclusion about what Soviet autonomy really meant late in the spring of 1920, it was clear that the Bashkirs' expectations far exceeded what Soviet power would grant.

Second, despite the steadfastness with which Lenin and Stalin upheld their commitment to national republics and recruiting non-Russian elites, much of Soviet nationality policy in 1917–1919 was characterized by improvisation, opportunistic political alliances, serious miscalculations, and local initiatives that structured and limited Moscow's options. This had already been made clear in 1918, as Moscow stumbled into its Bashkir policy. Lenin and Stalin's recognition of Bashkir autonomy in early 1919 was certainly an important intervention by Moscow into local affairs and perhaps even a brilliant concession at a critical moment in the civil war, but as a "policy" it was poorly conceived and atrociously implemented by the Red Army and led to a host of unanticipated conflicts, not only between Bashkirs and Russians locally but also between Tatars and Bashkirs over the fate of the Tatar-Bashkir republic. Moreover the critical treaty of March 1919 laid out the division of powers between center and republic in only the barest terms, leaving the field open for broad claims from both sides. One is tempted to conclude that Soviet leaders did not bother to define "autonomy" as a legal and not merely rhetorical term until the Bashkir crisis forced them to do so in 1920.

A third factor that conditioned the breakdown of cooperation was the continuing ability of local actors to obstruct the policies of the center and to shape them to their own ends. It is no exaggeration to say that in 1919, in Bashkortostan and in the neighboring provinces, ethnic Russian supporters of Lenin and Stalin's nationality policy could be counted in the tens at best. Russians in local Soviets and Communist party organs frequently opposed Bashkir national autonomy as a violation of proletarian internationalism and were reluctant to turn over power and resources to a cadre of leaders with proven anti-Bolshevik credentials. These ideological and political concerns were often supplemented by the attitudes of superiority over the "natives" characteristic of many Russians in the borderlands. Meanwhile, Validov's uncompromising anti-imperialism and advocacy of Bashkir sovereignty fueled a perception among both local Russians and the central authorities that Validov's group was seeking not membership in a federation—or junior partnership in an empire—but an independent state on the order of Finland.[54] Local Russians were understandably worried by the Bashkir leadership's long-term goals, particularly return of Bashkir land illegally seized before the revolution and removal of recent Russian immigrants. Even though the Bashrevkom did little or nothing to implement these policies, they lurked in the background and confirmed the colonizers' worst fears about the native.

It is clear that Lenin and Stalin's nationality policy did not exist in a vacuum but was only one among many priorities of the Bolshevik leadership. During the civil war, survival and preservation of the regime stood above other concerns, and to this were linked such policies as strict military discipline, enforced grain requisitioning, and brutal suppression of "counterrevolutionary" activities. At times, concessions to nationalist movements could serve these priorities, as when recognition of Bashkir autonomy severely weakened Kolchak's front in early 1919. In the end, however, a vigorously autonomous Bashkir republic ran afoul of the Bolshevik civil war agenda in economic, political, and military matters. What is perhaps most striking is that the center took so long to act. Although the Politburo followed the power struggle for control of the Bashkir republic closely, the supposed Bolshevik propensity for intervention and control showed itself rarely at first, and not exclusively on the side of local Russian communists. Lenin and Trotsky, in particular, recognized the validity of many of the Bashkir complaints about "Russian chauvinism" and seemed reluctant to antagonize their Bashkir allies, who could so adeptly exploit the (frequently lapsing) anti-imperialist consciences of their superiors. Bolshevik leaders seemed to come to the restriction of Bashkir autonomy in 1920 slowly and almost reluctantly. Nevertheless, given the intractability of social and ethnic conflicts in the borderlands and the disruptive results of allowing local initiatives on the part of both Russians and nationals to guide the evolution of Moscow's nationality policies, the central leadership concluded that it needed to play a much greater role in the national republics. This meant several things: carefully determining borders of the republics, spelling out the administrative and legal rules of the game, and, most of all, restricting local initiative by all parties and limiting the authority of local government. Only in this way could the notion of national autonomy be coordinated with other imperatives of the day: grain requisitioning, rational deployment of troops, and prevailing in a desperate civil war waged on multiple fronts, both external and internal. The zigzags of Soviet nationality policy during the civil war are fundamentally incomprehensible, and easily interpreted as random and arbitrary, without a clear understanding of this broader context.

Last, we cannot ignore the unprecedented levels of violence unleashed by revolutionary upheaval and the breakdown of civil order in the years after 1917. Armies crisscrossed Bashkortostan repeatedly during the civil war, leaving destruction and lawlessness in their wake. Natives, settlers, army deserters, and rival groups of political activists all found application of armed force, not skillful compromise, the preferred means of political intercourse. Bolshevik authorities in particular were prepared to mete out terrible punishments to anyone who opposed their rule. By the time Validov and his colleagues fled Bashkortostan in June 1920, they had seen Bashkir officers, soldiers, and peasants executed or massacred by Russian settlers, Red Army troops, and Cheka detachments on numerous occasions. Validov and his Bashkir troops certainly had blood on their hands as well, though this remains to be investigated. The point is that the Bashkir-Bolshevik political alliance of 1919–1920 was played out on a particularly bloody stage. The personal stakes were high in a game where slight missteps might carry fatal consequences; the psychological pressures on the players must have been intense. No wonder that when Validov's star began to fall within the Soviet establishment, he chose to head for the hills, rather than wait for the Cheka to come for him. In no small way, this polarized and dangerous atmosphere poisoned the relationship between the Bolsheviks and the Bashkir nationalists from the very beginning, so that the task of building interethnic harmony and overcoming the legacies of past imperialism—a professed goal of both sides, and difficult enough to achieve in peacetime—became a completely utopian dream in the face of the realities of the Russian civil war.

Notes

I would like to thank the International Research and Exchanges Board and the National Endowment for the Humanities for supporting research and study leading to this chapter. My gratitude goes out as well to Ronald Suny, Terry Martin, John Bushnell, and other participants in the CASPIC conference, and to Daniel Orlovsky for commenting on an earlier version of the paper.

1. N. G. O. Pereira, *White Siberia: The Politics of Civil War* (Montreal: McGill-Queen's University Press, 1996), pp. 132–133; Richard E. Pipes, "The First Experiment in Soviet Nationality Policy: The Bashkir Republic, 1917–1920," *Russian Review* 9 (1950): 303–319.

2. Recent local studies have identified a great variety of conditions, processes, and dynamics in both Russian provinces and ethnic borderlands during the Russian revolution and civil war, many of which had nationwide implications. See for example Diane Koenker, *Moscow Workers and the 1917 Revolution* (Princeton, N.J.: Princeton University Press, 1981); Donald J. Raleigh, *Revolution on the Volga: 1917 in Saratov* (Ithaca,

N.Y.: Cornell University Press, 1986); Ronald Grigor Suny, *The Baku Commune, 1917–1918: Class and Nationality in the Russian Revolution* (Princeton, N.J.: Princeton University Press, 1972); not to mention Alexander Rabinowitch's classic study of the impact of local Petrograd politics on the course of the all-Russian revolution, *The Bolsheviks Come to Power: The Revolution of 1917 in Petrograd* (New York: Norton, 1976).

3. An aging yet critical introduction to these issues is Serge A. Zenkovsky, *Pan-Turkism and Islam in Russia* (Cambridge, Mass.: Harvard University Press, 1960). Important works on prerevolutionary Bashkir history include Robert F. Baumann, "Subject Nationalities in the Military Service of Imperial Russia: The Case of the Bashkirs," *Slavic Review* 46 (1987): 489–502; Alton S. Donnelly, *The Russian Conquest of Bashkiria, 1552–1740: A Case Study in Imperialism* (New Haven, Conn.: Yale University Press, 1968); B. Kh. Iuldashbaev, *Istoriia formirovaniia bashkirskoi natsii: Dooktiabr'skii period* (Ufa: Bashkirskoe knizhnoe izdatel'stvo, 1972); and R. G. Kuzeev, *Proiskhozhdenie Bashkirskogo naroda* (Moscow: Nauka, 1974).

4. So called to distinguish it from Greater Bashkiria, which would have included Bashkirs to the west who lived interspersed with large numbers of Tatars, Russians, and other peoples. For reasons of political practicality, Validov and company put the Greater Bashkiria project on hold in 1917.

5. See the resolution on land passed by the Bashkir Kurultai in December 1917. TsGIARB (Tsentral'nyi gosudarstvennyi istoricheskii arkhiv Respubliki Bashkortostan, Ufa), f. 395r, op. 1, d. 7, ll. 10b-2. For more on the evolution of Bashkir nationalism and the events of 1917 and the years following, see Pipes, "The First Experiment in Soviet Nationality Policy"; Serge A. Zenkovsky, "The Tataro-Bashkir Feud of 1917–1920," *Indiana Slavic Studies* 2 (1958): 37–61; Stephen Blank, "The Struggle for Soviet Bashkiria, 1917–1923," *Nationalities Papers* 10 (1983): 1–26; Michael Rywkin, "The Autonomy of Bashkirs," *Central Asian Survey* 12, no. 1 (1993): 47–57; S. Atnagulov, *Bashkiriia* (Moscow: Gosudarstvennoe izdatel'stvo, 1925); and Daniel E. Schafer, "Building Nations and Building States: The Tatar-Bashkir Question in Revolutionary Russia, 1917–1920" (Ph.D. diss., University of Michigan, 1995).

6. Schafer, "Building Nations," pp. 173–222, 248–277.

7. Jonathan D. Smele, *Civil War in Siberia: The Anti-Bolshevik Government of Admiral Kolchak, 1918–1920* (Cambridge: Cambridge University Press, 1996), pp. 296–301; Schafer, "Building Nations," pp. 286–314.

8. Zenkovsky, *Pan-Turkism*, p. 99. During the Bashkir defection Validov told Red Army and Soviet officials that his force totaled, variously, 5,700 and from 5000 to 10,000. Later the number of Bashkir soldiers defecting in February 1919 was established as 6,556. See GARF (Gosudarstvennyi arkhiv Rossiiskoi federatsii, Moscow), f. 1318, op. 1, d. 45, ll. 20, 30, 65; M. L. Murtazin, *Bashkiriia i bashkirskie voiska v grazhdanskuiu voinu* (Moscow: Voennaia tipografiia upr. delami Narkomvoenmor i RVS, 1927), p. 71; and M. M. Kul'sharipov, *Z. Validov i obrazovanie Bashkirskoi Avtonomnoi Sovetskoi Respubliki (1917–1920 gg.)* (Ufa: Bashkirskoe knizhnoe izdatel'stvo, 1992), p. 129. On Muslim units in the Red Army, see GARF, f. 1318, op. 1, d. 45, l. 10.

9. RTsKhIDNI (Rossiiskii tsentr khraneniia i izucheniia dokumentov noveishchei istorii, Moscow), f. 17, op. 2, d. 11, l. 2 (Central Committee minutes, March 16, 1919). V. I. Lenin, *Polnoe sobranie sochinenii*, 5th ed., 57 vols. (Moscow: Izdatel'stvo politicheskoi literatury, 1974–1978), 38: 158, 183.

10. Yuri Slezkine, "The USSR as Communal Apartment, or How a Socialist State Promoted Ethnic Particularism," *Slavic Review* 53, no. 2 (1994): 414–452.

11. See the March 1918 decree in *Politika Sovetskoi vlasti po natsional'nym delam za tri goda: 1917-XI-1920* (Moscow: Gosudarstvennoe izdatel'stvo, 1920), pp. 100–101, from *Izvestiia VTsIK* (March 24, 1918) and in English in Schafer, "Building Nations," p. 468. On the repeal of the decree, see RTsKhIDNI, f. 17, op. 3, d. 48, l. 4; B. Kh. Iuldashbaev, ed., *Obrazovanie Bashkirskoi Avtonomnoi Sovetskoi Sotsialisticheskoi Respubliki: Sbornik dokumentov i materialov* (Ufa: Bashkirskoe knizhnoe izdatel'stvo, 1959), p. 423 (hereafter OBASSR).

12. V. Grishko, "The Establishment of a Soviet Volga-Tatar State," *East Turkic Review* no. 1 (1958): 55.

13. Alexandre Bennigsen and S. Enders Wimbush, *Muslims of the Soviet Empire: A Guide* (Bloomington: Indiana University Press, 1986), p. 248.

14. Azade-Ayse Rorlich, *The Volga Tatars: A Profile in National Resilience* (Stanford, Calif.: Hoover Institution Press, 1986), pp. 137–138. See also the perspective of the modern Tatar activist Aidar Khalim, in his *Kniga pechali, ili zapiski aborigena* (Vil'nius: Mokslas, 1991), pp. 160–161.

15. Bennigsen and Wimbush, *Muslims of the Soviet Empire*, p. 247.

16. See Fredrik Barth, ed., *Ethnic Groups and Boundaries* (Boston: Little, Brown, 1969), in particular the article by Gunnar Haaland, "Economic Determinants in Ethnic Processes."

17. On the former case, see for instance Robert Geraci, "Russian Orientalism at an impasse: Tsarist Education Policy and the 1910 Conference on Islam," in Daniel R. Brower and Edward J. Lazzerini, eds., *Russia's Orient: Imperial Borderlands and Peoples, 1700–1917* (Bloomington: Indiana University Press, 1997), pp. 138–161. A stunning example of the later is A. Arsharuni and Kh. Gabidullin, *Ocherki panislamizma i pantiurkizma v Rossii* (Moscow: Bezbozhnik, 1931).

18. Schafer, "Building Nations," pp. 226–277.

19. OBASSR, pp. 193–195; GARF, f. 1318, op. 17, d. 5, l. 121; *Zhizn' natsional'nostei*, February 16, 1919. See also the statement of the Bashkir government on negotiations, February 8, 1919. OBASSR, pp. 196–197; GARF, f. 1318, op. 1, d. 45, ll. 12–13; Zaki Validi Togan, *Vospominaniia: Bor'ba narodov Turkestana i drugikh vostochnykh musul'mantiurkov za natsional'noe bytie i sokhranenie kul'tury, Kniga I*, trans. G. Shafikov and A. Iuldashbaev (Ufa: Kitap, 1994), p. 283.

20. GARF, f. 1318, op. 17, d. 5, l. 120 (Lenin and Stalin to Nimvitskii, n.d., but apparently February 5 or 6 1919); *Zhizn' natsional'nostei*, February 16, 1919; Lenin, *Polnoe sobranie sochinenii*, 50: 252. The editors of Lenin's works note that in the original text, the first two sentences were in Stalin's hand; the last, in Lenin's. See also OBASSR, p. 880.

21. OBASSR, pp. 211–215, 223–225. A preliminary treaty was signed at Simbirsk on February 27, 1919.

22. OBASSR, pp. 216–222.

23. *Politika Sovetskoi vlasti po natsional'nym delam*, pp. 17–19; R. M. Raimov, *Obrazovanie Bashkirskoi Avtonomnoi Sovetskoi Sotsialisticheskoi Respubliki* (Moscow: Izdatel'stvo Akademii nauk, 1952), pp. 470–475; OBASSR, pp. 227–232. The treaty was first published in *Izvestiia VTsIK* and in *Zhizn' natsional'nostei* on March 23, 1919.

24. The Zlatoust plebiscite zone was added to the Bashkir republic in 1922, only

to be transferred to Cheliabinsk province later that year. The Sterlitamak plebiscite area joined Little Bashkiria in November 1920. It seems that in neither case was a plebiscite actually held. OBASSR, p. 883.

25. The Bashkirs themselves had worked through these issues in much more detail at their Kurultai of December 1917, as had Tatar federalists in the Millät Mejlisi, but their projects seem not to have been consulted.

26. Validov later indicated that the Red advance had recently cut off Bashkir forces from their Kazakh allies to the south, who were also considering defection. This left the Bashkirs completely surrounded by Red and White forces. Togan, *Vospominaniia*, p. 282.

27. Lenin's policy on not disarming Bashkir soldiers is found in Lenin, *Polnoe sobranie sochinenii*, 50:259, and confirmed in GARF, f. 1318, op. 1, d. 45, l. 26 (transcript of conversation between Sultan-Galiev and Validov, February 21). On local commanders' views of the Bashkirs see GARF, f. 1318, op. 1, d. 45, ll. 19–20 (Commander Vorob'ev of the Penza Division, in a communication to Validov, February 20) and the orders by Commander Zelenkov of the First Brigade of the Penza Division on February 16 that all defecting Bashkirs give up their weapons and cross the line with arms in the air (OBASSR, p. 202; GARF, f. 1318, op. 1, d. 45, l. 15). Validov's complaints about the incidents can be found in GARF, f. 1318, op. 1, d. 45, ll. 19–20, 27–33.

28. GARF, f. 1318, op. 1, d. 45, ll. 27–33. In response Stalin encouraged Validov to come to Moscow for direct talks.

29. TsGIARB, f. 395r, op. 1, d. 4, l. 48 (Bashrevkom minutes, March 3, 1919); RTsKhIDNI, f. 17, op. 65, d. 22, l. 221ob. (Iumagulov to Central Committee, June 4, 1919); GARF, f. 1318, op. 1, d. 45, ll. 42, 45–46, 62; TsGAOORB (Tsentral'nyi gosudarstvennyi arkhiv obshchestvennykh ob"edinenii Respubliki Bashkortostan, Ufa), f. 1832, op. 3, d. 379, ll. 69–70 (memoir of Mustafa Khalidov, n.d.). On the episode involving the Bashkir First Cavalry Regiment see Togan, *Vospominaniia*, pp. 293–294, and GARF, f. 1318, op. 1, d. 45, ll. 63, 57. Activities of the Preobrazhensk committee are described in GARF, f. 1318, op. 1, d. 45, ll. 61ob.–62.

30. Validov's lengthy report on the atrocities is found in GARF, f. 1318, op. 1, d. 45, ll. 58–66 (Validov to Stalin, May 3, 1919) and reprinted in Kul'sharipov, *Z. Validov*, pp. 128–139. See also Murtazin, *Bashkiriia i bashkirskie voiska*, pp. 207–211, and Togan, *Vospominaniia*, pp. 292–295. Iumagulov's version is found in GARF, f. 1318, op. 1, d. 45, l. 70 and RTsKhIDNI, f. 17, op. 65, d. 22, l. 227 (Kharis Iumagulov to Central Committee, et al., March 28, 1919).

31. See Smilga's report to the Central Committee, dated March 28, 1919, in RTsKhIDNI, f. 17, op. 65, d. 22, l. 201. On Gai's efforts to restore order, see GARF, f. 1318, op. 1, d. 45, l. 9 (Adigamov to Bashrevkom, n.d.) and l. 44; OBASSR, pp. 243–244. It does appear that some of the purpetrators of the atrocites were indeed arrested and put on trial, although the final disposition of their cases is unclear. Apparently unaware of his efforts to stop the bloodshed, Bashkirs concluded that Gai had ordered the repressions because, as an Armenian, he saw Muslims as his enemies. RTsKhIDNI, f. 17, op. 65, d. 22, l. 218; Togan, *Vospominaniia*, p. 293; Mirsaid Sultan-Galiev, *Stat'i, vystupleniia, dokumenty* (Kazan: Tatarskoe knizhnoe izdatel'stvo, 1992), p. 437. On continuing atrocities during the Red Army's summer 1919 advance into Bashkortostan, see RTsKhIDNI, f. 17, op. 65, d. 22, l. 218 (Kulaev and other members of the Bash-

revkom to Stalin, June 25, 1919). The report on Bashkir mobilization in Belebei district in July 1919 comes from TsGAOORB, f. 1832, op. 3, d. 240, l. 3 (undated memoir by Karavaev).

32. The sequence of events in Little Bashkiria between the coming of the Bash-revkom in August 1919 and the redefection of the Bashkir national leadership to the Whites in June 1920 is quite complex and is not analyzed in great detail here. See Pipes, "First Experiment in Soviet Nationality Policy"; Zenkovsky, "The Tataro-Bashkir Feud"; Blank, "Struggle for Soviet Bashkiria"; Rywkin, "Autonomy of Bash-kirs"; Atnagulov, *Bashkiriia;* Kul'sharipov, *Validov;* B. Kh. Iuldashbaev, *Natsional'nyi vo-pros v Bashkirii nakanune i v period Oktiabr'skoi revoliutsii* (Ufa: Izdatel'stvo Bashkirskogo universiteta, 1984); and OBASSR, pp. 295–513.

33. RTsKhIDNI, f. 17, op. 3, d. 22, l. 1 (Politburo minutes, August 23, 1919).

34. RTsKhIDNI, f. 5, op. 2, d. 283, l. 1 (Trotsky telegram to Central Committee, February 17, 1920).

35. On the Decree No. 1 and its consequences, see OBASSR, pp. 303–313; *Zhizn' natsional'nostei,* September 21, 1919; *Politika Sovetskoi vlasti po natsional'nym delam,* pp. 19–20; F. Samoilov, "Malaia Bashkiriia v 1918–1920 g.g. (Iz istorii odnogo opyta prime-neniia natsional noi programmy VKP)," *Proletarskaia revolutsiia,* no. 11 (1926), pp. 203–204; *Izvestiia Ufimskogo gubernskogo revoliutsionnogo komiteta,* September 13, 1919; and F. Samoilov, *Malaia Bashkiriia* (Moscow: Staryi Bol'shevik, 1933), p. 18. See also Zenkov-sky, "The Tataro-Bashkir Feud," pp. 48–49.

36. TsGIARB, f. 629r, op. 1, d. 7, ll. 21, 23, 64; GARF, f. 5677, op. 1, d. 273, l. 3.

37. TsGIARB, f. 629r, op. 1, d. 23, l. 98 (Bashkir representative at the VTsIK to VTsIK, 27 October 1919); ibid., d. 24, ll. 38–39 (new township list drafted by the Bashkir government in 1919); ibid., d. 23, l. 11 (Ilias Alkin and Suleiman Asmanovich to Bikbavov and Adigamov, October 24, 1919); ibid., l. 38 (Valitov to Adigamov, March 23, 1920); ibid., ll. 43–44 (Valitov to Adigamov, c. January 1920); RTsKhIDNI, f. 17, op. 65, d. 22, l. 187 (El'tsin to Kalinin, et al., January 14, 1920). Several documents on the territorial and jurisdictional disputes between Little Bashkiria and neighboring provinces in 1919 have been published in OBASSR, pp. 330–375.

38. Sadly, the petitions themselves have not been found. What we have instead is a series of Bashkir government dispatches listing those villages interested in joining Little Bashkiria. Petitions came from the Zlatoust, Ufa, Sterlitamak, and Belebei dis-tricts of Ufa province, from the Buzuluk and Buguruslan districts of Samara province, and from the Orenburg district of Orenburg province (TsGIARB, f. 629r, op. 1, d. 23, ll. 4–7, 17, 32–33; GARF, f. 5677, op. 1, d. 273, ll. 18–20, 23–26). For the views of the Bashkir Obkom and Ufa authorities, see OBASSR, pp. 362–363, 417. On the Dëma river episode, see OBASSR, pp. 363–364. Peasant dissatisfaction with food req-uisition policies in the provinces surrounding Little Bashkiria was vividly illustrated by the massive February 1920 uprising in Ufa province. Officials in Ufa estimated that 90 percent of the rebellious peasants were Muslims. See Tamurbek Davletshin, *Sovetskii Tatarstan: Teoriia i praktika leninskoi natsional'noi politiki* (London: Our Word Publishers), pp. 177–179; TsGIARB, f. 1r, op. 3, d. 83; OBASSR, 523.

39. RTsKhIDNI, f. 17, op. 3, d. 34, l. 1 (Politburo minutes, October 30, 1919); ibid., d. 58, l. 6 (Politburo minutes, January 23, 1920).

40. See for example Samoilov, "Malaia Bashkiriia v 1918–1920 g.g. (Iz opyta . . .),"

pp. 211, 213, and F. Samoilov, "Malaia Bashkiriia v 1918–1920 g.g. (Okonchanie)," *Proletarskaia revoliutsiia* no. 12 (1926): 188–189.

41. On the executions, see RTsKhIDNI, f. 17, op. 65, d. 22, l. 200 (Ufa provincial Cheka to all-Russian Cheka, September 19, 1919). The Sterlitamak Cheka incident is reported in RTsKhIDNI, f. 17, op. 65, d. 22, ll. 209–212 (El'tsin to All-Russian Cheka et al., September 29, 1919). Not unexpectedly, Bashkir leaders refuted charges they had used armed force. See RTsKhIDNI, f. 17, op. 65, d. 22, l. 207 (Iumagulov and Validov to Kalinin, October 8, 1919) and TsGIARB, f. 629r, op. 1, d. 7, l. 52 (Iumagulov to VTsIK, n.d.). The Central Committee concluded that the Bashrevkom had indeed used armed force to obtain illegal release of the three prisoners (RTsKhIDNI, f. 17, op. 65, d. 22, l. 206). See also the brief account in Samoilov, "Malaia Bashkiriia v 1918–1920 g.g. (Iz opyta . . .)," pp. 204–205.

42. RTsKhIDNI, f. 17, op. 3, d. 34, l. 1 (Politburo minutes, October 30, 1919); ibid., d. 48, l. 3 (Politburo minutes, December 13, 1919).

43. When the Politburo heard a report from Dzerzhinskii on the tense relations between the Soviet authorities in Ufa and the Bashrevkom ("which has at its disposal rather significant armed forces"), it resolved to accelerate the dispatch of the remaining Bashkir troops from Bashkortostan. RTsKhIDNI, f. 17, op. 3, d. 32, l. 2 (Politburo minutes, October 23, 1919).

44. Lenin, *Polnoe sobranie sochinenii*, 51:81.

45. See Artem's communication to Lenin and Frunze about the incident (January 17) and the Bashrevkom's explanations the next day in RTsKhIDNI, f. 17, op. 65, d. 22, ll. 194 and 193, respectively. Validov's version is in RTsKhIDNI, f. 5, op. 2, d. 192, l. 1.

46. RTsKhIDNI, f. 17, op. 65, d. 22, l. 185 (Shensen to Staff of Turkestan Front, et al., before January 19, 1919); RTsKhIDNI, f. 5, op. 1, d. 1227, ll. 1–2 (A. Nemtsov to Lenin, March 16, 1920)

47. RTsKhIDNI, f. 5, op. 1, d. 1409, ll. 2–3 (Trotsky to Lenin, January 26, 1920); RTsKhIDNI, f. 17, op. 3, d. 62, l. 1 (Politburo minutes, February 17, 1920). See the minutes of the March 1920 meeting in Samoilov, *Malaia Bashkiriia*, pp. 65–72, and Samoilov, "Malaia Bashkiriia v 1918–1920 g.g. (Okonchanie)," pp. 192–196.

48. Decree of the VTsIK "On the state organization of the Autonomous Soviet Bashkir Republic," *Izvestiia VTsIK*, May 22, 1920; *Politika Sovetskoi vlasti po natsional'nym delam*, p. 22.

49. Responsible, that is, to the Bashkir Central Executive Committee. In the version of the decree published in Soviet newspapers in 1920, the word "All-Russian" was mistakenly printed in the place of "Bashkir," leaving the impression that there was to be no autonomy left at all. OBASSR, pp. 487–488.

50. *Izvestiia*, May 29, 1920; *Pravda*, May 29, 1920; *Zhizn' natsional'nostei*, June 2, 1920; *Politika Sovetskoi vlasti po natsional'nym delam za tri goda. 1917-XI-1920* (Moscow: Gosudarstvennoe izdatel'stvo, 1920), pp. 101–102.

51. After several years of political activity among the Basmachi and in Afghanistan, Validov returned to his former academic pursuits of history and Turkology in Germany and later Turkey, where he took the surname Togan and lived until his death in 1970. On Validov's life and work, see A. M. Iuldashbaev, *Professor Akhmetzaki Validi Togan (Politicheskaia i nauchnaia deiatel'nost')* (Ufa: Bashkirskaia respublikanskaia organizatsiia obshchestva "Znanie," 1991).

52. Indeed, the head of the first Bashkir Sovnarkom selected in July 1920 was Gali

Shamigulov, a long-time foe of Bashkir autonomy who had once declared his "Bukharinist orientation" on the national question. TsGIARB, f. 629r, op. 1, d. 497, l. 52a; OBASSR, p. 524.

53. On the rebellions of 1920 and 1921, see OBASSR, pp. 554–583, 907; Atnagulov, *Bashkiriia*, pp. 73–74; Zenkovsky, "Tataro-Bashkir Feud," pp. 55–56; Richard E. Pipes, *The Formation of the Soviet Union: Communism and Nationalism, 1917–1923* (Cambridge: Cambridge University Press, 1957), pp. 317–318; TsGAOORB, f. 1832, op. 3, d. 116; RTsKhIDNI, f. 17, op. 3, d. 119, l. 1 (Politburo minutes, October 30, 1920); GARF, f. 1318, op. 1, d. 116, ll. 1–2 (petition by a member of the Obkom).

54. See the comment of Sultan-Galiev, writing in July 1918. Sultan-Galiev, *Stat'i, vystupleniia, dokumenty*, p. 73.

Nationalizing Backwardness

Gender, Empire, and Uzbek Identity

IN THE MODERN SENSE "NATIONS" are a very recent creation in the ethnic, cultural, and linguistic mosaic of Central Asia. How did they form? Perhaps oddly, Bolshevik leaders of the early Soviet period may have been the most directly responsible parties. Recent work by Yuri Slezkine, Ronald Suny, and others has argued that Bolshevik power, despite its "internationalist" pretensions, helped not only to prevent the fading away of nations but even to create them where none had existed before. A study of the struggle over family life in early Soviet Uzbekistan shows one way in which such nation-building took place on Stalin's watch.

As Gregory Massell demonstrated more than twenty years ago, Muslim women played a central part in Bolshevik analyses of, and approaches to, Central Asian society during the 1920s.[1] From Moscow's perspective, it seemed self-evident that such women, enormously oppressed by traditional Muslim codes of behavior that kept them veiled and secluded, represented potentially pivotal allies in the revolutionary cause. This analysis led Moscow's representatives in 1927 to instigate a *hujum* ["onslaught"], a full-frontal assault on the system of female seclusion that, it was hoped, would mobilize Muslim women on a massive scale. In the end, such hopes died stillborn; the vast majority of Central Asian women showed little interest in Bolshevik ideals or programs, and many of the few who did challenge traditional Muslim society paid dearly for doing so.

Recent theoretical insights combined with archival access in Tashkent and Moscow, however, makes it possible now to go much farther than Massell ever could in exploring the details and implications of the struggle over women's rights in Uzbekistan. Family and gender relations were fluid during the first decades after 1917, and their meanings were contested bitterly. While keeping in mind the multiplicity of groups and motives involved, in broadest terms the struggle that emerged can fairly be depicted as one that became, in the end, two-sided: between Bolshevik activists seeking ("modern") reform on the one hand and Muslims (made by the Bolsheviks into "traditionalists") resisting it on the other. Both argued fiercely for their respective visions of "proper" family relations, visions that hinged on diametrically opposed views of women's roles in the family and society. The contest was expressed in all arenas of social life, through a wide variety of discourses—legal, moral, artistic, economic, and hygienic, among others.

Both groups took everyday culture [*byt* in Russian, *turmush* in Uzbek] as their principal focus in the fight over what society should be. Social behaviors thus carried enormous implications, and private culture—as practiced in the intimate space of the family—became publicized and politicized. The various discourses generated by each side depicted gender roles and family relations as fundamental to social identities, even while they purported to disagree completely about just what the character of such roles and relations should be. Nevertheless, both groups agreed in general terms about *who* was being defined in this process, namely the Uzbek Muslims. And who were they? While several criteria could be employed—language, religion, history—one apparently easy and straightforward definition relied on family relations, and particularly on customary patterns of women's dress and social behavior, to answer the question. Specific variants of ostensibly "Muslim" behaviors—such as female seclusion, veiling, early marriage, polygyny, and brideprice—found themselves taken as emblematic of Central Asia's newly "national" cultural, religious, and social identities.

In brief, this chapter argues that certain ("customary") patterns of gender relations—and, in particular, specific forms of female dress and seclusion—were used, often quite effectively, as national "markers" in early Soviet Central Asia. For its own reasons, the party encouraged this development, seeing the creation of indigenous "nations" as a progressive step in Central Asia. At the same time, however, the Bolsheviks' remarkable success in creating distinct national identities quickly caught them on the horns of a dilemma. On the one hand, they had defined the new Uzbek nation in large part through its distinctive patterns of gender relations and customs of female seclusion, and especially through the heavy cotton-and-horsehair veils [*paranji* and *chachvon*] worn by Uzbek women. Yet, by the mid-1920s, they had also declared these same practices to be primitive, dirty, and oppressive—a combination that had two serious consequences. First, it meant that the Party had deemed the Uzbek nation *by definition* not to be capable of "modernity" or "civilization" in its current state, a judgment that in turn led directly to the decision to transform Uzbek society forcibly through its women (in the *hujum*). Second, this association of Uzbek national identity with social practices that had been targeted for eradication was a gift to those who opposed Soviet-style reform, allowing them to portray themselves as defenders of the "nation." The party thus inadvertently helped create a discourse of national-cultural resistance to its own women's liberation policies. The resulting contradictions plagued Soviet Uzbek authorities for decades, and in some ways their legacy may still be felt today.

The Orientalist "East" and Its Women

The equation of Central Asia with its women was not new in 1917. The image of an exotic, often veiled, woman had long symbolized Central Asia—indeed, the entire "East"—in Russian (and European) eyes. This ideal type, the "Eastern woman," was largely created by a series of Westerners who had visited the region and, once returned safely home, written about what they had seen. Some of these visitors had traveled to Turkestan, Khiva, and Bukhoro seeking adventure; others were pursuing scholarly ends and still others aimed to further diplomatic or military agendas. Whatever their purposes, the books they published proved popular, attracting an eager audience among educated society across Europe and Russia.

These writers drew a picture that was in many ways grim, showing a despotic, primitive, almost timeless Central Asia—yet one that was also alluringly exotic. As one of them put it, "the East is, and ever was from time immemorial, the land of the most striking contradictions."[2] The Russian observer Nikolai Muravev, writing about Khiva in 1822, described its "Uzbegs" as lazy, careless, and "extraordinarily dirty."[3] Fathers ruled their children with an iron hand, and life was governed by the dictates of religion. Unhappily, Muravev noted, the Uzbegs were "very low in the scale of enlightenment and education," being ignorant of nearly every Western science.[4] In the mid-1840s, Joseph Wolff, an English clergyman, visited Bukhoro in a well-publicized attempt to secure the release of two British soldiers held by its Khan. Wolff's mission failed, but his descriptions of a passive populace under a brutal ruler reached a wide audience.[5] A generation later, the Hungarian scholar Arminius Vámbéry, having disguised himself as a dervish to travel (he said) undetected, described the brutal tortures, ranging from starvation to eye gouging, inflicted by the Khivan authorities in their zeal to defend religious law. Apparently to underscore the shockingly barbarous character of the region, Vámbéry also included drawings of human heads being bought and sold.[6] The depth of Eastern savagery was not to be doubted, Vámbéry asserted, nor the power of its rulers: "In a country where pillage and murder, anarchy and lawlessness, are the rule, and not the exception, a sovereign has to maintain his authority by inspiring his subjects with the utmost dread and almost superstitious terror for his person; never with affection. Even those nearest to him fear him for his unlimited power."[7]

Readers familiar with the work of Edward Said and other postcolonial theorists will immediately recognize the Orientalist tropes in these descriptions.[8] Such writings frequently accompanied and underpinned colonial expansion, justifying European rule even while they served as a means of (European) self-definition. The Central Asian "East" is seen here as unenlightened and primitive, thus practically begging for the introduction of civilization and progress by the more advanced West (or at least by the somewhat more advanced Russia, which expanded into the region during the mid-nineteenth century). At the same time, the people of Turkestan are depicted as somehow less than European. History, it seemed, had passed them by: Central Asian society was alleged to be timeless and unchanging.

In 1887, the British cleric Henry Lansdell declared the Kazak steppe to offer an excellent exhibit of how people had lived at the time of the Old Testament, having what he called a "primeval character."[9] At the same time, Central Asian Muslims could not really act as autonomous individuals, since their lives were said to be governed by an unchanging religious fervor. As a result, the details of how these individual people thought—their differences and disagreements with one another, the nuances and changes in how they perceived the world and their place in it—became unimportant and received generally short shrift.

Yet European and Russian readers' fascination with Muslim Central Asia ran deeper than knowing how Western travelers had, through clever disguises, subterfuge, and bravery, entered the domains of Oriental despots and lived to tell the tale. The very character of everyday life in "the East," too, seemed impossibly exotic and alluring, and these writers spent page after page chronicling the strange customs that shaped Muslim society. Of particular interest in this regard were the details of how women lived in the East, and writers devoted considerable space to the topic. As George Curzon explained in 1889,

> I have frequently been asked since my return—*it is the question which an Englishman always seems to ask first*—what the women of Bokhara were like? I am utterly unable to say. I never saw the features of one between the ages of ten and fifty. The little girls ran about unveiled, in loose silk frocks, and wore their hair in long plaits escaping from a tiny skull-cap. Similarly the old hags were allowed to exhibit their innocuous charms, on the ground, I suppose, that they could excite no dangerous emotions. But the bulk of the female population were veiled in a manner that defied and even repelled scrutiny. For not only were the features concealed behind a heavy black horsehair veil, falling from the top of the head to the bosom, but their figures were loosely wrapped up in big blue cotton dressing-gowns, the sleeves of which are not used but are pinned together over the shoulders at the back and hang down to the ground, where under this shapeless mass of drapery appear a pair of feet encased in big leather boots.[10]

Female veiling and seclusion thus both illustrated and served as a metaphor for the more generalized despotism that characterized the region. In the same vein as Curzon, for instance, Vámbéry provided an extended description of the secluded life led by the Khan's wives in their harem.[11] Veils, harems, and polygyny all served as powerful symbols, redolent of a supposed Eastern essence. Women—their dress, social customs, and restrictions—served as a emblems of their society, being both seductive and repellent; once one understood them, these writers implied, one would understand the East.[12]

In the colonial context of tsarist Central Asia, it is not surprising to find women being used as symbols of their people. Recent scholarship has argued that cultural authenticity is often taken to inhere to the female sphere: gender and culture thus construct each other, and women are seen as markers of a society's identity.[13] But how much did these descriptions of an "Eastern woman" actually say about

Central Asia? The authors who constructed this archetype were themselves mostly outsiders to Muslim society—Russian, British, and Hungarian, among others. As such, their fixation with veiled women and harems as emblematic of one overarching, vague "East" reveals as much about themselves as it does about their supposed subject.[14] The creation of this primitive, despotic, and exotic East as an "Other"—as something utterly unlike Europe—served as a means of *self-definition*. For Russian writers, moreover, the ability to paint ethnographic pictures of "primitive" Central Asians may have helped bolster a sometimes shaky sense of Russia's proper place among the "enlightened" nations. Central Asia and its women, that is, provided Russia with a visible civilizing mission. As Dostoevskii was reported to have said in 1881, "In Europe we were Tatars, but in Asia we are Europeans."[15]

Virtually all of these writers were male, and some lacked knowledge of the local languages. Vámbéry may never have been permitted inside a harem, and Curzon admitted that he never saw the face of a woman of reproductive age. Despite such restrictions, these writers nevertheless claimed expert status on the most intimate customs of Muslim life. Vámbéry, for example, dwelled at length upon the local rituals of birth, marriage, and death, focusing especially on the roles played by women. He then explained why such ethnographic observations mattered: "Central Asia in this respect is wrapt in considerable obscurity. To attempt to dispel this darkness may therefore not be deemed superfluous; and, the savage Polynesian and Central African having resisted vainly the spirit of inquiry, we will in like manner raise the veil from the rude and suspicious Œzbeg."[16] His choice of image here—the veil—clearly served multiple purposes. Most obviously, for Vámbéry and his fellow authors, women represented a central site for the construction of knowledge about Central Asia, and thereby for the assertion of (European) scientific expertise and power.

At the same time, as Sarah Graham-Brown has argued in her study of photographic representations of Middle Eastern women, it is striking to see the same tropes—such as, especially, the harem and the veil—recurring throughout the accounts written by Western men decades, and even centuries, apart.[17] According to Curzon (quoted earlier), an Englishman's first question about Central Asia was always to ask what its women were like; plainly there was (and still is) an element of the erotic in the fascination wielded by the Muslim East. The harem, to which nearly all access was banned, drew Western readers' attention largely because of the sexualized mystery attached to it. By describing harem life, authors therefore permitted their readers a vicarious thrill in entering the innermost sanctum of the exotic East. Similarly, the veil, both enticing and shocking to Western readers, remained a constant focus of attention. It served both to demonstrate the power of patriarchal control over women and to raise a challenge to the imagination—these authors' detailed descriptions of Central Asian women's daily lives represented an attempt to solve the "mystery" of what lay behind the veil.[18] Given that the point of female seclusion was to bar other men from knowing precisely that, such descriptions thus again offered the reader an illicit thrill, promising vicarious access to the East's most protected (and erotic) domain.

Bolshevism and the Eastern Woman

As far as conceptions of Central Asia and its women were concerned, in many ways the Bolshevik assumption of power in 1917 brought few changes. At first, of course, other matters occupied party leaders' attention—most obviously, the need to fight and win a civil war. Yet even when they did devote time to thinking about Central Asia, one discerns a surprising degree of continuity across the supposed watershed of 1917. Many of the same tropes recurred, as Soviet writers—few of whom knew local languages, and even fewer of whom were raised Muslim—drew upon prerevolutionary traditions of describing the East through such overarching, formulaic images. In many respects, Bolshevik views sounded as much Orientalist as Marxist. Consider the description given in 1926 of Bukhoro ("the most typical Eastern city") by Serafima Liubimova, a prominent Russian women's activist who spent years working in Central Asia. After describing the city's charmingly "narrow, crooked little streets," the omnipresent mosques and minarets, and the bustling teahouses featuring exotic Eastern music and dancing, Liubimova declared that "All of this [strikes you] as soon as you take the first step away from the little Bukhoro train station—it makes the rest of the world fall away, and transports you to a fairy-tale world [*skazochnaia obstanovka*]."[19]

From such a perspective, Central Asia remained above all the Other, a land both attractive and repellent, seductive but at root primitive and despotic. As one foreign visitor sympathetic to the Soviet cause, Fannina Halle, later put it, "The Soviet East, like all Asia, like the whole East, whether Near or Far, is an alien, exotic land to our European feelings. And so any effort to grasp its alien quality emotionally is far better than all enumeration of names and figures, however systematic."[20] Russian writers and ethnographers produced descriptions of Muslim areas—along with photo books, museum exhibitions, even picture postcards—that confirmed such judgments for their home audience, painting with a very broad brush as they did so. Turkestan and the khanates of Bukhoro and Khiva were deemed backward [*otstalyie*] places, with low literacy rates and few children (and virtually no girls) even able to attend school; the poor health care and hygienic habits of the indigenous people sufficed to demonstrate the region's blighted, benighted nature. Even the food, it was said, tasted bad.[21]

In the eyes of these early Bolshevik observers, much of the explanation for these problems lay in the paramount importance of religion in Central Asian life. Ostensibly primitive, "barbaric" practices could thus be ascribed straightforwardly to Islam. Although the Qur'anic scriptures had been written in Arabic (a language understood by few Central Asians), and despite their great antiquity, these texts alone sufficed to explain why specific people acted in certain ways now, thirteen centuries later. Indeed, the supposedly primeval character of Central Asian Muslim society made it seem to these writers all the more reasonable to look far back in time for explanations—just as Lansdell had compared the Kazak nomads to the Hebrew patriarchs of Biblical times. Turkestan appeared to them not to have changed appreciably in centuries. The Central Asian East, Bolsheviks said, possessed a "medieval way of life" [*srednevekovyi byt*].[22]

After 1917 just as before it, the Muslim woman served as a principal illustration for such views. Alluring and sensual, yet simultaneously a primitive and oppressed victim of patriarchal despotism, she seemed to embody the very essence of her culture. Depictions of the allegedly horrific lives lived by women in pre-Soviet Central Asia pepper the documents of the early 1920s, contrasting vividly with an accompanying picture of Leninist liberation. Bolshevik activists and writers always started by drawing a grim portrait of life under Islamic *shariat* [religious law] and Central Asian *adat* [customary law]. According to them, before the revolution females had been treated as property, more like cattle than humans. Veiled while still girls—sometimes at age seven or eight—they were sold into marriage soon thereafter for a high brideprice [*qalin*]. (*Shariat* norms permitted a girl to be married at nine, and a boy at twelve, if their bodies were sufficiently developed; Bolshevik writers tended to overlook this stipulation in their expressions of disgust.) Soviet readers were told that often a young girl would be married to an old man, fifty years her senior, to be one of his many wives. She would soon be infected with syphilis or worse, and her health would never recover. Thereafter, the "harem life" kept her from education and productive labor, and thus from any hope of achieving economic independence and a measure of control over her life. Easily manipulated by her husband because of her ignorance, she most likely died young, wizened before her time.[23]

Once again, images of veiling and seclusion featured prominently to make this picture concrete. The power of Muslim patriarchy could, as before, best be appreciated by Western readers through the ideal type of an "Eastern woman," and more than anything else the veil conjured her to mind. Readers, after all, had come to expect such images. Accordingly, Soviet writers, just like their "bourgeois" counterparts, stressed the extent of female seclusion throughout Central Asia and drew their individual examples from regions (especially those later incorporated into the Uzbek SSR) with particularly strict customs in this regard. One prominent *Zhenotdel* official, Antonina Nukhrat, went so far as to say that the Uzbek woman "literally does not see the sun"; her colleague Kasparova described Central Asian houses bereft of any windows facing the street.[24] Serafima Liubimova told of fifty-year-old Uzbek women who had never left their own quarter of Toshkent and had never even heard of the European-style New City. The world known to these women, Liubimova asserted, rarely stretched beyond husband and kitchen. Barred even from the bazaar, they were required to wear heavy, horsehair veils that stretched from head to toe at any time that a strange man might appear, lest he spy even the smallest glimpse of their body.[25] The Orientalist tone of such accounts sounds remarkably like that of contemporary missionaries[26]—a similarity, indeed, not as strange as it may first appear.

Of course, the severe limits of this—as any—ideal type should be noted. No single "Eastern woman," however "typical" or emblematic, could possibly do justice to the multiplicity of, and variety among, all the peoples she supposedly represented. Her always-unchanging visage—veiled and oppressed, apparently from time immemorial—obscured the fluidity of any human society and, in particular, missed the tensions and social ferment that rocked Central Asia as it wrestled with the challenges of colonial control. Such limitations, starkly visible in the sweepingly general pre-1917 writings discussed, were no less apparent in early Soviet discussions of the "Eastern woman." Any such singular archetype could represent only a narrow subsection of Central Asian society, ignoring both regional and class distinctions. Strict harem-style seclusion was most common among the upper classes, for instance, where men could most easily afford to maintain a stable of wives. For its part, the heavy horsehair-and-cotton veil was neither universal nor timeless. Taking root in a modern form only during the mid-nineteenth century, *paranji* and *chachvon* were by 1917 common among urban women of the southern river basins. They could by then be found, albeit less frequently, in rural areas, but scarcely at all on the nomadic steppe, let alone among the many non-Muslim peoples (ranging from Caucasian mountain dwellers to Buddhist Buriats to Koreans living in Siberia) who also constituted part of the Soviet "East."

Inventing Uzbekistan: Defining an "Uzbek" Woman

Soviet writers thus drew upon their prerevolutionary heritage, constructing a Central Asian "East" both primitive and despotic—but enticing—through its women. At the same time, though, this colonial discourse was not static across 1917. Most obviously, of course, Bolshevik power brought a tendency to seek explanations of social dynamics through the Marxist lens of class struggle. Although not discussed at length here, this proclivity was as apparent in discussions of women's issues in Central Asia as it was elsewhere.[27] Two additional (and countervailing) discontinuities, however, are the focus of the rest of this paper. The first such shift, and the subject of this section, was the addition of a new tenet after 1917: women now were taken to signify a specific *nation* as well as the relatively undifferentiated "East." They thus played an important role—one encouraged by the party—in building separate national identities in Turkestan. But the second major shift, discussed in this chapter's final section, worked against such nation building: Soviet writers also increasingly treated indigenous women as emblematic of what was *wrong* with their nations, and as symbols of what had to be changed to make Central Asia "modern."

In most pre-1917 Russian discussions the word "national" [*natsional'nyi*], when applied to Central Asia, meant only "distinctive" and "non-Russian"—writers referred to "local national peculiarities," for instance. Its various Muslim inhabitants were thought of as tribes or groups, perhaps proto-nations or "nationalities," but certainly not as true *nations* on the level of Russians themselves. Under the Bolsheviks, however, such words began to take on a life of their own. While cases can be found of Soviet writers referring uncritically to one huge, expansive "East,"[28] it also became a state priority to parse this East into smaller bits. "National" no longer signified simply "native" or "distinct" but came to specify particular peoples within the multiethnic mosaic of Central Asia. (Even the term used to discuss the indigenous peoples as a whole—they were called the "principal local nationalities" [*mestnye osnovnye natsional'nosti*, or *MON*]—stressed multiplicity, rather than unity.[29])

Making Nations: Borders

Borders, by their nature, divide people. In Central Asia, however, they created people as well—when Soviet Turkestan was subdivided into several new republics in the mid-1920s, these boundaries helped produce half a dozen or so nations, among them the Uzbeks. The borders of "Uzbekistan" were not entirely invented—Soviet experts tried to follow lines of ethnic settlement, a desire visible in the irregular, twisting shape of the republic that emerged—but no such territorial unit had ever existed before. Although the term "Uzbek" had been used earlier,[30] moreover, it was not altogether clear who was one, or what the label meant. Great differences of culture, language, and religion plainly divided the people of "Uzbekistan." Once Bolshevik leaders had created geographical boundaries, then, and called them "national," their first job was to make such borders meaningful. This task, in turn, depended crucially on the ability to define through difference, which meant the ability to point out distinctions between the various new "nations."

What distinguished "Uzbeks" in Uzbekistan from other Muslims just across the border in, say, Kazakstan? In seeking answers to this question, the party hoped to define—in essence, to create—an Uzbek national identity from the ground up. The search for definitions led in many directions. Linguistic differences, for instance, were deemed to separate (Turkic) Uzbeks from (Persian) Tajiks. But, even within Turkic cultures, a whole range of careful distinctions could be drawn within the broader sphere of Islamic practice to make clear specific "national" differences among "Uzbeks," "Turkmen," "Kazaks," and others. One of the most promising avenues aimed to identify nations through distinctive customs of daily life [*byt*], focusing particularly on gendered patterns of family behavior. Women, in particular, became the normative figures of each distinct nationality. Having long served as cultural emblems, women stood (in Partha Chatterjee's terms) for the "inner" domain—family, home, spirituality—where the roots of cultural identity were taken to lie.[31] In the new republic of Uzbekistan, codes of female behavior, and especially of female veiling and seclusion, thus became the markers of a distinctly Uzbek, and not merely "Eastern," identity. At times, it seemed that a woman (and therefore her family) could be classified as

"Uzbek" merely because she veiled herself in a certain way. In a very real sense, then, the *paranji* became a *creator* of Uzbek identity.

In this way, the struggle over gender roles and family relations became a way to say what it meant to be "Uzbek," at a time when that identity was provisional, fragile, still very much under construction. The sharpest conflict over women's "liberation," it is worth remembering—the *hujum* of 1927—took place just after the "national demarcation" [*razmezhivanie*] of 1924–1925, when the several Central Asian republics were carved out of the former Turkestan ASSR. Modern "national" identities in the area were weak at best. "Uzbeks" and "Turkmen" had never before lived in separate, ethnically defined states. "Kyrgyz" and "Kazaks" had never been distinguished from each other. The region's common literary language was Chagatai; the native inhabitants of Uzbek towns were often called "Sarts," a name that fell into disuse after 1925. Constructing gender through such strict definitions became a way of constructing the nation, then; by casting the debate in these terms, party activists aided the process of nation-building. Indeed, Bolsheviks may have thought at the time that it would serve their interests to draw such sharp distinctions between Uzbeks and their neighbors; many scholars have portrayed the Central Asian *razmezhivanie* as a means of forestalling pan-Islamic or pan-Turkic loyalties.[32]

Given the complexities of local settlement patterns, ethnic and clan groups spilled across the new borders, and—contrary to the image of a unitary "East"—a wide variety of gender practices could be discerned among them. Such variety served the purpose of demarcation, however, since family relations of a certain type, generally practiced on or near the territory of the new Uzbek SSR, proved a convenient way of labeling a woman and her family as "Uzbek." Veils were one of the most vivid markers of identity, and Soviet writers policed the boundaries that resulted, carefully distinguishing among the various ("national") types of veils. One could identify Uzbeks living in largely Turkmen areas, for example, by their "characteristic" veils—that is, they wore a *paranji* rather than a *yashmak*—and by their different practices of female seclusion.[33] Uzbek and Kyrgyz families in the border area of Osh, or Uzbek and Kazak families in southern Kazakstan, could be—and were—separated along similar lines.[34] Indeed, the various leaders of the new Soviet republics contributed to this sharp delineation of "national" customs, since they could use such ethnographic distinctions to underpin land claims and argue for a redrawing and expansion of their own borders.[35]

Such strict definitions did not always fit the complex realities of Central Asian social practice, and some of the shortcomings were plain to see. Most obviously, not all women who seemed "Uzbek" by other criteria wore veils, nor were all veiled women Uzbek. Indigenous Jewish women in Bukhora, for example, wore the same *paranjis* and *chachvons* as their Muslim sisters and shared other customs as well, yet no one—neither Jews, Uzbeks, nor the party—argued that these women were ethnically "Uzbek" as a result.[36] Instead, Soviet writers mostly ignored Jewish women as they increasingly nationalized the veil as a specifically *Uzbek* form of dress. A handful of "European" women—mostly Russian orphans, born in Central Asia, who had married Muslim men—could also be found veiled, but this image was so exceptional that it only served to underscore the Otherness of Uzbek veiling in general.[37]

Tajik women presented a similar, but potentially more serious, problem, since the veils many of them wore appeared identical to the ostensibly "Uzbek" *paranji* and *chachvon*. Tajikistan remained part of the Uzbek SSR until 1929, so it may have been less important to draw a stark Uzbek/Tajik distinction—and when one was needed, linguistic differences could play a prominent role. But party writers went further in their effort to make the *paranji* and *chachvon* Uzbek national property, even portraying the veils worn by Tajik women as borrowed from the Uzbeks. How could that be so? Tajik women did not know how to make their own *paranjis*, these writers said, and therefore tended to buy them in the larger (Uzbek) cities. Moreover, only Tajik women in relatively "Uzbekified" areas did so. Such veils, they continued, were seen rarely in purely Tajik districts and even more infrequently in Tajik villages. Hence, they showed only the extent of Uzbek influence on Tajik society.[38] In the end, therefore, both *paranji* and *chachvon* were deemed to belong properly to the *uzbechka* alone. Creating borders, then, helped transform this veil from the symbol of a vaguely "Eastern" woman into a truly *national* emblem of the Uzbek people.

Marking Nations: Science

The new Soviet state, of course, employed a variety of tactics—it created different alphabets and literary languages, for example—to demarcate the new Central Asian nations. The use of gender to signify nationality, however, represented an particularly important plank of the nation-building project. It can be seen bolstering Uzbek identity in a variety of ways. The deployment of science in this regard was particularly striking, as Soviet "experts" set out to define precisely what it was that made a woman "Uzbek."[39] Working at the intersection of anthropology and biomedicine, scientists cooperated in this dual construction of gender and nation, lending support to the view that national-cultural distinctions in Central Asia were real. Through their authority, methods, and manner, moreover, they gave this opinion a reassuring cast of objectivity.

Some of this work was highly technical, such as investigations of "scientific" phrenology—that is, detailed studies of the different head sizes and shapes of various "nations." One V. K. Iasevich, for example, a physician at Central Asian State University, in 1925–1926 carried out a study of several hundred Uzbek women in Khorazm. His aim was to ascertain the unique biological characteristics of the Uzbek woman and, through her, of the Uzbek nation.[40] Iasevich's study involved a detailed questionnaire asked of each woman concerning her daily customs and life history, as well as complete physical and gynecological exams. Photographs were taken of some, supposedly "typical," subjects. Perhaps unsurprisingly, the study encountered significant difficulties—many subjects had never before seen European medical personnel and often were seized with terror at the sight of medical instruments. A few women fainted in front of the cameras. Many questionnaires and exams were left incomplete, a fact noted in passing by Iasevich as he pressed on with his scientific quest.[41]

In the end, Iasevich defined the Uzbek woman through the language of statistics and sexuality. His results, published in 1928 ("On the Question of the Constitutional and Anthropological Type of the Uzbek Woman of Khorazm"), included painstakingly detailed tables giving the statistical distributions of the measurements and descriptions of every conceivable body part—from spine curvature to skin tone to breast size—within the Uzbek female population of Khorazm. These distributions were compared with those of Russian, German, American, Jewish, and Norwegian women to demarcate national differences more clearly. The voyeuristic quality of his project was then completed with photographs of six nude (and clearly uncomfortable) women; Iasevich explained in dryly scientific language that they were meant as illustrations of the six principal body types found in Khorazm.[42]

If Iasevich's statistical tables were written for an audience of sociomedical specialists, other scientific work aimed at a wider audience. The well-known anthropologist L. V. Oshanin, for instance, was commissioned in 1926 to prepare a study called "The Daily Life and Anthropological Type of the Uzbek Woman." Financed and closely supervised by the Party's *Zhenotdel* and the government's *Narkompros*, this study in many ways resembled Iasevich's. Once again, several hundred Uzbek women—this time from Toshkent—were to be asked a series of questions about their daily lives and life histories and then subjected to detailed physical exams. The goal was to elucidate their biological essence, to isolate that in them which was "typical" of the Uzbek people. Such a study was needed, Oshanin argued, because the topic was completely unexamined, and people did not know what features and behaviors should be considered characteristically or definitively Uzbek.[43] His party and state overseers agreed on the topic's importance and asked only that his study, in addition to its scientific merit, be made as accessible as possible to a mass, popular readership. They repeatedly encouraged him, for example, to include photographs of "typical" Uzbek women and not to omit drawings of illustrative scenes from Uzbek *byt*, or daily life.[44]

One cannot help but be struck by the intrusive character of such studies. The anthropologists' questionnaires and exam records show an astounding attention to detail. Notwithstanding the deep cultural sensitivity to such questions in Central Asia, for Oshanin's study every conceivable body part (including the sexual organs) was to be measured and categorized, and quite possibly photographed. Each woman then faced a series of probing questions about the most intimate details of her family life: her age at sexual maturity, at first sexual act, at marriage, at childbirth, and so on.[45] These examinations represented a clear exercise of power: these scientists sought to gain an intimate knowledge of the most closely guarded areas of Uzbek family life, a knowledge that which could in turn be published to underpin their own claims to expertise. By using the language of science and discovery, then, they could justify what amounted to a form of cultural rape.

These studies served a second purpose, as well, one with a more constructive end: namely to offer a sharp definition of just what it meant to be "Uzbek" and to do so in a very concrete and visible way. Anthropological and biomedical studies concluded by pointing to physically distinguishing characteristics of this new nation, sometimes even calling it a separate "race." This scientific argument for a distinctive Uzbek identity was made to as wide an audience as possible, public museums were constructed and traveling exhibitions designed to illustrate, through women's *byt* and biology, the uniquely Uzbek features of the indigenous population.[46] Such scientific policing of the boundaries between Central Asian peoples continued for decades along these lines, often including photographic "evidence" of Uzbek distinctiveness through its women.[47] As such, scientists lent their voice and authority to a definition of who the Uzbeks were, thus helping to propagate a sense of national identity.

All of these Soviet efforts, taken together, did start to bear fruit by the mid- to late 1920s, albeit not exactly in the manner that the party intended. By that time an Uzbek national consciousness, however fitful and uneven, had begun to take root, a remarkable development that had momentous and lasting consequences for the region. Anyone hearing Uzbeks today denigrate their Turkmen (or Kazak or Kyrgyz) neighbors as "inferior" peoples would surely agree that a sense of national identity is one of the principal Soviet legacies to Central Asia in general, and to Uzbeks in particular. They did not cease to see themselves as Muslims, to be sure, any more than they stopped being members of a certain family or clan or inhabitants of a particular region.[48] But, for many, their matrix of personal identity gained a new component, that of the Uzbek nation, a component that took on an importance in its own right.

Just as the party had hoped, this sense of Uzbek identity was indeed based largely on customs of everyday life, and particularly on the supposedly distinctive veils and behaviors that defined an Uzbek woman.[49] The *paranji* and *chachvon* marked a woman as Uzbek, then, in the eyes of her countrymen (and-women), just as it had in the eyes of Soviet ethnographers and scientists. Her dress became *national*, expressive of entire communities; it literally embodied an identity, both for her and for those around her, saying who they were and who they were not. A woman's decision to wear Russian-style shoes, for instance, sometimes led even other women to denounce her as a prostitute who had abandoned her people; if she unveiled, she had by choice committed the ultimate transgression, renouncing her nationality to become "Russian."[50] Women and families who moved into the "European" New Cities were lambasted as national traitors: not only had they learned to speak Russian, but they had abandoned Uzbek ways of life, most vividly by unveiling and wearing "European" clothes. All that remained of their former selves, according to one observer, was their propensity to sit on the ground during meals.[51]

Such strict policing of the boundaries between national cultures went beyond what the party had intended, and led at times to actual hostility, both between

Uzbeks and Russians and among some of the indigenous "nations" of Central Asia themselves.[52] Soon the defense of each nation's cultural integrity was taken up by its own members, expressed largely in the same lexicon of *byt*—meaning family life and, especially, practices of female seclusion—that had been used by Soviet experts to define that nation in the first place. For example, one Uzbek man in Osh—a Communist party member, no less—felt particularly strongly about policing these national boundaries following his marriage in 1927. In order to ensure that his family and any future children would remain "Uzbek," he forced his new wife (who was herself listed as "Kyrgyz," apparently largely because she had not previously worn a veil) to don *paranji* and *chachvon*, a step that cost him his party membership card.[53] His willingness to risk such a potentially serious outcome, though, speaks eloquently to the importance he attached to issues of national identity and to the degree to which he saw his own identity as embodied in, and expressed through, his wife's *paranji*.

Clearly, therefore, many Muslim inhabitants of "Uzbekistan" responded favorably to Bolshevik attempts to create a new, "Uzbek" sense of identity through the intimate space of family relations. But with party and people cooperating in this construction of nationhood, how could the equation of nation with gender come to backfire against Moscow? The answer, and the subject of the remainder of this chapter, lies in the unintended consequences of the methods chosen by the party to bring "progress" and "modernity" to Central Asia. As already noted, specific gendered behaviors became synonymous with, and helped to define, a new, national Uzbek identity. Such behaviors encoded multiple meanings, though, and in addition to the "national" they took on diametrically opposed value judgments—being seen as "deviant" and in need of change by Bolshevik women's activists and as "devout" or "patriotic" and worthy of defense by Muslim conservatives and, now, Uzbek nationalists, as well. It was only a short step for the new Uzbek identity itself to assume the same, conflicting, moral connotations. From the Soviet perspective, then, "Uzbekness"—defined as it was through practices of veiling that seemed both primitive and oppressive—was a concept readily associated with notions of backwardness and even deviance, and it practically cried out to be changed, rehabilitated, and transformed. This equation of "Uzbek" with "deviant" in turn carried ominous implications for later relations between Bolshevik leaders and Uzbek society. It carried within itself the seeds of an unwelcome, if persistent association: that of Uzbek national identity on the one hand, and resistance to Soviet policies of women's "liberation" on the other.

Sovietizing Uzbekistan: Transforming the Uzbek Woman

A contradiction lay at the heart of the new Uzbek identity. Created largely by the Soviet state, it served a state purpose and was thus encouraged. Yet the very practices by which it was defined—veiling, seclusion, *qalin*—were seen as "back-

ward," "primitive," and "dark." An Uzbek woman was "Uzbek" partly because
she wore a *paranji* and *chachvon;* an Uzbek man, because his wife, mother, daughter, and sister did so. Both were encouraged to see themselves as Uzbeks and to
be proud of that identity. For the most part, Uzbeks themselves welcomed Soviet
efforts up to this point. Yet, in Soviet eyes, just as in the eyes of prerevolutionary
travelers, the same *paranjis* and *chachvons* that made Uzbek women distinct served
also to mark them as savages. The resulting contradiction—the apparent impossibility of being both "Uzbek," that is, true to one's culture, and "Soviet," that
is, modern and forward looking—certainly was not fully appreciated by the activists who set out to remake Uzbekistan in the mid-1920s through their *hujum*
against female seclusion.

A large part of the problem lay in the second discontinuity of colonial discourse
across 1917. The first, discussed earlier, was the addition of a specifically *national*
element to the connotations of the veiled "Eastern" woman. The second, discussed here, was the inability of Bolshevik activists to emulate tsarist officials, who
had—even while establishing a system of colonial rule—done comparatively little
to Central Asian culture besides marvel at its exotic strangeness. Bolshevik activists
marveled, too, even while denouncing their tsarist predecessors' allegedly exploitative, colonialist policies. At the same time, though, these Bolsheviks found it
impossible simply to leave Uzbekistan more or less alone. The point, after all, as
Marx had said, was to *change* the world, and it was simply unacceptable for Uzbek
women in a Soviet state still to be wearing heavy black veils in public. The party's
claim to rule in Central Asia was anchored on its emancipatory rhetoric, its
promise to help the oppressed, and this rhetoric seemed to apply particularly to
Uzbek women, long the symbols of oppression. Consider the dedication of a
booklet written in 1925 to commemorate the first five years of *Zhenotdel* work in
Central Asia:

> TO THOSE whose faces have for centuries been hidden from the sunshine;
> To those who have like slaves been chained to the women's courtyards and to
>   their husbands' *kibitki;*
> To those who have for a century learned the submissiveness of slaves;
> To those whom no one considered human before October;
> To the masses which have been raised by the crests of the October Revolution
>   to the status of women-citizens of the freest country in the world;
> To those who in their growing movement are forging a sacred loathing towards
>   the remnants of medieval servitude;
> To those who are advancing with every month, with every year into the cadres
>   of fighters for liberation;
> To these awakening women of the peoples of Central Asia, this collection is ded-
>   icated.[54]

Such rhetoric impelled party workers to attack the very veils that defined these
women as Uzbek in the first place. This logic of emancipation drove the ostensibly

anticolonialist Soviet government to launch a project of cultural transformation in Central Asia that far surpassed in intrusiveness anything that had been done by the tsarist state or, indeed, by many prior colonial regimes in other parts of the world.[55]

I have already argued that gender relations coded other social identities—Muslim, Uzbek, non-Russian—in a variety of discourses. Women's positions and status within the family, that is, served as national "markers." My focus now turns to the way in which these "markers" were held up by (generally non-Muslim, and often Russian) Bolshevik activists against a model of the ideal family and society and were found to be wanting. These activists drew their ideal from their own experience and theories, basing it on a vision of strict gender equality—a self-consciously modern, secular, European vision that was quite foreign to the views of much of Muslim Uzbek society. And, as will become plain, they made such judgments well before the *hujum* of 1927.

Most Russians living in Uzbekistan made a point of calling themselves "European," rather than "Russian"; in reports, statistics, and propaganda exhortations, they drew the contrast starkly between "European" and "local national" ways. (The "European" label was also claimed by other Slavs and, indeed, by nearly every non-Muslim group living in the area, with the exception of the indigenous Jewish community.) If anyone in Central Asia had to change, it was clear who it would be: "European" practices were the (modern) model to which (backward, primitive) Uzbeks would need to adjust.[56] Soviet evaluations of local customs, including the panoply of practices built up around female seclusion, found them in need of transformation, on the grounds that they lacked the requisite qualities of modern, "civilized" life. Uzbek customs, therefore, were made to appear both unhygienic and unjust, as the expressions of a social life that remained mired in the Middle Ages.

Dirty Nations:
Science, Hygiene, and the Uzbek Woman

The expertise of Soviet scientists and anthropologists could once again be deployed to support the depiction of Uzbek life as primitive. Such experts offered learned opinions in the years after 1917 that stressed the negative consequences of Uzbek social customs and portrayed them as emblematic of the despotic primitivism that allegedly characterized Uzbek culture. One finds detailed studies of the "harmful survivals" [*vrednye perezhitki*] that still structured Uzbek daily life and careful elucidation of the health and moral risks associated with them.[57] Hygiene was the particular concern of most such studies, since that was what Uzbeks supposedly lacked. Women once again served as exemplars of their people, in this case by showing the dirt, disease, and ignorance that gripped the Uzbek nation.

This dual conflation of women with dirt on the one hand and nation on the other can be seen wherever issues of health and hygiene were discussed.[58] Soviet experts construed virtually every aspect of an Uzbek woman's life to be dirty and unhealthful. (One commonly related statistic held that a demographic gap resulted, with Central Asia having only 889 women for every 1,000 men.) She married early, resulting in damage to her reproductive system and often causing her to contract several venereal diseases. Owing to her seclusion in the *ichkari* [women's quarter] of her home, she suffered a further deterioration in health from lack of exercise and insufficient exposure to sunshine and fresh air. She gave birth in horrendous conditions, and the rites that surrounded childbirth only increased the danger to her and her newborn child. She then raised her children in dirt and squalor, leading to astonishingly high rates of infant mortality. Any number of Uzbek child-care customs could be identified as dangerously unhygienic: the *beshik*, or cradle, came under particular fire because it permitted a mother to leave her child unattended for long stretches (strategically placed holes and tubes were meant to obviate the need for diapers) and thus stunted proper development. With a pitying eye, Serafima Liubimova described the cumulative effect of such primitive *byt*. After reporting that one large medical survey had found more than 45 percent of local women (9,772 of 21,626) to be seriously ill, she explained that the squalor of indigenous life was to blame:

> They are ill with syphilis, with rashes, with gynecological and skin diseases, with diseases of the eye. All of these sicknesses are connected by the fact that there is much filth in the *kibitkas* and *iurts;* by the fact that both the sick and the healthy drink and eat from the same dishes, [and] sit on common cushions and blankets; [by the fact that] for years at a time they do not wash their children, nor wash themselves, nor wash their clothes. According to one children's clinic in the Old City of Toshkent, 35% of the children in school never bathe at all.[59]

Dirt was everywhere; indeed, it seemed to characterize Central Asia and Central Asians. In such passages, one feels the horror of "European" activists like Liubimova, the sense that they were here to enlighten the savages, to transform the local way of life in Uzbekistan—and that they were doing it for the Uzbeks' own good.

Having painted such a dire picture of Uzbek *byt*, some party workers portrayed Soviet efforts to improve women's hygiene as a defense of the Uzbek nation. They based their reasoning on the need to transform Uzbek women into educated mothers able to raise strong, healthy children. In a speech of August 1925, for instance, Uzbek party secretary Ikramov attacked the ignorance and stupidity of local folk healers [*tabibs*], some of whom reportedly had advised syphilitic men that the only cure was to marry a young girl. After denouncing such "barbaric, frankly idiotic methods [of treatment]," Ikramov argued that they served as excellent illustrations of the prevailing conditions of everyday Uzbek life:

> If one pays strict attention to these facts, to the proper upbringing of the younger generation, then here one must start thinking about the fate of the

Uzbek nation, about the proper cultivation of this nation. One must pay serious attention to [the need to] prepare, raise, and foster cultured mothers. A girl of 14 years, or one of 15–16 years, cannot become a mother and produce children, cannot raise them, and besides this, the facts show that such a wife will be maimed and broken after her first births and will [thus] cease to satisfy her husband—from which [comes] polygamy, etc. The children of such a mother will be sick, and if all of this continues in the future, then nothing will come of it [but] the Uzbek nation will degenerate. It is necessary to consider this question seriously, to consider it from the point of view of the fate of the nation itself, of its culture and its material conditions. . . . [60]

At the same time, though, this call for protecting the nation through its mothers remained a contradictory theme in party discussions of women's issues. In order for mothers to improve and safeguard the Uzbek nation's future, after all, they would have to abandon many of the practices that made them both members and emblems of this same nation.

Most frequently, then, native women—in all their dirtiness and primitivism—served as shorthand for their nation, and thus as symbols of all that was *wrong* with it. Some native Communists in Turkmenistan reportedly divorced their wives in favor of "European" women because the latter were less "illiterate and unclean."[61] Party activists called Uzbek women uncultured and illiterate. According to Akhunbabaev, "It is impossible to compare European women with Uzbek women. The European woman understands something of cultural questions, and the Uzbek woman does not understand [them]."[62] Bolshevik activists thus focused their attention on basic efforts, for example, to teach Uzbek women to use soap.[63] Such hygiene campaigns could be justified on public health grounds, to be sure—but, in the eyes of European observers, they also served to underscore the primitivism of the unwashed Uzbek woman, and thereby her people's need to be led toward cleanliness and civilization.

Deviant Nations:
The Uzbek Woman and Her Veil

Given its centrality to images of the Uzbek woman, it comes as no surprise to find that the veil elicited a particularly heavy rhetorical attack. Soviet writers denounced the *paranji* in every way they could, launching their assault on several fronts even before the *hujum* of 1927 made such attacks official.[64] In their opinion the veil was an economic hindrance to women, preventing them from working effectively outside the home. It both kept women physically enslaved and symbolized the oppression under which they lived. These writers denounced the veil in florid terms, as they did the *ichkari*, as a "prison" from which Uzbek women had to be freed—and, since no one else appeared to be defending these young women from oppression, it fell to the party to do so.

The two most interesting lines of attack, which I will treat in turn, portrayed the veil as, first, dirty and, second, deviant. Criticisms of the veil's allegedly unhygienic character fit quite nicely with the general portrait, already described, of illness and disease in Uzbek daily life. Since Uzbek women's *byt* was thought to be redolent of filth, and since the *paranji* supposedly defined the Uzbek woman, it makes sense that this veil, too, would be judged unhealthy and dangerous. In fact, many Soviet doctors and propagandists argued that the *paranji* was to blame for the health problems that beset Uzbek women. According to one typical article written in 1925 by Liubimova ("The *Paranji* and Women's Health"), the veil kept Uzbek women from moving about and working outside, causing muscular weakness, flabby skin, and premature aging. This lack of exercise, Liubimova maintained, led to poor circulation and an accumulation of toxins, and, often, an early death.[65]

Liubimova became even more exercised as she traced a series of specific adverse health consequences to the *paranji*, many of which only came to light when the unfortunate Uzbek woman became a mother. Her weak muscles meant that she would probably have difficulty giving birth, Liubimova said; either mother or child might die in childbirth, and birth deformities were commonplace. Likewise, since according to Liubimova only a mother who moved about briskly and exercised could hope to produce healthy breast milk, the restricted lifestyle imposed by the *paranji* meant that Uzbek children consumed milk in which the "poisons" of village life had accumulated. Once a young daughter herself donned the veil, she was cut off from fresh air and sunshine and thus was rendered susceptible to various diseases: the *chachvon* was said to be to blame, because it did not permit fresh air to circulate, meaning that both poisonous carbon dioxide and harmful microbes were kept close to the face.[66]

Liubimova concluded by arguing that the *paranji* could fairly—if indirectly—be blamed for two other kinds of health problems. First, she argued, it produced ignorance, which itself could potentially be fatal. Veiled women, for instance, were particularly vulnerable to a range of venereal diseases: ignorant of modern medical knowledge, they understood neither the means of transmission, nor the symptoms, nor the treatments for such serious conditions as syphilis and gonorrhea. Liubimova noted that such diseases could be spread either sexually or through close quarters and unhygienic practices (such as eating from common dishes). Yet, their real cause, she argued, was the ignorance produced by the *paranji*. Women would contract a venereal disease from their husbands (who for his part had picked it up "somewhere"), not recognize the initial signs of infection ("Often, particularly [in] a semi-cultured [*malokul'turnaia*] woman, the disease proceeds unnoticed"), and then bemoan the curse of fate: stillbirth and/or permanent infertility. If their children lived, moreover, the chances were excellent that they, too, would be infected from birth.[67]

Second, the veil cut women off from the world physically, which indirectly caused additional medical troubles. It meant that an Uzbek woman could not leave her husband or her family even if she knew that staying would endanger her own health. It meant that she could not venture into the outside world to seek medical attention for any member of her family who fell ill or to take that person to a hospital. It meant that she could not take her infant for regular preventive care, leading to a much higher chance that the child would die young; nor, Liubimova might have added, could she accept medical treatment for herself from a male Soviet doctor. All of these tragedies and more Liubimova laid squarely at the foot of the *paranji*: "And so the *paranji* leaves the woman a flaccid, sickly body; weak lungs; difficult births; infertility and children sick from syphilis and gonorrhea; and an early, bitter old age."[68]

If attacks on the veil's health risks made the *paranji* seem dirty, criticism of its moral essence made it seem deviant. By casting the issue of whether an Uzbek woman should veil as a moral one, Soviet activists, intriguingly, tried to enter the argument against the *paranji*'s Uzbek Muslim defenders on the latters' own turf. The Bolshevik denigration of the veil, therefore, did not stop at the practical (its cumbersome weight, its propensity to spread germs). It went further, arguing that by its very essence the veil was spiritually harmful, morally unjust, and, in some sense, fundamentally evil. As one local Communist put it as early as 1924,

> Communism is as incompatible with the *chadra* of native women as a dark night [is with] the full, bright sunshine of day. The *chadra* is the shameful mark of [long,] hoary centuries of despotism and slavery, darkness and ignorance; and besides this, [it is] an obstacle on the path towards the revolutionary advancement of the global working class.
>
> From this perspective every *chadra* that is torn away from a [woman's] face signals the victory of new life over the musty past, the victory of culture and light—[that is, the victory of] communism.[69]

The veil thus served as the antithesis of all the party stood for: it served as darkness to the party's light, oppression to its liberation, ignorance to its wisdom. Whether one attributes such a view to the Enlightenment roots of the Bolsheviks' Marxist ethos or to the heritage of evangelical Europeanism shown by prerevolutionary Orientalists, it is unmistakable in the endless depictions of the *paranji* as a "prison" from which innocent women had to be freed.[70]

Sometimes this moral denigration took another line altogether, imputing a range oi character flaws to the act of donning of a *paranji*. In an almost religious way, the veil could be blamed for causing sinful behavior. A fascinating, albeit extreme, example can be seen in the words of an Uzbek Communist who in 1927 addressed a local congress in Andijon:

> Together with the growth of socialist elements in the economy, there will be a decline in the debauchery [*razvrat*] of women. Really, does the *paranji* protect against depravity? Nothing of the sort; to the contrary, it leads to yet more of the same. Almost everyone knows that various forms of dissipation thrive among those who wear the *paranji*. For example, the love of one woman for another: this unhealthy phenomenon is very widespread among Uzbek women, [and] from this fact you [can] see that the *paranji* does not at all ward off debauchery.[71]

Casting such moral aspersions on the veil and the women who wore it attacked the religious and moral defense of female seclusion at its heart. Rather than being the mark of devout piety, that is, from this perspective, the *paranji* was said to drive women toward immorality and deviance by turning them into lesbians.

Soviet writers thus constructed the veil as something dirty and unhealthy, as well as something that was at its root essentially evil, immoral, and unjust. It should therefore come as no surprise to find that the *hujum* of 1927 targeted the *paranji* above all else. After all, one party member had declared in 1925 that "Uzbek women are veiled, this has been their custom since ancient times; but as you can see, this is not normal. Thus it is necessary [for us] to take action so that they will remove their *chadras*."[72] The same *paranji* that had been used to define the Uzbek people, then, was in Soviet eyes held up against a European model and declared "not normal." In short, the very nation itself—the same Uzbek nation that had been built up and encouraged by the party—was implied through its women's veils to be both dirty and deviant. Hence, it became, in a crucial way, *wrong* to be Uzbek, at least in the party's eyes, insofar as "Uzbekness" was defined through the practices of daily life. Some Bolshevik workers were astonishingly frank about this, saying that their goal was to civilize the wild Uzbeks, to tame their fanaticism.[73] They apparently did not stop for long to consider whether such an aim, so reminiscent of pre-revolutionary missionary rhetoric, could be considered colonialist.

Conclusions and Legacies

This negative construction of the Uzbek woman and her *byt* both underpinned and impelled the party's determination to remake Central Asia, a determination expressed most vigorously in the *hujum* of 1927. In launching this assault on the system of female seclusion, party leaders aimed at nothing less than a thoroughgoing transformation of Uzbek culture and society, a transformation from primitivism to modernity that would be measured largely (although not entirely) by the emancipation of Uzbek women from their *paranjis*. As one writer put it in 1925,

> A formal revolution in municipal life is taking place. The old Asian cities (Toshkent, Bukhoro), consisting of wretched little cottages [*zhal'kie mazanki*], fashioned from clay and reeds, are earmarked for demolition. In their place will be built a new city of the European type, [which] although lacking in the picturesque "Eastern color," will on the other hand assure the native population light, air, and cleanliness. . . . The struggle for women's liberation, for throwing off the age-old, nightmarish *chadra* of horsehair completes the picture of enlightenment-propagandistic work now underway all across the territory of Soviet Central Asia.[74]

The sweeping ambition of this vision distinguished the Bolshevik brand of colonialism from its tsarist predecessor, and, indeed, the only real points of comparison, such as French efforts to remake Algeria, are equally modern phenomena.[75]

Party leaders thus called upon Uzbek women to cast off their veils in the name of equality and freedom, trusting that the lure and promise of a European model of emancipation would of its own accord attract the support and cooperation of millions of downtrodden women. The success of the campaign, these Bolsheviks thought, was thus ensured, because the interest of a veiled woman in her own "emancipation" seemed to be self-evident. In a few cases, this approach worked well—local Jewish women, for example, often wore the *paranji*, but they could sometimes be encouraged to emulate their European Jewish sisters by unveiling.[76] The party, however, had not invested enormous time and effort to associate Jewish women—even "Eastern" Jewish women—with the veil. As for Uzbek women, matters appeared altogether different, since the *paranji* and the *chachvon* had, in effect, been nationalized as Uzbek property. By definition, therefore, all Uzbek women wore the veil (it, in fact, *made* them Uzbek), so party activists no longer had any group analogous to European Jewish women to which they could point, no models of women simultaneously Uzbek and unveiled. These activists thus had no options beyond urging veiled Uzbek women to emulate foreign, European, women by casting off their *paranjïs*. In the context of a newly created national community, such advice was tantamount to telling them to abandon their people.

The conflicting associations of Uzbek women and their veils—nationally emblematic and thus good, disease ridden and primitive and thus bad—created all sorts of potential problems for Soviet power in Uzbekistan. Once veils had been made into emblems of backwardness, the *hujum* represented a logical culmination of the party's efforts to remake and civilize Central Asia. Yet the same party had also made veils into emblems of Uzbek nationality and had encouraged this national identity to develop and flourish, a fateful decision with unexpected consequences. Party leaders showed a remarkable disregard for the resulting contradictions. Soviet president Mikhail Kalinin displayed an astonishing degree of obliviousness, not to mention vulgarity, when he described his vision of the future in a speech delivered in early 1928:

> There will be, of course, women of the East, but they will not have their specific peculiarities [*osobennosti*]. They will not wear the *paranji*, they will not veil themselves, they will not live locked up the walls of their huts. [Liubimova calls out from the floor: remember *qalin*!] They will not be sold for *qalin*. As soon as a woman emerges into the light, when others see that, unveiled, she is not so beautiful, then they will not buy her. (*Laughter from the audience.*)
> . . . I think that the time is not far off when we will no longer associate the Eastern woman with the idea that she is a woman who wears the veil. I think that the time is not far off when this connection between the veil and the woman

of the East will disappear, and when we speak of the Eastern woman, this will signify only the territorial presence of this woman in the Eastern countries, and no more. There will be no other particular connotations [of the term]. So it seems to me that this time is not far off; [yet] I would like to make this not-too-distant day come still nearer. (*Applause from the audience.*)[77]

All "Eastern" women, therefore—and by extension the "East" itself—were expected to be stripped of any distinguishing features. By returning to the former vocabulary of an undifferentiated "East," moreover—and one with ugly women to boot—Kalinin obliterated such distinctions even as he spoke. The idea that this outcome might not appeal to nations such as the Uzbeks, who had only just acquired such a distinctive identity, did not appear to enter Kalinin's thinking.

The effects of this miscalculation soon became plain, as resistance to the *hujum* appeared almost instantaneously and quickly became a near-universal phenomenon.[78] The conflicting logic of constructing both nationality and backwardness through the same symbol meant that when the party's vision for modernizing Uzbekistan began with a *hujum* against the veil, Uzbek women and their *paranjis* served all too readily as a focus of cultural, religious, and now *national* resistance to Soviet incursions into Uzbek culture. Such resistance in turn meant that conflict expressed over the intimate space of Uzbek family life would only stir passions more deeply. From the Bolshevik perspective, the "national" thus became all the more "deviant" and worthy of attack. From the Uzbek point of view, the fact that such gender roles and family practices were equivalent to one's national identity gave another reason for Uzbeks to fight all the harder for their preservation—since, after all, the battle amounted to a struggle to preserve themselves as a people.

The results are plain in the Bolsheviks' utter, abject failure—at least during the 1920s and 1930s—to achieve the intended metamorphosis of Uzbek society by transforming local gender relations. Far from succeeding quickly, as intended (it was meant to unveil Uzbek women in time for the revolution's tenth anniversary in October 1927), the *hujum* gave way to a long, slow, uneven process of cultural change that lasted for two generations. Even at the height of Stalin's power, then, the party found that it could not *force* sociocultural change in Central Asia, not even within its own ranks. Local Communists may have proclaimed success in unveiling Uzbek women—and trumpeted that success as the primary exhibit of, and justification for, Soviet power—but *paranjis* could still be seen on the streets of some Uzbek cities well after World War II, and occasionally even into the 1960s. Indeed, following the breakup of the USSR in 1991, when a newly independent Uzbek state sought its own identity, it is striking to note a (mostly temporary, and certainly unplanned) reappearance of a modified version of the *paranji*. But this is not, in fact, as odd as it may seem. This chapter has argued that the veil as such a national symbol was, ironically, created in part by the party itself. It therefore represents one of the more contradictory, and certainly unintended, legacies of the Soviet period—in which a modernizing party could make such emblems of backwardness into markers of the Uzbek nation.

Notes

1. Gregory J. Massell, *The Surrogate Proletariat: Moslem Women and Revolutionary Strategies in Soviet Central Asia, 1919–1929* (Princeton, N.J.: Princeton University Press, 1974).

2. Arminius Vámbéry, *Sketches of Central Asia* (London: Allen, 1868), p. 93.

3. Reprinted and translated into English as Nikolay Murav'yov, *Journey to Khiva through the Turkoman Country* (London: Oguz Press, 1977), pp. 159–161.

4. Murav'yov, *Journey to Khiva*, pp. 163–166.

5. Joseph Wolff, *Narrative of a Mission to Bokhara in the Years 1843–1845 to Ascertain the Fate of Colonel Stoddart and Captain Connolly* (London: Parker, 1845), vol. 1, pp. 330–345.

6. Arminius Vámbéry, *Travels in Central Asia: Being the Account of a Journey from Teheran across the Turkoman Desert on the Eastern Shore of the Caspian to Khiva, Bokhara, and Samarcand Performed in the Year 1863* (New York: Harper, 1865), pp. 169–172.

7. Vámbéry, *Sketches of Central Asia*, pp. 90–91.

8. The *locus classicus* is Edward W. Said, *Orientalism* (New York: Vintage, 1978). See also his *Culture and Imperialism* (New York: Knopf, 1993).

9. Henry Lansdell, *Through Central Asia* (London: Sampson Low, 1887; repr., Nendeln/Liechtenstein: Kraus, 1978), pp. 127–142. He described the "Kirghese," meaning, in modern parlance, the Kazaks.

10. Quoted by Kathleen Hopkirk, *A Traveller's Companion to Central Asia* (London: Murray, 1993), p. 52, emphasis added.

11. Vámbéry, *Sketches of Central Asia*, p. 96. He also uses women to show the power of religion, telling what happened when one man tried to see a veiled woman: both he and the unlucky woman were stoned to death (Vámbéry, *Travels in Central Asia*, p. 170).

12. This implication was not unique to Central Asia. For similar developments in other parts of the Muslim world, see Sarah Graham-Brown, *Images of Women: The Portrayal of Women in Photography of the Middle East 1860–1950* (New York: Columbia University. Press, 1988), pp. 5–35.

13. See Lata Mani, *Contentious Traditions: The Debate on Sati in Colonial India, 1780–1833* (Ph.D. diss., University of California at Santa Cruz, 1989), and Deniz Kandiyoti, "Women, Islam, and the State: A Comparative Approach," in Juan R. I. Cole, ed., *Comparing Muslim Societies: Knowledge and the State in a World Civilization* (Ann Arbor: University of Michigan Press, 1992), pp. 237–260.

14. Exceptions do exist to this generally vague portrait of an undifferentiated "East" stretching halfway around the globe. Lansdell pointed out the difference between Kirghese [Kazak] and Sart veiling practices, and Vámbéry sometimes depicts a surprising degree of male-female interaction. (Lansdell, *Through Central Asia*, p. 131, and Vámbéry, *Sketches of Central Asia*, pp. 102–106.) The general picture, however, stressed regional similarities, with particular attention to female seclusion as a metaphor for despotism.

15. Quoted by Andreas Kappeler, *Rußland als Vielvölkerreich: Entstehung—Geschichte—Zerfall* (Munich: Beck, 1992), p. 176. For another theoretical perspective on the use of

gendered racial superiority in the "Othering" of colonized peoples, see Ann Laura Stoler, "Carnal Knowledge and Imperial Power: Gender, Race, and Morality in Colonial Asia," in Micaela di Leonardo, ed., *Gender at the Crossroads of Knowledge: Feminist Anthropology in the Postmodern Era* (Berkeley: University of California Press, 1991), pp. 51–101.

16. Vámbéry, *Sketches of Central Asia*, pp. 98–99. Similar claims of expertise by Western men, made in this case about African women, are questioned by Anne M. Jennings, *The Nubians of West Aswan: Village Women in the Midst of Change* (Boulder, Colo.: Rienner, 1995), p. 5.

17. This observation should not be taken to mean that this Western discourse on the East was always present, fully formed, and unchanging. Although its emergence is not the subject here, this discourse, too, came into being historically, with different men (and, more rarely, women) disagreeing about what features should be considered essential to it. While some of its tropes remained remarkably constant, others shifted over time, as is made clear later in this chapter.

18. Graham-Brown, *Images of Women*, pp. 70–91, 134–138. On the place of the veil in the Western imagination, see also Ludmilla Jordanova, *Sexual Visions: Images of Gender in Science and Medicine between the Eighteenth and Twentieth Centuries* (Madison: University of Wisconsin Press), pp. 87–97.

19. Serafima Timofeevna Liubimova, *Dnevnik zhenotdelki* (Toshkent: Sredazkniga, 1926), p. 21.

20. Fannina W. Halle, *Women in the Soviet East* trans. Margaret M. Green (New York: Dutton, 1938), p. 20.

21. For the allegations of backwardness, see GAUz, f. 86, op. 1, d. 8130, ll. 72–5; f. 94, op. 1, d. 200, ll. 16–17; and RTsKhIDNI, f. 62, op. 2, d. 775, ll. 6–7. Uzbek food was disparaged at GAUz, f. 9, op. 1, d. 3399, ll. 5–6. Unless noted otherwise, all subsequent citations from RTsKhIDNI are also from f. 62, op. 2, and thus specify only *delo* and *list*.

22. For one example of many in which the phrase is used, see a report written in 1925 by the Uzbek SSR's Commissariat of Enlightenment [*Narkompros*] at GAUz, f. 94, op. 1, d. 33, l. 134.

23. Elements of this portrait appear frequently throughout the published and archival Soviet records of the period. The litany given here appears in the following sources among others: RTsKhIDNI, d. 426, l. 56; d. 434, l. 25; d. 769, l. 44; d. 775, ll. 5–6 (from which the phrase "harem life" was taken); and d. 776, l. 90; PAUz, f. 60, op. 1, d. 4868, ll. 25–6; "Zhizn' musul'manki (primechaniia k stikhotvoreniiu 'Sartianka')," *Krestianka*, 1923, n. 8 (May), 40; Antonina Ivanovna Nukhrat, *Oktiabr' i zhenshchina Vostoka* (Moscow-Leningrad: Gosizdat, 1927); Antonina Ivanovna Nukhrat, *Oktiabr' i zhenshchina Vostoka* (Moscow: Partizdat, 1932); L. I. Klimovich, *Islam i zhenshchina* (Moscow: Obshchestvo po rasprostraneniiu politicheskikh i nauchnykh znanii RSFSR, 1958). For a particularly astonishing picture of Turkmen women being treated as wares—with the same woman being bought and sold several times over—see Antonina Ivanovna Nukhrat, "Zhenshchina na 2 s"ezde kolkhoznikov," *Revoliutsiia i natsional'nosti*, 1935, n. 3, 24–25.

24. Nukhrat, *Oktiabr i zhenshchina Vostoka* (1927), p. 19; and V. R. Kasparova, *Zhenshchina vostoka (obzor zhenskogo kommunisticheskogo dvizheniia na Vostoke)* (Leningrad: Priboi, 1925), p. 26.

25. Serafima Timofeevna Liubimova, *Sdvigi* (Toshkent: n.p., 1925), p. 6.

26. Consider the following description by two American missionaries, also published in 1926:

> In Bokhara the woman is described as conspicuous by her absence. No man ever sets eyes upon a lady not his own, for in the street she is nothing but a perambulating sack with a black horse-hair screen where her face is likely to be. The women live in a strictly separate part of the house, often having its own courtyard and its own pond. Only now and again one meets them at dawn or nightfall, stealing out furtively to fetch water. They shrink at the sight of a stranger and veil themselves in all haste. The children, of whom the usual quantity abounded, were suffering from sore eyes, a result of the all-pervading dirt amid which they live and the pestering flies which take advantage of defenceless babies.
>
> On the whole, women make the impression of children, and in the outlying districts, of savage children. They are inexpressibly filthy in the villages and are everywhere on a far lower social grade than the men. One may say that the highest woman in the land is inferior to the lowest man. "Woman is a cheap article in Bokhara. A man in search of a wife can get one in exchange for several sheep and a little money, or a horse as the case may be. Those higher in the social scale and better endowed with the world's goods know no restrictions except those imposed by their own conscience or caution."

(A. E. Zwemer and S. M. Zwemer, *Moslem Women* [West Medford, Mass.: Central Committee on the United Study of Foreign Missions, 1926], pp. 63–64.)

27. I treat the role of class ideology at length in chapter 3 of "Uzbek Women and the Veil: Gender and Power in Stalinist Central Asia" (Ph.D. diss., Stanford University, 1999). Suffice it here to point to two party discussions of women's issues in 1926 framed in terms of class: RTsKhIDNI, d. 769, l. 45, and d. 786, l. 5.

28. See for example Almatinskaia-Zelenina, *Iz mgly tysiacheletnii: Istoricheskii ocherk byta zhenschiny Vostoka* (Toshkent: Sredazkniga, 1926).

29. The term appeared frequently. One example is at GAUz, f. 86, op. 1, d. 5881, l. 168.

30. The name was used during the medieval period, although not necessarily with a clearly ethnic meaning. See James Critchlow, *Nationalism in Uzbekistan: A Soviet Republic's Road to Sovereignty* (Boulder, Colo.: Westview, 1991), p. 1, and Edward A. Allworth, *The Modern Uzbeks: From the Fourteenth Century to the Present: A Cultural History* (Stanford: Hoover Institution Press, 1990). Among the authors previously cited, Muravev had described "Uzbegs" as early as 1822. Wolff had mentioned the "Usbecks," while Vámbéry called them "Œzbegs."

31. Partha Chatterjee, *The Nation and Its Fragments: Colonial and Postcolonial Histories* (Princeton: Princeton University Press, 1993), pp. 6, 121.

32. Bolshevik activists could point to other reasons to encourage the growth of nations in Central Asia. From a Marxist perspective, Central Asia was a "feudal" or "precapitalist" area, meaning that nations (thought to be a product of capitalism) could be justified as progressive. Encouraging non-Russian nations to flourish also provided a useful contrast with the allegedly oppressive legacy of tsarist colonialism.

33. RTsKhIDNI, d. 775, l. 6, and PAUz, f. 60, op. 1, d. 4868, ll. 25–26. On the policing of national boundaries through women's dress, see the various booklets meant

to describe each nation's unique women. One on Uzbek women appeared as V. Moskalev, *Uzbechka* (Moscow: Okhrana materinstva i mladenchestva, 1928). Another series of such booklets was planned for 1930–1931; see GAUz, f. 9, op. 1, d. 3425, l. 11. For a later example of such national definitions, see the discussion of veiling practices at B. Pal'vanova, *Docheri sovetskogo Vostoka* (Moscow: Gosizd. pol. lit., 1961), p. 28.

34. For an example of secluded women in southern Kazakstan being deemed Uzbek in 1929, see GAUz, f. 9, op. 1, d. 3404, ll. 37–38. Such distinctions seemed to follow a circular logic: in Osh, for example, an unveiled Muslim woman must be Kyrgyz rather than Uzbek, because Kyrgyz women did not veil.

35. The republics squabbled among themselves over the details of these borders throughout the 1920s and beyond, often basing their arguments on ethnographic claims. Uzbek officials argued, for example, that the Uzbeks of Osh had been cut off by the border and that they should be reunited with their conationals in the Uzbek SSR. For an example of such arguments, see GAUz, f. 86, op. 1, d. 3423, ll. 47–59.

36. The veils of Bukhoran Jewish women are discussed at RTsKhIDNI, d. 787, l. 176, and d. 1157, ll. 24 and 38–40. (A contrary view—that these women were unveiled—was expressed by the Danish geographer Olufsen, who visited Bukhoro from 1896 to 1899. See Kathleen Hopkirk, *A Traveller's Companion to Central Asia* [London: Murray, 1993], p. 53.) These women were sold into early marriages much like Uzbek women according to GAUz, f. 86, op. 1, d. 2597, l. 1020b.

37. Such cases were reported in the newspapers to horrify a Russian readership. See, for instance, "Russkaia devochka pod parandzhei," *Pravda Vostoka*, April 10, 1927, n. 80 (1276), p. 3. For similar cases in 1929, see also RTsKhIDNI, d. 2072, l. 61, and d. 2073, ll. 26–29.

38. See RTsKhIDNI, d. 2054, l. 118, and Z. A. Shirokova, *Traditsionnaia i sovremennaia odezhda zhenshchin gornogo Tadzhikistana* (Dushanbe: Donish, 1976), pp. 81–85.

39. Note that a few studies of males proceeded along similar lines, such as A. P. Shishov, "Mal'chiki uzbeki. Antropometricheskoe issledovanie," *Meditsinskaia mysl' Uzbekistana*, n. 1 (January 1928): 16–41. Women of other ethnic groups were the subjects of similar investigations, further disaggregating the unitary "Eastern woman": see the studies of Tajik women at RTsKhIDNI, d. 812, ll. 34–105, and of Chechen women at S. Arsanov, "Chechnia," *Vlast' Sovetov*, n. 29–30 (July 25 1926): 27. Such anthropological investigations were defended in general terms as a worthy enterprise at GAUz, f. 86, op. 1, d. 5885, l. 7770b.

40. "It is necessary to stop [and study] the Uzbek woman because . . . [she] represents the most conservative element in the family, having long held on to and preserved tradition and the old style of life . . ." (V. K. Iasevich, "K voprosu o konstitutsional'nom i antropologicheskom tipe uzbechki Khorezma," *Meditsinskaia mysl' Uzbekistana*, n. 5 [February 1928]: 35).

41. Ibid., p. 35.

42. Ibid., p. 49. It does not seem far-fetched to see Iasevich's "scientific" investigation as overlaid with the erotic fantasies of earlier male visitors to the East, discussed earlier. For a discussion of such "scientific pornography," see Ann Laura Stoler, *Race and the Education of Desire: Foucault's History of Sexuality and the Colonial Order of Things* (Durham, N.C.: Duke University Press, 1995), pp. 183–190.

43. Plans for this study, which does not seem to have been published (although many of the examinations were carried out), are at GAUz, f. 94, op. 1, d. 797, ll. 89–890b, and also at RTsKhIDNI, d. 776, ll. 146–147.

44. On this encouragement, see RTsKhIDNI, d. 1201, ll. 56–58, and GAUz, f. 94, op. 1, d. 797, l. 88. Other records of the close attention paid this project by the *Zhenotdel* in particular may be found at RTsKhIDNI, d. 773, ll. 106–107 111, and d. 793, ll. 40, 63.

45. For a sample of the physical examination forms, see RTsKhIDNI, d. 776, ll. 143–144ob. A questionnaire on each woman's "social character" follows at l. 145.

46. On the use of exhibitions and museums to delineate such distinctions in Uzbekistan, see RTsKhIDNI, d. 774, l. 42; d. 793, l. 37, and d. 801, l. 60. For a theoretical perspective on such representations of other cultures, see Timothy Mitchell, *Colonising Egypt* (Cambridge: Cambridge University Press, 1988), chapter 1.

47. For a similar approach to these boundaries see V. Ia. Zezenkova, "Materialy po antropologii zhenshchin razlichnykh plemen i narodov Srednei Azii," in L. V. Oshanin and V. Ia. Zezenkova, *Voprosy etnogeza narodov Srednei Azii v svete dannykh antropologii. Sb. Statei* (Toshkent: AN UzSSR, 1953), pp. 57–60. Zezenkova, who carried out her work in 1944, also included a series of photographs of the different "types" of Uzbek women (pp. 89–111). Interestingly, just as Iasevich and Oshanin had before her, she sought to illustrate "the" Uzbek woman—in the singular—far more than variations among Uzbek women. Yet, to do so, she found herself showing a multiplicity of "types"—in the plural. The logical consequences for the concept of a single, ideal "Uzbek woman," however, remained unexplored.

48. Especially in the case of Islam, indeed—at least insofar as "Islam" was understood in Central Asia as a shorthand appellation not only for a religious faith but for an entire complex of (locally specific) cultural practices and ways of seeing the world—the new national identities were often intertwined (and sometimes conflated) in complicated ways with the old Muslim ones. Elizabeth Bacon quotes one ethnically Uzbek member of the party, for instance, as saying, "The Muslim religion is the Mother of the Uzbek people," and Gerhard Simon tells of the horror felt by a Kyrgyz audience when a native Communist disavowed any sense of himself as a Muslim on the grounds that he did not believe in God. Such a disavowal, in the eyes of his listeners, amounted to a renunciation of his identity as a Kyrgyz. Neither Simon nor Bacon, however, probe behind what seems to them the irrationality of such views— Simon calls the idea of a "non-believing Muslim" an "obvious oxymoron"—to appreciate the cultural intricacies of what "Islam" meant in Central Asia. See Gerhard Simon, *Nationalism and Policy toward the Nationalities in the Soviet Union: From Totalitarian Dictatorship to Post-Stalinist Society*, trans. Karen Forster Oswald Forster (Boulder, Colo.: Westview, 1991), p. 288, and Elizabeth E. Bacon, *Central Asians under Russian Rule: A Study in Culture Change* (Ithaca, N.Y.: Cornell University Press, 1966), p. 176.

49. Women have been seen as repositories of nationhood in other Muslim parts of the former Soviet Union, although generally only from a contemporary perspective. See particularly Gillian Tett, " 'Guardians of the Faith?': Gender and Religion in an (ex) Soviet Tajik Village," in Camillia Fawzi El-Solh and Judy Mabro, eds., *Muslim Women's Choices: Religious Belief and Social Reality* (Oxford: Berg, 1994), pp. 128–151, and also Nayereh Tohidi, "Soviet in Public, Azeri in Private: Gender, Islam, Nationalism in Soviet and Post-Soviet Azerbaijan," paper presented at the Middle East Studies Association of North America annual meeting, December 6–10, 1995, Washington, D.C.

50. See the records from 1925 and 1926 at RTsKhIDNI, d. 433, l. 36, and d. 776, l. 29.

51. RTsKhIDNI, d. 1202, l. 33.

52. Russian and Uzbek women could not work together in a factory at PAUz, f. 58, op. 2, d. 1371, ll. 23–25; an example of Uzbek-Jewish tension from 1924 is related at RTsKhIDNI, d. 162, l. 96ob.

53. RTsKhIDNI, d. 1684, l. 400b.

54. RTsKhIDNI, d. 427, l. 1; published as *Za piat' let* (Moscow: Tsentr. Izd. narodov SSSR, 1925). For similar rhetoric, see also PAUz, f. 60, op. 1, d. 2461, l. 2, and GAUz, f. 94, op. 1, d. 85, ll. 22–220b.

55. In India, for instance, the British colonial government had earlier faced an issue—the practice of *sati*, or widow burning—that in some ways paralleled the *paranji* in Central Asia. Both practices seemed abhorrent (albeit expressive of the indigenous population's low cultural level) to the colonial authorities. British authorities justified their opposition to *sati*, however, on the grounds that it contravened "true" Hindu practice. Finding and supporting Brahmin clerics willing to make such an argument— a group in some ways analogous to the *jadids* of Central Asia—the government could portray itself as a defender of native cultural authenticity. (See Mani, *Contentious Traditions*.) Soviet officials took the opposite approach in Central Asia, giving no quarter to potentially sympathetic voices within native society and instead introducing a model for social reform based entirely (or so they said) on an external, European ideal of women's rights. (See later discussion.) Unlike the British authorities, therefore, who had permitted a vigorous debate within Indian society over *sati* (making it possible for modern historians like Mani to reconstruct indigenous arguments in defense of the practice), Soviet leaders stifled where they could any discussion of the *paranji* in non-Soviet (such as religious) terms. Historians can only regret the lack of such materials today and are forced to look elsewhere for insights into Uzbek perspectives on veiling.

56. In one factory, for example, Uzbek women reportedly showed themselves as unable to work effectively or efficiently. The only exception was one *uzbechka* who had improved dramatically after being put to work directly between two "European" co-workers. The latters' superior example of skill and diligence apparently inspired her to raise her own level. (PAUz, f. 58, op. 2, d. 1371, ll. 23–25.)

57. Note that the language of "survivals" was explicit and unapologetic, seeing in these everyday customs vestiges of a developmental stage that "European" peoples had long since surpassed. From a Foucauldian perspective, the attention to health and dirt speaks to the Bolshevik state's efforts to claim for itself the mantle of "civilization" and to create a self-disciplined citizenry through the use of soap. For two party lists of all the various "harmful customs" crying out for study by Soviet scientists, see RTsKhIDNI, d. 1201, ll. 74–750b, and d. 1203, ll. 9–10.

58. Evidence for this paragraph is taken from GAUz, f. 737, op. 1, d. 185, l. 179; RTsKhIDNI, d. 769, l. 34; d. 775, ll. 6–8; d. 787, ll. 277–278; and d. 1211, l. 117; PAUz, f. 60, op. 1, d. 4868, ll. 25–26; Iasevich, "K voprosu"; and Serafima Timofeevna Liubimova, *Kommunist! Esli ty ne khochesh', chtoby narod vymiral, esli ty deistvitel'no zabotish'sia o razvitii narodnogo khoziaistva i kul'tury, esli ty ne bai, ne mulla i ne podderzhivaesh' mull i baev—ty dolzhen rabotat' po raskreposhcheniiu zhenshchin* (Toshkent: Izd. Zhenotdela SAB TsK RKP(b), 1925), p. 3.

59. Liubimova, *Kommunist!*, p. 3. Note that Liubimova is somewhat vague about her area: *kibitki* and *iurts* were nomadic steppe dwellings, not typical in Uzbekistan and certainly not in Toshkent.

60. RTsKhIDNI, d. 445, ll. 43–44. In its very title, Liubimova's just-quoted booklet

invokes a similar fear of the [Uzbek] *narod*'s becoming extinct. According to a different party report, also written in 1925, perversions such as those mentioned by Ikramov were "gnawing away at the health of the nation and leading to its degeneration." As this report put it, "An illiterate and enslaved mother cannot raise her children as healthy and cultured people. The facts of the degeneration and *kolechenie* of women speak to the threat to the very existence of the Uzbek nation" (GAUz, f. 94, op. 1, d. 223, ll. 121–122).

61. RTsKhIDNI, d. 1202, l. 59.

62. RTsKhIDNI, d. 1688, l. 25. See also d. 1239, l. 27.

63. Examples of this soap-and-water campaign can be found at RTsKhIDNI, d. 769, l. 44; d. 774, l. 63; d. 1204, l. 35; and f. 507, op. 2, d. 118, l. 59; and Moskalev, *Uzbechka*, p. 23. Hygiene was also applied as a judgment to other Central Asian nations—to Turkmen women at RTsKhIDNI, d. 799, l. 41, and to Tajik women at RTsKhIDNI, d. 812, ll. 75–76, 82.

64. The remainder of this paragraph is based on RTsKhIDNI, d. 427, l. 16; PAUz, f. 60, op. 1, d. 4981, l. 23; and Bibi Pal'vanova, *Docheri Sovetskogo Vostoka* (Moscow: Gospolitizdat, 1961), pp. 28–29.

65. Liubimova's unpublished article is at RTsKhIDNI, d. 429, ll. 43–47, and this part of her argument is from ll. 43–44. For another treatment of the veil's health risks, see the Uzbek-language booklet published under the same title by Ukraintsev in 1923. For an example of a doctors' meeting to discuss such risks, see A. Nikolaeva, "Protiv parandzhi i chachvana," *Pravda Vostoka*, n. 51 (1247) (2 March 1927): 3.

66. RTsKhIDNI, d. 429, ll. 44–45.

67. RTsKhIDNI, d. 429, l. 46.

68. RTsKhIDNI, d. 429, l. 47.

69. RTsKhIDNI, d. 427, l. 155.

70. Jean Starobinski, for instance, has argued that the Enlightenment sought above all else *transparency*, as expressed for example in its aim to unveil the secrets of nature— a perspective from which the *paranji* would certainly appear unwelcome, morally threatening, and not a little ominous. (Jean Starobinski, *Jean-Jacques Rousseau: Transparency and Obstruction*, trans. Arthur Goldhammer (Chicago: University of Chicago Press, 1988), especially pp. 65–80, 254–267.

71. GAUz, f. 837, op. 3, d. 150, ll. 138–139.

72. RTsKhIDNI, d. 436, l. 102.

73. GAUz, f. 86, op. 1, d. 2217, ll. 22–23.

74. V. A. Gurko-Kriazhin, "Poezdka v Zakavkaz'e i Sredniuiu Aziiu," *Novyi Vostok*, n. 7 (1925), 370.

75. Strikingly, French colonial authorities also chose an unveiling campaign to "gallicize" Algeria through its women. See David C. Gordon, *Women of Algeria: An Essay on Change* (Cambridge Mass.: Harvard University Press, 1968), pp. 56–59.

76. RTsKhIDNI, d. 787, l. 176.

77. GARF, f. 3316, op. 50, d. 14, ll. 4, 2. (Reverse pagination.) See also RTsKhIDNI, d. 449, l. 77.

78. Such resistance is discussed in the later chapters of Northrop, "Uzbek Women and the Veil."

PART IV

Stalinism and the Empire of Nations

The Forge of the Kazakh Proletariat?

The Turksib, Nativization, and Industrialization during Stalin's First Five-Year Plan

O**N DECEMBER 31, 1928, A POGROM ERUPTED** on the construction of the Turkestano-Siberian Railroad (the Turksib) at its northern railhead of Sergiopol'. Approximately four hundred Russian workers viciously beat any Kazakh they could lay their hands on, including their own coworkers. The attack at Sergiopol' was just one of a number of pogroms, beatings, and acts of "hooliganism" that dominated the construction of the Turksib. This ethnic hostility was a reaction to a second construction project by the Soviet government, the construction of a Kazakh working class. The animus of rank-and-file European workers toward the Kazakhs at Sergiopol' and elsewhere indicates that this project faced considerable resistance from the very proletariat the Kazakhs were supposed to join. Assimilating Kazakhs into the Soviet working class also engendered major resistance from the managers of the construction and from many Kazakhs themselves.

Despite this resistance, the Soviet regime pushed through a policy of hiring preferences, educational mandates, and political intervention that can be termed a type of affirmative action.[1] Moreover, the state deployed its full powers of coercion to discipline opponents of affirmative action. One of the leaders of the Sergiopol' riot was shot for his crimes, and numerous other workers, employees, and even highly placed Turksib managers were reprimanded, fired, or indicted for anti-Kazakh acts. Despite occasional high-level complicity by party, trade union, or construction officials in discrimination, the higher organs (even the Kazakh Party Committee, with its notoriously anti-Kazakh secretary, F. I. Goloshchekin) consistently combated "Great Power chauvinism" whenever it appeared on the construction site.

This strong state action to protect the rights of a previously oppressed minority gives an obviously beneficent appearance to the regime's nationalities policy. And yet, this same state promoted a different group of policies that had a nearly genocidal effect on Kazakhs: forced settlement and collectivization.[2] The brutal effects of these policies decimated the same pool of people the Soviet government took such pains to recruit, promote, and train as industrial workers on the Turksib. The paradox is obvious and troubling. How are we to understand the Soviet nationalities policy from these two examples? As a maker of nations or a breaker of nations?

To explore this conundrum, this chapter probes the Soviet Union's policies, particularly those of *korenizatsiia*, or nativization. Nativization was the core policy of an ambitious, complex, and prolonged effort by the Soviet state to build ethnically based nations within the context of a politically and economically unitary state. These policies, envisioned by Lenin and implemented consistently by Stalin, seem contradictory. In effect, they sought to subsume all nations within socialism by encouraging nations to flourish. Efforts at promoting national cultural autonomy extended even to attempts at linguistic assimilation of Russians—Soviet officials and managers were expected to learn the language of the titular nationality they served.[3]

The state's support for nativization, however, should not obscure the importance of individuals as agents, not simply as objects of the Soviet nationalities policy. While the regime could shatter Kazakh traditional identity by destroying their nomadic lifestyle, it could not conjure a native proletariat from thin air. Nativization, especially within industry, would provide a radically different social space for a new ethnic identity to develop. But how and even whether Kazakhs used this space depended on them. They could simply stay away from industrial employment. Moreover, the entire nativization program hinged on encouraging the managers and workers of Soviet industry to accept Kazakh "savages" as proletarians.

The success of Soviet nation building, then, became intimately tied to the industrialization drive of the pre–World War II Five-Year Plans. The construction of the Turksib railroad connecting Novosibirsk with Tashkent provides as good an environment to study this process as any. One of the great construction projects of the First Five-Year Plan (1928–1932), the Turksib embodied the Bolshevik ideal of "building socialism"—creating a modern, industrial society free of class, gender, or ethnic animosities. From December 1926 to January 1931, the railroad's 1,440 kilometers of roadbed were built by upward of thirty thousand workers. Perhaps more important, the railroad became an icon of the regime's commitment to end national oppression and ethnic "backwardness" through economic development and political mobilization.[4]

The Forge of a Kazakh Proletariat?

When construction of the Turksib commenced, Kazakhs already possessed a well-developed ethnic identity closely tied to their nomadic pastoral economy.[5] This Kazakh identity, tied as it was to nomadism, respect for traditional authorities, and clan divisions, was deeply troubling to both the regime and modernizing Kazakh intellectuals Communists rejected this identity, in part, because it seemed to reinforce the power of "exploiters" within Kazakh society.[6] Moreover, nomadism provided the majority of Kazakhs with only bare subsistence. Kazakh herds in the region of the Turksib averaged only 8.7 head of sheep per nomadic household. Given the accepted flock size for the minimum subsistence of a family—roughly sixty head—this figure indicates the extremely precarious condition of pastoralism in the region.[7] Yet, although their own economies were increasingly stressed, the nomads stuck stubbornly to their traditional way of life. They had few choices. Their subsistence economies left them few surpluses for the market, and their only source of income was to work for very low wages as a shepherd for a *bey*. As one official put it, "There are very few Kazakhs at work [i.e., as wage workers] and their wages are very low, sometimes less than one ruble a day." He added that such workers usually had to "economize" on food.[8] This penury, as well as deference to traditional authority, embodied the stagnation of nomadic pastoralism to supporters of nativization.

Many of these supporters were Kazakh intellectuals, often so-called National Communists, who had been coopted by Moscow and who embraced the revolution's call for ending economic backwardness.[9] Moscow's cooptation, unlike its practice in Russian areas of the Union, created a considerable overlap in Kazakhstan between the prerevolutionary Kazakh intelligentsia and postrevolutionary national party cadres. The need to nativize the local party and Soviet officialdom, coupled with the lack of any native attachment to Bolshevism, forced Moscow to be less particular in choosing its party cadres. This continuity, attenuated though it was, between Kazakhstan's prerevolutionary intelligentsia and its Soviet native elite provided a constituency for Kazakh development. Typical of such "National Communists" was T. R. Ryskulov, a leading Kazakh Communist, who played an important role in building the Turksib. Ryskulov dreamed of the Kazakhs leaping into modernity: "Leninism affirms the view that under the leadership of the laboring proletariat backward nations may be led to socialism without having to endure a long process of capitalist development."[10] Most leading Kazakhs agreed with Ryskulov. Kazakh party cadres consistently supported capital investment and industrial transformation of their societies to overcome "colonial exploitation."[11] The *aul* (the migratory encampment), rather than being a romantic embodiment of the people's culture, was a sort of embarrassing relic, or at least a stage of development to be quickly bypassed.[12]

Consequently, local leaders greeted the government's announcement of the Turksib's construction with enthusiasm as a method for transmitting socialist modernity to the "backward" steppe. As Ryskulov put it, "The railroad will undoubtedly bring culture and Soviet power into those areas where it is very dubious to talk of Soviet power."[13] There was some basis for such grandiose hopes. By one estimate, 35 percent of the Kazakh population lived within the immediate hinterland of the Turksib.[14] Both Moscow and the Kazakh government wanted to use the railroad's construction to "capture" this population for socialist production. To do so, they hoped to hire thousands of Kazakhs for the construction and to accustom them to industrial labor. If the Turksib's builders and operators were drawn primarily from the local population, a solid core of Kazakhs could be both settled and proletarianized, thereby offering a model for their nomadizing kin.[15] Even officials of the central commissariat charged with building the railroad, Narkomput' (Narodnyi Kommissariat Puti Soobshchenii—the People's Commissariat of Means of Communication), embraced this civilizational mission for the Turksib. Vladimir Shatov, the man in charge of the construction, viewed the Turksib as an embodiment of socialism's promise. Or, as he put it, "The Tsarist government feared bringing new life and culture to the East; This we have to do as Communists."[16] The Turksib would become, in an oft-used phrase of the time, "the forge of the new proletarian cadre of the Kazakh Republic."[17]

To ensure that the Turksib became this forge, local officials spearheaded an effort to get a hard employment quota for Kazakh workers.[18] Ryskulov, who headed the government's Committee to Aid the Construction of the Turksib, emerged as a tireless lobbyists for this goal.[19] Unfortunately, Narkomput' and the central organs, while enthusiastic about the "civilizational" mission of the Turksib, showed rather more coolness toward staffing the construction with natives. Despite its rhetoric, Narkomput' was far more interested in cost than in social engineering and thus resisted hiring untrained Kazakh tribesmen for construction. Initially, the Commissariat proposed importing 75 percent of its workers from European Russia and hiring only 25 percent of its workforce from the "local" (not native) population.[20]

The government and the Communist party of Kazakhstan strenuously resisted this plan. Tellingly, Narkomput' conceded only when it was convinced that Kazakh workers would be cheaper and more resistant to the region's ferocious weather and endemic diseases.[21] Even then, Narkomput' would not commit to a hard quota until ordered to do so by the Russian Republic's *Sovnarkom*.[22] In early 1928, Narkomput' and the Turksib's management signed an agreement with the Kazakh labor commissariat to hire 50 percent of its workers from the native population.[23] That enormous pressure had been brought to bear on the Commissariat to wring this quota out of it and that it still put economic efficiency above the regime's nativization plans boded ill for the program on the Turksib.

Even so, this agreement was a huge victory for the partisans of nativization. The building season in 1927 had been used primarily for surveys, which required few workers.[24] The 1928 plan, on the other hand, called for upwards of 25,000 workers. A quota of 12,500 Kazakh builders would represent a potent increase in the republic's native proletarians. To ensure that the quota was actually met, Kazakh nomads were allowed to register at labor exchanges with the same hiring priority as Red Army veterans and trade union members. Kazakhs took advantage of these new privileges in droves. As early as December 1927, 5,078 of the 9,653 men registered for work on the Turksib were Kazakh. It seemed that the Turksib was now prepared to forge its native proletariat.

Affirmative Action and Its Discontents

Unfortunately, for both Kazakh National Communists and the regime itself, this forging would be a difficult endeavor. The use of the Turksib as an instrument of nativization faced resistance from three major sources: the society to be transformed into workers, the managers of the Turksib who were to conduct the transformation, and the majority of European workers who were to acquiesce in this transformation. Of the three forms, the most diffuse and largely ineffectual resistance came from traditional Kazakh society. Surprisingly, the most sustained and intractable resistance generally came from the putative supporters of the Soviet regime, its proletarians.

Of the three sources of resistance, the Kazakhs had most reason to fear the Turksib. Railroads had not been kind to nomads, who had been dispossessed from land following the construction of the Trans-Siberian railroad. Additionally, the railnet had been instrumental in crushing the 1916 Steppe Revolt and the anti-Soviet *basmachi* movement during the civil war.[25] Even so, Kazakh society offered no unified response to construction. Reactions toward the Turksib ran the gamut from open revolt to active collusion. At one end of the spectrum were thousands of Kazakh construction workers, guides, teamsters, and camel drovers without whom the Turksib could not have been built. Most Kazakhs, however, were not so helpful. They covered up wells, stole surveyors' stakes, withheld carting services and supplies, and spread wild rumors against the construction.[26] Soon after the announcement of construction, for instance, rumors began to fly that the Turksib would displace Kazakhs from their pastures.[27] Although the Soviet authorities usually blamed these rumors on the machinations of mullahs and *beys* seeking to keep their people chained to the past, Kazakh resentment of the railroad was broadly based. Incidents such as stealing stakes and spreading malicious gossip were so pervasive that they must have represented the hostility of most *auly* to the railroad. Some *auly* actually fled when the Turksib's builders approached them.[28]

A few Kazakhs did not limit themselves to such desultory forms of resistance and fought the railroad openly. These were the *basmachis*, Muslim partisans committed to the overthrow of the Communist system. One Communist activist left an account of the actions of these bands on the northern section of construction:

[T]he *basmachis* had grown bold. They began to disconcert the workers and attack us in various ways. For instance, they would undermine the railroad ties to cause a train derailing even at slow speeds. The Turksib had difficulties with water and often we would wake up in the morning to discover our water tanks emptied and riddled with holes. The bandits became particularly impudent in the spring of 1930. They went as far as shooting at the workers finishing the railroad.[29]

These attacks, however, were worse than futile. The Turksib, thanks to its vast concentration of European workers, Communist cadres, and its own department of the Ob"edinnennoe Glavnoe Politicheskoe Upravlenie (OGPU), represented one of the most difficult targets for an open assault in all of Kazakhstan. A former Turksib worker recalled how *basmachi* bands were handled:

> The communists decided to form a fighting detachment to combat the bandits. From March to May 1930 I was its political commissar. Day and night we stayed in the saddle, tracking the elusive *basmachi*. Finally, in the region of the Lepsy and Matai settlements, we overtook them. The battle was short and merciless. That's when my ability to shoot a machine gun came in handy. The band was destroyed and I returned to construction.[30]

No *basmachi* attack ever caused the suspension of construction.

The policy of nativizing the Turksib, however, would be tested not so much in battles with *basmachis* as in the recruitment of Kazakh workers. Here, more difficult foes appeared—bureaucratic pettyfoggers, workers' chauvinists, and the rank-and-file Kazakh labor "flitters." Of these, Narkomput's bureaucrats initially represented the most serious roadblock to nativization. The Commissariat's managers waged a stubborn bureaucratic battle to undermine the government's prescriptions on nativization. In fact, most Turksib construction managers, especially its engineers and technical personnel, showed an unalloyed contempt for Kazakhs and the goals of nativization.

Many of the Turksib's managers had been trained prior to the revolution ("bourgeois specialists," in the parlance of the times), and the vast majority were European. These managers often carried strong prejudices against native workers. Most of this prejudice was masked in a rhetoric of efficiency—Turksib managers would often claim that Kazakhs simply did not know how to work. For instance, I. N. Borisov, head of Narkomput's Construction Division, said the Turksib's Kazakh navvies did "twenty per cent of what a good Russian worker would accomplish in previous times—a fifth. This is contemptible productivity."[31] At least Borisov believed that Kazakhs could, with time, become decent navvies. Other Commissariat personnel were less sanguine. Ryskulov complained early in 1928 that Turksib managers simply would not hire Kazakh workers: "There [on the construction site] they say that the Kazakhs are little suited for this type of work and, being weaker, they will earn less."[32] One section chief, engineer Gol'dman, bluntly stated this prejudice against hiring Kazakhs: "Kazakhs are very poor workers from whom nothing will ever come. A proletariat will never arise from such as them."[33] The Turksib's managers enumerated a long list of Kazakh production sins—they did not know how to use the tools, took too many tea breaks, and quit work suddenly.[34]

While these charges could be supported with examples, Kazakh production difficulties had less to do with laziness and stupidity than with sheer ignorance. Ryskulov pointed out that, when Kazakhs were given the same tools as Europeans and time to learn the proper techniques, both groups had comparable output. A Communist engineer agreed; most of his Kazakh workers quickly mastered the norms once trained.[35] Some Kazakh work gangs, in fact, achieved higher productivity than their European counterparts.[36] The journalist Vit. Fedorovich, on viewing a laboring mass of Kazakh navvies, wrote admiringly that "they worked just like automatons, these former nomads."[37]

The anti-Kazakh rhetoric of efficiency deployed by some Turksib managers was merely a screen for ethnic prejudice. Until 1929, the local construction managers largely ignored the labor regulations and hired whomever they chose. Often their choices had racist overtones and were justified in the most facetious ways. As late as 1930, one section chief, a "bourgeois" specialist, hired forty-six grooms, all European. When questioned on this, the chief claimed that Kazakhs worked poorly with horses, despite the fact that Kazakhs were practically born on horseback.[38] Moreover, as one disgruntled Kazakh noted, "The first to be fired are Kazakhs. The Russians remain even if they have the same skill level."[39] This practice of Kazakhs being "last in, first out" was so common that Shatov demanded repeatedly his managers cease the practice.[40]

Kazakh workers also faced other types of ethnic prejudice from their bosses. The bourgeois specialists, especially, often acted in an openly chauvinist manner. They had ways, as one activist put it, "to create an unfriendly work atmosphere for a Kazakh."[41] Kazakh workers suffered discrimination in work assignments and pay. Since most work was compensated in the form of piece-rates, the two forms of discrimination were intimately entwined. Europeans, for instance, almost always received the easier jobs and usually were the first chosen to receive new tools or be trained to work with new machinery.[42] Such systematic discrimination in assignments showed up in wages; Russians' wages were usually higher than the Kazakhs' by a ratio of three to one.[43] On occasion, this sort of ethnic favoritism was done quite openly, without even the fig leaf of different work assignments. For instance, in summer 1928, new Kazakh navvies were classified a rank lower than starting European navvies—despite the fact that both groups had no production experience. Thanks to such unfair ranking, the Kazakhs earned only two-thirds of the Europeans' wages in this case.[44]

As if such injustice were not trial enough, many European managers heaped all sorts of personal indignities on their Kazakh workers. One foreman became infamous for "acting towards Kazakh workers as if they were cattle." This foreman once struck a Kazakh for no apparent purpose. When the stricken Kazakh asked, "Why'd you belt me?" the foremen replied "Shut up, or I'll punch out your eyes!" Moreover, mockery and contempt oozed from his attitude toward his charges. He refused to take his Kazakhs up the line for their weekly bath: "Why do you Kazakhs need a bath? You can manage without a bath since there are fifty or sixty of you. Better to take twenty Russians!"[45] These actions, of course, produced indignation among Kazakh workers, who asked, "Aren't we workers like the others?"[46]

Discrimination was pervasive off the job, also. Kazakh living conditions were invariably inferior to the Europeans' poor accommodations. As a rule, they were the last to get whatever shelter, bedding, and other equipment was available.[47] Furthermore, Kazakhs suffered constant outrages at the Turksib's cooperative stores. They were ordered to the back of the line, received goods after the Europeans had first choice, had to accept bread that was cut with the same knife used to cut pork fat (anathema to the Kazakhs' religious practices), and withstood constant verbal abuse from the clerks.[48] Finally, technical specialists of the "older cut" established a sort of apartheid on the worksite; they built dining sheds for Kazakhs alone to eat in (separated from Europeans) because "Kazakhs smell bad."[49] The Turksib's trade union and party organs initially did little to impede this sort of open discrimination. Kazakhs made up only a small minority of either institution's membership.[50]

If managerial discrimination was humiliating and oppressive to the Turksib's native workers, the rage of their European coworkers could be terrifying. The Soviet affirmative-action program created a backlash among previously privileged workers of the dominant ethnicity. This backlash had its roots in the two identities the European workers brought with them to the Turksib. First, rank-and-file European workers resented nativization as a betrayal of the "ruling class." In the late 1920s, both the Soviet Union and Kazakhstan suffered from high levels of unemployment. Throughout the NEP, Soviet workers—mainly members of the trade unions—pushed hard for closed shops and discrimination against nonproletarians. The constant tension between "cadre" workers and peasant seasonal workers stemmed from this turf war, as well as the exclusion of women from most high-paying industrial jobs. Second, European workers brought a chauvinism to the Turksib just as virulent as that of their bosses. Mockery, violence, and race riots cannot be explained only by a desire to defend closed-shop policies. Many of the Turksib's European workers were racists.

That the government's decision to support a hiring quota for Kazakhs caused dissatisfaction among Europeans is hardly surprising, given the urban unemployment and rural underemployment that characterized the labor market in the mid-1920s. Throughout the early period of the Turksib's construction (until the beginning of 1930), the Soviet working class suffered very high unemployment rates. Unemployment was enormous in Kazakhstan, as well.[51] At the beginning of the First Five-Year Plan, in 1927, the labor exchanges in the Turksib's hinterland had thirty thousand registered unemployed, mostly Europeans cadre workers who had just lost their hiring preference to a bunch of thoroughly unproletarian nomads.[52] Even a huge project like the Turksib could not hope to provide jobs for all these men. Thirty thousand disgruntled job seekers turned out to be only the tip of the iceberg, however. When the government announced the building of the Turksib, a huge wave of unemployed from the central regions of the USSR flooded into the railheads at Lugovaia and Semipalatinsk. This so-called *samotyok* ("self-flow," i.e., getting a job without going through proper governmental channels) became a flood by 1928. As one observer noted, "On some days not scores but hundreds of workers would arrive at Lugovaia station."[53]

By early 1928, more than thirteen thousand unemployed European workers were milling around in Semipalatinsk, only too aware that "their" jobs had been taken by people they considered savages (the workforce was about 40 percent Kazakh at this time).[54] They responded with a campaign of intimidation and harassment against Kazakh job seekers. Kazakhs attempting to sign up for work on the Turksib routinely faced beatings by Europeans. In such an atmosphere, little was needed to transform individual beatings into a more general outburst of violence. This occurred in spring 1928, when an "unemployment riot" broke out in Semipalatinsk. A mob of unemployed went on a rampage and conducted a pogrom against the town's Kazakhs. The authorities quickly restored order once the mob's fury had spent itself—interestingly enough, with the aid of workers who had jobs. But the riot had made its point.

As Shatov himself observed, "It is extremely difficult to give preeminence to Kazakhs in such conditions."[55] To avoid such disturbances, the Turksib sacrificed its Kazakh quota for 1928.[56] Rather than half of the workforce, Kazakhs made up only 26.1 percent of the workforce on the Northern Construction Section during the height of the building season in August.[57] It is worth noting that on the Southern Construction, where there were no riots, the Kazakh share of the workforce was consistently lower than their share on the Northern Construction.[58] In fact, here Kazakhs did not even reach 20 percent of the workforce until September.[59] The correlation between the low percentage of hired Kazakhs and lack of riots is probably not coincidental.

Even if a Kazakh got a job on the Turksib, however, the perils of ethnic hatred still awaited him. In fact, the general ubiquity of "chauvinism" on the work site led to repeated calls by Shatov and the regime for such "abnormal" conditions to be stamped out.[60] These pronouncements had little effect—a general level of mockery and contempt toward Kazakhs pervaded the Turksib. One favorite bit of hooliganism was to smear pig fat forcibly on the lips or bread of Kazakh workers to mock their religion.[61] Such mockery was closely correlated to place. The club, the store line, the dining hall, all the places which European workers considered their domain, often acted as settings for racial slurs, mockery, and hooliganism.

Fist fights and the individual beating of Kazakhs occurred commonly at the worksite. In early February 1929, for instance, an assistant locomotive driver, Nikolai Chantsev, beat a Kazakh coal stoker, Zalei Iakubov, and tossed him from the cab of his moving locomotive.[62] As late as mid-1930, and despite a massive campaign to discipline such acts, individual beatings were frequent among certain trades (particularly conductors and brick workers), and *poboishchy*, or organized brawls, between Kazakhs and Europeans were endemic at such major work points as Tansyk.[63] While the fights were often labeled as hooliganism, ethnic insults usually preceded the blows.[64]

Mockery, discrimination, and even individual beatings, however, did not represent the most terrifying aspect of ethnic hostility on the Turksib. This distinction belongs to the mass attack by European workers on Kazakhs. Although there were several such mass beatings, the Sergiopol' pogrom that closed out 1928 had the most impact. The well-organized culmination of weeks of labor and racial unrest, the pogrom caused deep concern among the party and governmental elite about the future of the construction project.

Although the regime tried to blame the riot on counterrevolutionaries, in fact gandy dancers (rail layers), the Turksib's most touted "cadre" workers, made up the nucleus of the rioters. The riot, which involved more than four hundred workers, actually took over the town and attacked many other symbols of the regime (sacking the OGPU headquarters and besieging party offices, for instance). The rioters also attacked Kazakhs as beneficiaries of the regime's nativization policy.[65] More than fifty Kazakhs were seriously beaten, although none died. That nativization, not mere hooliganism, played a decisive role in fomenting the pogrom can be seen in the riot's aftermath, all accounts blame the trade unions for not sufficiently educating the European workers on the need for the Kazakh quota.[66]

Given all the hostility, the mockery, the discrimination, and the beatings, who could blame the Kazakhs for resisting the regime's plans to proletarianize them, either by avoiding the Turksib or by leaving it? Kazakhs were staying away or, worse, leaving after only a short stay. In 1928, Kazakh turnover on the Turksib was enormous. No firm figures were kept (in itself a revealing indication of how transient Kazakh labor must have been), but the partial data are suggestive. In 1927, for instance, one Construction Section reserved eight hundred jobs for Kazakhs and went through eight thousand to ten thousand workers trying to fill them. At one point, this section managed to hold Kazakh workers an average of only two to three days.[67] Another work point started out with two hundred Kazakhs and finished with seventy by the end of the season.[68]

To the administration, and especially to its non-Communist managers, this turnover became yet another indictment of the Kazakhs' lack of "production habits"—their basic allergy to "rational labor." Managers alleged that the Kazakhs' "nomadic inclinations" influenced them to work only long enough to make some pocket change and leave.[69] As one foreman complained, "You never know how many will show up for work each day. Yesterday they sign on, and today they leave once they find out they don't like the work or it's too hard."[70] Yet, like the argument that Kazakh workers could not meet European productivity levels, this explanation turned out to be something of a self-fulfilling prophecy. Kazakh turnover did in part stem from the Turksib's alien milieu for many Kazakhs; railroad building was not much like sheep herding. But Kazakhs had worked as railroad workers before and accommodated industrial work rhythms.[71]

Far more important in driving Kazakhs from the worksite was the pervasive atmosphere of discrimination, prejudice, and ethnic violence on the Turksib. In effect, rather than conducting *basmachi* raids or pulling up surveyors' stakes, Kazakhs "voted with their feet."

The Making of a Kazakh Working Class

If the nativization program on the Turksib had been frozen at the end of 1928, the halfway point of construction, a dismal picture would reveal itself. The policy's greatest success thus far had been the creation of a fertile arena for bureaucratic obstruction, racial violence, and Kazakh detachment from industrial society. But the nativization program would overcome all this, thanks to strong pressure from the highest reaches of the party and state apparatus.

The regime's response to the Sergiopol' riot left no doubt that it considered ethnic violence state treason, not interpersonal violence. It arrested a number of the pogrom's ringleaders and, after a well-publicized show trial, handed down strict sentences. One leader was shot, two others had their death sentences commuted to fifteen years, and fourteen others received long sentences in solitary confinement. One (presumably the government informant) was acquitted.[72] Moreover, the Kazakh party and government organs became increasingly intolerant of the Turksib's ineffective nativization policies. The new line from the higher authorities branded failure to meet the Kazakh hiring quota as arising not from "objective" difficulties, such as *samotyok* or Kazakh turnover, but from "subjective" deficiencies, especially the persistence of a "colonial attitude" toward the native population by Turksib managers.[73]

For its part, the Turksib's management belatedly recognized how dangerous ethnic hostility could be to its fulfillment of the production plan.[74] Shatov asked the trade unions, government oversight institutions, and the OGPU "to take the most decisive measures to immediately eliminate from work those unmasked as wreckers," that is, to initiate a purge. Soon, dozens of workers were fired for "counterrevolutionary" sentiments. This campaign, to be sure, did not end ethnic hostility or even mass beatings, but it clearly marked them as a dangerous political action.[75]

Shatov did not limit this supervision to workers. Henceforth, he warned, "all abnormalities, coarseness, red tape, and negligence towards Kazakhs" would be considered a dereliction of duty. Furthermore, he "would not allow the derision or maltreatment of [Kazakhs], ignoring their requests and needs, or speculation concerning their strangeness or cultural backwardness spoken in Russian." The Central Construction Administration promised that any employee guilty of such acts would be dismissed and that "any display of intolerance, chauvinism, or national antagonism will be prosecuted without mercy."[76] One publicist noted the new tone of vigilance: "There are still colonial elements which have stuck themselves onto the Turksib; they conceal themselves in a corner and only impotently, maliciously hiss as they see the Kazakhs gradually becoming accustomed to production. Of course, these elements don't dare speak out openly. Caddish behavior and petty hooliganism, these are the weapons of these scoundrels, which often finds a way to dark elements."[77] Clearly, overt acts of chauvinism by managers were now beyond the pale.

Moreover, the older generation of managers' relative immunity from political criteria suddenly evaporated in the political earthquake caused by the Shakhtyi Affair. By the end of 1928, the Turksib management had been thoroughly purged, the old bourgeois specialists giving way to so-called Red engineers, or managers who strongly endorsed the regime's social policies.[78] Now, managers would be held personally responsible for the ethnic hostility manifested in their production units. The Turksib's trade union asked for, and received, authority to single out and punish individual managers "perverting the government's policy on ethnic issues."[79] This authority found its first target in one of the Turksib's leading managers, the section chief Gol'dman, who was well known for his contempt for Kazakhs. Gol'dman not only suffered dismissal for tolerating discrimination against Kazakhs but was charged criminally as a counterrevolutionary.[80] Other managers also felt the wrath of Soviet power for such "defects."[81]

In addition to disciplining discriminatory managers, the Turksib made a concerted effort to recruit and integrate Kazakh workers at the construction site. Its first action was a dose of realism. Because of its abject failure to meet the 50 percent quota, the Turksib pleaded with central authorities for a more attainable number, especially since 20 percent of the Turksib's workforce requirement consisted of skilled positions that the Kazakhs could not fill. The government relented, and the 1929 quota was lowered to 30 percent. This new quota, however, would be monitored carefully.[82] In a second step, the Turksib "privatized" its recruitment efforts by paying recruiters 1.50 rubles for each Kazakh hired from the labor exchanges. This incentive overcame one of the most glaring failings of the old recruitment system—most Kazakhs lived far from the towns and labor exchanges, making it difficult for them to procure Turksib jobs. Under the new recruitment system, the Southern Construction quickly received its initial order of five thousand Kazakh recruits for the 1929 season.[83]

Simultaneously, a small but important group of European workers took it upon themselves to integrate Kazakhs into the worksite. These were the Turksib's activists, its "conscious workers," who openly identified with the regime's politics. They often took on causes unpopular with rank-and-file workers, like shock work and collectivization.[84] These crusaders now campaigned to overcome discrimination in production and in the barracks. One incident is demonstrative of this new activism. At the Southern Railhead, the Kazakh gandy dancers were subjected to a diet of only bread and water due to religious insensitivity. When a Komsomol gandy dancer complained that the Kazakhs could not eat the pork-laden meals of the Russians, the cafeteria management replied:

"And what are we supposed to do, cook in another pot especially for the Kazakhs? Should we get another wagon-kitchen for two cooking staffs in the track-laying camp? What about the budget?"

The *Komsomol* took his case to the rank and file gandy dancers: "We came to Kazakhstan to lead the Kazakhs from darkness. And they send these lads to learn from us. And we from the very first step separate from them like a Lord from a peasant. We skilled workers from Russia ought to get closer to Kazakh youth. We can still make over the young. Comrades, let's abstain from pork for a while and eat with the Kazakhs from one pot. Then they will little by little come to eat pork with us."

In fact, this suggestion earned the Komsomol only hostile glares from his co-workers (gandy dancers loved their pork fat). Nonetheless, a compromise position of handing out pork fat individually did earn unanimous consent.[85] This story tells much about the worker activists' methods and attitudes. First, rank-and-file workers considered them a bunch of puritan bootlickers, who nonetheless had to be placated because of their party connections. Second, there is no question here of "nativization"—Kazakhs were to be assimilated into the proletariat, and that meant the Russian proletariat ("they will little by little come to eat pork with us").

This Russification is evident in the way the conscious workers sought to overcome the language problem. A source of much mutual incomprehension on the Turksib, which in turn engendered condescension and indignation, was the language gulf on the construction. In 1928, very few Europeans spoke Kazakh, and small numbers of Kazakhs understood even the rudiments of Russian. As one technician complained, "We have a confusion of tongues like the Tower of Babel. . . . the naked savage comes to us and we can only communicate with him by signs."[86] The other side of this linguistic divide was equally frustrated:

In his native steppe, on the ancient pastures, on the tracks that a thousand times their camels have trod, the Kazakh coming to work on the Turksib has no tongue. All the managers are European. Almost none of them have mastered the Kazakh language. All the section and subsection chiefs cannot speak Kazakh. As a result the Kazakh navvies don't receive the proper direction in work, don't know what their piece-rates are, and cannot get competent advice or valuable specialized instruction.[87]

This was exactly the sort of situation nativization had been designed to avoid. Brigades of Turksib shock workers attacked the problem in their own way. They took on individual Kazakh workers and helped them learn Russian.[88] In fact, the first letters that most Kazakhs wrote on the Turksib in their "Liquidation of Illiteracy" bases were in Russian.[89] This is not to say that nativization was abandoned; courses in Kazakh for Russian line managers were greatly expanded, and a series of training classes cranked out foremen and gang bosses from among the worksite's Kazakhs.[90] Still, the road to social mobility ran through Russian language acquisition. Many of the memoirs of Kazakh workers who rose to prominence during and after the construction of the Turksib mentioned being taken under the wing of a "conscious" worker who taught them Russian, a trade, and how to comport oneself as a proletarian.[91]

These efforts by the Turksib's "conscious workers" were important because of their multiplier effects. Everything that shock workers did on site soon came to be expected from rank-and-file workers. So, just as every work gang had to eventually participate in socialist competition (or risk being branded "alien elements"), soon each brigade of European skilled workers found itself training a Kazakh apprentice. For instance, at Illiiskoe, a major depot, the local shock workers eventually forced every brigade to train a Kazakh pupil.[92] These efforts broke down the ethnic segregation of work brigades and trained substantial numbers of Kazakhs (about three thousand at the beginning of 1931) in European workers' craft skills.[93]

In such a way, Kazakh workers were induced to overcome their hesitancy to operate machinery. As a preindustrial people with little exposure to modern technology, the Kazakh approached machinery with a combination of fear and fascination. Visitors to *auly* along the Turksib were besieged with questions regarding machinery. Although these visitors were fond of pointing out the quaint, "primitive" names the Kazakhs used for machinery (*shaitan-arba*, or "Satan cart," for automobiles, "*kara-aigara*," or "black stallion," for train), still they could not but be impressed by the burst of curiosity.[94] Crowds invariably clustered around cars, while Kazakh clans from deep in the steppe would send out emissaries to report back on what a train really looked like. Fear, too, however, was present—a point invariably noted by Soviet commentators with habitual condescension: "They [the Kazakhs] are big babies. Once a section engineer arrived in a car and took it in his head to offer a ride to a good-sized Kazakh lad. He called over the Kazakh and had him sit down next to him. The car snorted and jerked. Suddenly the Kazakh yelled out, 'Ah, a Satan cart!' as if someone hurled a head in a basket at him."[95]

The process of mastering this fear of machinery for individual Kazakhs on the Turksib could, on occasion, be quite nervewracking. The Kazakh Tansyk avoided jackhammers as some sort of half-alive beast when he first came to the worksite. When his foreman ordered him to take up a jackhammer, the following scene played itself out: "Tansyk was silent. The hammer began to cut into the stone; it knocked off sparks, then shook Tansyk and tore out of his hands. Tansyk wanted to throw down the wild machine, but he was afraid to, and, white with terror from uncontrollable shaking, he continued to press on." Despite these terrors of the damned, Tansyk soon became a skilled jackhammer man; he could reassemble the tool from scratch and made the princely sum of five rubles per day in his new position.[96] Not only foremen and managers but shock workers made it their business to create such technically proficient Kazakhs.

The workers who placed Kazakhs under their tutelage could be irritants, as well as patrons. One union activist, for instance, began a campaign to control Kazakh leisure activity: "they [the Kazakhs] spend the day chattering by the *kumiss* shop and play cards in the evening." He wanted to end such frivolous activity in favor of literacy classes and "living newspapers" in the workers' club.[97] There was, indeed, nearly as much condescension in the conscious worker's approach to his Kazakh comrade as in the old "bourgeois" specialists' attitudes. The fundamental difference was that the specialist preferred to dismiss the Kazakh, while the conscious worker wanted to transform him.

These various recruitment techniques and the solicitude of the conscious workers achieved considerable success, especially in attracting young, impoverished Kazakh males to the Turksib.[98] These younger Kazakhs often became the construction site's best propagandists when they returned to their *auly* in the winter. One veteran of the railroad, the engineer Kozhevnikov, remembered that many Kazakhs had never seen a railroad but had heard of it from Kazakh navvies returning home.[99] Young men seemed to predominate among the new recruits. Sketchy statistics from late 1931 indicated that a full 30 percent of several stations' Kazakh workers were less twenty-three years old, and most were younger than thirty.[100] One foreman complained that he was getting workers as young as twelve with forged documents.[101] Because of the class war mentality of the time, as well as the constant purges, hiring preference went to Kazakhs without herds. Thus, primarily the *aul's* herdless *"jataki"* found their way onto the Turksib.[102]

These are exactly the Kazakhs who should have broken with *aul* traditionalism. As *"jataki"* without herds or social standing, these men faced bleak futures in the traditional Kazakh way of life. The Turksib offered these young men something sorely lacking in the *auly* until then—social mobility. Many came to the Turksib as unskilled navvies, received training for skilled positions, and eventually rose in the industrial hierarchy. A good example of this dynamic can be seen in the testimony of Uruspek Amangel'dinov. He arrived at site totally illiterate and unable to understand a single word of Russian:

> At that time I was the most curious of the lads in the *aul*. I became familiar with the builders so I became one of them. They persuaded me to come work with them, to hammer in the surveying pegs. The work did not require much wit, but I was in seventh heaven, especially when the route took us past my comrades in the *aul*. That's how I became the foster child of the builders. One of them taught me Russian, another taught me how to lay railroad ties quickly, and a third explained to me how to set up the steel rails. Soon they sent me, barely comprehending the first thing about letters, to the course for railway brigadiers and I studied for six whole months. Two years past, once again I studied in school and graduated as an assistant road master. And such attention, of course, was not put on me alone but to hundreds and thousands of Kazakh lads—future railroad workers.[103]

Amangel'dinov's impression of the Turksib as a huge engine for social mobility is borne out by the data. Already in mid-1929, on the Northern Construction nearly five hundred Kazakhs were enrolled in technical courses. In 1930 alone, sixty-nine "illiteracy eradication bases" taught more than 2,700 enrolled Kazakhs the rudiments of reading and writing.[104] Furthermore, to fulfill its huge demand for railroad workers, the Turksib adopted a crash training program that heavily recruited among Kazakhs. In summer 1930, among twenty distinct courses that enrolled 899 students, only 260 students were Europeans. The 1931 training plan was even more ambitious—2,470 trainees in all, with only 514 spots reserved for Europeans. This program soon became a massive in-house training effort to educate nearly seven thousand former construction workers to take permanent positions on the new railroad. In the years 1931–1934, the Turksib's courses and apprenticeship programs churned out 8,200 skilled workers, 4,500 of them Kazakhs.[105] The emphasis on training Kazakhs was not merely a political decision. The management found Kazakhs more likely to stay on at the Turksib than to relocate to another railroad, and, at least in some cases, they were more attentive students than the Europeans.[106]

More was involved in the attracting Kazakhs to the railroad, however, than "pull mechanisms," such as social mobility. Several very strong "push mechanisms" also acted on Kazakh jobseekers. As part of its "socialist offensive," the regime attacked traditional pastoral lifestyles with collectivization, forced settlement of nomads, and "dekulakization" of the average nomad. Kazakhs responded to this coercion by slaughtering their herds, attempting to emigrate from the Soviet Union, and taking themselves out of the agricultural economy.[107] Famine soon gripped the steppe. A tremendous tragedy, caused by ignorance, zealotry, and cruelty, undermined the entire nomadic lifestyle. In this environment, the Turksib's wages, especially its guaranteed rations, became increasingly attractive. While construction of the Turksib ended before the full impact of this downward spiral was felt, the years 1929–1930 already presented hardships enough for Kazakhs to want another option than "petite bourgeois" livestock herding.

This push and pull, along with the Turksib's increased attention to Kazakh recruitment, meant a marked increase in the numbers of Kazakhs working on the Turksib. In the 1928 season an average of 2,924 Kazakhs were employed per month on the Turksib; this figure rose to 6,310 in 1929 (the peak building season) and held at 5,417 in 1930 (see figure 1). Moreover, while only forty-three Kazakhs, on average, held management positions in 1928, by 1930 this number had tripled to 145. In 1930 alone, the number of Kazakh skilled workers rose from seventy to 503.

Despite this growth, many supporters of Kazakh affirmative action were disappointed. In April 1930, Ryskulov admitted that the Turksib's affirmative-action program was less than successful: "In this area we have done important work. Yet, neither in extent nor quality, have we guaranteed the fulfillment of the government's decrees on recruiting the local population to work on the Turksib."[108] This disappointment stems not from the numbers of Kazakhs working on the Turksib but from their percentage in the workforce. The Turksib rarely met even its lowered 30 percent quota for hiring Kazakhs. The number of Kazakhs at the worksite hovered between a quarter and a third of the workforce. Even if

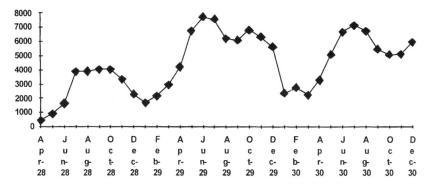

Figure 1. Number of Kazakhs Employed on the Turksib (Apr. 1928–Dec. 1930)

the quota is construed more narrowly as a percentage of workers instead of work-force (thereby omitting white-collar workers), the Turksib still failed to meet its quota, reaching a high of 27 percent in spring 1930.[109] Although considerable numbers of Kazakh workers were involved in the building of the Turksib (nearly seven thousand in June 1929), many more who might have been hired, and whom the Turksib had been ordered to hire, were not.

Two factors doomed the Turksib in its effort to maintain its quota. One was the helter-skelter dash to finish the railroad ahead of schedule as a gift to Stalin. The management accomplished this by greatly increasing the numbers of workers over the original labor plan. The 1929 labor plan had called for an average of sixteen thousand workers per month, rather than the twenty-two thousand that were used. Had the Turksib kept to the original figure and recruited the same number of Kazakhs, it would have easily met its quota of 37 percent. Kazakh recruitment tended to be overwhelmed by a desperate desire to grab hold of bodies, any bodies, to fulfill the construction plan. Those jobs, through the 1930 season, continued to be filled by *samotyok*. Second, Kazakh turnover, while de-clining, remained substantially higher than European turnover. In June 1929, Kazakh labor turnover, at 34.2 percent, was nearly double the European rate of 18.7 percent.[110] These factors greatly complicated the Turksib's efforts to reach its quota. One foreman probably spoke for the entire management when he said, "They tell us we have to use the locals as workers, give wages to the Kazakh poor, and involve the Kazakh nomad in the construction of the railroad. But it's not as easy to do as it seems."[111]

Nonetheless, the affirmative action program that made up the heart of nativ-ization was much more successful than these numbers might indicate. A whole cadre of Kazakhs first gained exposure to industrial civilization working on the railroad. Within a year of the railroad's opening, they already made up 22 percent of its skilled workers. Throughout the 1930s, Kazakhs constituted about one-third of the Turksib's labor force.[112] By 1940, seventy-nine locomotive engineers, 123 assistant engineers, and nearly two hundred train schedulers were Kazakhs.[113] By mid-decade Kazakhs had cracked the ranks of the higher technical specialties and white-collar employment on the railroad (they made up 8.2 percent of the technical staff and 8.7 percent of the white-collar workforce).[114]

Hidden in these statistics are several stunning success stories. Mukhtar Kaptagaev, for instance, arrived on the Turksib as an illiterate shepherd. He began work as a navvy, became a stonemason, and learned how to read. At this point, he asked to become a boiler stoker (or fireman), and from this position he learned how to become an engine driver, the worker aristocrat of the railroads. Kaptagaev's social rise did not end here, however. He became a leading Stakhanovite and was elected as a delegate to the USSR's Supreme Soviet.[115] Not every socially mobile Kazakh ended up as a delegate to the Supreme Soviet, but Kazakhs' advancement must have seemed substantial to them in any case. Another Kazakh alumnus of the Turksib, Dzhumagali Omarov, rose higher still. A former shepherd who came to the Turksib in 1927 as an "expediter" (in other words, a gopher), Omarov had already risen to the position of assistant section chief in April 1930. After a stint as an engine driver, he was sent to the Transport Academy in 1934, and at the end of the war he had become the railroad's second-in-command. In the years after the war, Omarov became the first Kazakh director of the railroad.[116] Thus, the Turksib not only produced a Kazakh working class but also opened up for Kazakhs the road to middle-class respectability and the industrial elite. This stories could be repeated for literally dozens of Kazakhs who would rise to the level of skilled worker, white-collar manager, and party cadre worker. In a sense, the construction turned out to be not simply the "forge of the Kazakh proletariat" but also the forge of Kazakhstan's *nomenklatura*.

The Turksib caused a cultural revolution among the Kazakh nomads it recruited. The very fact that it presented an alternative to traditional nomadism had a subversive effect on local Kazakh society. The Kazakhs on the Turksib, or so it was alleged, were much more likely to eschew the traditional religious holidays; they rarely used their wages to buy flocks.[117] More important, to the regime and to its supporters, the experience of the Turksib undercut traditional hierarchies and recast the identities of its Kazakh workers within the acceptable Marxist schema. A Kazakh journalist, Gashimbaev, saw the Turksib as a giant engine for raising class consciousness:

> Well, yes, at Dossier and Rider, at Karsakpai there are Kazakh workers but they are individuals, they are not from the depths of the steppe. But here there are thousands! . . . In a year, maybe in a month, these thousands of steppe dwellers will know that the clan is rubbish, a trap very convenient for *beys*, that there are only two clans—workers and exploiters. This will be such a "confiscation" of the *beys'* moral basis that it can hardly be compared to a propaganda campaign alone.[118]

As Gashimbaev had hoped, nomadic Kazakh entered the industrial workforce in huge numbers during the 1930s. By 1934, Kazakhs comprised 64 percent of the republic's coal miners, 74 percent of its oil workers, 44 percent of its nonferrous miners, and 82 percent of its leather workers.[119] By 1936, Kazakhs made up 41 percent of the republic's industrial workers. Considering that their weight in the republic's population had fallen to little more than 35 percent, these figures show excellent "saturation" of industry by the titular nationality.[120] The new railroad itself played a large role in this transformation, growing thirteen times over the course of the 1930s and 1940s.[121] According to the party line in the early 1950s: "As a result of Stalin's nationalities' policy and the fraternal aid of the Russian nation, Kazakhstan was transformed from a backward outpost of Tsarist Russia. It bypassed capitalist forms of development to become a mighty socialist agrarian and industrial economy with mechanized agriculture, and became one of the most important bases of the non-ferrous metallurgical industry."[122]

Yet this triumphal assertion tells only half the story, and that half not well. The very thing Ryskulov had warned against, the forced settlement of the nomads, occurred. The Soviet government did not simply create the conditions to attract Kazakhs to industry; it pushed the few survivors of the famine and dislocation of the early 1930s out of the only life many of them had known. The quickness of the transformation of Kazakhs from nomads to proletarians was accomplished not just through positive inducements but through a very violent dispossession. Millions starved or emigrated, millions more forever abandoned the nomadic lifestyle that had defined *Kazakshilik*—the quality of being Kazakh. Class and ethnic identity may perhaps be conceived as an "imagined community," but this identity is, of course, limited by what is imaginable. After the famine, the nomadic way of life sank into the realm of the unimaginable.

The Kazakhs certainly did forge a new identity in the industrial establishments of the 1930s, but not one that the Russians handed to them "by fraternal aid." As one trade union representative on the Turksib observed about his Kazakh membership, "they earned their place in the proletariat."[123] Kazakhs also really did seem to replace their clan and tribal affiliations with a new class identity. When S. M. Ivanov, one of Shatov's deputies, out of politeness, asked a Kazakh to name his clan, the Kazakh replied, "We are not from a clan, we are proletarians."[124] Although the temptation is to cast doubt on the veracity of this statement, we should not be so quick to dismiss it. Here, the question "Are we not workers, as well?" has been recast as an assertion of identity. Moreover, the Kazakh was not speaking in a politicized forum where propaganda-speak, or "speaking Bolshevik," could be expected. And Ivanov was genuinely surprised by the answer.

Should we be? Some evidence points to the assertion of new identities in the "forge" of the Turksib. Unlike in the surrounding countryside, clan competition among Kazakhs who worked on the Turksib was so low as to rarely earn mention. Kazakh workers generally were thrown into work gangs of mixed clan and tribal affiliation, yet this caused almost no difficulty on the worksite. Mixing Europeans and Kazakhs in such work gangs, as noted, was much more difficult. Why, however, did Ivanov's Kazakh call himself a proletarian, rather than a Kazakh? In

part, because of the highly charged ethnic atmosphere on the worksite, his ethnicity would have been self-evident and therefore unnecessary of comment. The
Kazakh quota, nativization, and vicious ethnic conflict all acted to strongly mark
ethnicity on the Turksib. And, of course, being a worker in a workers' state was
exactly the identity to which many of the Turksib's Kazakh employees most
aspired.

One might speculate that Ivanov's Kazakh identified himself as a proletarian
because a supraethnic identity such as "proletarian" allowed him to enter a privileged stratum without surrendering his ethnic identity. Unfortunately, such a neat
tradeoff was not possible. Despite the regime's emphasis on nativization, "conscious" Russian workers controlled the image of the proletarian. In this way,
Russification, in some ways more pernicious than racist hostility, came in the
back door of class. The roots of present-day Kazakhs' concerns with the *mank-
urty*—the large number of them who have assimilated to Russian language and
culture—lies not only in the destruction of Kazakh traditional society but also in
the peculiar effects of "nativization." A policy designed to overcome colonial
domination and to integrate "backward" nomads into wider socialist society was
in some ways spectacularly successful. Kazakhs did coalesce around a larger national identity, and many of them came to embrace a modern, industrial society.
Few other "empires" beside the Soviet Union could boast the numbers of native
elites trained to assume roles of political, cultural, and economic leadership in the
face of the sort of ethnic discrimination that pervaded the Turksib. One finds it
hard to imagine an Omarov finding such opportunities for social advancement
under tsarism. On the other hand, nativization colonized the Kazakh consciousness far more effectively than tsarism's malignant contempt of its nomads. Kazakh
traditional society was crushed with appalling brutality, and the refuge offered
Kazakhs, Soviet industry, could offer poor solace to those who saw their way of
life destroyed by an alien system. That Russification and assimilation to European
norms was the price for inclusion in this system should not surprise us—the
Kazakhs, despite the efforts of their National Communists, did not control the
rules of the industrial sphere into which they were thrust. The *basmachi* raids on
the Turksib represented a response to the Soviet nation and class-building project
just as legitimate as Omarov's. In the final analysis, the experience of the Turksib
indicates that Soviet nationalities policy acted as both a destroyer of nations and
a creator of a new Kazakh nation. Moreover, the Turksib project shows that the
formation of social identities, class or ethnic, is the product of a complex and
nuanced interaction among the state, social formations, and the individual—that
the communities are not only imagined but what is imaginable.

Notes

1. Terry Martin, *The Affirmative Action Empire: Ethnicity and the Soviet State, 1923–1939*
(Ithaca, N.Y.: Cornell University Press, 2001). Affirmative action need not be based

only on ethnicity. Indeed, the early Soviet state granted preferential treatment on the basis of class, gender, and age, as well as ethnicity. For class-based affirmative action see Sheila Fitzpatrick, *Education and Social Mobility in the Soviet Union, 1921–1934* (Cambridge: Cambridge University Press, 1979); V. Z. Drobizhev et al., *Sotsial'naia politika Sovetskogo gosudarstva: ukreplenie vedushchei roli rabochego klassa v sotsialisticheskom stroitel'stve* (Moskva: Mysl', 1985). For gender-based affirmative action see Gregory J. Massell, *The Surrogate Proletariat: Moslem Women and Revolutionary Strategies in Soviet Central Asia, 1919–1929* (Princeton, N.J.: Princeton University Press, 1974); Wendy Z. Goldman, *Women, the State and Revolution: Soviet Family Policy and Social Life, 1917–1936* (New York: Cambridge University Press, 1993), especially pp. 109–118. On preferential treatment for youth see Yuri Slezkine, "From Savages to Citizens: The Cultural Revolution in the Soviet Far North, 1928–1938," *Slavic Review* 51, no. 1 (Spring 1992): 52–76; William J. Chase, *Workers, Society and the Soviet State; Labor and Life in Moscow, 1918–1929* (Urbana: University of Illinois Press, 1987), pp. 150–153.

2. Upward of 1.75 million Kazakhs perished in the years 1931–1933, while more than 500,000 nomadic and seminomadic households were forced to abandon their traditional pastoral economies. Zh. Abylkhozin, M. Kozybaev, and M. Tatinov, "Kazakhstanskaia tragediia," *Voprosy istorii*, no. 7 (1989); Anatoly M. Khazanov, "Ethnic Stratification and Ethnic Competition in Kazakhstan," in his *After the USSR: Ethnicity, Nationalism, and Politics in the Commonwealth of Independent States* (Madison: University of Wisconsin Press, 1995), p. 158. Olcott states that 3.3 million Kazakhs died and another 1.2 million were driven into exile by famine but gives no source for these figures; Martha Brill Olcott, "Ceremony and Substance: The Illusion of Unity in Central Asia," in Michael Mandelbaum, ed., *Central Asia and the World: Kazakhstan, Uzbekistan, Tajikistan, Kyrgyzstan, and Turkmenistan* (New York: Council on Foreign Relations Press, 1994), p. 19. Both Maksudov and Ellman argue for a lower figure, around 1.3 to 1.5 million. See Sergei Maksudov, *Poteri naseleniia SSSR* (Benson, Ver.:, 1989); Michael Ellman, *Soviet Studies* 51 (1990): 812–813; Ellman, *Soviet Studies* (1992): 914. Finally, a semiauthoritative number of famine victims was published by *Izvestiia* on June 11, 1991. Here the number of dead was placed at 2.5 million. Cited in *Tak eto Bylo: Natsional'nye repressii v SSSR 1919–1952 gody*, vol. I (Moskva: Insan, 1993), p. 41. For more on the famine see T. Nusipbaev and N. Zhiengaliev, eds., *Golod v Kazakhskoi stepi* (Na kazakhskom, russkom iazikakh) (Almaty: Kazak universitet, 1991).

3. For cogent and sophisticated discussions of the genesis and implementation of the Soviet Nationalities policy see Yuri Slezkine, "The USSR as a Communal Apartment, or How a Socialist State Promoted Ethnic Particularism," *Slavic Review* 53, no. 2 (Summer 1994): 414–452; Terry Martin, *The Affirmative Action Empire*, pp. 15–63; Gerhard Simon, *Nationalism and Policy toward the Nationalities in the Soviet Union; From Totalitarian Dictatorship to Post-Stalinist Society* (Boulder, Colo.: Westview, 1986), pp. 20–70; Ronald Grigor Suny, *The Revenge of the Past: Nationalism, Revolution, and the Collapse of the Soviet Union* (Stanford: Stanford University Press, 1993), pp. 84–126.

4. The Turksib produced the usual First Five-Year Plan flurry of pamphlets, popular accounts, literary works, and other artistic representations of the Great Leap Forward. The work of Ilf and Petrov for *Gudok* on the subject is probably the most enduring. Typically, the best representation of the Turksib is their farcical lampoon of the dignitaries sent out on a special train to watch the "golden spike" ceremony in *The Golden Calf*. See I. Ilf and E. Petrov, "Zolotoi telenok," in *Sobrianie sochinenii*, vol.

2 (Moskva: Khudozhestvennoe izdatel'stvo, 1961), pp. 289–328. The movie *Turksib* became one of the iconic films of Stalinist cinema through its representation of Communism's goal of transforming the "backward East." See Jay Leyda, *Kino: A History of the Russian and Soviet Film* (London: Allen & Unwin, 1960), pp. 260–261.

5. For the well-developed Kazakh ethnic identity see Kemal H. Karpat, "The Roots of Kazakh Nationalism: Ethnicity, Islam, or Land?" in Marco Buttino, ed., *In a Collapsing Empire: Underdevelopment, Ethnic Conflicts and Nationalisms in the Soviet Union* (Milan: Feltrinelli, 1993); Shirin Akiner, *The Formation of Kazakh Identity: From Tribe to Nation-State* (London: Royal Institute of International Affairs, 1995). On the use of the common ethnonym as a signifier of collective identity "Kazak," see Akiner, *The Formation of Kazakh Identity*, p. 11; T. A. Zhdanko, "Ethnic Communities with Survivals of Clan and Tribal Structure in Central Asia and Kazakhstan in the Nineteenth and Early Twentieth Century," in Wolfgang Weisslender, ed., *The Nomadic Alternative: Modes and Models of Interaction in the African-Asian Deserts and Steppes* (The Hague: Mouton, 1978), p. 142. On the common literary tradition creating a "fiction" of Kazakhness, especially the oral tradition, see Thomas G. Winner, *The Oral Art and Literature of the Kazakhs of Central Asia* (Durham, N.C.: Duke University Press, 1958), pp. 26–29, 45–47; on the common literary language see Isabelle Kreindler, "Ibrahim Altynsarin, Nikolai Ilminskii and the Kazakh National Awakening," *Central Asian Survey* 2, no. 3 (November 1983): 99–116. For good discussions of nomadism's importance to Kazakh identity see Martha Brill Olcott, *The Kazakhs* (Stanford: Hoover Institute Press, 1987), pp. 76–79; and Akiner, *The Formation of Kazakh Identity*, p. 15–16.

6. A Soviet journalist's account of traditional power relations in an *aul* near the Turksib shows clearly why it would upset Marxist sensibilities. He reported the remarks of a *bey* (a wealthy herder often considered equivalent to a *kulak* in Bolshevik demonology) who owned eight hundred rams, 120 horses, and many camels and steers. The *bey*, enunciating values quite consonant with the Kazakh political system of deference for age and authority, bragged, "In my clan there are no disobedient. All the poor and middling serve me." The quote was reported with outrage. S. Volk, *Turksib: Ocherki stroiki* (Moskva: Molodaia Gvardia, 1930), p. 54.

7. RGAE, fond 1884, opis' 80, delo 244, ll. 9–30: Zhurnal zasedanii podkomissii po novym putiam soobshcheniia, 12/2/26, no. 31; ll. 138–59: Doklad Kollegii, "O Turkestan-Sibirskoi Magistrali," 1/27; ibid., delo 251, ll. 20–46: Doklad, "Turkestano-Sibirskaia zhel. doroga"; ibid., delo 349, ll. 56–84: Doklad A. B. Khalatova Sov-NarKomu RSFSR, 2/4/27, "Materialy k postroike Semirechenskoi zheldor"; ibid., delo 351a, ll. 2–3: Rezoliutsiia po khoziaistvenno-operatsionnomu planu na 1926/27g, 2/2/27; ibid., ll. 4–20: Doklad sostoianiia sel'skogo khoziaistva, zhivotnovodstva, veterinarnogo dela, lesnogo khoziaistva Dzhetysu v 1925–26 godu; ibid., ll. 138–159: Doklad Kollegii, "O Turkestan-Sibirskoi Magistrali," 1/27.

8. TsGA Kaz SSR, f. 131 (Kaz TsP Stroitelei), op. 1, d. 10, ll. 108–110.

9. In fact, many of leaders of the so-called bourgeois nationalist Kazakh Alash Orda movement staffed government and party staffs in Kazakhstan well into the 1920s. Moscow needed native bodies, and it was none too picky about how it got them. Sometimes, bare literacy and a lack of open antagonism to the new regime was sufficient. As F. I. Goloshchekin, Moscow's viceroy in Kazakhstan, stated somewhat plaintively in 1927, the krai party had "recruited into the Party, Soviet, union and economic apparatus all the literate and half-literate Kazakhs that we have." Martin, *The Affirmative Action Empire*, p. 197.

10. Hélène Carrère d'Encausse, "The National Republics Lose their Independence," in Edward Allworth, ed., *Central Asia: A Century of Russian Rule* (New York: Columbia University Press, 1967), pp. 259–260; V. M. Ustinov, *Sluzhenie narodu*, pp. 34–40; "O 'formirovanii Kazakhskoi natsii' i Kazakhskom Proletariate," in Ryskulov, *Izbrannye trudy*, pp. 119–126; on Ryskulov's hope of "leaping over historical stages," see Tulepbaev, *Sotsialisticheskie agrarnye preobrazheniia*, pp. 12–13, 54. For the quote, see G. F. Dakhshleiger, *V. I. Lenin i problemy Kazakhstanskoi istoriografii* (Alma-Ata: Nauka, 1978), p. 123.

11. Even those Kazakhs accused of being under the influence of *beys* and mullahs, such as S. Sadvokasov, did not reject the need for "forced industrialization." In fact, Sadvokasov wrote a stinging denunciation of Soviet investment policy as a continuation of Tsarist colonialism in 1926. See S. B. Baishev, ed., *Istoriia industrializatsii Kazakskoi SSR* (1926–1931gg.), vol. 1 (Alma-Ata: Nauka, 1967), pp. 206–208. There was a wide range of opinions within Kazakhstan's party, but generally Kazakh members, like the "leftist" Sadvokasov and the "rightist" S. Khodzhanov, supported modernization. European officials, such as Goloshchekin, were more likely to stress the prematurity of industrialization for such a "primitive" population, despite the party program. Such men supported industrialization, but they simply took the "Great Power chauvinist position" that Kazakhs should not be the primary beneficiaries of such a program. See N. Dzhagfarov, "Natsional'no-uklonizm: Mify i real'nost'," in *O proshlom—dlia bydushchego: Nekotorye aktual'nye problemy istorii Kompartii Kazakhstana v svete glasnosti* (Alma-Ata: Kmzakhstan (1990), pp. 167–176, 180–181. For an impartial, if deeply uninformed account of the divisions within Kazakhstan's party, see "Natsional'nye momenty politiki v Kazakhstane," *Arkhiv Trotskogo* vol. 2, pp. 197–199. For similar attitudes in favor of industrialization among Ukrainian and Uzbek national Communists see George Liber, *Soviet Nationality Policy, Urban Growth, and Identity Change in the Ukrianian SSR, 1923–1934* (Cambridge: Cambridge University Press, 1992), pp. 114–115; Simon, *Nationalism and Policy*, p. 96.

12. For a sense of the condescension towards nomadism see Volk's description of a migratory *aul* he met during his perambulations around the Turksib; Volk, *Turksib: Ocherki stroiki*, pp. 41–42.

13. GosArkhiv UMVD po Semipalatinskoi oblasti, f. 74 (OkrIspolKom), op. 1, d. 19, ll. 385–413; Stenogramma rasshirennogo zasedaniia Prezidiuma KomSoda, 6/19/28.

14. A. Bekkulov and K. Mizambekov, *Stal'nye magistrali Kazakhstana* (Alma-Ata: Kazakhskoe Gosudarstvennoe Izdatel'stvo, 1960), p. 24.

15. RGAE, fond 1884, opis' 80, delo 244, l. 243; Vypiska iz Protokola No. 13 zasedaniia Soveta Narodnykh Kazakskoi ASSR ot 12/29/26; RGAE, f. 1884 (NarKomPutSoob), op. 80, d. 351b, ll. 142–162; Stenogramma zasedaniia Komiteta Sodeistviia, 12/22/27; Respublikanskii Partiinyi arkhiv Kazakhstana (PartArkhiv), f. 185 (PolitOtdel Turksiba), op. 1, ed. khr 1, ll. 7–10; Rezoliutsiia po dokladu o polozhenii Kazakskoi rabochei sily i mezhnatsional'nykh vzaimootnosheniiakh na postroike iuzhnoi chasti Turksiba, 7/29; TsGA Kaz SSR, f. 1129 (Uprav. Turksiba), op. 8, d. 53, ll. 88; Prikaz No. 429, "O korenizatsii," 2/19/30.

16. "Priezd tov. Shatov v Alma-Ata," *Dzhetysuiskaia iskra*, no. 34(183), 4/7/27, p. 1.

17. Grigorii Dakhsleiger, *Turksib—Pervenets sotsialisticheskoi industrializatsii* (Alma-Ata: Izdatel'stvo Akademii nauka Kazakhshoi SSR, 1958), p. 49.

18. RGAE, fond 1884, op. 80, d. 244, ll. 134–5: Protokol NKTrud RSFSR, 1/29/27; TsGA Kaz SSR, fond 138, op. 1, d. 1246, ll. 98–99: Protokol No. 14 zasedaniia prezidiuma KazSovProfa, 2/22/27

19. RGAE, fond 1884, op. 80, d. 351b, ll. 142–162: Stenogramma zasedaniia Komiteta Sodeistviia, 12/22/27.

20. This reliance on "imported labor" seems to have been ubiquitous in the 1920s. Roger Pethybridge, *One Step Backwards, Two Steps Forward: Soviet Society and Politics in the New Economic Policy* (Oxford: Clarendon Press, 1990), p. 397.

21. "K postroike Semirechenskoi zh. d.; Nadbor rabochikh budet proizveden na meste," *Dzhetysuiskaia iskra*, no. 3 (152), 10/1/27, p. 5; see also RGAE, fond 1884, opis' 80, delo 351a, ll. 55–56: Prot. No. 3 zasedaniia KomSoda, 5/vi.27 goda; M. Kh. Asylbekov, "O deiatel'nosti Komiteta sodeistviia postroiki Turkestano-Sibirskoi zheleznoi dorogi," *Izvestiia AN Kaz SSR*, Seriia obshchestvennaia nauka, 6 (1969), pp. 39–40; GosArkhiv UMVD po Semipalatinskoi oblasti, f. 74 (OkrIspolKom), op. 1, d. 19, ll. 385–413: Stenogramma rasshirennogo zasedaniia Prezidiuma KomSoda, 6/19/28; "Vse vnimanie stroitel'stvu," *Dzhetysuiskaia iskra*, no. 48 (197), 5/15/27, p. 3.

22. RGAE, fond 1884, opis' 80, delo 351(b), ll. 66–69: Postanovlenie Sovet Narodnykh Komissarov RSFSR, 12/10/27; "Po SSSR; Pravitel'stvo SSSR o Turk.-Sibe," *Dzhetysuiskaia iskra*, 1927, no. 138 (287), 12/15/27, p. 1.

23. In August there were only 3,408 workers on the Turksib, 40 percent of whom were Kazakhs. RGAE, fond 1884, op. 80, d. 351b, ll. 210–214: Svodka No 5 vyderzhek iz pechati (*Sovetskaia step'*, 1/8/28, "Dzhetysu dait 10,300 rabochikh."); TsGA Kaz SSR, fond 131, op. 3, d. 2, ll. 14–37: Resheniia KraiKomom po Turksibu; ibid., delo 91, ll. 12–22: Protokol No. 6/67 zasedaniia KSPS, 2/7/28.

24. RGAE, fond 1884, op. 80, d. 351b, ll. 47–53: Pis'mo Borisova Rudzutaku, 10/24/27.

25. Sokol, *The Revolt of 1916*, 33–43; Olcott, *The Kazakhs*, 83–99. On the 1916 Revolt see Sokol, *The Revolt of 1916*, pp. 111, 114–128; On the *basmachis* see Olcott, *The Kazakhs*, p. 152; Iu. A. Poliakov and A. I. Chuganov, *Konets basmachestva* (Moskva: "Nauka," 1976).

26. Dakhshleiger, *Turksib—Pervenets sotsialisticheskoi industrializatsii*, p. 45; O. Romancherko, *Kogda otstupaiut gory (O stroitel'stve Turksibe)*, (Mosrow: Politicheskaia literatury, 1968), p. 44.

27. Dakhshleiger, *Turksib—Pervenets sotsialisticheskoi industrializatsii*, p. 45; Romancherko, *Kogda otstupaiut gory (O stroitel'stve Turksibe)*, p. 29

28. Romancherko, *Kogda otstupaiut gory (O stroitel'stve Turksibe)*, p. 30.

29. I. Kruch, "Mne vypalo schast'e," in N. S. Nikitin (compiler), *Turksib—Magistral' sotsializma: Sbornik podgotovlen po initiative i pri aktivnom uchastii veteranov Turksiba* (Alma-Ata: Kazakhstan, 1986), pp. 155–156. These *basmachi* raids were probably not directed against the Turksib per se but rather were an outgrowth of the population's resistance to Stalin's collectivization drive. Lynne Viola notes that this resistance was particularly well organized in Central Asia and peaked at the same time that attacks on the Turksib were most prevalent. See Lynne Viola, *Peasant Rebels under Stalin: Collectivization and the Culture of Peasant Resistance* (Oxford: Oxford University Press, 1996), pp. 159–160.

30. Kruch, "Mne vypalo schast'e," pp. 155–156.

31. RGAE, fond 1884, opis' 80, delo 351a, ll. 220–242; Stenogramma plenuma KomSoda, 9/28/27.

32. GosArkhiv UMVD po Semipalatinskoi oblasti, f. 74 (Semip. OkrIspolKom), op. 1, d. 19, ll. 385–413; Stenogramma rasshirennogo zasedaniia Prezidiuma Kom-Soda, 6/19/28; see also TsGA Kaz SSR, f. 83 (Kaz NarKomTrud), op. 1, d. 289, ll. 8–21.

33. TsGA Kaz SSR, f. 239 (DorProfSozh Turksiba), op. 1, d. 3, ll. 136–143; Protokol obshchego uzlovogo sobraniia (Aiaguza), 8/28/30.

34. Volk, *Turksib: Ocherki stroiki*, pp. 55–56.

35. E. Kotenov, "Vesna 1929-go goda na Pervoi Stroitel'noi Uchastke," Z. Ostrovskii (compiler), *Turksib: Sbornik statei uchastnikov stroitel'stva Turkestano-sibirskoi zheleznoi dorogi (Moscow*: TransPechat', 1930), p. 221.

36. A. Tavashev, "Rol' Turksib v proletarianizatsii Kazakhstana," in Z. Ostrovskii (compiler). *Turksib: Sbornik statei*, Moscow p. 40.

37. Viti Fedorovich, *Konets pustyni: Ocherki*, Moscow: Federatsiia, 1931), p. 122.

38. TsGA Kaz SSR, fond 131, opis' 2, delo 54, ll. 155–157; Protokol No. 21 zasedaniia Pravleniia DorLinOtdela VSSR Turksiba, 12/29/30.

39. TsGA Kaz SSR, f. 131 (Kaz TsP Stroitelei), op. 1, d. 109, ll. 2–5. Protokol No. 10 rasshirennogo zasedaniia Orgbiuro LinOtdel SevTurksiba, 9/28/27.

40. TsGA Kaz SSR, f. 131 (Kaz TsP Stroitelei), op. 1, d. 109, ll. 54–57; Protokol No. 8 zasedaniia Pravleniia LinOtdela SevTurksiba, 5/18/28; TsGA Kaz SSR, f. 1129 (Uprav. Turksiba), op. 8, d. 50, l. 34; Prikaz SevTurksiba No. 18, "Ob uvolnenii Kazakov," 1/19/29; PartArkhiv, f. 185 (PolitOtdel Turksiba), op. 1, ed., khr. 3, ll. 148–150.

41. Tok, "V mery administrator," *Priirtyshskaia pravda*, no. 21 (272), 1/26/30, p. 3.

42. GosArkhiv UMVD po semipalatinskoi oblasti, fond 577, delo 12, ll. 18–20; Protokol No. 6/17 zasedaniia Semipalatinskogo Komiteta Sodeistviia, 4/10/29; Partiinyi Arkhiv, fond 185, opis' 1, ed. khr. 3, ll. 1–4; Protokol No. 1 zasedaniia Biuro RaiKoma VKP (b) IuzhTurksibstroia, "Rezolutssiia o korenizatsii," 2/27/29.

43. TsGA Kaz SSR, f. 83 (Kaz NarKomTrud), op. 1, d. 289, ll. 64–65; "Postanovlenie SNK KazASSR ot 2 oktiabria 1428 po protokolu Komiteta Sodeistviia stroitel'stvu Turksiba, No. 4.

44. V. Beliakov, "Rabochii vopros na Turksibe," *Sovetskii step'*, no. 225 (1430), 10/10/28, 2–3.

45. The words "Russian" and "European" were used interchangeably on the Turksib, as were "native" and "Kazakh." The "Russians" in question could have actually been Ukrainian navvies, who were employed in great numbers on the Turksib. *Priirtyshskaia pravda*, no. 21 (272), 1/26/30, p. 3.

46. Literally dozens of such managerial chauvinists could be enumerated on the Turksib. See also A. Briskin, *Na Iuzhturksibe: Ocherki Turksiba* (Alma-ata: Kazizdat', 1930), pp. 13–4.

47. Respublikanskii Partiinyi arkhiv Kazakhstana (PartArkhiv), f. 185 (PolitOtdel Turksiba), op. 1, ed. khr 1, ll. 7–10; Rezoliutsiia po dokladu o polozhenii Kazakskoi rabochei sily i mezhnatsional'nykh vzaimootnosheniiakh na postroike iuzhnoi chasti Turksiba, 7/29; PartArkhiv, f. 185 (PolitOtdel Turksiba), op. 1, ed. khr. 3, ll. 1–4; Protokol No. 1 zasedaniia Biuro RaiKoma VKP (b) IuzhTurksibstroia, "Rezolutssiia o korenizatsii," 2/27/29, PartArkhiv, f. 185 (PolitOtdel Turksiba), op. 1, ed. khr. 3, ll. 67–68; Protokol No. 22 zasedaniia Biuro RaiKoma VKP(b) IuzhTurksibstroia, 6/30/29, "Rezoliutsiia o korenizatsii;" Briskin, *Na Iuzhturksibe*, pp. 13–4.

48. GosArkhiv UMVD po Semipalatinskoi oblasti, f. 577 (Semip. Okr KK/RKI), op. 1, d. 12, ll. 18–20. Respublikanskii Partiinyi arkhiv Kazakhstana (PartArkhiv), f. 185 (PolitOtdel Turksiba), op. 1, ed. khr 1, ll. 7–10; Rezoliutsiia po dokladu o polozhenii Kazakskoi rabochei sily i mezhnatsional'nykh vzaimootnosheniiakh na postroike iuzhnoi chasti Turksiba, 7/29. TsGA Kaz SSR, fond 131, opis' 2, delo 33, ll. 174–183; Protokol zasedaniia aktiva rabochikh i sluzhashchikh pri RK No. 23 pri punkte Lepsy, 9/14/29. TsGA Kaz SSR, f. 1129 (Uprav. Turksiba), op. 8, d. 79, ll. 146–147; Prikaz No. 750 Turksiba, "O korenizatsii," 11/30/30.

49. Volk, *Turksib: Ocherki stroiki*, p. 55. Given the paucity of bathing facilities on the Turksib, it is doubtful anyone gave off a pleasant odor.

50. On the Kazakh membership of the Unions see TsGA Kaz SSR, f. 239 (DorProfSozh Turksiba), op. 2, d. 33, ll. 199b-204; PartArkhiv, f. 185 (PolitOtdel Turksiba), op. 1, ed. khr. 3, ll. 67–68; Protokol No. 22 zasedaniia Biuro RaiKoma VKP(b) IuzhTurksibstroia, 6/30/29, "Rezoliutsiia o korenizatsii." On the party's Kazakh saturation see PartArkhiv, f. 185 (PolitOtdel Turksiba), op. 1, ed. khr. 6, ll. 1–17; Protokoly No. 4, 6, 7, 7(a), 8, 9 zasedanii priemochnoi komissii po priemu v kandidaty i perevody v deistvitel'nye chleny VKP(b) pri raionnogo komiteta VKP (b) IuzhTurksiba, 8/3, 9/29, 10/14, 11/1, 11/18, 12/25/29.

51. TsGA Kaz SSR, f. 131 (Kaz TsP Stroitelei), op. 1, d. 295, ll. 214–222; "O vovlechenii kazakhov v profdvizhenii (nametka tezisov)," 4/29.

52. V. F. Kopeikin "Rabochii universitet," in *Turksib: Magistral' sotsializma*, p. 111.

53. A. Popov, "Pervye rel'sy v Lugovoi," in *Turksib: Sbornik statei* (Alma-Ata, 1985), p. 85.

54. GosArkhiv UMVD po Semipalatinskoi oblasti, f. 74 (Semip. OkrIspolKom) op. 1, d. 19, ll. 253–280; Stenogramma zasedaniia KomSoda Kaz ASSR, 8/28/28.

55. GosArkhiv UMVD po Semipalatinskoi oblasti, f. 74 (Semip. OkrIspolKom) op. 1, d. 19, ll. 253–280; Stenogramma zasedaniia KomSoda Kaz ASSR, 8/28/28.

56. GosArkhiv UMVD po semipalatinskoi oblasti, fond 141, opis' 17, delo 290, ll. 1–23; Stenogramma zasedaniia Semipalatinskogo Komiteta Sodeistviia, 8/28/29.

57. TsGA Kaz SSR, f. 83 (Kaz NarKomTrud), op. 1, d. 289, ll. 1–5; Protokol No. 21 zasedaniia kollegii Narkomtruda RSFSR, 8/25–8/28; TsGA Kaz SSR, f. 83 (Kaz NarKomTrud), op. 1, d. 289, ll. 64–65; "Postanovlenie SNK KazASSR ot 2 oktiabria 1428 po protokolu Komiteta Sodeistviia stroitel'stvu Turksiba, No. 4; d. 246, TsGA Kaz SSR, f. 83 (Kaz NarKomTrud), op. 1, d. 289, ll. 96–117; Doklad fraktsii VKP(b) TsP VSSR Kaz ob osnovnykh momentakh rabot;, TsGA Kaz SSR, f. 83 (Kaz NarKomTrud), op. 1, d. 226, l. 40; Gos Arkhiv UMVD po Semipalatinskoi oblasti, f. 577 (Semip. Okr KK/RKI) op. 1, d. 12, ll. 33–35; Kopeikin, "Rabochii universitet," p. 111.

58. TsGA Kaz SSR, f. 83 (Kaz NarKomTrud), op. 1, d. 289, ll. 1–5; Protokol No. 21 zasedaniia kollegii Narkomtruda RSFSR, 8/25–8/28; TsGA Kaz SSR, f. 83 (KazNarKomTrud), op. 1, d. 289, ll. 64–65; "Postanovlenie SNK KazASSR ot 2 oktiabria 1428 po protokolu Komiteta Sodeistviia stroitel'stvu Turksiba, No. 4; d. 246, TsGA Kaz SSR, f. 83 (Kaz NarKomTrud), op. 1, d. 289, ll. 96–117; Doklad fraktsii VKP(b) TsP VSSR Kaz ob osnovnykh momentakh rabot; TsGA Kaz SSR, f. 83 (Kaz NarKomTrud), op. 1, d. 226, l. 40; GosArkhiv UMVD po Semipalatinskoi oblasti, f. 577 (Semip. Okr KK/RKI) op. 1, d. 12, ll. 33–35; Kopeikin, "Rabochii universitet," p. 111.

59. RGAE, fond 1884, opis' 80, delo 559, ll. 170–174; Poiasnitel'naia zapiska k likvidatsion. otchetu Turksiba (Semip.-Lug.).

60. TsGA Kaz SSR, f. 131 (Kaz TsP Stroitelei), op. 3, d. 1, ll. 96–99; Protokol No. 6 zasedaniia komissii KazKraiKoma i KSPS ot 7-go septiabria, 1928-go goda; TsGA Kaz SSR, f. 131 (Kaz TsP Stroitelei), op. 1, d. 325, ll. 63–65; Rezoliutsiia 2-go Lineinogo S"ezda VSSR po organizatsionnym voprosam, 7/29; TsGA Kaz SSR, f. 131 (Kaz TsP Stroitelei), op. 2, d. 67, ll. 65–93; "Protokol No. 1-go dorozhnogo sleta udarnikov stroitelei Turkestano-Sibirskoi zh. d. otkrybshegosia 30 noiabr 1930 goda."

61. PartArkhiv, f. 185 (PolitOtdel Turksiba), op. 1, ed. khr. 1, ll. 7–10; Rezoliutsiia po dokladu o polozhenii Kazakskoi rabochei sily i mezhnatsional'nykh vzaimootnosheniiakh na postroike iuzhnoi chasti Turksiba, 7/29; Volk, *Turksib: Ocherki stroiki*, p. 55.

62. TsGA Kaz SSR, f. 1129 (Uprav. Turksiba), op. 8, d. 50, l. 69; "Ob izbienii Kazakhskogo."

63. TsGA Kaz SSR, f. 131 (Kaz TsP Stroitelei), op. 2, d. 28, ll. 196–203; f. 239 (DorProfSozh Turksiba), op. 1, d. 3, ll. 136–143; Protokol obshchego uzlovogo sobraniia (Aiaguza), 8/28/30.

64. Fedorovich, *Konets pustyni*, pp. 42–43.

65. TsGA Kaz SSR, f. 131 (Kaz TsP Stroitelei), op. 1, d. 285, ll. 19–26; Vyvody i predlozheniia PartKomissii po obsledovanymu Aiaguzskoi partorganizatsii v sviazi s natsional'nymi treniami, imeiushchimi mesto na linii Turksiba, early 1929.

66. TsGA Kaz SSR, f. 131 (Kaz TsP Stroitelei), op. 1, d. 285, ll. 19–26; TsGA Kaz SSR, f. 138 (Kaz SovProfSoiuzov), op. 1, d. 2098, ll. 17–21; Protokol No. 66/147 Prezidiuma KSPS'a, 1/17/29.

67. GosArkhiv UMVD po Semipalatinskoi oblasti, f. 74 (Semip. OkrIspolKom) op. 1, d. 20, ll. 182–183; "Kratkii doklad po voprosu nabora i ispol'zovaniia rabochei sily na postroike v stroitel'nyi sezon 1926/1927 goda i poriadke privlecheniia v 1927/28 g." 9/27; RGAE, f. 1884 (NarKomPutSoob), op. 80, d. 251, ll. 259–261; TsGA Kaz SSR, f. 131 (Kaz TsP Stroitelei), op. 1, d. 325, ll. 12–14; Protokol No. 8/42 zasedaniia Pravleniia LinOtdela SevTurksiba, 3/1/29.

68. GosArkhiv UMVD po Semipalatinskoi oblasti, f. 74 (Semip. OkrIspolKom), op. 1, d. 19, ll. 337–343; Protokol zasedaniia Dzhetysuiskogo KomSoda, 10/4/28.

69. GosArkhiv UMVD po semipalatinskoi oblasti, fond 577, delo 12, ll. 33–35; Protokol No. 1 (12) zasedaniia Semipalatinskogo Komiteta Sodeistviia, 1/17/29.

70. Zinaida Rikhter, *Semafory v pustyne* (Moscow: Mulodaia Gvardiia, 1929), p. 218.

71. Contrary to most accounts of the building of the Turksib, Kazakhs as a whole were not completely new to railroad construction. In fact, on the Central Asian Railroad's spur line to Ekibastus, "almost all the earthwork was done by Kazakh-Kirgiz workers on foot or with horses." By all accounts, conditions on this construction were horrendous. See Dakhshleiger, *Turksib—Pervenets sotsialisticheskoi industrializatsii*, p. 11.

72. TsGA Kaz SSR, f. 131 (Kaz TsP Stroitelei), op. 1, d. 246, ll. 94–96; Doklad Biuro Fraktsii VKP(b) Tsentral'nogo Pravleniia soiuza stroitel'nykh rabochikh o Sergiopol'skim sobytiiakh (Budreiko); TsGA Kaz SSR, f. 131 (Kaz TsP Stroitelei), op. 1, d. 285, ll. 19–26; Vyvody i predlozheniia PartKomissii po obsledovanymu Aiaguzskoi partorganizatsii v sviazi s natsional'nymi treniami, imeiushchimi mesto na linii Turksba, early 1929; TsGA Kaz SSR, f. 1129 (Uprav. Turksiba), op. 8, d. 51, l. 161; Prikaz No. 78 IuzhTurksiba, "O vnimatel'nom otnoshenii k nuzhdam rabochikh stroitel'stva i nedopushchenii natsional'noi rozni," 3/19/29; "Proletarskii sud vypolnil tre-

bovanie proletarskikh mass; O sudom nakazanii vinovnikov izbieniia Kazakov v Sergiopole," *Dzhetysuiskaia iskra*, no. 16 (454), 2/10/29, p. 1.

73. RGAE, fond 1884, opis' 80, delo 251, ll. 259–261; Protokol No. 12 obshchego sobraniia rabochikh Upravleniia postroika IuzhTurksiba, 11/12/28; RGAE, fond 1884, opis' 80, delo 253, ll. 256–259; "Protokol No. 12 obshchego sobraniia rabochikh i sluzhashchikh Uprav. Postroiki IuzhTurksiba, 11/26/28.

74. TsGA Kaz SSR, fond 1129, opis' 8, delo 50, l. 12; "Prikaz No. 7 SevTurksiba, 1/11/29, "O sobytiiakh v Sergiopole 31 dekiabria."

75. TsGA Kaz SSR, f. 131 (Kaz TsP Stroitelei), op. 1, d. 246, ll. 94–95; Doklad Biuro Fraktsii VKP(b) Tsentral'nogo Pravleniia soiuza stroitel'nykh rabochikh o Sergiopol'skim sobytiiakh (Budreiko); TsGA Kaz SSR, f. 131 (Kaz TsP Stroitelei), op. 1, d. 285, ll. 19–26; Vyvody i predlozheniia PartKomissii po obsledovanymu Aiaguzskoi partorganizatsii v sviazi s natsional'nymi treniami, imeiushchimi mesto na linii Turksba, early 1929; TsGA Kaz SSR, fond 138 (Kaz SovProfSoiuzov), op. 1. d. 2098, ll. 17–21; Protokol No. 66/147 Prezidiuma KSPS'a, 1/17/29.

76. TsGA Kaz SSR, fond 1129, opis' 8, delo 50, l. 12; "Prikaz No. 7 SevTurksiba, 1/11/29, "Osobytiiakh v Sergiopole 31 dekiabria."

77. Briskin, *Na Iuzhturksibe*, p. 13–14.

78. For details on this transformation see Matt Payne, *Working on Stalin's Railroad: Turksib and the Building of Socialism, 1926–1931* (Pittsburgh: University of Pittsburgh Press, forthcoming), ch. 4.

79. TsGA Kaz SSR, fond 131, opis' 1, delo 328, ll. 48–53; Protokol No. 23/2 zasedaniia Pravleniia LinOtdela SevTurksiba, 1/14/30.

80. TsGA RK, f. 131, op. 2, d. 53, ll. 67–76; ibid., f. 239, op. 1, d.b, ll. 136–14 ibid., f. 112 op.8, d.80, ll. 146–147.

81. TsGA Kaz SSR, f. 131 (Kaz TsP Stroitelei), op. 1, d. 246, l. 77; TsGA Kaz SSR, f. 131 (Kaz TsP Stroitelei), op. 1, d. 325, ll. 110–111; TsGA Kaz SSR, fond 131, opis' 2, delo 53, ll. 18; Prikaz No. 24 po upravleniiu i liniiu Turksib zh. d. 1/8/31, "O velikoderzhavnom shavanizme."

82. GosArkhiv UMVD po semipalatinskoi oblasti, fond 577, delo 12, ll. 33–35; Protokol No. 1 (12) zasedaniia Semipalatinskogo Komiteta Sodeistviia, 1/17/29; TsGA Kaz SSR, fond 131, opis' 1, delo 325, l. 55; Protokol No. 3 zasedaniia Pravleniia LinOtdela SevTurksiba, 6/29(?).

83. TsGA Kaz SSR, f. 83 (Kaz NarKomTrud), op. 1, d. 285, ll. 8–21; Doklad, "O rezul'tatakh obsledovaniia voprosov Truda na Turksibe i, v sviazi s stroitel'stvom Turksiba, raboty mestnikh organov Truda," 8/1/28; TsGA Kaz SSR, fond 83, opis' 1, delo 289, ll. 306–308; Doklad NKTruda KSSR, "O verbovke rabochei sily dlia stroitel'stva Turksiba," 1/29.

84. See Lewis H. Siegelbaum, *Stakhanovism and the Politics of Production in the USSR, 1935–1941* (Cambridge: Cambridge University Press, 1988), pp. 40–53; Hiroaki Kuromiya, "The Crisis of Proletarian Identity in the Soviet Factory, 1928–1929," *Slavic Review* 44, no. 2 (Summer 1985): 280–297; Kuromiya, *Stalin's Industrial Revolution; Politics and Workers, 1928–1932* (Cambridge: Cambridge University Press, 1988), pp. 78–137; Tim McDaniel, *Autocracy, Capitalism, and Revolution in Russia* (Berkeley: University of California Press, 1988), pp. 183–212.

85. Volk, *Turksib: Ocherki stroiki*, pp. 58–59.

86. Fedorovich, *Konets pustyni: Ocherki*, p. 65.

87. Gashimbaev, "Na stroike Turksiba," *Sovetskaia step'*, no. 168 (1373), 7/26/28, p. 3.

88. Romancherko, *Kogda otstupaiut gory*, p. 45.

89. Kopeikin, "Rabochii universitet," and K. Kadyrbaev, "Rabotali i uchali," in *Turksib—Magistral' sotsializma*, pp. 111–112, 141.

90. Volk, *Turksib: Ocherki stroiki*, p. 57.

91. See for instance the stories of Kazakh promotees in S. Ivanov, "Na bystrine . . . ," *Gudok*, no. 287 (12564), 12/13/66, p. 2; G. Maralbaev, "Rozhdennyi Oktiabrem," *Zaria Kommunizma*, no. 44 (4307), 3/4/70, p. 3; Dakhshleiger, *Turksib—Pervenets sotsialisticheskoi industrializatsii*, p. 111; Romancherko, *Kogda otstupaiut gory*, p. 31.

92. Dakhshleiger, *Turksib—Pervenets sotsialisticheskoi industrializatsii*, p. 109.

93. M. Kh. Asylbekov, *Formirovanie I razvitie kadrov zheleznodorozhnikov Kazakhstana, 1917–1977gg.* (Alma-Ata: Nauka, 1973), p. 95.

94. Volk, *Turksib: Ocherki stroiki*, pp. 3–4; One such poem allegedly ran "The black stallion flies, like a bird, with the smoke of a dragon. / It exhales, like a boiling samovar, giving off a column of steam. / The black breast of the land shakes from the passage of Kara-aigr, the land delights in its iron force. / Grateful, he bears to her from afar, such things as she has never seen: / Moscow goods, cars, and books. / What wise man bethought and created you, kara-aigr? / It is our Soviet Power that has given you to us. / Befor we heard only of you from fairy tales. / What kind of ignoramus could argure against your benefits?" While one should be dubious about the authencity of such obviously proregime poetry, the larger point that Kazakhs were singing about the Turksib as something novel and fascinating seems supportable to me.

95. Fedorovich, *Konets pustyni: Ocherki*, p. 66.

96. Aleksei Kozhevnikov, "Tansyk," in *Turksib: Magistral' sotsializma*, p. 201.

97. Iuga, "Net raboty sredi Kazakov," *Priirtyshskaia pravda*, no. 150 (250), 7/3/28, p. 3.

98. TsGA Kaz SSR, fond 131, opis' 2, delo 33, ll. 199b–204; "Otchet o rabote Pravleniia LinOtdela za stroisezona 1929 goda."

99. Ot Turksiba so zapoliarnykh trass; Piatiletkami rozhdennye," *Zvezda Priirtysh'ia*, no. 56–57 (7463), 3.18.67, p. 4.

100. Asylbekov, *Formirovanie I razvitie kadrov zheleznodorozhnikov Kazakhstana*, p. 95.

101. Rikhter, *Semafory v pustyne*, p. 218.

102. "Synu bagache ne mesto sredi rabochikh," *Priirtyshskaia pravda*, no. 135 (235), 6/15/28, p. 3.

103. Ia. Petrov, "Eto uzhe istoriia," *Ogni Alatau*, no. 68, 8/4/63, p. 4.

104. Dakhshleiger, *Turksib—Pervenets sotsialisticheskoi industrializatsii*, p. 109.

105. Kopeikin, "Rabochii universitet," in *Turksib: Magistral' sotsializma*, p. 112.

106. Volk, *Turksib: Ocherki stroiki*, p. 57.

107. RTsKhIDNI, fond 17, opis' 3, delo 697; Protokol No. 35 PB TsK VKP(b), punkt 22, 7/26/28; The standard English language source for the collectivization campaign is Martha Brill Olcott, "The Collectivization Drive in Kazakhstan," *Russian Review* 40, no. 2 (April 1981): 122–43; see also Olcott, *The Kazakhs*, pp. 179–187; The standard Soviet accounts include A. B. Tursunbaev, *Kollektivizatsiia sel'skogo Kazakhstana, 1926–1941 gg.* (Alma-Ata, 1967); idem, "Perekhod k sodelosti kochevnikov i polukochevnikov Srednei Azii i Kazakhstana," *Trudy institut etnografii* 91 (1973): 223–234.

108. T. Ryskulov, "Turksib i snabzhenie srednem Azii," *Priirtyshskaia pravda*, no. 73 (774), 4/1/30, p. 3.

109. RGAE, fond 1884, opis' 80, delo 559, ll. 170–174; Poiasnitel'naia zapiska k likvidatsion. otchetu Turksiba (Semip.-Lug.)

110. RGAE, fond 1884, opis' 80, delo 559, ll. 170–174; Poiasnitel'naia zapiska k likvidatsion. otchetu Turksiba (Semip.-Lug.)

111. Rikhter, *Semafory v pustyne*, p. 218.

112. TsGA Kaz SSR, fond 239, opis' 1, delo 282, l. 10; Protokol zasedaniia DorKom po provedeniiu korenizatsii, kazakizatsii i osedaniia, 12/16/31.

113. RGAE, fond 1884, opis' 31, delo 2346, ll. 24-obv.; Doklad, "X let raboty Turkestano-Sibirskoi zh. d."

114. Asylbekov, *Formirovanie i razvitie kadrov zheleznodorozhnikov Kazakhstana*, pp. 104–105.

115. S. Ivanov, "Na bystrine . . . ," p. 2; G. Maralbaev, "Rozhdennyi Oktiabrem," *Zaria Kommunizma*, no. 44 (4307), 3/4/70, p. 3.

116. G. Isakov, "Zhit' znachit' stroit', Rasskazy o komandirakh," *Gudok*, no. 195 (17030), 8/23/81, p. 2; S. Ivanov, "Na bystrine . . . ," p. 2; G. Maralbaev, "Rozhdennyi Oktiabrem," *Zaria Kommunizma*, no. 44 (4307), 3/4/70, p. 3; K. Filippov, "Turksibu—piatnadtsat' let," *Kazakhstanskaia pravda*, no. 82 (5207), 4/29/45, p. 3; TsGA Kaz SSR, fond 131, opis' 2, delo 20, ll. 10–11; "Protokol No. 38/17 zasedanii Pravlenii Sev-Turksiba, 4/20/30."

117. Volk, *Turksib: Ocherki stroiki*, pp. 45–47; Romancherko, *Kogda otstupaiut gory*, p. 44; Tavashev, "Rol' Turksib v proletarianizatsii Kazakhstana," *Turksib: Sbornik statei*, p. 40.

118. Gashimbaev, "Kolybel' Kazakhskovo proletariata," *Sovetskaia step'*, no. 177 (1382), 8/6/28, p. 2.

119. Baishev, *Istoriia industrializatsiia Kazakhskoi SSR*, p. 17.

120. *Istoriia Kazakhskoi SSR: s drevneishikh vremen do nashikh dnei*, tom 4, 522; These gains, unfortunately, were not maintained. The relocation of industry during the war, the postwar nuclear and space program, the heavy use of Gulag labor, Khrushchev's Virgin Lands Program, and Brezhnev's reliance on imported cadres to run the oil industry all tended to isolate native Kazakhs from industrial employment. A robust, urban middle class developed thanks to the regime's nativization policy but this Russian-speaking, urban-dwelling, modernized middle class soon found a growing rift opening between it and the mass of Kazakhs who were still relatively poorly educated, rural, and Kazakh speakers. For these developments see Anatoly M. Khazanov, "Ethnic Stratification and Ethnic Competition in Kazakhstan," in *After the USSR: Ethnicity, Nationalism, and Politics in the Commonwealth of Independent States* (Madison: University of Wisconsin Press, 1995), pp. 156–174.

121. A. Bekkulov and K. Mizambekov, *Stal'nye magistrali Kazakhstana*, p. 27.

122. M. N. Mezinov, "Slavnoe dvadtsatiletie," *Dvadtsat' let Turkestano-sibirskoi zheleznoi doroge* (Alma-Ata: KazIzdat, 1950), pp. 5–10.

123. B. Budreika, "Turksib—shkola profsoiuznoi raboty," *Turksib: Sbornik statei*, p. 95.

124. Volk, *Turksib: Ocherki stroiki*, p. 57.

Nation-Building or Russification?

*Obligatory Russian Instruction in the Soviet
Non-Russian School, 1938–1953*

FUNDAMENTAL TO STALIN'S "REVOLUTION FROM ABOVE" in the late 1920s and 1930s were policies of state-building and industrialization. Such policies logically led to efforts to create a culturally uniform Soviet population, an important basis of which would be universal knowledge of the Russian language.[1] Accordingly, a government decree of March 13, 1938, made Russian language and literature obligatory subjects in all Soviet non-Russian schools.[2] Yet the means to achieve Soviet uniformity through the Russian language were by no means obvious. Native-language schooling for the non-Russian population had been official policy since 1918. Committed to mass education, the Stalin regime not only retained native-language instruction in non-Russian schools but sought to extend it.[3] Finding a balance between native and Russian languages in the curriculum proved to be difficult. After the 1938 decree on obligatory Russian instruction, Stalin himself was unable, or unwilling, to signal where that balance should be. As a result, Russian-language instruction in non-Russian schools remained poor as educational officials and party bureaucrats alike dithered over the changes that might improve it. An examination of the drafting and implementation of the decree on obligatory Russian instruction reveals that contradictions and conflict beset the regime's language policy in non-Russian schools after 1938 and that the very nature of the Soviet multinational state remained ambiguous to its rulers. Requiring Russian for non-Russian children implied that the Soviet Union was becoming more like a unitary nation-state, one that demanded a common culture for its population. Continuing to support non-Russian languages meant that the USSR would retain characteristics of an "affirmative action empire" by supporting distinct ethnic cultures.[4]

Soviet educational authorities had always emphasized the importance of including Russian as a subject in non-Russian schools. It was the most obvious common language for the USSR because it was the most "developed."[5] Russian was, according to Lenin's widow and Deputy Commissar of Education N. K. Krupskaia, "the language of a revolutionary people with a huge literature in all areas of knowledge" and "the means of communication among various small nationalities." Krupskaia liked to emphasize that only wealthy non-Russians had been able to study the language before the revolution, whereas afterward it was available to all.[6] Knowledge of the Russian language was crucial if non-Russians were to pursue advanced education. Educators often complained that the lack of Russian was what hindered non-Russian students most of all once they embarked on vocational or higher education.[7]

Central educational authorities held that it was the responsibility of local authorities to include Russian in the curriculum if there was demand for it.[8] There was, however, no union-wide requirement to teach Russian in non-Russian schools. Notwithstanding the increasing centralization and coordination of education policy that started in the early 1930s, the non-Russian republics and regions continued to issue schedules and curricula independently.[9] The model schedule circulated in 1932 was common to all schools regardless of their language of instruction; it mandated "native" language instruction from the first grade and "second" language instruction from the third. In most cases, the second language was Russian, but in some schools for ethnic minorities children studied the language of the majority nationality. In the Tatar Autonomous Republic (ASSR), for example, schoolchildren in Chuvash-language schools studied Tatar as the second language.[10] In Ukraine and Belorussia, Polish, German, and Yiddish-language schools, among others, did not start teaching Russian until the fifth grade, owing to the need to teach Ukrainian or Belorussian, as well.[11] There was no common class schedule for all non-Russian schools in the Russian Federation (RSFSR) until the 1934–1935 school year, when Russian language and literature were established as distinct subjects for the first time. Russian instruction was then supposed to begin in the second grade, when children were nine years old.[12] In the 1935–1936 and 1937–1938 school years, time devoted to the Russian language was further increased.[13]

There is considerable evidence that non-Russian educational authorities had serious difficulties teaching Russian in their schools in the 1930s. At the All-Russian Conference on Non-Russian Textbooks, in April 1933, it was reported that "insufficiently trained people are often sent to be teachers of Russian" and that the graduates of the seven-year school "in fact do not know the Russian language." Those very graduates were candidates for training as primary-school teachers.[14] Most teachers of Russian had graduated from institutions where the language of instruction was the native one. Textbooks and methodological literature were lacking. Students in higher educational institutions were using textbooks produced for second and third graders.[15] Some central officials accused local authorities of "local nationalism" for ignoring Russian entirely.[16]

Although the Commissariat of Education (Narkompros) had long worried about the poor state of Russian instruction in non-Russian schools, the decision to mandate it came from a higher authority.[17] Stalin himself raised the issue of making Russian instruction obligatory in all Soviet schools at a Plenum of the Central Committee (TsK) in October 1937, allegedly because of the impending infusion of non-Russian soldiers into the Red Army. This would result from changes in the military service law, which no longer exempted certain non-Russian nationalities from conscription.[18] This "army of the whole Union" required a common language. As Stalin put it, "There is one language in which all citizens of the USSR can more or less express themselves—that is Russian. So we concluded that it should be obligatory. It would be good if all citizens drafted into the army could express themselves in Russian just a little, so that if some division or other was transferred, say an Uzbek one to Samara, it could converse with the population." Stalin's straightforward logic immediately ran into a complex reality. "We consulted with Narkompros," he complained, "but we couldn't get a clear answer: here Russian is studied as an obligatory subject from the second grade, there from the third, somewhere else from the fourth, and elsewhere not at all. . . . They claim that the law is vague." So "the Politburo" ordered Narkompros to work out a law that would standardize Russian-language instruction in all Soviet non-Russian schools.[19]

Stalin's emphasis at the plenum was on the practical need for non-Russians to learn Russian. In the tense atmosphere of the Great Terror, however, the political role of Russian took center stage, as the pedagogical reasons for teaching non-Russian students the language were relegated to a secondary position in official propaganda. Indeed, in the paranoid, xenophobic, and increasingly Russocentric atmosphere of the late 1930s, the decision to make Russian obligatory appeared to indicate that the Stalin regime had decided on a policy of Russifying non-Russian schools.[20] A press campaign attacking so-called bourgeois nationalists for consciously sabotaging Russian instruction in the non-Russian school followed Stalin's remarks at the TsK plenum.[21] Discussion at the Fifth Plenum of the Central Committee of the Communist Youth League, in February 1938, reinforced the theme of a nefarious plot to deny non-Russian students the benefits of the Russian language. In the course of 1936–1937, according to the representative from the Chuvash ASSR, "all the literature in Russian" was removed, because those who had created it turned out to be "enemies" or "bourgeois nationalists." An Uzbek official asserted that "not a single teacher of the Russian language for non-Russian schools" had been trained since the establishment of Soviet Uzbekistan. Anyone who raised the question, he claimed, had been called a "Great-Russian chauvinist."[22]

In such an atmosphere, it should not be surprising that Narkompros's initial proposals tended to be radical. Responsibility for proposing a law fell upon People's Commissar of Education P. A. Tiurkin, recently appointed to replace the arrested A. S. Bubnov, who, among many other things, was accused of sabotaging non-Russian schools.[23] Following the lead of the press campaign, Tiurkin condemned non-Russian "bourgeois nationalism" and produced considerable evidence to suggest that the state of Russian-language instruction in the non-Russian schools of the RSFSR was nothing short of disastrous. Having issued schedules that "in practice excluded the teaching of the Russian language," Tiurkin claimed, his predecessors were guilty of years of "wrecking." When Russian was initially included in the curriculum, in 1934, it had been allotted "an extremely insignificant number of hours (4 hours a week per grade)." The increases ordered subsequently were also insufficient when compared with the time allotted to Russian in *Russian* schools. Worse, "even these class schedules were not implemented. In many schools of certain autonomous republics and regions, the Russian language was not taught at all in the 1936–1937 school year."[24] Narkompros specialists, who believed that the amount of time devoted to Russian in the RSFSR non-Russian school—five hours per week for the second through six grades, decreasing thereafter—was insufficient, supported Tiurkin. A number of "leading schools," in violation of official policy, had introduced Russian in the form of conversational lessons in the first grade. These specialists recommended implementation of this method on a wider basis.[25] The situation in the union republics, according to Tiurkin, was worse than in the RSFSR. Of Turkmenistan's 728 schools, Russian was taught in 321. Of Kirgiziia's 667 primary schools, the language was taught in 189. Of Kazakhstan's 255 incomplete-secondary and 75 secondary schools, it was taught in only thirty-nine and seven, respectively. In those schools in which Russian was taught, Tiurkin claimed, the level of instruction was "extremely unsatisfactory." Complicating matters, Russian instruction began in different grades in different union republics.[26]

A shortage of teachers and textbooks was one reason for these failings. According to Tiurkin, Narkompros had failed to supervise the training of non-Russian schoolteachers ("not a few were counter-revolutionary elements, bourgeois nationalists and criminals") and had only begun to manage textbook publishing for non-Russian schools in 1933.[27] The methods of teaching Russian in non-Russian schools were not taught in the majority of teacher-training institutions.[28] Impressionistic evidence provided by Narkompros specialists indicated that Russian was taught poorly in non-Russian schools when it was taught at all: "Typically the teachers of the non-Russian school, who teach in the native language and also teach children Russian, know the languages very badly themselves, speak and read with many distortions, [and] commit a large number of gross spelling mistakes." Indeed, Narkompros representatives had to speak to teachers of Russian in the Tatar ASSR through an interpreter! Narkompros itself provided no support to such teachers: "No one gives them any kind of methodological help and no one has checked their work for years. They don't know how or what to study. They have no copies of the curriculum. There are no schedules, no textbooks, and no methodological instructions of any kind."[29]

Consistent with the goal of standardizing the educational process, textbooks for most subjects were written in Moscow in Russian and translated into the other languages of instruction. This was not the case for Russian-language textbooks for non-Russian schools, a practice that Tiurkin attacked especially harshly:

> The previous leadership of Narkompros RSFSR and of many other union republics consciously cultivated the harmful practice of creating so-called independent Russian-language textbooks for each people [*narodnost'*] separately. This harmful line was 'motivated' by linguistic differences . . . which allegedly did not make it possible to create good unified textbooks for all the non-Russian schools of the country. As a result, in the majority of non-Russian schools there are no textbooks now, and many of those which exist are at an extremely low conceptual, scholarly and, methodological level. . . . [30]

A reviewer of twenty-one Russian-language textbooks for non-Russian schools complained that each author had their own curriculum in mind and that they treated Russian as a "foreign language," rather than the "second native tongue" it was supposed to be.[31]

The result of these shortcomings was that non-Russian schoolchildren were illiterate in Russian, a goal, Tiurkin noted, of the "Trotskyite-Bukharinites." Indeed, a report Tiurkin had received from Narkompros specialists purported to present evidence that certain educational officials of the union republics, since arrested, had consciously sought to undermine Russian instruction. In 1935, the Narkompros of the Tadzhik SSR objected to a slight increase in hours devoted to Russian and to beginning instruction in the second grade, because "ninety-nine percent of primary-school teachers do not know the Russian language." The Narkompros of the Kara-Kalpak ASSR wanted to remove Russian entirely from the curriculum for the same reason.[32]

Given his evidence, and the political causes he found for it, Tiurkin suggested a radically Russifying direction. His first proposal, considered by the Orgburo on January 2, 1938, recommended that Russian be introduced immediately in the spring 1938 semester in all non-Russian schools as a subject "on an equal basis with the native language."[33] After conferring with representatives of the union republics on February 14, Tiurkin produced a second proposal, which was considered at a meeting of the Orgburo on February 16. This draft mandated Russian instruction from the first grade in all non-Russian schools and in teacher-training institutions, to begin with the fall 1938 semester, and provided measures to train and re-train teachers of Russian.[34]

In response to Tiurkin's recommendations, the Orgburo formed a committee to examine his second proposal.[35] Stalin, however, rejected Tiurkin's proposals as moving too far in the direction of Russification and instead ordered the Politburo to establish a commission under A. A. Zhdanov to work out a draft decree.[36] In his opening remarks at the March 8 meeting of this commission, Zhdanov noted that "we still do not have a prepared proposal on this question," thus indicating that Tiurkin's drafts would not do. Zhdanov also raised an entirely new issue, which he attributed to Stalin: "I think that what Comrade Stalin pointed out must be included in the draft—that there must be no suppression of, or limitation on, the native language, so as to warn all organizations that Russian is to be a subject of study, not a medium of instruction."[37] Indeed, Stalin also insisted that teachers of Russian know the native language of students, an indication that he did not intend the decree to signal a retreat on native-language education.[38]

Zhdanov's commission discussed technical issues, such as the grade at which Russian instruction would begun, how to create new textbooks, and how to overcome the shortage of teachers. The leaders of the autonomous and union republics had convinced Zhdanov—against the claims of Tiurkin and Narkompros specialists—that it was unnecessary to devote more time to Russian in the class schedules. Sufficient hours were devoted to the subject, but often these were not put to good use because of the lack of teachers. Similarly, they proposed that students in primary schools start Russian in the second grade, while those in the seven-year and secondary schools would start in the third.[39] Both of these decisions would complicate Russian-instruction in non-Russian schools in the coming years. They were also the first example of successful efforts by union-republican officials to temper Russifying tendencies at the center. The commission entrusted Zhdanov, Tiurkin, and L. P. Beriia to draft a final proposal. On March 11, Zhdanov presented this to Stalin, who made minimal changes; the decree was promulgated on March 13.[40]

Prefaced by a ritualistic condemnation of "bourgeois nationalists," the decree offered three reasons for mandating Russian language instruction: (1) the need for a common language in a multinational state seeking further economic and cultural development; (2) the importance of Russian for the advanced training of non-Russian cadres; and (3) the requirements of defense. It detailed very specific expectations for knowledge of the Russian language for graduates of the fourth, seventh, and tenth grades, and standardized the schedule for Russian language and literature in all non-Russian schools. By ordering that textbooks be written locally, with the advice of specialists sent by Narkompros from the center, the decree also rejected Tiurkin's demand that universal textbooks be drafted for all non-Russian schools, regardless of their language of instruction. Most important for the fate of future debates on language policy, the decree closed with Stalin's warning that attempts to convert Russian from a subject of study to the language of instruction were "harmful" and could be only temporary.

The final version of the decree was thus a defeat for proponents of a radical Russification of the non-Russian schools. All of Tiurkin's recommendations—that Russian instruction begin in the first grade, be given to the subject and to the native language, and that standardized textbooks be produced—were rejected or ignored by Zhdanov's commission. Native-language schools in most union republics did see an increase in the time devoted to the Russian language, but the decree actually led to a *decrease* in the number of hours devoted to Russian in the non-Russian schools of the RSFSR, compared to schedules for years past. The fact that Russian instruction had previously begun in the second grade in the incomplete-secondary and secondary schools but now would begin in the third grade also meant a reduction in the overall time devoted to Russian in these schools. Non-Russian schoolchildren in the RSFSR needed Russian instruction most because many non-Russian schools of the RSFSR taught in Russian after the fourth grade. These students, therefore, would be no better prepared to continue their education now than before.[41]

Authorities in the autonomous republics immediately recognized this problem and sought to change the terms of the decree, to no avail. A request by the North Ossetian ASSR to begin Russian instruction earlier, and to increase the projected time devoted to Russian, was actually *rejected* by the Orgburo.[42] When the Commissar of Education of Iakutiia requested clarification as to why the number of hours for Russian was actually to be reduced in the 1938–1939 school year, compared to 1937–1938, Tiurkin responded that this was because of the need to increase the number of hours devoted to the native language and literature and to other subjects.[43] There was, in fact, a significant increase in the projected time allotted for native language and literature in the non-Russian school of the RSFSR in the 1938–1939 school year, as Narkompros itself noted when explaining the new schedule.[44] Other measures, such as developing dedicated programs for training Russian instructors in the non-Russian school or publishing specialized journals, were also overlooked in the decree. At the same time, there is evidence that some local authorities violated the decree and maintained Russian in the second grade of the incomplete-secondary and secondary schools.[45]

That specific measures were outlined in the decree did not guarantee, of course, that Russian would be taught, or taught well, in all non-Russian schools in the coming years. The financial resources devoted to the measure were insufficient. The shortage of competent teachers could not be remedied in so short a time and would be exacerbated during the coming war. Most non-Russian republics and regions were required to print their own textbooks. Since their publishing resources were often very limited, textbook shortages would continue to plague non-Russian schools.

It soon became clear that the center was unable, or unwilling, to provide the financial support needed by the union and autonomous republics if the decree were to be fulfilled. The republics requested large supplements to their budgets, while the People's Commissariat of Finance (Narkomfin) reduced practically every request it received.[46] Narkomfin sought to standardize the costs and provisions of implementing the decree's measures across all republics. When Georgia observed that devoting additional hours to Russian would mean an overall increase in students' time in school, with a concomitant increase in teachers' salaries, Narkomfin dismissed the demand; the class schedules would have to be adjusted so as to preserve the number of hours.[47] Worse, Narkomfin took its time reconciling the budgetary allocations. Although most republics responded by mid-April with their financial needs, Narkomfin did not issue its final decisions until June. The

Council of People's Commissars tardy allocation of funds on June 28 likewise hampered the payment of teachers and students in summer teacher-training courses and of textbook writers.

Much of the preparation for implementing the decree fell upon Narkompros. It had to send specialists to the regions and republics to teach short-term teacher-training courses and to help write textbooks, to draft curricula for the entire Soviet Union, and to ensure that certain textbooks were printed. It also was required to provide teachers for permanent posting in the Central Asian republics. Not all of these targets were met. In the midst of all this, Tiurkin realized that the decree had failed to distinguish between the six-day urban and the seven-day rural schools. This required drafting yet another class schedule for the latter.[48] Despite the rushed measures and the lack of funding, much was accomplished between April and August 1938, at least on paper. According to aggregate statistics provided by the TsK Schools Department, 19,975 teachers were trained in the short-term courses, and a further 36,855 were retrained. Forty-one new departments of Russian language and literature were opened at universities and pedagogical institutions. Azerbaijan, Kazakhstan, and Kirgiziia, especially, still lacked sufficient teachers, and paper shortages meant that in many republics textbooks had not been printed on time.[49]

But money, teachers, and textbooks were just the tip of the iceberg. Another factor complicating all aspects of instruction in non-Russian schools was the switch from the Latin to the Cyrillic alphabet between 1939 and 1941. Although the Orgburo was approving the alphabet switches at the same time that it was considering the issue of mandatory Russian-language instruction—and, indeed, one of the explicit reasons for the switches was to make it easier for non-Russians to learn Russian—it did not attempt to coordinate the two processes.[50] For the RSFSR alone in the 1939–1940 school year, thirty-seven such alphabets were being created; this required the reprinting of textbooks that had only just been rewritten the year before.[51] Though they were supposed to be completed in time for the beginning of the 1939–1940 school year, the texts were delayed, and many schools were forced to continue to use the Latin-based books. The haste with which Cyrillicization was implemented led to spelling inconsistencies among different textbooks.[52] Worse yet, some republics sought to alter the new cyrillic alphabets just one year after they had been approved, necessitating reprinting of textbooks yet again.[53]

In the face of such difficulties, it should come as no surprise that Russian was not taught in all non-Russian schools by the start of the 1938–1939 school year. Rural schools especially suffered. In Azerbaijan, for example, Russian was taught in only 40–50 percent of all rural primary schools in that school year; in Armenia the figure was 70–80 percent. Educational officials were faced with the choice of hiring either native teachers who had completed only a short-term course in Russian or Russian teachers who did not know the native language. They often chose the latter, despite the center's insistence that "as a rule" the teacher of Russian must know the students' native language. As of December 1938, in Azerbaijan more than 20 percent of teachers of Russian did not speak the native language of students; in Dagestan the figure was 100 percent for urban schools, and almost 20 percent for rural primary schools.[54]

Where native teachers were employed to teach Russian, the quality of instruction often suffered from their poor training. In May 1939, the newspaper of Narkompros and the Teachers' Union, *Uchitel'skaia gazeta*, reported the following about a school in Tadzhikistan: "In the fourth grade of the Barzobskii primary school, Russian is taught by Comrade Aliev, who cannot answer a question about what kind of lesson [he is teaching] today without an interpreter. Lacking an elementary knowledge of the Russian language, naturally [he] cannot offer his students anything. There are more than a few such illiterate teachers of Russian in Tadzhikistan."[55] As a temporary measure to guarantee that all schools were staffed, Tadzhikistan had established "traveling teachers," each of whom taught Russian in several rural primary schools.[56] Since they were Russian, and, "as a rule, Russian teachers, even those who have taught in the schools of the republic for several years, do not know the Tadzhik language," this "seriously lowered the effectiveness" of instruction. The situation in Turkmenistan was no better. As of April 1939, 1,500 of 5,000 Turkmen teachers had not known Russian at all at the end of the previous academic year.[57] The Buriat authorities reported that, although all primary school teachers "spoke" Russian, "many of them make horrible mistakes in word-stress [and] pronounce sounds incorrectly." In general, their students studied grammar but had little practice in speaking the Russian language.[58]

In March 1940, the RSFSR planning agency, Gosplan, reported that Russian instruction remained "unsatisfactory" in the non-Russian schools of the republic.[59] Lack of textbooks continued to be a problem. The Chuvash ASSR, to take an example, had fulfilled only 39 percent of the 1939 plan for publishing Russian-language textbooks. But the decisive factor was the "extremely insignificant training of teachers who teach Russian." Gosplan cited examples from the Chuvash, Checheno-Ingushetian, North Ossetian, Tatar, Bashkir, and Buriat-Mongol autonomous republics. The quality of Russian instruction in the teacher-training institutions, which would supply new teachers, was also poor. Control over Russian instruction suffered because local school inspectors did not speak Russian and thus could not evaluate the effectiveness of instruction.

In September 1940, Narkompros acknowledged numerous problems in Russian-language instruction in non-Russian schools. Textbook production was a disaster. As of August 1, 1940, only 400 of 1,013 titles had been printed for the coming school year, mainly because of the lack of paper. Russian was still not taught in a number of schools because of the teacher shortage. Indeed, the new commissar, V. P. Potemkin, admitted that the training of non-Russian teachers was "completely unsatisfactory" and blamed Narkompros and local authorities for failing to fill teacher-training institutions with non-Russian students. Thus, at the Bashkir Pedagogical Institute, Bashkirs represented only 83, and Tatars 132, of 790 students; in the Kabardino-Balkar Pedagogical Institute, Kabardins and

Balkars were 67 of 342; and in the Chechen-Ingush Pedagogical Institute, Chechens and Ingush were only 15 of 221.[60] To overcome the shortfall of teachers, Narkompros proposed spending more money to establish special preparatory courses for non-Russian students who planned to become teachers. Almost a billion rubles had been spent on teacher training and retraining in the RSFSR in 1940 alone, however, and dropout rates at such institutions remained quite high. For this reason, Narkomfin rejected any new expenditure for teacher training.[61]

In July 1940, the TsK issued yet another decree on Russian-language instruction, this time addressing not schoolchildren but rather the problem of poor knowledge of Russian among army recruits. There were 152,766 such recruits, mainly from Central Asia and Transcaucasia, who did not speak Russian at all as of July 1, 1940.[62] Insofar as the army did not have the resources or infrastructure to accomplish the task, Commissar of Defense S. K. Timoshenko demanded that educational authorities of the union republics take measures to teach Russian to future draftees. The TsK so ordered, with the result that many Russian teachers were taken from schools and sent to teach special courses for recruits.[63]

During World War II, the shortage of teachers worsened, as many were conscripted or were recruited to better-paid work. Potemkin reported to TsK Secretary A. S. Shcherbakov in June 1943 that Dagestan alone would require 1,500 new teachers for the coming school year, but the six teacher-training institutions of the republic were to graduate only seventy.[64] In the following month, the Council of Peoples' Commissars did issue a decree aimed at rectifying the teacher shortage throughout the USSR. Teachers' salaries were increased, students at teacher-training institutions were provided with stipends and free tuition, and other organizations were ordered to cooperate with Narkompros in returning teachers to the schools. But the long-term prognosis for training teachers of the non-Russian nationalities remained bleak.[65]

It would indeed have been surprising if the hurried measures for training teachers and publishing textbooks had solved the problems facing the non-Russian school. In memoranda to Narkompros in the summer and fall of 1940, several autonomous republics had suggested solutions for addressing the teacher and textbook problem. But, almost universally, they also demanded changes in the class schedules mandated by the 1938 decree. Most requested that Russian instruction begin in all types of schools at the second-grade level. The Bashkir and the Tatar authorities went so far as to demand that the amount of classroom time for Russian in non-Russian schools be the same as that in Russian schools.[66] Narkompros agreed that the schedules had to be changed and dutifully appealed to the TsK. But the TsK rejected proposals to introduce Russian at an earlier grade and to synchronize the beginning of instruction in all types of schools several times between 1940 and 1945. Narkompros proposed a decree in September 1940 that would have begun instruction in the second grade in all non-Russian schools.[67] Potemkin wrote to the TsK in March 1941, requesting approval for this. The TsK Schools Department supported him, as did the other union republics with the exception of Ukraine and Georgia. Perhaps because of this opposition, nothing came of the proposal.[68]

Unable to address the deficits of teachers and textbooks during the war, educational authorities continued to focus on the schedules. In February 1943, the TsK Schools Department wrote Secretaries A. A. Andreev and Shcherbakov that "Five years of experience shows that the difference in beginning instruction of Russian in different types of schools leads to students of grades one to four . . . entering the fifth grade with completely different levels of knowledge of the Russian language." The department proposed beginning Russian instruction with conversational lessons in the second semester of the first grade in all schools, an idea, it will be remembered, that had been supported by Narkompros specialists back in 1938. G. F. Aleksandrov, the head of the TsK Propaganda and Agitation Directorate and thus responsible for education matters, also agreed that "the greatest specialists declare in unison" that Russian instruction should be started earlier. Furthermore, "It can hardly be considered expedient that in the schools of the autonomous and union republics, apart from the native and Russian languages, students also study English or German. In practice this nearly always results in students of these schools knowing neither Russian nor English or German properly. It is necessary to establish the study of languages in non-Russian schools such that students study Russian above all." Even this appeal, tinged with Russian chauvinism, did not find its mark. Aleksandrov's proposal, which included mandating the study of Russian from the first grade in all non-Russian schools, and "reconsidering" the inclusion of foreign languages in their curricula, never even made it to the agenda of the TsK Secretariat.[69] In September 1945, Potemkin once again wrote Secretary G. M. Malenkov about Narkompros's longstanding proposals. On Malenkov's orders, the TsK Schools Department responded to Potemkin's request with a memorandum asserting that it had proposed measures to improve the teaching of Russian in non-Russian schools, noting pointedly that Malenkov himself had determined that "further work on this question [is] premature" and so his proposal had been put aside."[70]

If the regime had truly been engaged in a policy of "Russification," it would be surprising that proposals designed to improve Russian instruction in the schools of the non-Russian peoples continued to flounder in the bureaucracy of the Central Committee. Since other fundamental changes in educational policy were adopted during the war—such as the decision to begin instruction with seven- rather than eight-year-olds and the introduction of gender segregation in the classroom—one cannot explain this inaction by the difficulties of the war itself.[71] Rather, increasing the amount of time devoted to Russian in non-Russian schools remained a controversial issue at the highest levels of the regime because it opened the question of a retreat on native-language education and the relaxation of standardized school requirements in other subjects.

In the immediate postwar years, frustrated by the inability of Narkompros to improve the situation, officials of the autonomous republics in the RSFSR appealed directly to the TsK to demand changes in the 1938 arrangements. They emphasized that poor knowledge of the Russian language was responsible for holding back non-Russian students from furthering their education.[72] For example, for the 1945–1946 school year, 840 spaces in higher education were planned for new students in Dagestan, but only 150 students graduated from the tenth grade in the republic, of whom only 70 were non-Russians.[73] Limited changes to the schedules of non-Russian schools were finally adopted in 1946. A "preparatory grade" for seven-year-olds was established in certain regions, mainly where native-language instruction was limited to the primary grades. Narkompros justified the measure by the fact that the four-year system did not sufficiently prepare students for instruction in Russian beginning in the fifth grade.[74] The change nearly doubled the amount of Russian taught in such schools. It was, however, temporary. If indeed native-language instruction were to be extended in such schools beyond the fourth grade, then the new five-year system would become unnecessary.

Insofar as the introduction of the five-year school was limited in scope, the idea of a blanket solution to the problem of Russian instruction remained on the agenda.[75] As the tenth anniversary of the decree of March 13 approached in 1948, the Central Committee apparatus prepared several proposals. N. N. Iakovlev, head of the TsK Schools department from 1943 to 1948, offered the first postwar proposal to substantially change educational policies for all non-Russian schools. His plan would have ended native-language education entirely in non-Russian schools of the autonomous republics and regions after grade four and thus represented a challenge to the very policy of native-language education. It would have "permitted" the union republics to begin instruction of certain subjects—history, geography, mathematics, physics, "and others"—*in* Russian in grades 8–10.[76] Iakovlev's memorandum played upon the theme that lack of Russian was the cause of poor non-Russian student performance and provided the usual statistics of the shortage of non-Russian students in higher education.[77]

Iakovlev's ideas resonated with the RSFSR Minister of Education, A. A. Voznesenskii, who was appointed in January 1948. One of the new Minister's main tasks was to improve the workings of non-Russian schools, which had been strongly attacked in a survey produced by a special TsK Commission upon his appointment.[78] Voznesenskii determined that insufficient class hours were devoted to Russian and proposed that foreign language be made an optional subject in non-Russian schools; Russian then would replace English, French, or German in their curricula.[79] Many officials of the autonomous republics and regions supported this "radical solution" to an "age-old problem," as Voznesenskii described it, because foreign languages were often not taught in their schools anyway because of a lack of teachers. However, when he proposed that non-Russian applicants to higher-educational institutions be exempted from entrance exams in a foreign language, he was opposed by representatives of the union republics at the Cultural Bureau of the Council of Ministers. At a May 13, 1949, meeting, the Ukrainian Deputy Minister of Education called it "an incorrect proposal. . . . I can't understand why this was proposed."[80]

There is thus evidence that the educational authorities of the union republics resisted extensive revisions to the 1938 arrangements, just as they had tempered Russifying tendencies a decade earlier. In 1946, the Deputy Minister of Education of Uzbekistan insisted that time devoted to Russian assigned by the 1938 schedules was sufficient but that better teacher training was needed.[81] A major increase in time devoted to Russian would inevitably mean either burdening non-Russian schoolchildren with more classroom time than their Russian counterparts or reducing time devoted to other subjects, such as foreign language and native language and literature. Many of the union republics did not support such changes. Debates among them on the pages of *Uchitel'skaia gazeta* resulted in disagreement on such issues as whether to start Russian-language instruction in earlier grades. The Minister of Education of Georgia proposed starting Russian in the second grade. Many officials of the autonomous republics opposed this, wanting to start it earlier.[82] After the war, some union republics did tinker with their schedules. Secondary education was extended to eleven years in Georgia in 1946, primarily to create more time for Russian instruction.[83] Azerbaijan introduced Russian as a subject in all schools from the second grade in 1947.[84] The Central Asian republics also gradually introduced Russian instruction in the second or first grades.[85] As early as the 1946–1947 school year, Uzbekistan introduced conversation lessons in the first year in fifty schools as an experiment.[86] But none of these measures retreated on native-language education, something that the radical Russifiers, such as Voznesenskii and Iakovlev, believed to be necessary if Russian language instruction was to improve.

Officials of the autonomous republics and regions supported Voznesenskii and Iakovlev because they felt pressure from parents to improve Russian instruction, which would ensure educational opportunity for their children. As Narkompros specialists explained, some non-Russian parents preferred to send their children to Russian schools because of the poor quality of Russian instruction in non-Russian schools. Local educational administrators would then "take the path of least resistance [and] exhibit the incorrect and harmful tendency of converting Russian from a subject of study to the language of instruction."[87] But this "spontaneous" trend of retreating on native-language education for the sake of Russian instruction also had its firm opponents at the center, who relied on Stalin's closing words in the 1938 decree. F. F. Sovetkin, a leading specialist on Russian-language instruction in non-Russian schools at the RSFSR Academy of Pedagogical Sciences, declared, at a 1948 conference, that "discussions" about switching from native-language instruction to Russian-language instruction were "improper": "[W]e must remember the decision of March 13, 1938. . . . No one has abolished this decision. . . . [T]he Central Committee and Sovnarkom emphasized that the native language is the main [one] for teaching in schools of the non-Russian republics and regions. . . . Upon this basis one may judge how to approach the proposal of moving instruction from the native language to Russian."[88]

Directly or indirectly, Sovetkin's words were heeded. Ten years after the initial decree making Russian instruction obligatory, the radical Russifying line was again rejected. When the TsK apparatus was reorganized in 1948, Iakovlev was replaced by L. S. Dubrovina. In a case unrelated to his duties as Minister of Education, Vozenesenskii was arrested and summarily executed in the 1949 "Leningrad Affair."[89] In contrast to her predecessors, Dubrovina considered the question of native-language education in non-Russian schools to be nonnegotiable. Her proposal to improve the non-Russian schools conspicuously only treated the RSFSR, thus avoiding the potential opposition of the other union republics, and took a number of autonomous republics and regions to task for retreating from full native-language education.[90] The Secretariat considered her proposal, which emphasized improved teacher training and textbook production, on June 24, 1949. But there remained disagreement among regional officials on standardizing new measures. Unable to get agreement from all the parties, Secretary M. A. Suslov decided to leave specific changes to the discretion of the republics themselves.[91] No new TsK decision would be forthcoming.

Some adjustments were soon made in the autonomous republics. In 1950, first-year conversational Russian lessons were introduced in Mordoviia. Sovetkin explained that he and fifteen other specialists had spent six weeks investigating the "special conditions" there. Mordovians had lived long among Russians and hence were more familiar with their language. Mordovian literature was "undeveloped," so time for Russian could be found in the schedule at its expense. Sovetkin emphasized that this was an exception to the March 1938 rule that Russian instruction would normally begin in the second or third grade and that "no one has the right to change the situation." Of course, by this time first-year courses were already becoming the rule, rather than the exception. Other autonomous republics became "envious," in Sovetkin's words, and requested approval for similar changes.[92] The TsK permitted this in each instance that local authorities requested it.[93]

Although all of these changes in class schedules did increase the amount of Russian taught in non-Russian schools, proposals for a more radical shift in policy were defeated after more than a decade of foot dragging and indecision. In large part, this was a consequence of the regime's equally serious commitment to native-language education and the support this principle enjoyed from union-republican officials.

The centralization and standardization of Russian instruction as far as possible was an important goal of officials at the center. It was important not only that Russian be taught to all non-Russian schoolchildren but that it be taught in the same way. Of course, owing to linguistic differences, such standardization was not completely possible; this fact was recognized in the mandate that textbooks be differentiated according to language. But the curriculum, regardless of linguistic differences, was to be issued by Narkompros for all non-Russian schools in the USSR. The amount of time devoted to Russian was to be the same. And the expectations for students' linguistic competency in Russian were to be the same. This insistence on standardization, which dominated the drafting of the

1938 decree on obligatory Russian instruction, created complications in teaching Russian to many non-Russian children because of the very diversity of the USSR.

Equally important, the center did not dedicate sufficient resources to implement the demand that all non-Russians learn Russian. As it tinkered on the margins of class schedules, the regime held fast on native-language education. A more drastic revision of the decree in the direction of Russification, such as Voznesenskii and Iakovlev proposed, required the intervention of Stalin himself, since he was personally responsible for the original decision. As we have seen, no such revision was forthcoming. Perhaps the reason for this is that Stalin withdrew from the more mundane affairs of state in the postwar years. More likely, he did not believe that increased Russification was politically or practically desirable. Only after his death, with the educational reforms of 1958, would the regime move fully in the direction of Russification. After 1958, native-language education in the autonomous republics and regions was reduced, and a new type of school introduced—the non-Russian school with Russian as the language of instruction—in which native language and literature remained only a subject. Non-Russian parents were then officially given the choice of sending their children to Russian-language schools.[94] As Isabelle Kreindler has argued, it was only *after* 1953 that the Russian language "took center stage as most official efforts [were] devoted to expanding its role as *the* language of the 'new historical community—the Soviet people.' "[95]

The contradictory signals sent by the Stalin regime on language policy in non-Russian school reveals that a coherent understanding of the nature of the Soviet multinational state itself remained lacking in these years. On the one hand, the regime promoted Russian as a common language and a force for making the non-Russian peoples "Soviet." On the other hand, the regime was unwilling to retreat on native-language education sufficiently to ensure that young people would learn Russian first and foremost. The conflicting signals from the top frustrated educational officials and parents alike and temper the image of a Stalinist policy of "Russification."

Notes

I appreciate the comments of Yuri Slezkine, David Brandenberger, Terry Martin, Monica Rico, the participants in the conference "Empire and Nation in the Soviet Union," and an editor at Oxford University Press on earlier versions of this article. The research on which it is based was funded by the Berkeley Program in Soviet and Post-Soviet Studies, the Department of History, and the Macarthur-Mellon Program on the Politics of Cultural Identity, Institute of International Studies, University of California, Berkeley.

1. Industrialization, as Ernest Gellner argued, tends to require a standardized, interchangeable population with a "common conceptual currency." Likewise, the rulers of the modern state have an interest in what David Laitin calls "language ration-

alization," because a common language for state institutions reduces the costs of governance and facilitates administrative transparency. See Gellner, *Nations and Nationalism* (Ithaca, N.Y.: Cornell University Press, 1983), p. 34; Laitin, *Language Repertoires and State Construction in Africa* (Cambridge: Cambridge University Press, 1992), pp. 9–12; and Laitin, *Identity in Transition: The Russian-Speaking Population in the Near Abroad* (Ithaca, N.Y.: Cornell University Press, 1998).

2. Rossiiskii tsentr khraneniia i izucheniia dokumentov noveishei istorii (RTsKhIDNI) 17/3/997/103–107 (Protocol of the Politburo 59/166); GARF r-5446/1/144/18 (copy in collection of Council of Peoples' Commissars). The decree was never published, but similar decrees of regional and republican institutions were. See, for example, *Sovetskaia Kirgiziia*, April 12, 1938, p. 1; *Kazakhstanskaia pravda*, April 6, 1938, p. 1; *Pravda vostoka*, April 5, 1938, p. 1. Local versions of the law were mentioned widely in the press and were included in official compendiums of government decrees. See *Kul'turnaia zhizn' v SSSR, 1928–1941. Khronika* (Moscow: Nauka 1976), p. 606, note 6.

3. I examine the problems of native-language education in the non-Russian school in chapter 4 of my Ph.D. dissertation, "Stalin's Nations: Soviet Nationality Policy between Planning and Primordialism, 1936–1953" (University of California, Berkeley, 1999).

4. The term comes from Terry D. Martin, "An Affirmative Action Empire: Ethnicity and the Soviet State," (Ph.D. diss., University of Chicago, 1996).

5. I. Davydov, "O probleme iazykov v prosvetitel'noi rabote sredi natsional'nostei," *Prosveshchenie natsional'nostei*, no. 1 (1929): 26–27. Similarly, G. V. Gasilov, "Vseobshchee obuchenie sredi natsmen (Itogi Vserossiiskogo Soveshchaniia)," G. V. Gasilov, ed., in *Prosveshchenie natsional'nykh men'shinstv v RSFSR* (Moscow: Tsentrizdat, 1928), pp. 38, 43. On Soviet developmental ideas as they applied to language, see Michael G. Smith, *Language and Power in the Creation of the USSR, 1917–1953* (Berlin: Mouton de Gruyter, 1998).

6. RTsKhIDNI 12/1/444/47 (October 1934 memorandum on teaching Russian to non-Russian applicants to higher education).

7. Gosudarstvennyi arkhiv Rossiiskoi federatsii (GARF) r-3316/30;872;116 (June 8, 1937, report on training of non-Russian cadres in Kirgiziia, Kazakhstan, and Bashkiriia).

8. G. V. Gasilov, "O postroenii plana vseobshchego obucheniia sredi natsmen (Stenogramma doklada i zakliuchitel'nogo slova na Soveshchanii Avtonomnykh Respublik v fevrale 1928 goda)," in G. V. Gasilov, ed., *Prosveshchenie natsional'nykh men'shinstv v RSFSR*, p. 210. Similarly, M. Epshtein, "O nekotorykh voprosakh kul'turnoi revoliutsii," *Prosveshchenie natsional'nostei*, no. 7–8 (1931): 52.

9. Class schedules (*uchebnye plany*) indicated the number of hours devoted to each subject weekly. School curricula (*uchebnye programmy*) outlined the content of instruction. In the mid-1930s, the union republics gradually began to bring their class schedules in accordance with those of the RSFSR. On Soviet educational policies in the 1930s in general see Sheila Fitzpatrick, *Education and Social Mobility in the Soviet Union, 1921–1934* (Cambridge: Cambridge University Press, 1979); and Mark Stephen Johnson, "Russian Educators, the Stalinist Party-State and the Politics of Soviet Education, 1929–1939" (Ph.D. diss., Columbia University, 1995).

10. RTsKhIDNI 17/114/833/26. For the 1932 class schedule see N. A. Konstantinov and E. N. Medynskii, *Ocherki po istorii sovetskoi shkoly RSFSR za 30 let* (Moscow: Uchpedgiz, 1948), p. 245.

11. Most Soviet educators rejected the idea of teaching more than two languages in primary school. I. Davydov, "O probleme iazykov," p. 28.

12. *Sbornik prikazov i rasporiazhenii po Narkomprosu RSFSR*, no. 26 (September 10, 1935): 9–11.

13. Ibid., and 1937, no. 18 (September 15): 9, 14–16.

14. "Vserossiiskoe soveshchanie po natsuchebniku," *Prosveshchenie natsional'nostei*, no. 4 (1933): 11.

15. P. Sharenkov, "O prepodavanii russkogo iazyka v shkolakh Armenii," *Prosveshchenie natsional'nostei*, no. 2 (1935): 45–47.

16. F. Krongauz, "Sostoianie i perspektivy vseobucha v natsional'nykh raionakh RSFSR," *Prosveshchenie natsional'nostei*, no. 1 (1934): 26.

17. Unless otherwise specified, "Narkompros" refers to Narkompros RSFSR. Although it was officially designated a "Ministry" in 1946, I retain use of the earlier term for consistency.

18. Territorial units were phased out after 1935; ethnic formations were abolished in 1938. See Roger R. Reese, *Stalin's Reluctant Soldiers: A Social History of the Red Army, 1924–1941* (Lawrence: University Press of Kansas, 1996), chapter 1; and RTsKhIDNI 17/3/997/95–96 (Protocol of the Politburo59/95, March 7, 1938, on abolition of ethnic military units).

19. RTsKhIDNI 17/2/628/121–122 (October 12, 1937).

20. This is the most common view in the literature. See, for example, Gerhard Simon, *Nationalism and Policy toward the Nationalities in the Soviet Union*, trans. Karen and Oswald Forster (Boulder, Colo.: Westview Press, 1991), pp. 150–152; and Yaroslav Bilinsky, "Education of the Non-Russian Peoples in the USSR, 1917–1967: An Essay," *Slavic Review* 27 (1968): 418.

21. "Russkii iazyk v shkolakh Kryma," *Pravda*, January 10, 1938, p. 3; "Russkii iazyk v shkolakh Ukrainy," *Pravda*, March 26, 1938; "Russkii iazyk v karel'skoi shkole," *Pravda*, April 9, 1938; "Zamechatel'noe orudie sotsialisticheskoi kul'tury," *Izvestiia*, April 14, 1938, p. 1. Attacks on bourgeois nationalism in general became a prominent theme in the press starting in September 1937. See Terry D. Martin, "An Affirmative-Action Empire," pp. 858–864.

22. Tsentr khraneniia dokumentov molodezhnykh organizatsii (TsKhDMO) 1/2/134/36 (Uzbekistan), 130 (Checheno-Ingushetiia) (February 16, 1938); 1/2/135/78 (Chuvash ASSR) (February 17, 1938).

23. Under interrogation, Bubnov "admitted" to collaborating with "bourgeois nationalists" in the union republics. See the documents about his arrest in V. F. Koliazin, comp., *"Vernite mne svobodu!" Deateli literatury i iskusstva Rossii i Germanii—zhertvy stalinskogo terrora* (Moscow: Medium, 1997), pp. 78–95.

24. For example, in Dagestan, of 984 primary, incomplete-secondary, and secondary schools, Russian instruction occurred in only 190 schools. In Checheno-Ingushetiia, Russian was taught in only 508 of 1,351 classes. RTsKhIDNI 17/114/833/26–27 (Tiurkin to Orgburo, no date).

25. GARF a-2306/69/2437/12 (Apaverdov and Sovetkin to Tiurkin and Artiukhin, no date); authorship of the document is noted at GARF a-2306/69/2435/6 (January 13, 1938).

26. RTsKhIDNI 17/114/840/76–77 (Tiurkin to Zhdanov and Andreev, no date). Russian instruction began in the non-Russian schools of the RSFSR, and in Ukrainian schools in the Ukrainian SSR, in the second grade. In most schools of the titular

nationalities of other union republics, it began in the third, while in ethnic-minority schools of those republics it often began later.

27. According to Tiurkin, in the 1936–1937 school year almost 60 percent of the teachers in primary schools of in the autonomous republics of the RSFSR lacked a completed secondary education (18,649 of 31,000). RTsKhIDNI 17/114/833/30 (Tiurkin to Orgburo, no date).

28. RTsKhIDNI 17/114/840/79 (Tiurkin to Zhdanov and Andreev, no date).

29. GARF a-2306/69/2437/8–10 (Apaverdov and Sovetkin to Tiurkin and Artiukhin, no date).

30. RTsKhIDNI 17/114/840/79 (Tiurkin to Zhdanov and Andreev, no date).

31. K. A., "Negodnye uchebniki," *Russkii iazyk v shkole*, no. 1 (1938): 61–66.

32. GARF a-2306/69/2437/2 (Apaverdov and Sovetkin to Tiurkin and Artiukhin, no date). For similar evidence, see E. I. Monoszon, "Russkii iazyk v shkolakh natsional'nykh respublik i oblastei," *Sovetskaia pedagogika*, no. 5 (1938): 76–79.

33. RTsKhIDNI 17/114/635/2 (Protocol of the Orgburo 77/2); ibid., 17/114/833/25 (draft law presented to the Orgburo).

34. RTsKhIDNI 17/114/639/13 (Protocol of the Orgburo 81/13); 17/114/840/84–87 (draft law).

35. RTsKhIDNI 17/114/639/13 (Protocol 81/13 of the Orgburo, February 16, 1938).

36. RTsKhIDNI 17/3/997/19 (Protocol of the Politburo 59/96, March 7, 1938). The commission included Zhdanov, Tiurkin, and representatives of the union and autonomous republics.

37. RTsKhIDNI 77/1/857/1 (partial transcript of meeting of Zhdanov Commission, March 8, 1938).

38. Ibid., p. 3.

39. The assumption was that children in the seven-year and the secondary schools would study Russian language and literature over a longer period than those in the primary schools. Georgia was permitted to begin Russian-instruction in the third grade in all types of schools, allegedly because of the large number of secondary schools in the republic.

40. Stalin removed "great" from the phrase "Great Russian people" in the decree's introduction and converted it from a decree of the TsK alone to a joint decree of the TsK and the Council of People's Commissars (SNK). For Stalin's changes see the draft at RTsKhIDNI 17/163/1187/91–97. I thank Oleg Khlevniuk for helping me to differentiate between Stalin's handwriting and that of his secretary, Poskrebyshev.

41. A student with four years of primary education from a non-Russian school in the RSFSR would receive 406 hours of instruction according to the 1938 schedule, whereas the 1935 schedule would have given 432, and the 1937 schedule provided for 612. *Sbornik prikazov i rasporiazhenii po Narkomprosu RSFSR*: 1935, no. 26 (September 10): 9–11; 1937, no. 18 (September 15): 9, 14–16; 1938, no. 16 (August 30): 6–13.

42. RTsKhIDNI 17/114/646/38 (Protocol of the Orgburo 88/193g, June 24, 1938). The Orgburo also rejected a request of the Volga German authorities to abolish the study of English or French and replace it with Russian. RTsKhIDNI 17/114/644/65 (Protocol of the Orgburo 86/343g, May 7, 1938.

43. GARF a-2306/69/2435/78 (April 22, 1938).

44. *Sbornik prikazov i rasporiazhenii po Narkomprosu RSFSR*, no. 16 (1938): 6.

45. According to incomplete figures, as of December 1, 1938, Russian was taught in the second grade of 25 percent of such urban non-Russian schools and 13 percent of rural schools in the RSFSR. Rossiskii gosudarstvennyi arkhiv ekonomiki (RGAE) 1562/17/728/1.

46. GARF r-5446/22/760/90–101 (Narkomfin Zverev to SNK SSSR, June 11, 1938). A copy of the decree of the SNK SSSR appropriating these funds is at ibid., 110.

47. Georgia had requested more than 2.7 million rubles to cover costs connected with the measure; of these, 1.4 million were dedicated to offsetting the costs of increasing the number of school hours. In the end they received 565,000 rubles. GARF r-5446/22/766/2–6 (G. Sturua to SNK SSSR, July 8, 1938, and Zverev's response).

48. Narkompros sent only 145, rather than 220, instructors to the non-Russian regions for special short-term courses for non-Russian teachers. As of the end of July, only 839 of 1000 teachers destined for Central Asia had been sent. Weekly hours for Russian, as for all subjects, differed between rural and urban schools, owing to fact that rural schools operated on a shorter school year and a seven-day, rather than six-day, system. Yearly totals were the same, however, and the differences between the two were soon abandoned. GARF a-259/36/185/4 (Tiurkin to Bulganin [Chair, RSFSR Sovnarkom]), July 26, 1938; RTsKhIDNI 17/114/863/190–194 (Tiurkin to Zhdanov and Andreev, July 13, 1938).

49. RTsKhIDNI 17/114/863/221–226 (Zhukov [Head of Schools Department] to Zhdanov, August 26, 1938).

50. For much of the North Caucasus this was done in late 1937; for other groups, approval was given in the first few months of 1938. For example: RTsKhIDNI 17/116/633/49 (Protocol 75/267g of the Orgburo, November 20, 1937 [Adygei]); ibid. 17/114/635/52 (Protocol 77/320g of the Orgburo, December 26, 1937 [Chechens and Ingush]); GARF r-1235/141/2030127 (Protocol 87 of the Presidium of VTsIK, October 2, 1937 [Dagestan peoples]); RTsKhIDNI 17/114/640/18 (Protocol 82/55g, 56g of the Orgburo, February 22, 1938 [Kalmyks, Nogai, Karachai, Abazins]); 17/114/644/16, Protocol 86/55g of the Orgburo [Crimean Tatars, North Ossetia]).

51. "Itogi proshlogo i zadachi novogo, 1939–1940 uchebnogo goda. Doklad Narkoma prosveshcheniia tov. P. A. Tiurkina na Vserossiiskom soveshchanii aktiva uchitelei i rukovodiashchikh rabotnikov narodnogo obrazovaniia," *Sovetskaia pedagogika*, no. 10 (1939): 23.

52. F. F. Sovetkin, "Rodnoi iazyk v natsional'noi shkole," in F. F. Sovetkin, ed., *Natsional'nye shkoly RSFSR za 40 let* (Moscow: Izdatel'stvo Akademii pedagogicheskikh nauk, 1958), p. 17.

53. In early 1941, the Bashkir authorities petitioned to make changes to the Cyrillic alphabet that had been approved in 1939; Narkompros objected that textbooks in the new alphabet had been printed already. GARF a-2306/69/2755/65–66. The Tatar authorities made adjustments to the new alphabet (approved in 1939) in January 1941 without informing either Narkompros or the Institute of Language and Alphabets of the Academy of Sciences. Ibid., p. 80.

54. RGAE 1562/17/728/4–10, 29. Figures for the Central Asian republics, if they are to be believed, were much better. Ibid., pp. 32–35.

55. T. Chugai, "Russkii iazyk v tadzhikskoi shkole," *Uchitel'skaia gazeta*, May 19 1939, p. 3.

56. The normal practice was for one teacher to teach all subjects in the primary (i.e., first four) grades.

57. L. Kurbanov, "Dve problemy narodnogo obrazovaniia v Turkmenii," *Uchitel'skaia gazeta*, April 9 1939, p. 3.

58. GARF a–259/38/350/31, 36 (report on Russian-language instruction in Buriat schools for 1939–1940).

59. GARF a–259/38/350/63–70 (Kordiukov to SNK RSFSR, June 16, 1940). See also A. Grigor'ian, "Russkii iazyk v nerusskikh shkolakh," *Pravda*, November 16, 1940, p. 3.

60. GARF a–259/38/350/20–21 (V. Potemkin to SNK RSFSR, September 2, 1940).

61. GARF a–259/38/350/13–14 (A. Safronov to SNK RSFSR, September 11, 1940).

62. RTsKhIDNI 17/117/125/42 (Bushuev to Malenkov, July 20, 1940).

63. Ibid., 45 (Timoshenko to Malenkov, May 26, 1940); ibid., 17/116/45/92 (Protocol of the Secretariat 44/415g).

64. RTsKhIDNI 17/125/135/490b (Potemkin to Shcherbakov, June 4, 1943).

65. In October 1941 in the various teacher-training institutions of the RSFSR, there were still few non-Russians. Only 23 Bashkirs, 194 Tatars, 8 Kabardins, and 1 Iakut were studying at Pedagogical and Teachers' Institutes at that time. RTsKhIDNI 17/125/135/52. These were the only figures Narkompros could offer as late as June 1943.

66. GARF a–259/38/350/8, 61 (Tinchurin to SNK RSFSR, October 9, 1940; Vagapov to SNK RSFSR, July 23, 1940).

67. GARF a–259/38/350/16–27 (Potemkin to SNK RSFSR, September 2, 1940).

68. RTsKhIDNI 17/126/3/43–45, 47–48 (Potemkin to Bushuev, March 31, 1941; Bushuev to Andreev, Zhdanov, and Malenkov, April 27, 1941).

69. RTsKhIDNI 17/126/7/1–14 (Memoranda exchanged among Mikhailov, Potemkin, Pivovarova, Andreev, Malenkov, and Shcherbakov, February–April, 1943).

70. RTsKhIDNI 17/126/21/177–178 (Potemkin to Malenkov, September 27, 1945; Iakovlev to Malenkov, October 26, 1945). See also the proposal sent by Aleksandrov, Potemkin, N. Mikhailov, and Iakovlev to Andreev and Shcherbakov, at RTsKhIDNI 17/125/342/7–8.

71. On these changes, see John Dunstan, *Soviet Schooling in the Second World War* (London: Macmillan, 1997), pp. 170–178.

72. RTsKhIDNI 17/126/23–49–51 (North Osetiia, November 1, 1945); GARF a–259/6/3232/145–146 (North Ossetia). RTsKhIDNI 17/126/23/6–9 (Dagestan, June 18, 1945); RTsKhIDNI 17/126/23/11–18 (Kabardin ASSR, October 2, 1945).

73. GARF a–259/6/3258/26–27 (June 14, 1946).

74. GARF a–259/6/3258/1 (Copy of Decree No. 521 of RSFSR Council of Ministers, August 11, 1946). The decree applied to the Kabardin, Dagestan, Buriat-Mongol, Iakut, and North Ossetian autonomous republics and to the Oirot, Cherkess, Adygei, Khakass, and Tuvan autonomous regions.

75. Indeed, the Central Committee rejected the introduction of a preparatory grade in Udmurt schools on the pretext that there were enough Russians in the Udmurt ASSR to provide the necessary environment for Udmurt schoolchildren to learn Russian. RTsKhIDNI 17/125/558/84 (Iakovlev to Zhdanov, September 26, 1947).

76. See the memorandum of Iakovlev to Zhdanov, Suslov, and Popov at RTs-KhIDNI 17/125/558/85–91 (August 5, 1947).

77. RTsKhIDNI 17/125/626/65–70 (Iakovlev and Shepilov to Suslov, February 12, 1948).

78. RTsKhIDNI 17/125/626/142. Both Iakovlev and Voznesenskii played a major role in this survey.

79. RTsKhIDNI 17/132/50/76–79 (Voznesenskii to Malenkov, November 16, 1948). See also his remarks at conference with local officials to discuss improving textbook production for non-Russian schools at GARF a–2306/71/126/28 (July 29, 1948).

80. GARF r–5446/75/7/43 (May 13, 1949). Only the Kazakh Minister of Education supported the idea at this meeting.

81. E. Rachinskaia, "Nashi prakticheskie mery. O prepodavanii russkogo iazyka v uzbekskikh shkolakh," *Uchitel'skaia gazeta*, April 10 1946, p. 3.

82. A series of articles appeared in the newspaper in June, July, and August 1947.

83. "V odinatsatykh klassakh shkol Gruzii," *Uchitel'skaia gazeta*, September 28, 1946, p. 4; V. Kupradze (Minister of Education, GSSR), "Pervyi opyt odinatsatletnykh shkol," December 2, 1948, p. 2. The change required Politburo agreement. RTs-KhIDNI 17/3/1057/19 (Protocol 50/60, March 28, 1946).

84. RTsKhIDNI 17/125/558/150–154.

85. RTsKhIDNI 17/88/919/5–6 (Kazakhstan, 1948); RTsKhIDNI 17/132/369/25 (Kirgiziia, 1950).

86. E. Rachinskaia, "Nashi prakticheskie mery."

87. GARF a–2306/71/365/47 (Memorandum on native and Russian-instruction in RSFSR non-Russian schools, no later than December 23, 1949). In the 1949–1950 school year, 26 percent of non-Russian students in the RSFSR were studying in Russian schools. GARF a–2306/71/779/1 (report on non-Russian schools for the 1949–1950 school year, no date).

88. GARF a–2306/71/120/68–69.

89. By a decision of the Politburo, Voznesenskii was removed for "mistakes in work and incorrect methods of leadership" and replaced by I. A. Kairov. RTsKhIDNI 17/3/1077/23 (Protocol of the Politburo 70/147, July 12, 1949). He suffered because of his politically influential brother, the Politburo member N. A. Voznesenskii, who was one of the main targets of the 1949 purge in Leningrad.

90. The initial draft of her proposal is at RTsKhIDNI 17/132/189/3–11 (no date [1949]). The final version was cosubmitted with Shepilov, RTsKhIDNI 17/118/435/51–58 (June 21, 1949).

91. RTsKhIDNI 17/118/435/64.

92. GARF a–2306/71/769/19–20 (Meeting of Non-Russian Schools Section at the All-Russian Conference of Teachers, August 15, 1950).

93. Suslov ordered the RSFSR Council of Ministers to deal with the issue. GARF a–259/6/8182/17.

94. For the 1958 reforms and their impact see Yaroslav Bilinsky, "The Soviet Education Laws of 1958–59 and Soviet Nationality Policy," *Soviet Studies* 14, no. 2 (1962): 138–157; Brian D. Silver, "Social Mobilization and the Russification of Soviet Nationalities," *American Political Science Review* 68, no. 1 (1974): 45–66; and Silver, "The Status of National Minority Languages in Soviet Education: An Assesment of Recent Changes," *Soviet Studies* 26, no. 1 (1974): 28–40.

95. Isabelle T. Kreindler, "Soviet Language Planning Since 1953," in *Language Planning in the Soviet Union*, ed. Michael Kirkwood (London: Macmillan, 1989), p. 46. According to Kreindler, this shift was "camouflaged by the relatively free atmosphere that prevailed under Khrushchev." Under Brezhnev, that camouflage would disappear completely. Ibid., 51.

". . . It Is Imperative to Advance Russian Nationalism as the First Priority"

Debates within the Stalinist Ideological Establishment, 1941–1945

FACED WITH THE THREAT OF WAR and the need for societal mobilization, Soviet ideologists assumed an increasingly pragmatic, populist posture during the mid- to late 1930s. Prerevolutionary historical imagery was deployed to popularize the reigning Marxist-Leninist ideology, something that led in 1937 to the rehabilitation of Peter the Great, Aleksandr Nevskii, and other beloved heroes, myths, and iconography from the Russian national past. An initiative that at times threatened to compromise the regime's commitment to internationalism and class consciousness, such a volte-face was viewed within the party hierarchy as the most expedient way to mobilize popular patriotic sentiments and loyalty among the USSR's poorly educated citizenry.[1]

The outbreak of hostilities with Germany in 1941 led to an escalation of such Russocentric agitational rhetoric. That said, it would be a mistake to see this as a linear or rationalized process.[2] Instead, the pages of the central press during the first days and weeks of the war reveal a cacophony of contradictory rallying calls, which were only gradually arranged into a more effective propaganda campaign. What can explain the idiosyncrasies of the official line between 1941 and 1945? The fact that relevant archives are either incomplete or inaccessible complicates a conventional approach to the analysis of wartime propaganda dynamics. For this reason, this chapter takes a somewhat unconventional approach to the question by focusing on the evolution of the official prewar historiographic line.

275

I have argued elsewhere that Soviet ideology's assumption of an increasingly Russocentric, etatist posture during the mid- to late 1930s took place without ever fully breaking with the previous two decades of militant proletarian internationalism. This seemingly awkward balancing act represented an attempt within the party hierarchy to popularize its central Marxist convictions with the help of more accessible, non-Marxist thematics drawn from a traditional vocabulary of Russian historical imagery.[3] A policy that might be referred to as "the search of a usable past,"[4] this aspect of the prewar propaganda line was quite populist in essence.

But panic destabilized this peculiar ideological equilibrium after June 22, 1941. The German invasion forced party ideologists to scramble for potent new slogans at a time when there was little encouraging news to report from the front. Returning to their "search for a usable past," wartime ideologists found themselves stymied by disagreements over how best to adapt the post-1937 line to the new context. Stemming from the awkward ideological dualism of the late 1930s, these disagreements belied an emergent schism within the ideological establishment that pitted idealistic "internationalist" holdovers from the prewar period against a new breed of pragmatic neonationalistic etatists.[5] This situation ultimately precipitated a series of open conflicts among party propagandists and "court" historians, in addition to underlying the puzzling instability in the official wartime line.

After beginning with a survey of propaganda during the first year of the war, this chapter then shifts focus to concentrate on the ideologists and historians responsible for the propaganda's articulation. A story of factional infighting and ideological disarray, this analysis reveals the extent to which pragmatism and Russocentrism divided Soviet propagandists after the start of the war. Examining these debates, this chapter explains how ideological zigzags between 1941 and 1943 ultimately coalesced during the last two years of the war into a hegemonic party line that would outlast the Stalinist period itself.

It should come as no great surprise that in the days and weeks following June 22, 1941, one of the principal objectives of Soviet propaganda organs was to reassure the Soviet public that the Red Army could cope with the German invasion. Official communiqués attempted to blunt the news of the surprise attack in a rather striking way, however. For instance, V. M. Molotov, the Soviet Commissar of Foreign Affairs, announced by radio on the first day of hostilities that

> This is *not the first time* that our people have been forced to deal with an arrogant enemy invader. *Long ago* our people responded to Napoleon's campaign against Russia with a patriotic [*otechestvennaia*] war[6] and Napoleon was defeated and came to his end. The same will happen with the vain Hitler, who is proclaiming a new campaign against our country. The Red Army and all of our people will *once again* lead a victorious patriotic war for our motherland, honor, and freedom.[7]

Such a blurring together of the tsarist and Soviet past—unheard of a decade earlier—became commonplace as calls for the defense of the socialist motherland were complemented by discussions of epic martial traditions [*boevye traditsii*], many of which were prerevolutionary in origin. Prominent historians were enlisted to detail the rich military history of the Soviet peoples throughout the ages, particularly Aleksandr Nevskii's 1242 victory over the Teutonic knights and Mikhail Kutuzov's routing of Napoleon in the War of 1812.[8] This writing was complicated, however, by the contradictions involved in rehabilitating figures who were first and foremost representatives of the old regime, and much of the initial work hesitantly focused on battles that featured great leaders, rather than on the great leaders themselves. Nevertheless, the priorities of the campaign were clear; as A. M. Dubrovskii has recently noted, "the pocket-sized paperback and pamphlet describing outstanding Russian military leaders—something which would fit into a political officer's field kit—was the most widespread of all historical genres during these years."[9] Although much of this initial publishing revolved around Russian themes, some historians made a considerable effort to develop agitational literature for the other Soviet ethnic groups, as well.[10]

Such rousing talk of military valor was aimed at civilians on the home front as much as it was at soldiers in the field. After all, party authorities knew that there was unrest among industrial workers, even in Moscow. Worse, peasants in the provinces were reported to be remarkably sanguine about the German advance: "What's it to us? It'll only be bad for the Jews and communists. There might even be a bit more order [*mozhet bol'she poriadka budet*]."[11] Rumors cast non-Russian ethnic groups as even being prepared to greet the Nazi forces with open arms.[12] Such sentiments forced propaganda organs to search for broader themes with more universal appeal. Traditional rallying calls revolving around "Soviet" themes (e.g., socialism, the personality cult) were promptly deemphasized in favor of a new repertoire of slogans that played upon emotions ranging from pride and revenge to the desire to protect friends, family, and motherland. Jeffrey Brooks notes that "patriotism and national identity" became key issues, as well.[13] Not coincidentally, I. V. Stalin spent considerable time during his first wartime speech on July 3 addressing precisely these themes, lauding in particular the friendship of the Soviet peoples and warning some twelve different Soviet ethnic groups of Hitler's plans to enslave them.[14]

But if mention of the "Friendship of the Peoples" was quite common during the opening months of the war, appeals to Soviet patriotism tended to favor Russian-oriented themes. Not only were most of the tsarist-era heroes and battles highlighted in the press implicitly Russian, but, a month into the war, *Pravda* explicitly referred to "the great Russian people" as *primus inter pares*, "the first among the equal peoples of the USSR."[15] Such statements would continue during the coming months. Despite impressions to the contrary, however, it would be incorrect to conclude that these tendencies stemmed from central directives declaring Russian nationalist themes to be the order of the day. Instead, the inertia of prewar Russocentrism and the limited availability of inspirational literature on the non-Russian peoples apparently produced these results by default.[16] This tendency, in turn, was encouraged by the fact that much of the desperate fighting

was taking place on Russian soil. In an absence of central directives, state publishing—as loath as ever to innovate—ritualistically combined old clichés with
snippets of new wartime speeches, while waiting for initiative from above.[17]

This situation clarified itself only five months into the war during the twenty-
fourth anniversary of the October 1917 revolution. Stalin's public statements at
such events were typically considered weathervanes for determining the "correct"
line, and, for those looking for direction, his November 7 Red Square speech was
hardly subtle. Urging his audience to "draw inspiration from the valiant example
of our great ancestors," Stalin rattled off a long list of exclusively Russian prerevolutionary heroes who were to define patriotic conduct during the war: Aleksandr Nevskii, Dmitrii Donskoi, Kuz'ma Minin, Dmitrii Pozharskii, Aleksandr
Suvorov, and Mikhail Kutuzov.[18] Taking prewar tendencies to the extreme, all
of Stalin's examples were defenders of the old regime, if not outright counterrevolutionaries. Authoritative nonetheless, Stalin's pantheon of heroes was reprinted in its original order over and over during the coming years.[19] Attendant
pamphlets and curricular materials followed in massive numbers early in 1942.[20]

Although few new heroes were ever added to Stalin's original Soviet Olym-
pus,[21] his November 7 association of "our great ancestors" with an exclusively
Russian cast of characters spurred a different genre of agitation. For instance,
Em. Iaroslavskii, a senior party historian, quickly published an article in *Pravda*
notable for its nationalistic language and content. Announcing that the Bolsheviks
were the "lawful heirs to the Russian people's great and honorable past," the
article constructed an analogy between the party's leading role in the state and
the Russian people's position "at the head of the other peoples of the USSR."
Needless to say, this linear relationship between the Russian people and Bolshevism whitewashed other ethnic groups' contributions to the society and blurred
the difference between Russian empire and Soviet socialist union.[22] Weeks later,
the Central Committee ideology chief, A. S. Shcherbakov, made a similar statement about the war effort: "the Russian people—the first among equals in the
USSR's family of peoples—are bearing the main burden of the struggle with the
German occupiers."[23] Lowell Tillett summarizes such pronouncements well:
"Whatever the fine points of distinction may have been between the new Soviet
patriotism and old Russian nationalism, they were soon lost sight of in the great
emergency. . . . Without much regard for what Marx or Lenin had said on the
subject [of patriotism], Soviet ideologists called for emphasis on prerevolutionary
military greatness—which meant Russian greatness, almost to the exclusion of
the other nationalities."[24]

By early summer 1942, the martial traditions campaign had worked itself into
a frenzy. In the press, Iaroslavskii and G. F. Aleksandrov, the head of the Central
Committee's Directorate of Propaganda and Agitation (Agitprop), repeatedly
stressed the importance of popular heroes and military history in stimulating
patriotic sentiments. A *Pravda* editorial in the fall announced that such inspirational stories were a "mighty fighting weapon, forged and honed in the past for
the great battles of the present and future."[25] At roughly the same time, new

military decorations named after epic martial heroes like Suvorov, Nevskii, and Kutuzov were unveiled, their symbolic value confirmed by the simultaneous appearance of articles profiling their namesakes in the central press.[26]

Although the swelling prominence of a rather nationalistic propaganda line between 1941 and 1942 is clear in hindsight, it is also important to acknowledge the nuances of the developing situation. One commentator wisely cautions that Russocentrism was only "one of the straws in the wind";[27] other dimensions of wartime propaganda revolved around military clashes, individual acts of heroism, the home front, the allied powers, atrocities committed by German forces, and the bankruptcy of Nazi ideology. Perhaps more important, it would be inaccurate to conclude that the emerging line eclipsed earlier calls for work on non-Russian martial traditions during the first several years of the war. Not only did non-Russian subjects appear from time to time in the central press (and with greater frequency in the republican dailies), but authorities called repeatedly for *increases* in the production of propaganda material concerning the non-Russian peoples. Criticizing republican publishing houses for "an almost total lack of literature on national [that is, non-Russian] heroes," the authors of a 1942 article in the prominent journal *Propagandist* pointed to the fact that, among these peoples, "there exists a burning desire to know more about the heroism of their ancestors and about the participation of their sons in patriotic wars of liberation."[28] In other words, the growing Russocentrism should be considered more of a tendency during the first years of the war than an articulate central line.

Why did wartime agitational efforts zigzag so wildly from Russian nationalist rhetoric to an interest in non-Russian martial traditions? Inconsistent leadership and a renewed "search for a usable past" among historian-ideologists probably provides part of the answer. In the wake of Iaroslavskii's and Aleksandrov's fervent articles on history and patriotism, many historians looked to the Russian imperial past for inspirational imagery and historical parables. Many found Stalin's November 7 speech and the daily content of the party press to indicate that a wide variety of names from the tsarist era now qualified for rehabilitation, even if they had had nothing to do with revolutionary movements or Marxist theory. Amateur historians submitted articles to the periodical *Istoricheskii zhurnal* on tsarist generals like A. P. Ermolov and M. D. Skobelev[29] and called for the abandonment of the prewar period's fascination with rebels like Ernel'ian Pugachev, Sten'ka Razin, and Shamil'. After all, argued Kh. G. Adzhemian, historiography containing unpatriotic or anti-Russian dimensions ought to be superseded by a new emphasis on "great power" [*velikoderzhavnye*] traditions, a proposal that was suspiciously reminiscent of the tsarist era.[30]

Established historians also took the changes to be indicative of a new official line. A. V. Efimov and A. I. Iakovlev—both prominent specialists on the modern period—began recruiting scholars in 1942 for the preparation of a new volume on historiography that promised to detail a more patriotic "national" line. Rumors hinted that they were even flirting with the idea of rehabilitating P. N. Miliukov, V. O. Kliuchevskii, and other non-Marxist prerevolutionary historians.[31] S. K. Bushuev's biography of M. D. Gorchakov—nominated in 1943 for a coveted Stalin prize—popularized a figure known as much for his participation in the crushing of nineteenth-century Polish and Hungarian popular revolts as for his Russian patriotism and strong anti-German sentiments. Later in the war, the same author would call for the reversal of what he referred to as the 1930s' "national nihilism," something that in practice apparently required the reassessment of such odious figures as A. A. Arakcheev, M. N. Katkov, and K. P. Pobedonostsev,[32] as well as the doctrine of Slavophilism. According to Bushuev, much of the existing historiography on tsarist foreign policy—especially that on Alexander I and the "Gendarme of Europe," Nicholas I—needed to be revised in order to present events in a more positive light.[33] Nineteenth-century Polish revolts, in turn, were to be treated less enthusiastically in view of the geopolitical "inviability" of the modern Polish state.[34] If Bushuev was quite militant, his colleague Iakovlev was considerably more radical, as is evident from his remarks during a 1944 discussion of the public school history curriculum:

> It seems to me that it is imperative to advance Russian nationalism as the first priority. We respect the [non-Russian] ethnicities [narodnosti] who have entered into our union and we relate to them with love. Still, Russian history was done by Russians and it seems to me that every textbook about Russia ought to be constructed with this leitmotif—what precisely from this point of view [was necessary] for the Russian people's successes, for their development, for understanding the suffering they endured, and for characterizing their general path. . . . The theme of national development so brilliantly evident throughout Solov'ev's[35] and Kliuchevskii's courses on Russian history ought to be passed on to every textbook editor. It seems to me that combining this with an interest in the hundred ethnicities which entered into our state is incorrect. . . . The basic idea is clear: we Russians want the history of the Russian people and the history of Russian institutions, in Russian conditions. It seems to me that celebrating the fact that the Kirgiz slaughtered Russians at some point or that Shamil' was able to halt Nicholas I would be inappropriate in a textbook.[36]

Although an outgrowth of prewar Russocentrism, Bushuev's and Iakovlev's nationalist sentiments were nevertheless unprecedented in their disregard for class analysis and the "Friendship of the Peoples" ethic.

If somewhat less Russocentric, other historians took the etatism of the 1930s to new heights. P. P. Smirnov and E. V. Tarle personified this tendency insofar as they tended to treat the subject of territorial expansionism under the old regime with a high degree of pragmatism. Acknowledging that Soviet historians' longstanding critique of tsarist-era colonialism had played a crucial role in the toppling of the old regime in 1917, Smirnov argued that the present war now required historiographical exigencies of its own. In particular, Smirnov declared that it was time to recognize the accomplishments of those who had built Russia into a "great power" [derzhava] capable of resisting Hitler.[37] E. V. Tarle went somewhat further in a series of lectures in Moscow, Leningrad, and Saratov, proposing to "clarify" the meaning of "Observations" made in 1934 by Stalin, A. A. Zhdanov, and S. M. Kirov that had labeled imperial Russia both "the Gendarme of Europe" and a "prison of the peoples." These critiques, of tsarist foreign and colonial policy, respectively, had long been mainstays of Soviet historiography. Now, however, Tarle argued that the gendarme thesis required nuancing in light of a recent article of Stalin's in the journal *Bol'shevik*. After all, Stalin had apparently argued that since *all* nineteenth-century European powers had been forces of reaction, St. Petersburg was not to be considered uniquely counterrevolutionary. Accordingly, if nineteenth-century tsarist foreign policy was no longer to be considered distinctive or egregious in comparison with that of Russia's neighbors, historians should cease referring to the Romanov empire as *the* Gendarme of Europe.[38] While not challenging the "prison of the peoples" paradigm as directly as the gendarme thesis, Tarle agreed with Smirnov that territorial expansion under the tsars had significantly enhanced the USSR's ability to defend its aggregate population against the German threat. This "territoriality thesis" won Tarle considerable acclaim, despite the fact that it contradicted a long-standing official condemnation of tsarist-era colonialism.[39] While neither Smirnov nor Tarle was blunt enough to declare that "the end justifies the means," their efforts to put the empire's colonial past in perspective departed markedly from the tenets that had guided Soviet historiography more than over two decades.

If historians like Iakovlev, Bushuev, and Tarle expanded upon the Russocentric, etatist tendencies of the post-1937 line, it should be emphasized that many others hesitated to stray from prewar historiographic positions. Although it is somewhat awkward to refer to such scholars as true "internationalists," insofar as their writing tended to advance Russians' claims to ethnic primacy,[40] equally visible in their work was a stubborn reluctance to entirely abandon class analysis.[41] Perhaps more important, many of them were also engaged in the development of historiography on the non-Russian peoples. The first major wartime study to emerge from these efforts, A. M. Pankratova's *History of the Kazakh SSR from the Earliest Times to Our Days*,[42] published in 1943, epitomized the sentiments of these scholars. "In our opinion," recalled Pankratova's collaborator N. M. Druzhinin decades later, "it was necessary to highlight the heroic past of not just the Russian people, but of the Kazakh people [as well,] among whom we lived and with whom we amicably worked."[43]

A controversial project from beginning to end, *History of the Kazakh SSR* ultimately determined the fate of the entire genre of wartime propaganda oriented around non-Russian history. Written in Alma-Ata by thirty-three scholars of local and all-Union prominence, the volume was earnestly advertised by its editorial brigade as an account of Russo-Kazakh cooperation in the struggle against tsarism that provided needed material on Kazakh martial traditions. A response to *Propagandist's* call in 1942 for work on non-Russian themes, this volume was also a revisionist treatment of Central Asian history. In particular, the book denied the applicability of the so-called lesser evil theory[44] to the tsarist colonization of Kazakhstan by contrasting the violence of its military conquest to the more "progressive" assimilation of Ukraine and Georgia. Such a principled position was necessary, according to Pankratova, because "casting tsarist colonizers as the bearers of progress and freedom would mean that we would be unable to describe the Great October Revolution as the liberator of our country's peoples." Introducing the volume with a largely negative characterization of tsarist colonial policy, Pankratova and her editorial brigade devoted a significant portion of their work to an examination of an array of revolts against St. Petersburg's rule.[45]

As one of the first major pieces of post-1937 scholarship to concern a non-Russian republic, *History of the Kazakh SSR* was nominated for a Stalin prize in 1943 as soon as it rolled off the presses. Selected to review the book for the Stalin prize committee, A. I. Iakovlev composed what was generally a favorable review. Nevertheless, he objected to tsarist colonial policy's being described in terms similar to those used to discuss the cross-border raiding that emanated from the Khiva and Kokand emirates. Contending that imperial expansion had been defense oriented, justifiable, and therefore implicitly "progressive," he also questioned the emphasis placed on Kazakh resistance to tsarist rule. Generally, he concluded, the book demonstrated "a lack of good will, not just in relation to the policies of the Russian imperial state, but in relation to the Russian people themselves."[46]

Because Iakovlev's review threatened *History of the Kazakh SSR*'s Stalin prize nomination, Pankratova and her colleagues protested directly to V. P. Potemkin at the history section of the Stalin prize committee late in 1943. Arguing that Iakovlev's objections were logically unsound and that their book contributed to the ongoing war effort by boosting Kazakh morale, Pankratova cited Lenin,[47] Stalin,[48] the 1934 "Observations," and various other party directives on historiography in her brigade's defense.[49] Elaborate objections were made in particular to Iakovlev's classification of Russian imperial expansion in Kazakhstan as progressive and defense oriented. According to Pankratova, Iakovlev was incorrect in thinking that, if the gathering of Russian lands under Ivan Kalita, Ivan III, and Ivan IV was to be considered progressive, so too should territorial expansion in the seventeenth through the nineteenth centuries. To illustrate her point, she cited a simplistic statement on the issue that Iakovlev had supposedly made at a recent meeting: "the Russian tsars, according to the inevitable laws of history, followed the general Russian tendency of supporting the security of the Russian borders and the Russian population." Such apologetic treatments of tsarist expansionism, according to Pankratova, came close to contradicting Lenin's unambiguously negative evaluation of colonialism as an economic system. Justifying their book's stress on revolts against the tsarist colonial administration, Pankratova explained that Kazakh resistance to Russian tsarism often turned into revolts against local indigenous elites, thus indicating that ethnic consciousness was inseparable from class consciousness. In regard to the book's alleged pitting of Kazakh against Russian, she suggested that Iakovlev had overlooked documented cooperation between the two peoples in the form of Kazakh support of Russian rebels such as Pugachev and Russian peasant participation in indigenous Kazakh revolts. Pankratova concluded by denouncing Iakovlev's review for contradicting official policy, "as it deals a blow to the friendship of the peoples, denying the peoples of the USSR their martial traditions and heroes and even their right to their own history."[50]

Although Potemkin probably read the letter from Pankratova and her colleagues, he did not take any steps to restore the book's Stalin prize nomination. This failure to react frustrated Pankratova enough for her to ask Aleksandrov and P. N. Fedoseev at Agitprop for a reassessment of the book early in 1944. Aleksandrov's refusal was instructive: "(1) the book is anti-Russian, as the authors' sympathies are on the side of those revolting against tsarism and there is no effort to exonerate Russia; (2) the book is written without acknowledgment of the fact that Kazakhstan stood outside of history and that it was Russia that brought [the Kazakhs] into the ranks of the historical peoples."[51]

Furious with this undisguised display of Russian chauvinism, Pankratova protested to Zhdanov, detailing not only issues concerning *History of the Kazakh SSR*, but also denouncing rivals, including Iakovlev, Efimov, Bushuev, Adzhemian, and the entire Agitprop administration. She argued that, while revising M. N. Pokrovskii's[52] wholly negative characterization of Russian colonialism was necessary, it was questionable whether the valor or Russian ethnicity of certain infamous tsarist officials automatically justified a reappraisal of their activities. She also questioned whether it was legitimate to deny the heroism of non-Russian rebels just because they had distinguished themselves while resisting tsarist colonialism or Russian ethnic dominance: "I am especially worried by this last tendency, which could have major consequences of the most negative kind among the peoples of our motherland. In all the Soviet republics at the present time, books are being written intensively about the individual peoples. Interest has increased dramatically [among non-Russians] concerning their national history, their heroic past, and all those who have fought for freedom and independence." She argued that books like *History of the Kazakh SSR* were capable of discussing the realities of tsarist colonialism and the military traditions of the non-Russian peoples, while at the same time propagandizing "the friendship of the peoples and [their] respect and love for the great Russian people." Begging Zhdanov to reverse Aleksandrov's decision, Pankratova warned that the retraction of the Stalin prize nomination "would deeply insult the Kazakh republic's leadership . . . one can't deny the Kazakh people their heroic martial traditions and declare them to be a people without a history."[53] Several weeks later, she appealed to Shcherbakov, phrasing her argument somewhat differently in terms of how her book helped "to propagandize the Soviet peoples' martial and heroic traditions in the national units of the Red Army."[54]

Indicative of the ongoing struggle on the Soviet historical front, Pankratova's efforts to save her monograph in early 1944 were parried by Aleksandrov and the Agitprop administration, who were moving to outflank their critics and regain control over the official line. According to established practice, this was to be accomplished through the convening of a conference where contested issues would be debated and resolved. Conclusions would then be disseminated through the publication of the conference's proceedings in the journal *Pod znamenem mark-sizma*. Apparently, the discussion was to be wide ranging—various accounts suggest that both *History of the Kazakh SSR* and Tarle's territoriality thesis were to be publicly debated. "Among propagandists and teachers," according to one rumor, "[people] have begun talking about a 'reappraisal' of the most important and commonly accepted concepts in the historical sciences. Of particular interest is whether the [1934] 'Observations' of Comrades Stalin, Kirov and Zhdanov on historical questions have become 'obsolete' [*ustareli*]." Oddly enough, despite the fact that several Kazakh specialists traveled all the way to Moscow in spring 1944 in order to defend their work, Agitprop failed to convene even an informal discussion.[55]

If Pankratova's initial complaints earlier that year had had little visible effect on the state of affairs in the history profession, a letter of hers in mid-May finally caught the party hierarchy's attention. Why this letter elicited a response after so many calls had gone unanswered is unclear, perhaps the reason was the letter's addressees (Stalin, Zhdanov, G. M. Malenkov, and Shcherbakov), its length (nearly twenty typewritten pages), its ribald content,[56] or its perfect timing.[57] In any case, Pankratova reiterated in this new letter that Agitprop was mismanaging the historical front at a time when popular interest in history was rising at an unprecedented rate. As a result, not only were historians indulging in what she considered to be non-Marxist heresies, but both the novelist A. N. Tolstoi and the film director S. M. Eisenstein had been allowed to seriously exaggerate Ivan the Terrible's populist tendencies, a contagion that had affected artistic representations of Alexander I and A. A. Brusilov, as well.[58] According to Pankratova, schoolchildren were particularly confused by the valorization of Brusilov, as this World War I general's claim to fame was based on his defense of a regime that Lenin was plotting to overthrow! Frustrated by years of indecision concerning the official line, Pankratova asked the Central Committee to clarify things through the convocation of a meeting to discuss not only *History of Kazakh SSR*, but the state of the discipline as a whole.[59]

Pankratova was not the only one frustrated by the status quo, however. Having failed to convene the Agitprop conference, Aleksandrov proposed correctives of his own in a series of internal memos during March and April 1944. Although he was careful to balance his analysis with criticism of Iakovlev and Adzhemian, much of his rhetoric was directed against historians such as Pankratova, who were resisting the Russocentric line. Broadsiding *History of the Kazakh SSR*, a similar volume entitled *Sketches on the History of Bashkiriia*, and a number of recent textbooks, Aleksandrov hissed that these works were not only unpatriotic but bore all the telltale signs of ideological heresy:

In Soviet historical literature, the influence of the Pokrovskii school [which condemned the tsarist experience] is still very evident. In textbooks on [the

history of] the USSR and different historical works, there is insufficient illu-
mination of the most important moments in our people's heroic past and the
lives and deeds of outstanding Russian military commanders, scientists, and
state figures.

The influence of the Pokrovskii school also finds its expression in the fact
that the non-Russian peoples' unification with Russia is appraised as an absolute
evil by historians examining it independently of the concrete circumstances in
which it took place. The interrelationship between the Russian people and the
other peoples of Russia is looked at solely in the context of tsarist colonial
policies. In the *History of the Kazakh SSR* and *Sketches on the History of Bashkiriia*,
the history of Kazakhstan and Bashkiriia is limited, by and large, to the history
of Kazakh and Bashkir revolts against Russia.[60]

Aleksandrov's memo concluded with sentiments similar to Pankratova's—the
time had come for the Central Committee to intervene—although he envisioned
the latter body simply ratifying recommendations being prepared by Agitprop.

If these memos reveal considerable tension within the Soviet ideological establishment during March and April 1944, Pankratova's explosive letter to Stalin,
Zhdanov, Malenkov, and Shcherbakov in May drove Aleksandrov into a frenzy.
He quickly returned fire with a volley of ad hominem attacks entitled "On Serious
Shortcomings and Anti-Leninist Mistakes in the Work of Several Soviet Historians," a memo coauthored with two Agitprop insiders, Fedoseev and P. N. Pos-
pelov. Echoing earlier salvos, this fusillade was aimed not only at Pankratova and
her "unpatriotic" colleagues but at Iakovlev, Tarle, and Adzhemian, who had
allegedly broken with Marxist historical materialism in their promotion of what
was described as "Great Power chauvinism" [*velikoderzhavnyi shovinizm*] and even
"restorationist" [*restavratorskie*] views![61] If earlier Aleksandrov had tended to side
with this latter group against Pankratova, by May 1944 his strategy had changed.
By declaring "a plague on both your houses," he apparently hoped to style himself
as nonpartisan and capable of correcting excesses at either end of the polarized
discipline.

But Aleksandrov's loss of control over the historians had not gone unnoticed,
and the Central Committee instead moved to convene a history conference of its
own during the early summer 1944.[62] Malenkov noted during his keynote speech
that "the Central Committee discussed the issue and decided that it was imperative to meet with leading scholars in order to talk about controversial issues and
develop [a set of] *principal positions for all historians*."[63] Despite this ambitious agenda,
however, the conference turned out rather inconclusively. Although Shcherbakov's continuous presence as chair was complemented by the occasional appearance of Malenkov or A. A. Andreev, truly authoritative commentary from the
party hierarchs was brief and unmemorable. The futility of the enterprise was
compounded by the fact that the historians bickered fiercely among themselves,
not only during the sessions but behind the scenes, as well, via written appeals to
Shcherbakov and Stalin.[64] Disbanding early in July after five sessions, the confer-

ence participants left with the understanding that the Central Committee would make an announcement about the state of affairs on the historical front in short order.[65]

But such a panacea never appeared. Asked to compose a Politburo resolution that would mend the ideological schism, Aleksandrov drafted a document that essentially repeated his partisan observations from earlier that spring. Unsatisfied, Shcherbakov rejected it.[66] The initiative for the project then shifted to Zhdanov, who had just arrived in Moscow from Leningrad and who had missed the conference entirely.[67] Over the next several months, Zhdanov would write and rewrite a series of theses on the subject, consulting repeatedly with Stalin, the conference stenogram, and the various recommendations made by Aleksandrov and Pankratova. While preserving Agitprop's conceptualization of the problem at hand as a question of two non-Marxist heresies—a "bourgeois-monarchist" Miliukovite school (Efimov, Iakovlev, Tarle) and a "sociologizing" Pokrovskiian school (Pankratova et al.)—Zhdanov proved to be considerably more critical of the former than the latter.[68] In particular, he objected to the indiscriminate blurring of tsarist and Soviet history.[69] After a number of redactions, however, work on the draft ground to a halt before it could ever see light as a formal statement on party ideology. Puzzlingly, the results of this major conference were limited to a minor Central Committee resolution, a speech, and the publication of a handful of book reviews during the coming year.[70]

This failure to issue a formal resolution on the history conference confounded historians in 1944–1945 and has remained a source of considerable debate in the years since.[71] Pankratova may have alienated her patrons early that fall by a major lapse in judgment.[72] Stalin may have wanted to protect his client Tarle[73] or to focus exclusively on defeating Hitler.[74] Equally likely, however, the Red Army's expulsion of German troops from the Soviet heartland during summer 1944 simply reduced the need for mobilizational exigencies like the promotion of non-Russian martial traditions.[75] Perhaps non-Russian history itself (and with it, *History of the Kazakh SSR*) had simply lapsed into obsolescence?

Circumstantial evidence seems to favor the latter argument, according to which the party hierarchy simply lost interest in non-Russian historical subjects after the Red Army crossed over the frontier into Poland in July 1944. Particularly revealing is the Central Committee's prompt passage of a series of minor resolutions between 1944 and 1945 that criticized wartime propaganda in Kazakhstan, Tatarstan, and Bashkiriia.[76] In language similar to Iakovlev's critique of *History of the Kazakh SSR*, these resolutions condemned scholarly, artistic, and literary activity that represented these regions' experience under medieval Mongol rule as a "renaissance" and discussed their rebelliousness under the Russian tsars in congratulatory terms. Such rulings suggest that the party hierarchy had decided that it was time to put an end to republican historical sloganeering that was promoting non-Russian heroes at the Russian people's expense. Shortly thereafter, Aleksandrov attacked the wartime publication of a medieval Tatar epic, claiming that "nationalistic ideas foreign to the Tatar people are expressed in the tale *Idegei*. In it, a powerful feudal lord of the Golden Horde and an enemy of the Russian people is described as a national hero." Comparing Idegei (alt. Edigei) to the notorious fourteenth-century khans Mamai and Tokhtamysh, in so far as he had "aimed to revive the former might of the Golden Horde through campaigns into Russian lands," Aleksandrov bitterly scolded those who had authorized the epic's publication.[77] During the first postwar years, the Central Committee would criticize numerous other republican and province-level [*obkom*] party organizations for similar wartime publications.[78]

The war, then, is key to understanding the waning fortunes of the non-Russian genre of historical propaganda. If such subjects had been encouraged within certain circles between 1941 and 1943, after mid-1944 they were savaged one by one for trafficking in non-Russian nationalism and for ignoring the age-old symbiosis that had purportedly united the non-Russian peoples with their Russian brethren. In other words, once the exigencies of 1941–1943 had faded, party ideology reverted to an extreme version of the post-1937 line on the Russian people's ethnic primacy within Soviet society. This agenda was confirmed by Stalin early in the postwar period in his infamous toast to the Russian people at a Kremlin reception for Red Army commanders:

> Comrades, allow me to raise one more final toast.
> I would like to raise a toast to the health of our Soviet people and, most of all, to the Russian people. [*Loud, continuous applause, shouts of "hooray!"*]
> I drink, most of all, to the health of the Russian people because they are the most outstanding nation of all the nations entering into the Soviet Union.
> I raise a toast to the health of the Russian people because they earned general recognition during the war as the Soviet Union's leading force among all the peoples of our country.
> I raise a toast to the health of the Russian people not just because they are the leading people, but because they have a clear mind, hardy character and patience. . . . [79]

Implicitly contrasting the loyalty of the Russian people to that of the rest of Soviet society, Stalin's May 1945 toast ratified the late wartime restoration of an ethnic hierarchy and in fact encouraged propagandists to focus *exclusively* on the Russian people and their historic greatness during the early postwar years.

As well as a question of timing and exigency, the wane of wartime non-Russian historical propaganda was also a function of the increasing pervasiveness of Russocentrism in Soviet society between 1941 and 1945—a dynamic that at times resembled a vicious circle. Official pronouncements between 1941 and 1942 that described the Russian people as the first among equals and the USSR's principle fighting force contributed to a high level of Russian-oriented propaganda and press coverage. Over time, this rhetoric gradually eclipsed discussion of non-Russian heroism, allowing the prevailing wisdom to develop on the popular level that the Russian people were bearing the horrendous cost of the struggle alone.[80]

Such sentiments within the party hierarchy reinforced the imperative of Russo-centric propaganda,[81] precipitating initiatives that in turn further exacerbated the situation on the ground. Discussion of non-Russian heroism in the press might have slowed this escalation of Russian exceptionalism,[82] but neglect of such subjects during the late 1930s meant that little was ready for release when the opportunity presented itself between 1941 and 1942. Although some sophisticated material like *History of the Kazakh SSR* and *Sketches on the History of Bashkiriia* became available in 1943, by that time it was already too late.[83] What's more, the inertia of wartime Russocentrism and the fading exigencies of war meant that, by 1944, such work was beginning to be viewed within the party hierarchy as not only increasingly irrelevant but misguided. As a result, despite the concerted effort of a number of highly placed ideologists and court historians like Pankratova, the post-1937 line emerged from the wartime experience much more Russocentric and particularist than it had been before the outset of the conflict.

In sum, if the first appearance of Russocentric etatism as an articulate ideological line dates to the second half of the 1930s, this sloganeering underwent a profound transformation in the four years following June 22, 1941. Prewar propaganda had existed within a quarter-century's continuum of ubiquitous proletarian internationalist rhetoric. Despite the fact that the latter themes had waned over the course of the mid to late 1930s, they nevertheless remained intrinsic elements of prewar official discourse. In the wake of the German invasion, such a contradiction in the official line divided party ideologists from court historians. Some pragmatists promoted a nativist, nationalistic genre of propaganda—a seemingly heretical move that dovetailed with the Soviet state's iconoclastic alliance with former adversaries within the capitalist world and the Church. Other idealists remained stubbornly committed to the official line that had been developed in the late 1930s and actively participated in the wartime mobilization of both the Russian and *non-Russian* peoples. At times, debate was remarkably polarized and acrimonious as neonationalists clashed with their "internationalist" rivals. This schism ultimately confounded even the party hierarchy itself in the wake of the 1944 history conference.

Although the party leadership never directly resolved this impasse, a number of wartime dynamics ultimately contributed to an oblique resolution of the crisis. The fading imperative of non-Russian propaganda and the heavy atmosphere of wartime Russocentrism meant that, by 1944, the position advanced by Pankratova and her allies had lapsed into obsolescence. Although these scholars might have found support in Zhdanov's theses on historiography, the party hierarchy's failure to issue a ruling on the conference instead allowed a series of minor Central Committee, republican, and obkom resolutions to solidify the now unambiguously Russocentric line. The title of Pankratova's first postwar book—*The Great Russian People*—epitomizes with bitter irony her acceptance of this new historiographical orthodoxy as much as it indicates the postwar agenda for the historical discipline as a whole.[84]

Notes

The title of this chapter is derived from a statement made by A. I. Iakovlev, a prominent Soviet historian, to a group of educators in 1944 (see note 36). Research was supported in part by a grant from the International Research and Exchanges Board (IREX), with funds provided by the National Endowment for the Humanities and the United States Department of State, which administers the Russian, Eurasian, and East European Research Program (Title VIII). The article likewise benefited from communications with A. M. Dubrovskii, Serhy Yekelchyk, Maureen Perrie, Jeffrey Rossman, Katia Dianina, Barbara Keys, George Enteen, and the editors of this volume. Conclusions and errors contained herein remain the sole responsibility of the author.

1. D. L. Brandenberger and A. M. Dubrovsky, " 'The People Need a Tsar:' the Emergence of National Bolshevism as Stalinist Ideology, 1931–1941," *Europe-Asia Studies* 50, no. 5 (1998): 873–892; David Brandenberger, "The 'Short Course' to Modernity: Stalinist History Textbooks, Mass Culture and the Formation of Popular Russian National Identity, 1934–1955" (Ph.D. diss., Harvard University, 1999), especially chapters 2–3. Chauvinistic aspects of this campaign, which have been frequently used to label Stalin, A. A. Zhdanov and others as closet Russian nationalists, are in fact better understood as fallout from the party hierarchy's perhaps excessively cynical and calculating rehabilitation of tsarist heroes, legends, and regalia.

2. The party hierarchy's mobilization of Russian national symbols is often discussed in rather unproblematized terms. See Harold Swayze, *Political Control of Literature in the USSR, 1946–1959* (Cambridge, Mass.: Harvard University Press, 1962), p. 28; Lowell Tillett, *The Great Friendship: Soviet Historians on the Non-Russian Nationalities* (Chapel Hill: University of North Carolina Press, 1969), pp. 49–61; Christel Lane, *The Rites of Rulers: Ritual in Industrial Society— the Soviet Case* (Cambridge: Cambridge University Press, 1981), p. 181; Alexander Werth, *Russia at War, 1941–1945* (New York: Carrol and Graf, 1984), pp. 120, 249–50; Vera S. Dunham, *In Stalin's Time: Middleclass Values in Soviet Fiction* (Durham, N.C.: Duke University Press, 1990), pp. 12, 17, 41, 66; Stephen K. Carter, *Russian Nationalism: Yesterday, Today, Tomorrow* (New York: Printer 1990), p. 51; John Barber and Mark Harrison, *The Soviet Home Front, 1941–1945: A Social and Economic History of the USSR in World War II* (London: Longman, 1991), p. 69; Nina Tumarkin, *The Living and the Dead: The Rise and Fall of the Cult of World War II in Russia* (New York: Basic Books, 1994), p. 63; Victoria E. Bonnell, *Iconography of Power: Soviet Political Posters under Lenin and Stalin* (Berkeley: University of California Press, 1997), 255–257.

3. Brandenberger, "The 'Short Course' to Modernity."

4. This phrase stems from a famous 1965 essay reprinted in Henry Steele Commager, *The Search for a Usable Past and Other Essays in Historiography* (New York: Knopf, 1967), pp. 3–27.

5. In contrast to the propagandists of the late 1930s, certain leading wartime figures verged on legitimating the idea of Russian self-rule. Such a political program by nature is inherently nationalistic. See Ernest Gellner, *Nations and Nationalism* (Ithaca: N.Y.: Cornell University Press, 1983), p. 1.

6. This conflict, long referred to as "the War of 1812" by Soviet scholars, had had its tsarist title restored in 1940. See M. V. Nechkina, ed., *Istoriia SSSR*, 2 vols., (Moscow: Gosudarstuennve Sotsial'No-Economiclle Sokl Izdatel Stvo, 1940), 2: 76.

7. Italics added. "Vystuplenie po radio Predsedatelia Soveta narodnykh komissarov SSSR i Narodnogo komissara inostrannykh del tov. V. M. Molotova," *Pravda*, June 23, 1941, p. 1. Stalin and other members of the Politburo took part in the editing of the speech (with the exception of A. A. Zhdanov, who was caught unawares on vacation in Sochi at the start of the war). See *Sto sorok besed s Molotovym: iz dnevnika F. Chueva* (Moscow: Tecca, 1991), pp. 51, 38.

8. Also receiving prominent mention, of course, was the more recent expulsion of German forces from Ukraine and Belorussia in 1918. See Em. Iaroslavskii, "Velikaia Otechestvennaia voina Sovetskogo Soiuza," *Pravda*, June 23, 1941, p. 4; "Dadim sokrushitel'nyi otpor fashistskim varvaram," ibid., June 24, 1941, 1; M. Khozin, "O khvastlivoi vydumke zaznavshegosia vraga," ibid., June 25, 1941, p. 4; "Nashe delo pravoe—vrag budet razbit," ibid., June 26, 1941, p. 1; "Izverg Gitler—liutyi vrag russkogo naroda," ibid., July 13, 1941, p. 4; S. V. Bakhrushin, *Geroicheskoe proshloe slavian* (Moscow: Ailademiia Nauk S SSR, 1941).

On the first day of the war, a Central Committee meeting called for war-oriented publishing from the Academy of Sciences' Institute of History. Within days, production plans at the Academy of Sciences and the State Political Publishing House had been reworked to accommodate the new priorities. Typical was the call at the State Instructional Pedagogical Publishing House amid massive cutbacks for "proposals on five or six books in the Pupil's Library series illuminating the heroism of the Russian people and their historical past, e.g., 'The Battle on the Ice,' 'the expulsion of Napoleon from Russia,' 'Peter I and his times,' etc." See G. D. Burdei, *Istorik i voina, 1941–1945* (Saratov: Izdatel' stvo Saratovskogo Instatuta, 1991), p. 148; Gosudarstvennyi arkhiv Rossiiskoi federatsii (TsGA, hereafter GARF) f. 2306, op. 69, d. 2785, ll. 10–11. A year later, the priorities remained the same—see Rossiiskii tsent khraneniia i izucheniia dokumentov noveishei istorii (hereafter RTsKhIDNI), f. 89, op. 3, d. 10, ll. 200b, 1250b, 1260b.

9. A. M. Dubrovskii, *S. V. Bakhrushin i ego vremia* (Moscow: Izdatel'stvo Rossiiskogo instituta Druszhby Narodov, 1992), p. 119. On historians' wartime publication planning sessions, see Burdei, *Istorik i voina*, pp. 148–49.

10. See RTsKhIDNI, f. 89, op. 3, d. 10, ll. 12–120b; "Pis'mo Skvortsovu ot Pankratovoi i.t.d" (March 12, 1943), ibid., f. 17, op. 125, d. 224, ll. 12–120b; N. M. Druzhinin, *Vospominaniia i mysli istorika*, 2d ed. (Moscow, 1979), pp. 66–67; " 'Idegeevo poboishche' TsK VKP(b)," *Rodina* no. 3–4 (1997): 117. This process was accelerated by the mass evacuations of scholars to Central Asia in late 1941 and 1942.

11. *Moskva voennaia: memuary i arkhivnye dokumenty, 1941–1945* (Moscow: Musborarkhiv, 1995), pp. 49–50; RTsKhIDNI, f. 17, op. 125, d. 85, l. 79; Harvard Project on the Soviet Social System, interview no. 13, schedule A, vol. 2, 42.

12. *Iosif Stalin—Lavrentiiu Beriia: "Ikh nado deportirovat' "—dokumenty, fakty, kommentarii* (Moscow: Druzhba Narodon, 1992), pp. 86–7, 99–100, 129–134; *Sto sorok besed s Molotovym: iz dnevnika F. Chueva*, p. 277; "Udary v spinu Krasnoi Armii nanosili v 1941–1942gg. vooruzhennye chechenskie natsionalisty," *Voenno-istoricheskii zhurnal* no. 1 (1997): 60–62; etc.

13. Jeffrey Brooks, *"Pravda Goes to War,"* in Richard Stites, ed., *Culture and Entertainment in Wartime Russia* (Bloomington: Indiana University Press 1995), p. 14. Brooks claims in this article that "Russian . . . themes were a minor part of the larger discourse and articles about 'Holy Russia,' which made a great impression on some foreign

observers, were infrequent amidst the daily news of the war" (pp. 20–21). The fact that this contention does not appear in his 1999 monograph *"Thank You, Comrade Stalin": Soviet Public Culture from Revolution to Cold War* (Princeton: Princeton University Press, 1999) seems to indicate that he no longer supports such an untenable position.

14. "Vystuplenie po radio Predsedatelia Gosudarstvennogo komiteta oborony tovarishcha I. V. Stalina," *Pravda*, July 3, 1941, p. 1.

15. "Velikaia druzhba narodov SSSR," ibid., July 29, 1941, p. 1.

16. For more on this analysis, see Brandenberger, "The 'Short Course' to Modernity," chapters 3, 8–9. The persuasiveness of prewar russocentrism is revealed by the fact that authors from Vs. Vishnevskii to N. M. Druzhinin responded to the German invasion with agitational essays that emphasized historic Russian military prowess even before receiving explicit instructions. See D. I. Ortenberg, *Iiun'-dekabr' sorok pervogo: rasskaz-khronika* (Moscow: Sovetskii pisateli, 1986), p. 9; Druzhinin, *Vospominaniia i mysli istorika*, pp. 62–66. On these articles, see also Brooks, *"Thank You, Comrade Stalin,"* p. 160.

17. The "first among equals" cliché, for instance, would appear in numerous articles, including "Sem'ia narodov SSSR—edinyi, nerushimyi lager'," *Pravda*, December 29, 1941, p. 1; V. Kruzhkov, "Velikaia sila leninsko-stalinskoi druzhby narodov," ibid., February 21, 1942, p. 3; and "Doklad tov. A. S. Shcherbakova 21 ianvaria 1942 goda," *Bol'shevik* no. 2 (1942): 10.

18. See "Rech' Predsedatelia Gosudarstvennogo komiteta oborony i Narodnogo komissara oborony tov. I. V. Stalina," *Pravda*, November 8, 1941, p. 1. On the eve of the anniversary, Stalin had provided a different list of heroes while detailing the German leadership's intentions to lead a savage war: "these people, without conscience and honor, [these] people, with the morals of animals, have the audacity to call for the extermination of the great Russian nation, the nation of Plekhanov and Lenin, Belinskii and Chernyshevskii, Pushkin and Tolstoi, Glinka and Tchaikovsky, Gor'kii and Chekhov, Sechenov and Pavlov, Repin and Surikov, Suvorov and Kutuzov!" "Doklad Predsedatelia Gosudarstvennogo komiteta oborony tovarishcha I. V. Stalina," ibid., November 7, 1941, p. 2.

19. *Pravda* editorials frequently reprinted the list of heroes verbatim (e.g., November 10, December 27, and February 11, 1942). Shortly after Stalin's speech, individual figures drawn from the heroic pantheon were featured in *Pravda* in an ongoing series: Minin and Pozharskii (November 25), Aleksandr Nevskii (December 24), etc.

20. Pamphlets are detailed in S. Bushuev, "Muzhestvennye obrazy nashikh velikikh predkov," *Bol'shevik*, no. 7–8 (1942): 57–64. Pankratova specifically mentioned the role of Stalin's November 7, 1941, speech in the formation of the wartime curriculum. See A. M. Pankratova, ed., *Prepodavanie istorii v usloviiakh Velikoi Otechestvennoi voiny: metodicheskoe posobie dlia uchitelei srednikh shkol Kazakhskoi SSR*, part I, *Istoriia SSSR*, (Alma Ata: Kazogiz, 1942), p. 11.

21. Fascinatingly, *Propagandist*'s calls in 1942 for rehabilitations of non-Russian heroes were largely ignored, as was the Belorussian Communist Party's bitter criticism of V. I. Picheta's *Geroicheskoe proshloe belorusskogo naroda* for downplaying or ignoring altogether various Belorussian heroes. See Tillett, *The Great Friendship*, p. 65; M. Morozov and V. Slutskaia, "Broshiury mestnykh izdatel'stv o geroicheskom proshlom nashego naroda i o geroiakh velikoi otechestvennoi voiny," *Propagandist*, no. 17 (1942): 46–48; and RTsKhIDNI, f. 17, op. 125, d. 224, l. 65.

22. Em. Iaroslavskii, "Bol'sheviki—prodolzhateli luchshikh patrioticheskikh trad-itsii russkogo naroda," *Pravda*, December 27, 1941, p. 3.

23. "Doklad A. S. Shcherbakova," p. 10. See also Kruzhkov, "Velikaia sila leninsko-stalinskoi druzhby narodov," p. 3. See note 81.

24. Tillett, *The Great Friendship*, p. 61.

25. Em. Iaroslavskii, "O blizhaishikh zadachakh istoricheskoi nauki v SSSR," *Istoricheskii zhurnal* no. 6 (1942): 17–24; Iaroslacskii, "Za boevuiu, dokhodchivuiu, pravdivuiu agitatsiiu," *Pravda*, July 10, 1942, p. 2; G. [F.] Aleksandrov, "Otechestvennaia voina sovetskogo naroda i zadachi obshchestvennykh nauk," *Bol'shevik*, no. 9 (1942): 35–47; Aleksandrov, "O reshaiushchikh usloviiakh pobedy nad vragom," *Pravda*, July 13, 1942, p. 4.

26. In addition to the articles and editorials about the decorations, see "Aleksandr Nevskii," *Pravda*, July 30, 1942, p. 3; "Mikhail Kutuzov," ibid., July 31, 1942, p. 3; "Aleksandr Suvorov," ibid., August 2, 1942, p. 3. During the war, portraits of Suvorov and Kutuzov were hung in Stalin's spartan Kremlin office next to Marx, Engels, and Lenin. See V. Malyshev, "Proidet desiatok let, i eti vstrechi ne vosstanovish' uzhe v pamiati," *Istochnik*, no. 5 (1997): 121; G. K. Zhukov, *Vospominaniia i razmyshleniia*, vol. 1 (Moscow: Novosti 1974), p. 343; *Sto sorok besed s Molotovym: iz dnevnika F. Chueva*, p. 292.

27. Tillett, *The Great Friendship*, p. 65. See also Brooks, *"Thank You, Comrade Stalin": Soviet Public Culture from Revolution to Cold War*, chapter 7.

28. Morozov and Slutskaia, "Broshiury mestnykh izdatel'stv o geroicheskom proshlom nashego naroda i o geroiakh Velikoi Otechestvennoi voiny," pp. 46–48. Interestingly, the article parenthetically cautioned that the celebration of non-Russian heroes should be confined to those who epitomized cooperative struggle against foreign invaders (apparently a veiled statement warning against discussing resistance against Russian colonialism in positive terms).

29. A. P. Ermolov (1777–1861) and M. D. Skobelev (1843–1882) were notorious for their roles in the colonial administration of the Caucasus and Central Asia, respectively.

30. RTsKhIDNI, f. 17, op. 125, d. 224, ll. 4–5; ibid., l. 1060b; RTsKhIDNI, f. 88, op. 1, d. 1049, ll. 47–50; ibid., f. 17, op. 125, op. 225, ll. 15–85.

31. P. N. Miliukov (1859–1943) and V. O. Kliuchevskii (1841–1911) were prominent liberal prerevolutionary historians. The idea of such a collection of articles was apparently first suggested by S. K. Bushuev in April 1942. Ibid., f. 89, op. 3, d. 10, l. 8. Efimov's interest in revising prewar historiography brought him into conflict with more cautious scholars when late in September 1942, he criticized A. M. Pankratova's contribution to the *Twenty-five Years of the Historical Sciences in the USSR* collection in September 1942 for maligning the accomplishments of prerevolutionary historians. He even reportedly proposed, at a meeting of the Institute of History, that the war's united front with bourgeois foreign powers and the "old [domestic] bourgeoisie and churchmen [*tserkovniki*]" *required* a more respectful treatment of prerevolutionary history and historiography. Furious with Efimov and other former students of Kliuchevskii "who openly boast of their affiliation with that school," Pankratova promptly wrote a thinly veiled denunciation to Agitprop in an attempt to derail her rival. Apparently also split on the issue, Agitprop failed to arbitrate the dispute, Iaroslavskii perhaps siding with Pankratova against Aleksandrov. Her piece was ultimately published in *Dvadtsat' piat' let istoricheskikh nauk v SSSR* (Moscow: Aicodemii Adauk SSSR, 1942). RTsKhIDNI, f.

17, op. 125, d. 224, l. 11–110b; ibid., ll. 2–3. Pankratova justified her objections to prerevolutionary historiography by arguing that it had failed to stimulate genuinely patriotic sentiments on the popular level between 1914 and 1917. See ibid., f. 89, op. 3, d. 10, l. 6.

32. Known for their conservative support of the autocracy, A. A. Arakcheev (1769–1834) was a general, M. N. Katkov (1818–1887) a publisher, and K. P. Pobedonostsev (1827–1907) the Procurator of the Synod.

33. Referring to an article of Stalin's published in early 1941, Bushuev contended that because *all* European powers had been forces of reaction in the nineteenth century, St. Petersburg should not be singled out for condemnation. See I. [V.] Stalin, "O stat'e Engel'sa 'Vneshniaia politika russkogo tsarizma,' " *Bol'shevik*, no. 9 (1941): 3–4. Stalin had originally written the article as a letter to his Politburo colleagues on July 19, 1934. For a draft of the *Bol'shevik* article, see RTsKhIDNI, f. 77, op. 1, d. 906, ll. 44–52, esp. 42–43; see also A. Latyshev, "Kak Stalin Engel'sa svergal," *Rossiiskaia gazeta*, December 22, 1992, p. 4.

34. (March 2, 1944), RTsKhIDNI, f. 17, op. 125, d. 224, ll. 3–4; ibid., l. 106. Efimov's modern history division of Moscow State University's history department had led the nomination of Bushuev's book, the introduction of which stressed that it had been written explicitly in defense of the "national position of Russian historiography." This inflammatory line was removed before the book's second edition came off the presses, see S. K. Bushuev, *A. M. Gorchakov: iz istorii russkoi diplomatii*, vol. 1 (Moscow: Arademiia Nauk SSSR, 1944).

35. Vl. Solov'ev (1853–1900), a religious philosopher and historian.

36. RTsKhIDNI, f. 88, op. 1, d. 1049, l. 9; ibid., ll. 5–50b. Tarle agreed, noting sarcastically that, despite Shamil's valorous conduct, "he was the head of a primitive theocracy—is it really that bad that today we are governed by the Stalin Constitution and not Shamil'?" (70b).

37. Ibid., f. 17, op. 125, d. 224, ll. 710b–72.

38. Although subtly Russocentric, the 1934 "Observations" were considerably more critical of the negative dimensions of tsarist rule than party directives would be in subsequent years. Tarle's interpretation of Stalin's 1941 article is somewhat exaggerated; while Stalin *did* note that all major European states were reactionary, he also affirmed the original thesis of the "Observations," that tsarist representatives had led the fight to crush revolution in nineteenth-century Europe. See I. Stalin, A. Zhdanov, and S. Kirov, "Zamechaniia po povodu konspekta uchebnika po 'Istorii SSSR'," *Pravda*, January 27, 1936, p. 2; "O stat'e Engel'sa 'Vneshniaia politika russkogo tsarizma,' " pp. 3–4. A more conventional reading of Stalin's thesis is presented in *Istoriia diplomatii*, vol. 1 (Moscow: Gosudarstvennoe sutsialino-'konomicheskoe iztatel'stvo, 1941), pp. 299–300. See also note 33.

39. Reconstructing Tarle's thesis is complicated by the subjective way in which he and Pankratova describe it in various documents. See RTsKhIDNI, f. 88, op. 1, d. 1049, ll. 16–25; ibid., f. 17, op. 125, d. 225, ll. 134–141, 142–165; ibid., d. 224, ll. 720b–73; ibid., ll. 1040b-1050b; ibid., d. 225, ll. 166–168.

40. See, for instance, Pankratova, *Prepodavanie istorii v usloviiakh Velikoi Otechestvennoi voiny*, pp. 4–8; M. Nechkina, *Istoricheskaia traditsiia russkogo voennogo geroizma* (Moscow: Akademiia Nauk SSSR, 1942), p. 198. See also RTsKhIDNI, f. 89, op. 3, d. 10, l. 120b.

41. S. V. Bakhrushin, for one, felt uneasy about Efimov's 1942 historiography project. Somewhat later, I. I. Mints and A. L. Sidorov challenged Tarle on his proposals to revise the 1934 "Observations" of Stalin, Zhdanov, and Kirov and to abandon class analysis. See ibid., f. 17, op. 125, d. 224, ll. 670b, 70–710b, 720b.

42. M. Abdykalykov and A. Pankratova eds., *Istoriia Kazakhskoi SSR s drevneishikh vremen do nashikh dnei* (Alma-Ata:Kazogiz, 1943). M. Abdykalykov was ideology chief of the Kazakh communist party.

43. Druzhinin, *Vospominaniia i mysli istorika*, p. 66. For other discussions of wartime efforts among the non-Russian peoples, see Serguei Ekeltchik [Serhy Yekelchyk], "History, Culture and Nationhood under High Stalinism: Soviet Ukraine, 1939–1954" (Ph.D. diss., University of Alberta, 2000), pp. 33–104; and George Liber, *Triple Exposure: Alexander Dovzhenko's Ukrainian Visions, Soviet Illusions and Stalinist Realities*, unpublished manuscript, 2000, chapter 9.

44. First advanced by A. A. Zhdanov in December 1936 to justify the incorporation of Georgia and Ukraine into the Russian empire, the "lesser evil" theory observed that these states had ceased to be geopolitically viable entities. According to Zhdanov, they preferred the "lesser evil" of integration into the Russian empire over similar arrangements with Persia, the Ottoman empire, or Poland because of the cultural and religious commonalities that they shared with their northerly Orthodox neighbor. The concept was subsequently expanded to favor annexation by leading regional powers over annexation by more backward powers. Brandenberger and Dubrovsky, " 'The People Need a Tsar': The Emergence of National Bolshevism as Stalinist Ideology," pp. 878 and notes 47–48.

45. While not denying the Leninist thesis that colonialism was "progressive," in so far as it expanded the amount of territory united under the fragile capitalist canopy, Pankratova stubbornly insisted that all European-led enlightenment in Kazakhstan followed the 1917 October revolution. "Pis'mo Skvortsovu ot Pankratovoi i.t.d." (March 13, 1943), RTsKhIDNI, f. 17, op. 125, d. 224, ll. 12–2100b, 26–35, especially 17–18; "Pis'mo Zhdanovu ot Pankratovoi" (March 2, 1944), ibid., ll. 9–10.

46. See ibid., ll. 23–25, citation on 240b; see also ibid., f. 88, op. 1, d. 1049, ll. 51–2.

47. Oblique references are made to "O natsional'noi gordosti velikorossov," "O karikature na Marksizm," "O broshiure Iuniusa," "Vozzvanie o voine," and "Sotsializm i voina" in *Sochineniia*, vol. 18 (Moscow: Partizdat, 1936), pp. 80–84, 181–185, 199.

48. Oblique references are made to "K voprosu o proletarskom metode razresheniia natsional'nogo voprosa" in *Marksizm i natsional'no-kolonial'nyi vopros: sbornik izbrannykh statei i rechei* (Moscow: Partizdat, 1934), p. 189.

49. Although somewhat Russocentric, party directives in 1934 and 1937 demanded that attention also be given to the colonial oppression of national minorities within the *ancien régime*'s "prison of the peoples." This militancy would fade later in the 1930s. See Stalin, Zhdanov, and Kirov, "Zamechaniia po povodu konspekta uchebnika po 'Istorii SSSR'," p. 2; "Postanovlenie zhiuri pravitel'stvennoi komissii po konkursu na luchshii uchebnik dlia 3 i 4 klassov srednei shkoly po istorii SSSR," *Pravda*, August 22, 1937, p. 2; Brandenberger, "The 'Short Course' to Modernity," 62–88, 375–377, etc.

50. RTsKhIDNI, f. 17, op. 125, d. 224, ll.. 36–430b, citation on l. 43; ibid., l. 4; ibid., l. 240b.

51. Ibid., l. 8; ibid., l. 74. Aleksandrov's reference to the notion of "world-historical peoples" is drawn from Hegel's *Philosophy of History*.

52. The dean of Soviet Marxist historiography during the 1920s, M. N. Pokrovskii presided over a materialist school of thought sometimes termed "sociology." Both Pokrovskii and his "school" were scathingly critical of tsarist colonialism and the Russian people's role in the administration of the empire. The about-face in party ideology during the mid to late 1930s led to the abandonment of this line.

53. RTsKhIDNI, f. 17, op. 125, d. 224, ll. 1–10, citations on ll. 7, 10.

54. Ibid., l. 22.

55. Ibid., ll. 72–74ob. The fact that Agitprop's Aleksandrov came under heavy fire in April 1944 at a philosophy conference may explain the fiasco. See note 57.

56. While S. V. Konstantinov is probably not far from the mark in observing that Pankratova's last letter was "composed in the best denunciatory traditions of the time," his attempt to single her out for criticism is less fair. The atmosphere in the profession was such that hyperbole formed an inherent part of the discipline's vernacular, so much so that separating rhetoric and posturing from genuine positions in the various debates is a haphazard process for contemporary scholars. Equally problematic is Konstantinov's chastising of Panktratova for "elevating to the level of indisputable evidence the retelling of personal conversations and things overheard while listening at the keyhole" in light of the fact that he bases *his* analysis of the affair almost exclusively on her correspondence. See S. V. Konstantinov, "Nesostoiavshaiasia rasprava (o soveshchanii istorikov v TsK VKP(b) v mae-iiule 1944 goda)," in *Vlast' i obshchestvennye organizatsii Rossii v pervoi treti XX stoletiia* (Moscow: n.p., 1994), pp. 254–268, esp. p. 256 and notes p. 29–36.

57. Kostyrchenko notes that it was no coincidence that Pankratova wrote to Stalin, Zhdanov, Malenkov, and Shcherbakov again after Aleksandrov came under fire during a Central Committee–orchestrated philosophy conference and in the subsequent Politburo resolution of May 1, 1944, "O nedostatkakh v nauchnoi rabote v oblasti filosofii." See RTsKhIDNI, f. 17, op. 125, d. 254, ll. 6–30, 31–47 62–71,; G. Kostyrchenko, *V plenu u krasnogo faraona: politicheskie presledovaniia evreev v SSSR v poslednee stalinskoe desiatiletie—dokumental'noe issledovanie* (Moscow: Mezhdunarudnye otnosheniia, 1994), pp. 21–22. Kostyrchenko's assertion of a patron-client relationship between Shcherbakov and Aleksandrov seems more tenuous, as Pankratova appealed to the former for support against the latter on several occasions.

58. A. N. Tolstoi and S. M. Eisenstein had developed a play and film script, respectively, concerning the reign of Ivan IV. Alexander I had apparently been mishandled in the film *Kutuzov*, while Brusilov had been distorted in I. Sel'vinskii's play *General Brusilov* and in several unrelated mass brochures.

59. RTsKhIDNI, f. 17, op. 125, d. 224, ll. 66ob–70.

60. Ibid., d. 221, ll. 71–72. On Pokrovskii's "school," see note 52.
In a subsequent shorter draft of the memo, Aleksandrov reiterated his dissatisfaction with the treatment of Russian heroes and the non-Russian colonial experience without mentioning Iakovlev. See "Meropriiatiia po uluchsheniiu propagandy i agitatsii partiinykh organizatsii" (April 10, 1944), ibid., l. 101.

61. "O ser'eznykh nedostatkakh i antileninskikh oshibkakh v rabote nekotorykh sovetskikh istorikov" (May 18, 1944), ibid., f. 88, op. 1, d. 1053, ll. 1–21; "O nastroeniiakh velikoderzhavnogo shovinizma sredi chasti istorikov," ibid., ll. 23–27. Aleksan-

drov's cover letter to the Central Committee which accompanies his memos, contained a series of personal insults aimed at Pankratova, with whom it apparently had been "impossible to discuss any sort of question," as the latter would "distort all the recommendations of the Agitprop staff and in such a perverted form spread them virtually throughout Moscow." "Spravka po voprosam pis'ma Pankratovoi v TsK VKP(b)" (May 18, 1944), ibid., f. 17, op. 125, d. 224, l. 90.

62. The earliest to call for a history conference had been Tarle, on January 3, 1944—see "Stenogramma soveshchaniia istoricheskoi obshchestvennosti," *ibid.*, f. 88, op. 1, d. 1049, l. 7. That Tarle and Aleksandrov had both lobbied for such a conference in early 1944 tends to discount Pankratova's subsequent claim that her efforts eventually brought it about. That said, it may have been Pankratova's complaints that caused the Central Committee to take responsibility for the conference rather than leave it up to Agitprop.

63. "Pis'mo druz'iam ot Pankratovoi" (June 15, 1944), ibid., f. 17, op. 125, d. 224, l. 1050b.

64. Perhaps because it seemed that Shcherbakov was favoring Pankratova's faction, Syromiatnikov and Tarle protested to him in written form, Efimov petitioned both Shcherbakov and Stalin, and Adzhemian sent letters to Stalin and the Politburo as a whole. See "Pis'mo Shcherbakovu ot Syromiatnikova" (June 10 and 14, 1944), ibid., d. 223, ll. 166–85; "Pis'mo Shcherbakovu ot Tarle" (July 10, 1944), ibid., d. 225, ll. 169–710b; "Pis'mo Shcherbakovu ot Efimova" (June 27, 1944), ibid., ll. 75–82; "Pis'mo Stalinu ot Efimova" ([May 1944]), ibid., f. 88, op. 1, d. 1050, ll. 42–50b; "Pis'mo Stalinu ot Efimova" ([June 1944]), ibid., f. 17, op. 125, d. 225, ll. 67–74; "Pis'mo Stalinu ot Adzhemiana" (July 9, 1944), ibid., d. 223, l. 81; "Pis'mo v Politbiuro ot Adzhemiana" (July 11, 1944), ibid., ll. 82–3.

65. "Stenogramma (prodolzhenie soveshchaniia po voprosam istorii)" (July 8, 1944), ibid., f. 88, op. 1, d. 1051, l. 254. *Voprosy istorii* has published the stenogram of the entire conference; see Iu. N. Amiantov's introduction and the serialized transcript in "Stenogramma soveshchaniia po voprosam istorii SSSR v TsK VKP(b) v 1944 godu," *Voprosy istorii*, nos. 2–7, 9 (1996): 47–87, 82–113, 65–94, 77–107, 70–88, 47–78. For analysis of the conference, see Burdei, *Istorik i voina*, pp. 152–159; Konstantinov, "Nesostoiavshaiasia rasprava," pp. 254–68; G. Bordiugov and V. Bukharaev, "Natsional'naia istoricheskaia mysl' v usloviiakh sovetskogo vremeni," in K. Aimermakher and G. Bordiugov, eds., *Natsional'nye istorii v sovetskom i postsovetskom gosudarstvakh* (Moscow: AIRO-XX, 1999), p. 41.

66. RTsKhIDNI, f. 17, op. 125, d. 222, ll. 1–10. Shcherbakov scrawled "this won't do" [*ne goditsia*] in the margin.

67. Kostyrchenko is likely correct in asserting that Zhdanov's participation was motivated by personal frustration with Aleksandrov, as well as a continuing interest in the historical profession. Zhdanov made special note of Pankratova's criticism of Agitprop by underlining related passages in her letter to Zhdanov on May 12, 1944. See the copy stored at RTsKhIDNI under f. 77, op. 1, d. 971, ll. 2, 3; Kostyrchenko, *V plenu u krasnogo faraona: politicheskie presledovaniia evreev v SSSR v poslednee stalinskoe desiatiletie*, pp. 21–22.

68. Note Zhdanov's underlining of Pankratova's passages criticizing Adzhemian in her letter of May 12, 1944—RTsKhIDNI, f. 77, op. 1, d. 971, ll. 5–6, 7. On the "Miliukovite" and Pokrovskii "schools," see notes 31 and 52, respectively. For a detailed analysis of Zhdanov's editing and re-editing of the Central Committee's draft

ruling on the conference's proceedings, see A. M. Dubrovskii and D. L. Brandenberger, "Itogovyi partiinyi dokument soveshchaniia istorikov v TsK VKP(b) v 1944g. (Istoriia sozdaniia tektsa)," in *Arkheograficheskii ezhegodnik za 1998* (Moscow: Nauka, 1999), pp. 148–163.

69. While affirming the leading role of the Russian people, Zhdanov linked this prominence exclusively to the Stalinist thesis that the Russian working class had played a decisive role in the emancipation of all the Soviet peoples. Declaring that Russian tsarism was not to be exonerated and that the "prison of the peoples" thesis was to remain in force, Zhdanov at the same time reined in those scholars who resisted the broad application of the "lesser evil" thesis: "Some of our historians apparently do not understand that there is a *principle difference* between *recognizing the progressiveness* of this or that historical phenomenon and [actually] *endorsing it*. Feudalism was superior in contrast to tribal social structure. However, while noting the progressive nature of the exchange of one means of production to another, one economic formation for another, Marxists have never concluded that it was necessary to support capitalism." See RTsKhIDNI, f. 17, op. 125, d. 222, l. 44.

70. See Central Committee resolution of July 2, 1945, "Ob istoricheskom zhurnale," ibid., op. 3, d. 1053, l. 10, discussed in "Zadachi zhurnala 'Voprosy istorii'," *Voprosy istorii*, no. 1 (1945): 3–5; S. V. Bakhrushin, "Kniga B. I Syromiatnikova 'Reguliarnoe gosudarstvo Petra I'," *Bolshevik* no. 22 (1944): 54–59; Bakhrushin, "O rabote A. I. Iakovleva 'Kholopstvo i kholopy v Moskovskom gosudarstve v XVII v.'," ibid, no. 3–4 (1945): 73–77; M. A. Morozov, "Ob 'Istorii Kazakhskoi SSR'," ibid., no. 6 (1945): 74–80; N. N. Iakovlev, "O knige E. V. Tarle 'Krymskaia voina'," ibid., no. 13 (1945): 63–72; G. F. Aleksandrov, "O nekotorykh zadachakh obshchestvennykh nauk," ibid., no. 14 (1945): 12–29.

71. See the literature cited in note 65.

72. Although Pankratova emerged relatively unscathed from the conference (especially in contrast to her rivals), Aleksandrov seized the opportunity to deal her a crushing blow in fall 1944. Perhaps overly confident, Pankratova had indiscreetly sent a newsletter of sorts to her former students throughout the USSR during the conference that contained not only her sardonic commentary on the proceedings but copies of her letters to the Central Committee. When one of these students turned his packet over to the Saratov oblast' party committee, it quickly landed on Aleksandrov's desk in Moscow because of Pankratova's ill-advised circulation of unofficial and confidential information. Summarily accused of distributing secret materials and engaging in factional activity [*gruppovshchina*], Pankratova was promptly called in for a dressing down by Zhdanov and Shcherbakov early in September 1944 and dismissed from her post as deputy director of the Academy of Science's Institute of History. In order to save her career, she reversed herself on the issue of progressive expansion and the "lesser evil" theory—in all likelihood coached by Zhdanov—and apologized for lobbying against Aleksandrov. See RTsKhIDNI, f. 17, op. 125, d. 224, ll. 104–118; see also ll. 119–137; ibid., l. 103; ibid., ll. 138–140; ibid., l. 142; ibid., ll. 143–146ob.

73. It is widely believed that Stalin facilitated Tarle's professional rehabilitation after the historian was exiled to Kazakhstan in 1931 in connection with a series of purges among the scholarly intelligentsia. See Burdei, *Istorik i voina*, pp. 180–187; B. S. Kaganovich, *Evgenii Viktorovich Tarle i peterburgskaia shkola istorikov* (St. Petersburg: Izdatel'stvd "Nikolai Bulanin," 1995), pp. 45–60.

74. Dubrovskii and Brandenberger, "Itogovyi partiinyi dokument soveshchaniia istorikov v TsK VKP(b) v 1944g.," pp. 148–163.

75. Such an argument is made in passing in Anton Antonov-Ovseyenko, *The Time of Stalin: Portrait of a Tyranny*, trans. by George Saunders (New York: Harper and Row, 1981), p. 290.

76. Even before the history conference, the Kazakh party organization had been criticized in the Central Committee resolution of April 1, 1944, "O rabote TsK KP(b)Kazakhstana," which was followed up by calls for further investigation on October 26, 1945. See RTsKhIDNI, f. 17, op. 125, d. 340, ll. 78–85; ibid., d. 311, ll. 108–130; ibid., ll. 131–143; ibid., l. 144.

The Tatar and Bashkir party organizations were savaged in the Central Committee resolutions of August 9, 1944, "O sostoianii i merakh uluchsheniia massovo-politicheskoi i ideologicheskoi raboty v Tatarskoi partiinoi organizatsii," and January 27, 1945, "O sostoianii i merakh uluchsheniia agitatsionno-propagandistskoi raboty v Bashkirskoi partiinoi organizatsii," in *KPSS v rezoliutsiiakh i resheniiakh s"ezdov, konferentsii i plenumov TsK*, vol. 6 (Moscow: Gosudarstvennoe izdatel'stvo politicheskoi literatury 1971), pp. 113–120, 130–134. Each of these moves forced their respective party organizations to pass resolutions of their own; see, for instance, the Tatar obkom resolution of October 6, 1944, "Ob oshibkakh i nedostatkakh v rabote Tatarskogo nauchno-issledovatel'skogo instituta iazyka, literatury i istorii," reprinted in " 'Idegeevo poboish-che' TsK VKP(b)," *Rodina*, no. 3–4 (1997): 116–117, and a discussion of a similar Kazakh resolution in "O podgotovke 2-go izdaniia 'Istorii Kazakhskoi SSR'," *Bol'shevik Kazakhstana*, no. 6 (1945): 49–51.

77. Aleksandrov, "O nekotorykh zadachakh obshchestvennykh nauk," pp. 17, 18. Mamai and Tokhtamysh led bloody raids into the territory of northern Rus' in the late fourteenth century. Mamai was defeated at the Battle of Kulikovo Field, in 1380, by Dmitrii Donskoi, but Tokhtamysh succeeded in sacking Moscow two years later.

78. Brandenberger, "The 'Short Course' to Modernity," chapter 10.

79. I. V. Stalin, "Vystuplenie I. V. Stalina na prieme v Kremle v chest' komanduiushchikh voiskami Krasnoi armii, 24 maia 1945 goda," in *O Velikoi Otechestvennoi voine Sovetskogo Soiuza* (Moscow: Gosudarstvennoe izdatel'stvo politicheskoi literatury, 1947), p. 197. Elena Zubkova underestimates the importance of this speech in her *Poslevoennoe sovetskoe obshchestvo: politika i povsednevnost'*, *1945–1953* (Moscow: Rosspen, 2000), p. 36.

80. Although official figures have never been released, losses in the war seem to have been more or less proportional to the ethnic breakdown of the USSR's population. See Gerhard Simon, *Nationalismus und Nationalitätenpolitik in der Sowjetunion: Von der totalitären Diktatur zur nachstalinschen Gesellschaft* (Baden-Baden: Nomos, 1986), pp. 213–215.

81. For examples of the party hierarchy's wartime interest in promoting "Russianness" and downplaying other cultural influences, see D. L. Babichenko, ed., *"Literaturnyi front": Istoriia politicheskoi tsenzury, 1932–1946—Sbornik dokumentov* (Moscow: Entsiklopediia Rossiiskikh dereven, 1994), pp. 77–155; Kostyrchenko, *V plenu u krasnogo faraona: politicheskie presledovaniia evreev v SSSR v poslednee stalinskoe desiatiletie*, especially pp. 9–18.

82. The correspondent A. N. Stepanov made precisely such a suggestion to his editor at the newspaper *Krasnaia zvezda*: "It would be really good if it were possible to print a couple of articles on Jewish Heroes of the Soviet Union, military commanders

and generals. That would inject a refreshing current into many people's minds."
RTsKhIDNI, f. 17, op. 125, d. 190, l. 16.

83. For more on this argument, see Brandenberger, "The 'Short Course' to Modernity," chapters 8–9.

84. A. M. Pankratova, *Velikii russkii narod* (Moscow: Gosudarstuennoe izdatel'stvo
politicheskoi literatury, 1948).

Index